Praise for *The Lion*

T0249167

"It is a rousing book and an important one.

"A compelling account of the achievement and feelings of an outnumbered people armed with enough competence, determination, weapons, and courage to prevent a promised annihilation." —*Baltimore Jewish Times*

"This is a great book with lots of details, great research, and an excellent narrative. Fans of military history will especially enjoy this book as it covers many aspects of the war, from the generals and politicians to the guys in the trenches." —BlogCritics.com

"You don't have to be a history buff to be riveted by this book. Like the Israeli population, most of the interviewees were not religious, but they believed: This is the Promised Land—the eternal homeland of the Jewish People, tracing all the way back to Abraham. And we'll do what is necessary to protect it. Eye-opening and deeply moving, *The Lion's Gate* could make a believer out of anyone." —*The Jewish Press*

"The headlines out of Israel today are echoes of the saga that Pressfield has told so well in the pages of *The Lion's Gate*." —*Jewish Journal*

"There are few books these days that you put down breathless, with tears in your eyes, thinking, 'These were men; would that I have been with them.' Unless it's a Steve Pressfield book. Bestselling author Steven Pressfield's latest book, *The Lion's Gate*, is such a book. An oral history of 1967's famed 'Six Day War' when Moshe Dayan led the newly formed Israeli Defense Forces in a preemptive strike against the massed forces of Egypt, Jordan, Syria, and Iraq, Pressfield has moved out of his comfort zone of historical fiction and tackled the challenging field of more current history, where the participants are alive, but their memories of troops in combat and engagements often differ." —*Leatherneck*

"*The Lion's Gate* is one of Pressfield's finest books. In the backs-against-the-wall theme of *Gates of Fire*'s Spartans at Thermopylae, Pressfield relates the true story of an entire country's courage while facing overwhelming odds. You won't put it down unfinished." —*Marine Corps Gazette*

"Not only does the first-person perspective that each of the interviews provide lend an edge and intensity to the conflict that is unmatched by any other history book I have read, but the excellent selection the author has included gives an outstanding summary of the events of the Six Day War. A truly superb work that truly elucidates a relatively obscure subject."

—*San Francisco Book Review*

SENTINEL

THE LION'S GATE

Steven Pressfield is the author of five works of nonfiction and eight of fiction, including the bestsellers *Gates of Fire* and *The Legend of Bagger Vance*. Mr. Pressfield is cofounder and partner in Black Irish Books, publisher of his bestselling backlist classic on creativity, *The War of Art*. His Wednesday column on www.stevenpressfield.com is among the most popular writing blogs on the web.

Also by Steven Pressfield

FICTION

The Profession

Killing Rommel

The Afghan Campaign

The Virtues of War

Last of the Amazons

Tides of War

Gates of Fire

The Legend of Bagger Vance

NONFICTION

The Authentic Swing

Turning Pro

The Warrior Ethos

Do the Work

The War of Art

THE
LION'S GATE

ON THE FRONT LINES OF THE SIX DAY WAR

STEVEN
PRESSFIELD

SENTINEL

SENTINEL

Published by the Penguin Group
Penguin Group (USA) LLC
375 Hudson Street
New York, New York 10014

USA I Canada I UK I Ireland I Australia I New Zealand I India I South Africa I China
penguin.com
A Penguin Random House Company

First published in the United States of America by Sentinel,
a member of Penguin Group (USA) LLC, 2014
This paperback edition published 2015

Map design by Christy Henspetter.
Graphics by Jasmine Quinsier.

Photograph credits appear on pages 411–12.

Pressfield, Steven, author.
The lion's gate : on the front lines of the Six-Day War / Steven Pressfield.
pages cm
Includes bibliographical references and index.
ISBN 978-1-59523-091-1 (hardback)
ISBN 978-1-59523-119-2 (pbk.)
1. Israel-Arab War, 1967. I. Title.
DS127.7.P74 2014
956.04'6—dc23
2014004328

Printed in the United States of America

Set in Sabon
Designed by Spring Hoteling

This book is dedicated with respect and
deep appreciation to Lou Lenart,

Captain, U.S. Marine Corps, 1940–1947,
Israel Air Force, 1948–1954.

Lenart with his F4U Corsair at the battle for Okinawa, 1945.

CONTENTS

A NOTE ON
HYBRID HISTORY

Before I address what this book is, let me state what it is not. It is not a comprehensive history of the Six Day War. Entire battles have been left out. Critical contextual material such as the international diplomatic and political state of affairs prior to the war, the point of view of the Arabs, even the history of the Jewish people, has been included only as it touches upon the testimony of the central personalities of this piece, the war veterans themselves. Even within the Israel Defense Forces (IDF), units whose contributions to victory were essential—the Golani Brigade, Ugda Yoffe, the Harel and Jerusalem Brigades, the Sayeret Matkal, the navy, and many others—receive only passing mention.

The Lion's Gate tracks the experiences of a limited number of IDF units—Mirage Squadron 119 of the air force, the 7th Armored Brigade (in particular its Reconnaissance Company), Helicopter Squadron 124, Paratroop Battalion 71, and several others. Even within these formations, only a limited number of individuals are profiled. The book's primary material comes from sixty-three interviews I conducted in Israel, France, and the United States, totaling about 370 hours. The focus is deliberately personal, subjective, and idiosyncratic.

Nor does this book pretend to document the "facts" of the war. The meat of this narrative is the testimony of soldiers and airmen. It is their memories. Memory can be a tricky animal. Is it "truth"? Is it "history"? Is it "fact"?

I am less concerned with these questions, which are ultimately unanswerable, than with the human reality in the moment. What fascinates me is the subjective immediacy of the event. I want to be in the cockpit, inside the tank, under the helmet. What is important to me is the event *as the man or woman experienced it*.

Memory, we know, is notoriously unreliable. Memory can be self-serving, self-glorifying, self-exonerating. Memory fades. People forget. Memory contains gaps and blank spots.

Then there is the Rashomon effect. The attentive reader will discover instances in this book where three individuals present three different versions of the identical event in which all three participated. This phenomenon happened during the interviews themselves. When I spoke with more than one person at a time, one friend would often contradict another. "No, that happened before dark. Don't you remember?"

The reader must keep these considerations in mind when evaluating the accounts presented in these pages.

A word, too, about the treatment of material within the interviews. In some instances the interviewee's speech is transcribed verbatim. In others, I have edited, inverted order, altered tense, used time compression, and employed other narrative devices. The interviews were conducted in English. For most participants, English is a second or third language. Several interviews involved translation on the spot by my colleague Danny Grossman. In configuring the material for use in this book, I have sometimes retro-imagined the interviewee's prose as if it had been spoken in his or her primary language.

Books. A number of the individuals interviewed—Yael Dayan, Ruth Dayan, Eliezer "Cheetah" Cohen, Uzi Eilam, Ran Ronen, Giora Romm, Morele Bar-On, Avigdor Kahalani, and others—have themselves written works in full or in part about the Six Day War. I have, with these writers' permission, interpolated material from their published works into these spoken narratives.

One unit featured in this book is the Reconnaissance Company of the 7th Armored Brigade. Members of this group produced a documentary, *We Looked Death in the Eye . . .*, about their experiences in the 1967 War. I have employed the same practice with this film as I have with books, taking certain quotes spoken on camera and integrating them into the individual speakers' narrations.

I must alert the reader to another intentional violation of the conventions of history writing. Moshe Dayan died in 1981. I conducted my interviews during 2011 and 2012. Clearly I could not have spoken with Dayan. Yet I have written "his" chapters in the first person, as if in his own words.

Why am I calling this book "hybrid history"? Because I have elected in its composition to employ techniques from a number of disciplines—from journalism and academic history, from conventional nonfiction and narrative nonfiction, and from New Journalism.

The Dayan chapters must be considered the latter. Dayan did not dictate these sentences into my tape recorder. They are not his testimony or his recounting of events. However, I have made every effort to be as true to the historical Moshe Dayan as my limitations of knowledge and imagination permit.

Fortunately Dayan left an autobiography, a diary of the Sinai Campaign of 1956, an extraordinary personal testament titled *Living with the Bible,* and a number of other published works. In addition, many excellent biographies exist, penned by his colleagues and contemporaries. I was privileged as well to interview a number of individuals who were extremely close to Dayan: his first wife, Ruth; his daughter, Yael; his nephew Uzi; as well as associates and fellow officers Neora Matalon-Barnoach, Shlomo Gazit, Morele Bar-On, Michael Bar-Zohar, Aharon Yadlin, and Zalman Shoval. That being said, the reader should bear in mind while reading the Dayan chapters that I have at some points crossed the line into pure speculation.

On my office shelves sit 107 books about the Six Day War and its antecedents. Why write another? The answer is I wanted to tell the subjective story, the on-the-ground and in-the-air saga, in a way I have not seen it told before, even if it meant taking liberties with academic and journalistic conventions.

The swift passage of the years is a factor as well. Many of the veterans interviewed for this book are in their late sixties; no few are in their seventies, eighties, or nineties. They may not tell their stories on the record again.

I am a Jew. I wanted to tell the story of this Jewish war, fought by Jews for the preservation of the Jewish nation and the Jewish people. I don't pretend to be impartial. At the same time, I have tried, despite license taken, to tell the story straight.

I alone am responsible for the structure, theme, and editorial choices in this book. I chose what to put first and what to put last, what to leave in and what to leave out. The veterans honored me by telling me their stories, but responsibility for the final shape and content of this work rests with me alone.

STEVEN PRESSFIELD

2014

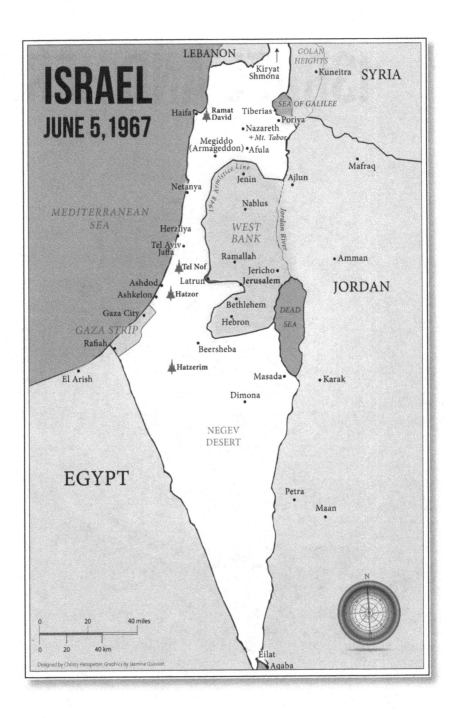

ISRAEL AND HER E

ATLANTIC
OCEAN

MOROCCO

• Rabat

Algiers •

Tunis •

TUNISIA

MEDITERRA

Tripoli •

Benghazi •

ALGERIA

LIBYA

MAURITANIA

MALI

NIGER

CHAD

MiG-21 fighter-interceptor

0   200   400 miles

0   400 km

Designed by Christy Henspetter. Graphics by Jasmine Quinsier.

Founded in 1964, the thirteen-member United Arab Command was the military arm of the Arab League.

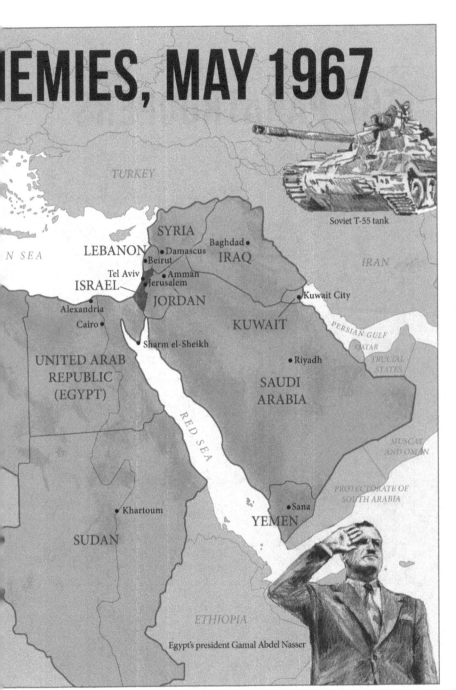

EMIES, MAY 1967

Soviet T-55 tank

Egypt's president Gamal Abdel Nasser

Its aim was, in the phrase of U.S. Brigadier General S. L. A. Marshall, the "elimination of Israel."

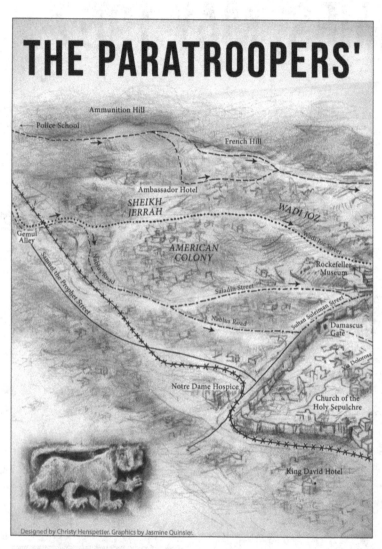

THE PARATROOPERS'

Ammunition Hill

Police School

French Hill

Ambassador Hotel

SHEIKH JERRAH

WADI JOZ

Gemul Alley

AMERICAN COLONY

Rockefeller Museum

Saladin Street

Sultan Suleiman Street

Nablus Road

Damascus Gate

Notre Dame Hospice

Church of the Holy Sepulchre

King David Hotel

Designed by Christy Henspetter. Graphics by Jasmine Quinsier.

TROOP MOVEMENTS

•••••••••••••••••••••••• Battalion 71

– – – – – – – – – – – – – Battalion 66

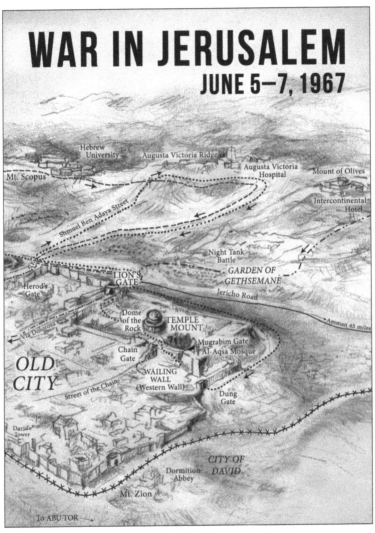

WAR IN JERUSALEM
JUNE 5–7, 1967

Hebrew University
Augusta Victoria Ridge
Augusta Victoria Hospital
Mount of Olives
Mt. Scopus
Intercontinental Hotel
Shmuel Ben Adaya Street
Night Tank Battle
GARDEN OF GETHSEMANE
LION'S GATE
Jericho Road
Herod's Gate
Amman 45 miles
Via Dolorosa
Dome of the Rock
TEMPLE MOUNT
Chain Gate
Mugrabim Gate
Al-Aqsa Mosque
OLD CITY
WAILING WALL (Western Wall)
Street of the Chain
Dung Gate
David's Tower
CITY OF DAVID
Dormition Abbey
Mt. Zion
To ABU TOR

— ·—·—·—·—·— Battalion 28

— ··—··—··—··— Brigade 55 Headquarters

✶✶✶✶✶✶✶✶✶✶ 1948 Armistice Line

And it shall be that if the king learns of any nation and people seeking to take away violently anything that belongs to Israel, he shall send unto the captains of thousands and of hundreds stationed in the cities of Israel, and they shall send to him one tenth of the host to go with him to war against their enemies, and they shall go forth with him. And if a great host comes against the land of Israel, they shall send him one fifth of the men of war. And if a king with chariots and horse and a great host come against Israel, they shall send him one third of the men of war, and the two thirds that are left shall keep the ward at their cities and borders so that no company shall come into their land. And if the battle goes sorely with him, they shall send him one half of the host, the soldiers, and one half of the host shall not be cut off from their cities.

From the 2,000-year-old Temple Scroll, recovered
one day after the liberation of Jerusalem, 7 June 1967

BOOK ONE

THE WAITING

1.

TWO BROTHERS

Three weeks before the war, I went to visit my brother Nechemiah in Jerusalem. He and I were born there. The city is our home.

Major Eliezer "Cheetah" Cohen is a pilot and commander of Squadron 124, Israel's first and leading helicopter formation.

Nechemiah was twenty-four years old then, a captain in the Sayeret Matkal, Israel's special forces. Along with Ehud Barak, the future prime minister, he was the most decorated soldier in the army. Nechemiah had been awarded five medals for valor—one Medal of Distinguished Service and four Chief of Staff Citations.

Nechemiah had been promoted from lieutenant four months earlier, transferred to the elite 35th Paratroop Brigade, and made a company commander. This was to give him experience commanding formations larger than the twelve-man teams of the special forces.

The date of our visit was May 15, Independence Day. My wife, Ela, and I had gone with our children to the parade in West Jerusalem. Nechemiah phoned and invited us to come out to his command post for a visit. "It's safe," he said. "Bring the kids."

Nechemiah's outpost was at Abu Tor, in the middle of no-man's-land. Abu Tor is the highest hill immediately south of the Old City. The site controls access by road from Jordan and dominates the southern approach to Old Jerusalem.

Nechemiah had about fifty paratroopers in posts along the armistice line, four or five in each. He had set up his headquarters in a beautiful old red-stone villa, which had been abandoned for almost twenty years, since the fighting in 1948. All around the house were barbed wire, barricades, machine-gun posts. Signs read DANGER—MINES. It was a gorgeous spot in the middle of a junkyard.

Down the hill were posts and fortifications of the Arab Legion. These were King Hussein's elite troops, British trained, wearing their famous red-and-white-checked keffiyehs. My kids were thrilled to see enemy soldiers so close.

Nechemiah and I spent two hours together. We went up on the villa's high, flat roof. The site looked like any other field outpost occupied by young soldiers—sandbags and high-powered binoculars, cases of combat rations, bedrolls tucked into corners, a half circle of rucksacks with weapons and helmets ready for action.

You must understand that Nechemiah and I come from a very humble family. We grew up playing in alleys and side streets and on the stony hillsides of a city we could not claim as our own. Jerusalem was under British rule then. There was no Israel. We Jews had no country.

When the state was founded in 1948, the army of Jordan won the battle for Jerusalem. The Arab Legion drove our forces out of the Old City, burned over fifty synagogues, killed every Jew they could find.

Nechemiah and I understood this and hated it, even as boys. When we grew up we became soldiers and officers. We ceased talking like angry children and began planning like military professionals. Nechemiah is a paratrooper, I am a pilot. It's up to us. We have to do the job.

This is how we saw the situation, Nechemiah and I, on the roof of the villa above no-man's-land. We both knew that war was coming. "Does it frustrate you, brother," I asked, "to be stuck here in Jerusalem when the fighting will surely be in Sinai or Syria?"

Our understanding in that moment was that war would not come to the Holy City. Jordan wouldn't risk attacking Israel; she might lose. And Israel could not make the first move. The outside world would never let her.

From our rooftop, my brother and I could see the poplar grove above the Western Wall—our people's most sacred site—so close it seemed we could almost touch it, yet cut off from us by barbed wire and minefields and the combat posts of the Arab Legion.

"Look there, brother," I said. "I can spit and reach Mount Moriah, where Abraham bound Isaac. There you see David's Tower and what is left of the Jewish Quarter of the Old City. All this is ours. What is stopping us from taking it, *ahuyah*?" I employed the Arabic word for brother, which we all used in our family. "Are we waiting for the United Nations or the world powers to give us permission? The Jordanians don't hold the Old City by ancient right. It was never part of their country. They seized it by force in 1948!"

I asked Nechemiah what he thought the Americans would do in our place. Would their army sit still for one minute if a foreign power occupied Pennsylvania Avenue? Would the British stand idly by if another nation held even one lane of London? What would the Russians do? I can hear my brother's answer as if he were standing before me now. "Ahuyah," he said, "if war comes, it will come to Jerusalem too. We are going to liberate the Old City."

I didn't believe him. I thought to myself, This is only a dream. Every combat alert at the time was against the Egyptians, the Syrians, the Iraqis. Never against the Jordanians.

"It will happen," my brother said. "You will see."

We embraced then and took our leave. That was the last time I saw Nechemiah alive.

My younger brother—I am older by eight years—was ordered with his company to join the main body of the 35th Paratroop Brigade along the frontier with Egypt. He was killed in Gaza on the first day of the war.

My helicopter squadron was assigned that day to fly medevac missions in northern Sinai and the Gaza Strip. The emergency call came over my own squadron radio net: "Mass casualties near Gaza City."

I dispatched one of my pilots, Reuven Levy, to handle the evacuation. It never occurred to me that my brother could be among the dead. He was too good, too smart. Nothing could happen to him.

Levy was ordered by an officer on-site to say nothing to me about Nechemiah's death. "Cheetah is a critical squadron commander," Levy was told. "The nation needs him operating at full capacity."

So I flew night and day throughout the war, in Gaza and Sinai, in the West Bank and Jerusalem and on the Golan Heights, and knew nothing of what had happened to my brother.

On the last day, when all Israel was flooding into liberated Jerusalem to touch the stones and behold the miracle that many had believed would never come to pass, I was in the office of the base commander at Tel Nof Air Base, being informed at last that my brother had not survived to witness this day. In that hour, my world ended.

2.

THE VOICE OF THUNDER

The state of Israel is the size of New Jersey. The combined landmass of its twenty Arab enemy states is more than a million square miles larger than the rest of the United States.

In 1967, the population of Israel was 2.7 million. Many were immigrants recently evicted from Arab countries of North Africa and the Middle East. These newcomers possessed few skills that could be used in the defense of the nation. Most could not even speak Hebrew. The state of Israel existed within a sea of 122 million Arabs, outnumbered by more than forty to one.

Lieutenant Zeev Barkai is the twenty-three-year-old operations officer of Paratroop Battalion 71. He is a kibbutznik from Kibbutz Kinneret on the Sea of Galilee. He will be awarded the Itur HaOz, Israel's second-highest decoration for valor, for his actions during the Six Day War.

In 1967, there was no TV station in Israel. We had only one radio station, Kol Israel, the Voice of Israel. But we could see Arab TV. There was a station in Jordan and one in Egypt, along with the Voice of Thunder out of Cairo, an all-day radio broadcast (in occasionally laughable Hebrew) whose normal propaganda had been cranked up now to crisis-hysteria level, seeking to terrify the Israeli populace.

Jews, the Arab people have decided to rid Palestine of your presence. Therefore pack your bags and flee before death overtakes you. Tel Aviv will be a ruin. Our bombs will hit their targets. Where will you run to, Zionists?

You tried to laugh this stuff off, but it got to you. Remember the song "The End," by Jim Morrison and the Doors? It was popular then. There was a line that said something like "This is the end, my friend, this is the end." That's what those weeks felt like.

Cairo TV played endless footage of Arab mobs in the streets, carrying banners and chanting, "Kill the Jews!" and "Death to the Zionists!" The Voice of Thunder quoted Azzam Pasha of the Arab League from 1948:

> *This will be a war of extermination and a momentous massacre, which will be spoken of like the Mongolian massacres and the Crusades.*

The Arab world had a leader then—Gamal Abdel Nasser, the president of Egypt—such as it had not had in the modern era before or since. (Egypt was then still officially the United Arab Republic, though its partner, Syria, had withdrawn from the union in 1961.)

Nasser's vision was pan-Arabism: one state stretching from Central Asia across the Middle East and Africa to the Atlantic. He wanted a modern Arab world, secular, socialist, armed with the latest weapons and equipped with the newest technology. To that end, Egypt and Syria had allied themselves with the Soviet Union, which was then at the peak of its wealth and power.

President Gamal Abdel Nasser, left, with army chief
Abdel Hakim Amer and Egyptian pilots a few days before the war.

Nasser's Russian-supplied air force possessed 480 combat aircraft, all jets, including 180 MiG-17s and MiG-15s, 80 MiG-19s, and 130 of the latest MiG-21s, capable of flying at twice the speed of sound. In addition, the EAF had 20 Sukhoi-7 fighter-bombers and 70 Tupolev-16 and Ilyushin-28 bombers, plus 90 Ilyushin and Antonov transport planes and 60 helicopters. Israel had no bombers at all. The Syrian Air Force augmented Egypt's with 120 more Soviet-built planes, including MiG-19s and MiG-21s. The Iraqis could contribute 200 more.

Egyptian armor consisted of roughly 1,200 tanks, including 300 new Soviet T-54s and 200 of the even newer T-55s. These were the same tanks the Russian Army used. Syria possessed 550 more Soviet tanks, and Iraq added 630, for a total of 2,400, not counting Lebanon's pledged 130 and 100 more from Saudi Arabia. Against this, Israel's armored brigades could put into the field only 800 tanks—250 British Centurions, 200 American M48 Pattons, plus 150 light AMX-13s and 200 Super Shermans, World War II tanks up-gunned and reconfigured for desert fighting.

Into Sinai over the past month Nasser had poured 950 tanks, 1,100 armored personnel carriers, 1,000 artillery pieces, and 100,000 troops. The Egyptian and Syrian air forces were trained by Soviet instructors. Air defense radar was Soviet built and Soviet installed; in many cases it was Soviet manned. Egypt's ground defenses in Sinai—minefields, artillery "boxes," and bunker emplacements—were built by and designed by Soviet engineers according to the latest Soviet military doctrine.

The bone in Nasser's throat was us. At the Arab League Summit in 1964, thirteen nations under Nasser's leadership had created the United Arab Command, a military entity pledged to eradicate "the Zionist entity." The word "Israel" appeared on no Arab maps.

My unit was called up on May 21. The way it works in Israel is you belong to the reserves. Israel's standing army then consisted of only three brigades. The IDF is a reservist army. For the force to reach full strength, reserve units are mobilized, meaning their men must leave their civilian jobs and report for military duty. The whole economy grinds to a halt.

My friend Yoram Zamosh, our "A" Company commander, was driving a tractor when a taxi came to mobilize him—the army sent cabs for officers. Zamosh's radioman, Moshe Milo, was plowing a field too, on his Caterpillar D4. He was a sergeant; a bus collected him along with the other enlisted men on the kibbutz. Yoram and Moshe both had to run for home, with no time even to say good-bye. Just grab a toothbrush, leave a note, and go.

Our battalion assembled at a place called Camp Israel next to Lod airfield, outside Tel Aviv. Paratroop units need to be near airfields for obvious reasons. Tel Nof Air Base was the main facility for paratrooper training. A fence divided the base into two parts. On one side were the swimming pool, the cinema, and the ice cream shop. That was the pilots' side. On the other side were the jump towers, the obstacle course, and the barracks. That was our side.

Three-quarters of the men in our battalion came from kibbutzim or moshavim (-*im* is a suffix indicating plural in Hebrew). A kibbutz is a communal farm where all land and goods are held in common. A moshav is similar, except individual families are permitted to possess and farm their own piece of land.

On kibbutzim in those days children were raised not by their parents but communally. They lived in a "Children's House" and grew up, supervised by their teachers and caretakers, among the other children. The pioneer ideals were still very much in practice then. All kibbutz members were equals. No one got a salary. Meals were taken in the communal dining hall.

Some kibbutzim had only one telephone. The idea of owning your own car was unheard of. The typical kibbutz might possess a couple of old clunkers—a Peugeot or Deux Chevaux or an Israeli-made Studebaker Lark. If you needed to drive somewhere—say, into the city to see a doctor—you put your name on a list and hoped the committee gave you the keys. We rode buses or bicycles or walked. Everybody walked.

A kibbutz could be tough sometimes. When our battalion commander, Uzi Eilam, was twenty years old and had completed his first army service, he wanted to study at the Technion, the Israel Institute of Technology in Haifa. Uzi was already an outstanding leader. Clearly he was destined for big things. The kibbutz took a vote and turned him down. They wanted him at home, working the land.

People think that Israelis of that era were religious. That's not true. On the kibbutz in those days the ethic was socialist, communal, Zionist—not antireligious but definitely nonreligious. Moshe Dayan, who was born on Israel's first kibbutz, Deganiah Alef, had never had a bar mitzvah. Many of us were like that. We could light a candle, but we knew only a handful of prayers.

In Israel the fifties and early sixties were called *Tekufat HaTzena,* the "period of austerity." The economy was struggling to absorb hundreds of thousands of immigrants, many of whom had been expelled from Arab countries. These were often poor and lacking Western skills or education.

On the kibbutz, at least we had enough to eat. You can tell someone who grew up during the Austere Period because their teeth have no cavities. No one could afford such luxuries as sugar or candy.

Israel, as I said, is small. On the kibbutz farms where I and Zamosh and Milo and others of our battalion grew up, you felt like you were living in Kansas. Yet Tel Aviv—our Manhattan—was only an hour and a half away.

At our base near Lod, the brigade began training in earnest. We were so new, we had never even jumped as a brigade. Soon we would be jumping in combat, the rumors said, in Sinai. We lived in shelter halves—two-man tents—in orchards under orange and lemon trees and listened at night on our transistors to the Voice of Thunder. The news was full of stories of Nasser's troop and tank buildup in Sinai. The UN had a peacekeeping force in the desert. Would they stop him? On May 18 Nasser ordered them out and they went. By May 22 he had closed the Straits of Tiran, sealing off our port of Eilat.

Would there be war? On May 24 we were ordered to stand ready; D-day would be the next morning. That order was rescinded, then repeated on May 25, 26, and 27, and again on May 29 and 30. Each time we stood down, the politicians gave a different excuse. They were "seeking a negotiated settlement" or "exhausting all diplomatic options." Mostly they were trying to get the Russians to tell Nasser to back off or to convince the Americans or the British and the French to come in on our side.

When you're a twenty-three-year-old lieutenant, you care nothing for any of this. All you know is that every day that passes without the government making a decision gives the enemy more time to prepare, more time to bring up tanks and guns, more time to dig in and fortify. Every twenty-four hours means more of us will die.

I remember getting a twelve-hour pass to go home because my mother had taken sick. I hitchhiked but got left off about fifteen kilometers short as darkness was falling. From the road I could look east down the valley toward Jordan. King Hussein's army had 176 new American Patton tanks; from the border they could reach my kibbutz in under an hour. Syrian armor could roll down from the Golan Heights and be overrunning our defenses even sooner.

Where I stood was only a few kilometers past the ruins of ancient Megiddo—Armageddon of the Bible. I tried not to think of it, but that song by the Doors kept playing in my head.

3.

DOWN IN THE DESERT

I was living in Athens when I got a cable from my father asking me to come home at once. It was understood that no Israeli would wish to be elsewhere when the nation was in danger. For my father, who understood the political and military dynamics of the Middle East as well as any man, to write such a note could mean only one thing: war was imminent.

Yael Dayan is the twenty-seven-year-old daughter of former army chief of staff Moshe Dayan. She has published two well-received novels, as well as essays and journalism, and has acquired a measure of celebrity in the European press. She is also a segen mishne, *a second lieutenant, in the reserve forces of the IDF.*

I flew back on BEA to Lod, the British-built airfield that would become Ben-Gurion International. My mother picked me up. The date was May 25, 1967. We drove to the mobilization center in Tel Aviv, where I presented my military identification and requested to be sent south, to the Egyptian front. The desk sergeant smiled. "And where do you think everyone else wants to go?"

But my request was approved.

Driving home, my mother and I listened to Nasser's latest radio harangue, in which the Egyptian president declared that "our ultimate objective will be the destruction of Israel."

Nasser announced that the armies of Egypt and Syria were now under unified command. He invited Jordan to join. Egypt's president was, he said, in daily contact with the leaders of a dozen other Arab states, every one of which had pledged troops, arms, or money.

I had dinner with my father that night. He had been visiting the fighting units at the front and was in high spirits. He joked that I had achieved in two hours what he had been unable to accomplish in two weeks: the acquisition of an actual job.

I asked him in what capacity he had been touring the forward units.

"As a uniformed soldier, accompanied by a conducting officer," he said. Ezer Weizman, who was IDF chief of operations (and my father's brother-in-law; Ezer's wife, Reumah, was my mother's sister), had gotten my father mobilized, though without rank or authority. "I show up as a simple pain in the neck."

He had met with Ezer that morning, my father said, and later with his dear friend Meir Amit, who was Israel's chief of intelligence. Egypt now had nearly a thousand tanks in Sinai, threatening our southern border. If you were offered a post, Amit had asked my father, would you take it? Dayan gave him this note for Prime Minister Levi Eshkol:

> Dear Eshkol,
>
> I have asked Ezer Weizman to arrange my formal mobilization for active service so that my presence in an army unit will be legal and proper. If you or the chief of staff consider that I may be of help in this war by being given a specific task, I shall, of course, accept. If not, I shall continue in the meantime to be attached to combat units so that I may see developments at close quarters and be able to express practical views on the strength of the army and on what may be done.
>
> Moshe Dayan
> 25.5.67.

We talked about my assignment. I had been detailed as a correspondent to the *ugda* of General Ariel Sharon, which was dug in now at Nitzana on the Egyptian frontier.

An *ugda* is a formation unique to the Israeli Army. Approximately the size of a division, it is configured of independent brigades for the purpose of accomplishing a specific objective or confronting a particular foe. An ugda is a onetime formation. It takes its name from its commander. On the Sinai border, the army had mobilized three. In the north, Ugda Tal (No. 84) under General Israel Tal; in the center, Ugda Yoffe (No. 31) under General Avraham Yoffe; in the south, Ugda Sharon (No. 38) under General Arik

Sharon. An independent armored brigade, the 8th, under Colonel Albert Mendler, was positioned farther south, opposite Kuntilla.

My father had been out of the army for ten years, but in the public mind he remained the hero of the '56 Sinai Campaign and the paragon of the Israeli fighting commander. While we dined, guests continually approached the table, no few in obvious states of agitation.

"When will the government call you, Moshe?"

"Will they make you minister of defense?"

"The people are behind you, General Dayan."

I asked my father if he expected to be given a command by Prime Minister Eshkol.

Yael Dayan.

"He will call you before he calls me!"

My father spoke of the distinction between "intent" and "objective." In any military order, intent is inscribed above and supersedes objective.

The issue with Eshkol, he said, was that his intent was to preserve Israel *at any cost*. To that end, the prime minister set the nation at the beck and call of the Western powers, specifically the United States, while stalling and refusing to make a decision based on our strength alone.

But the prime minister's intent, my father said, cannot be to preserve Israel at the price of sacrificing her fighting spirit and independence of action.

"To bang on the powers' doors is to cut off our own balls. We know it and Nasser knows it. What has kept Israel safe for ten years is our enemies' fear to strike us. The prime minister's intent must be 'to preserve the nation *by destroying the forces arrayed against it.*'"

We are being bullied, my father said, and the only way to handle a bully is to punch him in the face.

"What would you do?" I asked.

"Strike now. As soon as possible. Meet the enemy straight-up and destroy him. There is no other way."

Outside, my father's car was waiting. The hour was nearly midnight. He was leaving for the headquarters of Southern Command in Beersheba.

"The prime minister will address the nation in a couple of days," I said. At the mobilization offices, I had heard of a radio speech planned for the evening of May 29. "Will you listen?"

"Yes," Moshe Dayan said. "But without relish."

4.

THE DEATH BURST

The last thing on my mind was Eshkol's speech. I supposed I would listen when it came on. But my job was to kill MiGs, not to worry about politics. I was so deeply absorbed in my own flying and training that nothing could penetrate the bubble.

Lieutenant Giora Romm is a twenty-two-year-old fighter pilot with Squadron 119 based at Tel Nof Air Base. He will become the first and only "ace" of the Six Day War, shooting down five MiGs.

Every fighter squadron, and probably every operational unit in the world, breaks down into two generations: the old guys—the captains and majors at the top of the food chain—and the young lieutenants at the bottom.

The captains and majors are the senior pilots, the squadron commander and his deputies. In Squadron 119, these are the fliers with operational experience. They had fought in the Sinai Campaign of '56. They had flown reconnaissance missions over Egypt and Syria and Jordan. They had experienced "triple-A"—antiaircraft artillery. They had engaged in dogfights. They had made kills.

We young guys had done none of that. We tried to imagine what war was like, but the feat was beyond us. To us, war was a cinematic mash-up of Pierre Clostermann memoirs and old Battle of Britain movies.

The old guys were married and had families; they lived in the colony of bungalows in the administrative part of the base. They had cars and washing machines. Their wives took care of everything for them. I was twenty-two. I was six feet two and weighed 154 pounds. I shared a room in the bachelor officers' quarters with another pilot, Avramik Salmon. I had no wife. My car was at home with my parents in Tel Aviv. I rode a bicycle. I did my laundry at Ran Ronen's house, our squadron commander.

His wife, Heruta, helped all of us. She hung our socks and flight suits on the line out back and folded them up in neat piles, which we collected later.

Every pilot thinks his squadron is the best. I did and still do. Here's a story that will tell you about our commander, Ran Ronen:

In training for air-to-air combat, a kill is awarded based on the film in the gun camera. You must have one full second with your pipper—the gunsight—zeroed on the body of the plane you're competing against. But at that time a practice called "demonstration shots" was permitted. You were allowed to cite gun camera film even if you were not in a sure-kill position and you had not held your sights on the target for a full second. The purpose of this practice was simply to demonstrate at the end of the day, in the briefing room with Ran and the other pilots, that you had been on the other guy's tail and not the other way around.

One day Ran called the squadron together. "This is bullshit!" he said in that voice that could make you jump six inches out of your chair. From now on, Ran declared, pilots would be allowed to activate the gun camera only when the competing plane was dead center in our sights—a certain kill. And we had to keep that plane in the bull's-eye for a full second, sixteen consecutive frames of film.

The pilots groaned when they heard this. Do you know how hard it is to keep an enemy in your gunsights for a full second?

"I have no compassion for you," declared Ran. The sure-kill, sixteen-frame standard would now be called "the death burst."

If you wanted to be credited with a kill, you had to produce the death burst.

The next day, when the squadron went up to practice dogfighting, skill levels elevated by 40 percent. It was amazing. Every pilot raised his game. You had to. There was no other way to achieve the death burst.

When I was fifteen, I applied for and was accepted into a new military boarding school associated with the Reali School in Haifa. The Reali School was the elite high school in Israel. The military school was a secondary school version of West Point. We attended classes at Reali in the morning and underwent our military training in the afternoon.

I don't believe there is an institution in Israel today that can measure up to the standards of that school. Why did I want to go there? I wanted to test myself. At that time in Israel the ideal to which an individual aspired was inclusion as part of a "serving elite." The best of the best were not motivated by money or fame. Their aim was to serve the nation, to sacrifice their lives if necessary. At the military boarding school, it was assumed that every graduate would volunteer for a fighting unit, the more elite, the better. We studied, we played sports, we trekked. We hiked all over Israel. We were unbelievably strong physically. But what was even more powerful were the principles that the school hammered into our skulls.

First: Complete the mission.

The phrase in Hebrew is *Dvekut baMesima*.

Mesima is "mission"; *dvekut* means "glued to." The mission is everything. At all costs, it must be carried through to completion. I remember running up the Snake Trail at Masada one summer at 110 degrees Fahrenheit with two of my classmates. Each of us would sooner have died than be the first to call, "Hey, slow down!"

Second: Whatever you do, do it to your utmost. The way you tie your shoes. The way you navigate at night. Nothing is academic.

Third: *En brera.* "No alternative."

We are Jews; we are surrounded by enemies who seek our destruction and the extermination of our people. There is no alternative to victory.

In Squadron 119, Ran led us according to these principles. Complete the mission. Perform every action to perfection. Follow through at any cost.

Then there was one final principle, which was, and remains to this day, the secret weapon of IAF fighting doctrine. Here is how it was taught to me:

I was talking with an older pilot. He asked me what I considered to be Ezer Weizman's most important contribution to the air force. Ezer was the IAF's boldest and most flamboyant commander.

"That's easy," I said. "He got us seventy-two Mirages." Meaning the magnificent French-built warplanes that we flew in our squadron.

"No, Giora," the veteran said. "Ezer introduced the culture of the ruthlessly candid debriefing."

At the end of each training day, the squadron met in the briefing room. Ran stood up front. He went over every mistake we had made that day—not just those of the young pilots, but his own as well. He was fearless in his self-criticism, and he made us speak up with equal candor. If you had screwed up, you admitted it and took your medicine. Ego meant nothing. Improvement was everything.

An operational squadron flies only one type of plane. In the IAF of '67 these were all French made: twin-engined Vautour fighter-bombers; single-engine Ouragans that looked like American F-84 Thunderjets; the subsonic Mystères and supersonic Super Mystères; and the pride of the air force, the Dassault Mirage IIIC fighter-interceptor.

How do I feel about the Mirage? I'll tell you a story:

After the war, when the Mirage was replaced by the American F-4 Phantom, I moved on to a Phantom squadron. One day the ground crew was pushing my plane into its cell when we accidentally dinged one wingtip. As punishment my squadron commander grounded me. I phoned a friend, the commander of a Mirage squadron. He invited me to come and fly.

When I settled into the Mirage cockpit, tears welled in my eyes.

The Mirage is an aircraft like no other. You sit up front and high. You can see everything. The controls are close, and they respond to a touch. You fly a Mirage with your fingertips.

A Mirage is fast. When you light the afterburner, the aircraft leaps. And it's beautiful. It has that Coca-Cola body. Delta wings. Silver. The engine may be prone to flameouts and compressor stalls, and you had to land with your nose so high you could barely see the runway, and without flaps (the delta wings had none), but in the vertical dimension the Mirage was untouchable. Nothing in the sky was a match for her.

We were training to attack Egypt. The enemy had fourteen major fields in Sinai, the Nile delta, and the south. Each IAF squadron had its target list—primaries and secondaries. You had to know them all. The planes would attack in formations of four. In ours and the two other Mirage squadrons—the 101 at Hatzor and the 117 at Ramat David—each aircraft would be armed with two 500-kilogram (1,100-pound) bombs. The bombs would be dropped at specific points on specific runways at an hour and minute that was calculated precisely to coincide with attacks by every other squadron in the air force on every other Egyptian field.

The bombing runs would be followed by three passes of strafing in a 270-degree pattern, alternating the turning direction twice. Meaning you struck first from, say, the north, then the east or west, then the south or north. With our 30-millimeter cannons we would attack enemy aircraft on the ground. We knew where every plane was parked and at what hours the pilots returned from their early morning patrols.

Every squadron in the Israel Air Force would participate in the attack. Only 12 planes out of 202 would be held back to defend the nation's skies. Every machine that could fly would participate, including the ancient Fouga Magisters from the flight school. The Fougas would be outfitted with rockets to attack ground targets and to provide close air support for the infantry and armor.

How do you turn 202 planes into 404? By the skill of the maintenance crews on the ground. In most air forces 75 percent would be a spectacular combat readiness figure, meaning that seventy-five out of a hundred planes were fit to fly. On 5 June '67 the IAF had 100 percent of its aircraft ready for takeoff. Our ground crews could turn a plane around in minutes. They could squeeze four or five sorties out of every plane every day. On paper the enemy may have had more aircraft, but we could put more planes into the air.

By mid-May Nasser had closed the Straits of Tiran. Egypt was sending more and more tanks into Sinai. Squadron 119 was ordered to move onto the base full-time. Training hours went from ten to twelve to fourteen. When we weren't flying, we were briefing or debriefing or studying our tasks and our assignments.

For me, this was heaven.

What had motivated me to become a fighter pilot? To seek single combat in the sky. To test myself at what was, to my mind, the pinnacle of skill, resourcefulness, and daring.

There was only one moment during the waiting period when I felt fear. News came that the Egyptian 4th Armored Division had been deployed to Sinai. The 4th, we all knew, was Nasser's crack division, equipped with the heaviest and most modern Soviet tanks. I was at a military dinner and found myself for a moment beside Motti Hod, the air force chief.

"Motti," I said—only in Israel can a twenty-two-year-old lieutenant address the commander of the air force not just by his first name but by his nickname. "What do you think about the Egyptian 4th Division moving forward in Sinai? Should we be frightened?"

"Giora, this is news I have prayed for. Let Nasser bring *all* his divisions forward. The more he brings, the more we will destroy."

I thought, Wow, that is an interesting way of looking at things! It turned me around completely.

So as the evening of the prime minister's address approached, I was more worried about my laundry than about what Levi Eshkol had to say to the nation. Would Ran's wife have time to get my socks and skivvies into the washing machine? I was really concerned about this.

Let the rest of the country agonize over politics and diplomacy and whether or not the Americans were going to ride to our rescue. I refused to lose sleep over this. I had my Mirage. I knew how to fly it and with luck I was going to get the chance. That was all I knew and all I cared to know.

5.

PALSAR SEVEN

The waiting goes on. Our company is stationed among rolling dunes near Kerem Shalom, a kibbutz on the Gaza Strip/Egypt frontier. It's hot. A hundred Fahrenheit by nine in the morning.

Eli Rikovitz is a twenty-one-year-old lieutenant, a platoon commander in the Recon Company of the 7th Armored Brigade. He will be awarded the Itur HaMofet, the Medal of Distinguished Service, for his actions during the Six Day War.

An armored brigade in ready position spreads out over miles. Each morning at 03:30 the entire formation—hundreds of tanks, half-tracks, and support vehicles—is awake and at full alert, helmets on, chin straps buckled, all engines roaring, all radio nets open. We are waiting for the Egyptians to attack at dawn. When they don't, we stand down.

If there is a formula for driving young soldiers nuts, this is it.

A reconnaissance company's job is to find the enemy and to lead our tanks. We drive American CJ-5 jeeps, souped up to our own standards. What this means is we steal from other units all the extra fuel, ammo, and rations we can load onto the makeshift racks that we've welded onto our jeeps. When the tires start sinking into the sand, we know we've put on too much.

Across the border from us waits the Egyptian 7th Division, with four more divisions behind it in central Sinai. In the Gaza Strip, a few kilometers northeast of our position, is another enemy division, the Palestinian, as well as a near-division-size task force, the Shazli Force, named after its commander, General Saad Shazli—of nine thousand men and two hundred tanks and guns.

We are one division, Ugda Tal, with two others—Sharon's and Yoffe's—to our south.

Our company, Palsar Seven, will be the first to cross the border. We will lead the tanks of the 7th Armored Brigade. The plan is for the brigade's two armored battalions to strike north from Kerem Shalom on the Israeli side toward Rafiah Junction on the Egyptian. There the main road turns west toward El Arish in Sinai. El Arish is our ultimate objective.

Can we do it?

We are full of confidence.

We are all young in the Recon Company because we're regular army. Reserves are older—twenty-two to fifty. To be in a regular outfit means you're serving your compulsory service. You're a kid. You went in at eighteen. The oldest guy in Palsar Seven is our company commander, Ori Orr. He's twenty-eight. I'm twenty-one.

"Palsar" is an acronym for *Plugat Siyur*, which simply means "reconnaissance company." "Seven" means we're part of the 7th Armored Brigade. The guys in my platoon are so young that we don't have wives. Only a few have girlfriends. When we send postcards home, we write to our parents.

My mom and dad live in Zahala, a suburb of Tel Aviv built for army and defense ministry personnel. Yitzhak Rabin, the army chief of staff, is our neighbor. Growing up, my friends and I would catch rides to school with him. He's a good guy. I used to swim at night in the Zahala pool; Rabin would be there doing laps. Moshe Dayan's house is two streets over.

My mother sends me articles from the newspapers, *Haaretz* ("The Land") and *Maariv* ("Evening"). The editorials are full of calls for Prime Minister Eshkol's resignation, or at least for him to give up his post as minister of defense. People are demanding a unity government. Here in the desert we don't give a damn about such stuff. Let us fight. We're young and we believe we're bulletproof.

Every few days, word comes that we're going to attack. Tomorrow is D-day, we are told. There have been eight D-days so far, maybe nine—I can't remember. Each time we are told the attack code and the time of H-hour. New plans are issued, based on the positions to which the Egyptian forces have moved during the previous night.

Our job in Recon is to guide the tanks to their new ready positions. This is done after dark, to avoid observation by the enemy's air force or by his long-range observation posts. A tank alone in the dark will nosedive into the first ditch it comes to. Our jeeps guide them. It usually takes till two or three in the morning. We snooze under blankets in the sand or in our vehicles. The three-thirty wakeup comes; every engine fires up, every soldier runs through whatever mental stuff he does to get himself ready to face his own death.

Then the word comes: Stand down.

I have two guys in my outfit who are natural comics: Gabi Gazit and Benzi Zur. They're both about twenty. To Gabi and Benzi, I am an old man. They ask me for advice about sex and marriage. What do I know? They ask about death. "You tell me," I say.

We are all friends in Recon.

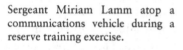

Miriam Lamm is pilot Giora Romm's fiancée. She is a sergeant, twenty-two years old, a code specialist in the headquarters group of Ugda Tal:

I am among the few women with the combat troops. My fiancé, Giora, is a fighter pilot in Mirage Squadron 119. I'm a coder/decoder, part of General Tal's com-

Sergeant Miriam Lamm atop a communications vehicle during a reserve training exercise.

mand group. I will ride in an armored half-track when and if war comes and we cross the border.

Our section's half-track, unlike those of the combat troops, is enclosed. I don't like it. I know I should feel safe inside this armored box, but I'd rather see what's going on outside. I feel like I'm in a coffin.

My father is in the reserves. He's fifty-one. Men love being in the reserves; it makes them feel proud. Three weeks ago, two officers in uniform came to our door with a notice, Call-up Order No. 8. This is the hottest, most urgent category of mobilization order. My father hurried to grab his gear. But the officers said, "We are here for your daughter, Sergeant Miriam Lamm."

My dad was crestfallen.

Call-up Order No. 8 meant you had to leave right that moment. You went with the officers.

I said good-bye, feeling so bad for my father, and went to join Tal's division.

Menachem Shoval is a nineteen-year-old trooper in the Recon Company of the 7th Armored Brigade, part of Ugda Tal:

In Israel when you turn eighteen the army takes you and puts you wherever it needs you or wherever your tests say you will do best. But you can volunteer before then, if you want, for special units like the paratroops or the Sayeret Matkal. I have always wanted Recon. The Recon company of an armored brigade is an elite unit. You're supposed to pass a battery of physical and intelligence tests, which, of course, you must. But the real selection process is *chaver mayvee chaver*, "a friend brings a friend."

I have not yet completed my training. This worries me a little. Our company may be in action soon. I wish I had had more time to learn everything I'm supposed to know.

In the American army, I understand, a recruit goes through basic training, then advanced training in his military specialty. Only after that is he assigned to a unit.

That's not how it works in Israel. In the IDF you go straight to your actual outfit. The outfit trains you from scratch. Our formation, the Recon Company of the 7th Armored Brigade, has been training all over Israel. We learn how to operate on foot and in jeeps, day and night, in all types of weather. You live rough. Camps have no cooks, no laundry, no hot showers. The team whips up its own chow and washes its own clothes. You're trained by the same guys you'll be serving with. You live in tents or trailers that are more like hobo jungles than military bases.

Navigation exercises are the meat of Recon training. Night nav. Have you ever seen a "blind map"? It shows topography only. No roads, no cities, no landmarks.

The object of a night navigation march is to trek from one prescribed point to another in a sequence that may include ten or twelve stations. This is the hardest thing I have ever done. One station may be a rock. Just a rock. You have to find it in the dark in the middle of nowhere and then write in your notebook what you have discovered. A white X, say, painted on the underside of the rock. The next station may be a kilometer away, or ten kilometers. You have to complete the circuit before the sun comes up.

To observe a great navigator like Eli Rikovitz or Amos Ayalon, the Recon platoon commanders, is like watching Beethoven. These guys read a map like you or I read a book. They don't scratch their heads, they don't furrow their brows. They look and see. This is amazing to me.

Will we use any of these skills when we cross the Egyptian border? I don't know. Nobody does. Will war come? Can we win?

Intelligence reports keep coming in saying that the Egyptians have brought up Stalin tanks, a whole brigade, to block the approaches south of Rafiah—the very area our outfit is slated to attack. Stalin tanks are the heaviest Russian armor from World War II. A Stalin tank packs a 122-millimeter main gun. The cannons on our Pattons are 90-millimeters and on our Centurions 105-millimeters. Stalin tanks were designed by the Russians to knock out the heaviest German tanks, the huge Tigers and Panthers. I can't imagine what damage a 122-millimeter gun can do.

6.

NAOMI'S TRENCH

My husband is mobilized on May 21. The unit he commands, Paratroop Battalion 71, is one of the last to get orders, though clearly the call-up is imminent. Uzi has been meeting with his company commanders in our living room all week. I serve coffee and sweet rolls, while the officers spread maps on the floor and on top of the piano.

Dr. Naomi Eilam is a pediatric physician serving in the department of health. Her responsibilities include two villages of new immigrants, Yemenite Jews, to which she commutes under armed guard because of fedayeen incursions from Jordan. She is twenty-nine years old and has been married to her husband, Uzi, since 1954.

I have been an army wife for almost thirteen years and have come to hate the word "operational." It means that my husband is somewhere across the border, usually at night on a reprisal operation, or in some other position where he may be wounded or killed. Uzi has already been shot twice, once by our own forces. Not even Israeli wives get used to that.

Uzi fought in the Sinai Campaign in '56, the victory that all of Israel believed had bought us a decade or more of peace. Even when our forces were compelled by the Americans and the Russians to withdraw from Sinai in 1957, Israelis acceded to the necessity with cautious optimism. UN peacekeepers took over our soldiers' posts in Sinai. The desert became a demilitarized zone, a buffer between us and the Egyptians. Nasser could no longer move bombers or tanks close to our border. The Great Powers guaranteed it. They would hold their shield over Israel. Beneath this, we dared to feel safe.

Suddenly in '67 everything changed.

On May 15, Israel's Independence Day, the radio reported Egyptian divisions moving into Sinai. Neighbors and friends reacted with shock. Nasser can't do that, can he? The UN is supposed to stop him.

But each day brought further Egyptian incursions.

On May 18, Nasser ordered the United Nations out of Sinai entirely. Our ambassadors appealed to the Security Council. Surely Secretary-General U Thant will stand up to these Egyptian provocations. But two days later UN peacekeepers were packing up their equipment and pulling out.

More Egyptian divisions rolled into Sinai. Nasser had long since nationalized the Suez Canal; now he sent paratroopers to seize Sharm el-Sheikh, closing the Gulf of Aqaba to Israeli shipping. Our port of Eilat had been cut off by this clear and flagrant act of war.

The Arab world exploded with joy. Nasser's boldness ignited anti-Israeli passions across North Africa and the entire Middle East. Mobs filled the streets in a dozen Arab nations, chanting, "Kill the Jews!" and "Death to the Zionists!" Syria, Iraq, and Saudi Arabia pledged troops to Nasser. So did Lebanon, Libya, Tunisia, and Morocco.

How could this be happening? Where were our allies? The Americans, mired in Vietnam, dilated and demurred. The State Department claimed to have literally lost the 1956 letter in which Secretary of State John Foster Dulles had guaranteed Israel's territorial integrity.

France, after her costly war in Algeria, had adopted a strategy of befriending the Arabs. When our foreign minister, Abba Eban, called upon Charles de Gaulle to honor France's post-Sinai pledge to stand by Israel, the French president rebuffed him with contempt. "That was 1957," he said. "This is 1967."

That same night, France cut off all arms shipments to Israel.

As for Great Britain, the hearts of her people may have been in the right place, but the nation's politicians had tied their hopes for Middle East oil and influence to their former client states Jordan, Iraq, and Saudi Arabia. Whitehall was not keen to shed British blood in defense of a couple of million pain-in-the-neck Jews who had last made headlines in London in 1946 when their underground fighters blew up British military headquarters in Jerusalem's King David Hotel.

In the suburb of Yehud, where Uzi and I lived, homes started emptying as husband after husband was called up for war. I drove into Tel Aviv one morning and found Allenby Street so deserted that I could walk across at midblock, an act that would have been suicidal two weeks earlier.

Families were leaving the country. I knew two in our neighborhood. The airport at Lod was so busy with outbound flights that a grim joke began circulating: "Will the last one out please turn off the lights?"

Along Dizengoff Street in Tel Aviv, shopkeepers were shuttering their businesses. Doorways had been sandbagged, windows taped or shielded by roll-down iron gates. I had been nine years old during the War of Independence in 1948. I remember Egyptian Spitfires attacking Tel Aviv unopposed (Israel had not even a single antiaircraft gun), dropping bombs and making strafing runs down civilian streets.

This time would be far worse. Nasser had Soviet bombers, Ilyushins and Tupolevs. If the city started to burn, who or what could stop it? Half the fire trucks had been mobilized. Even the city buses were gone. Almost all had been activated as transport for the troops. Taxis had been called up as well, along with bread vans, milk trucks, even dump trucks and panel vans. The one truck I saw from the Tnuva Dairy was carrying reservists.

City parks and soccer fields were being consecrated as graveyards. There seemed to be blood drive tables in every office building. Hotel lobbies had been made over into casualty collection centers. In a drugstore I was handed a mimeographed sheet—instructions for the identification and burial of the dead.

Uzi dug a trench in our backyard. He is an engineer so he did it exactly per specifications, with a zigzag at the halfway point so that if a bomb or mortar shell landed at one end, the blast wouldn't kill you at the other.

Digging trenches at Gan Shmuel.

The first morning when the sirens sounded, I was alone in the kitchen with the baby. I grabbed her, in her diaper, and dashed out to the trench in my robe. I had left the coffee percolator going. I remember thinking, Do I dare go back inside to turn it off?

Finally, after about fifteen minutes sitting there in the trench, just me and the baby, I decided it was silly and went back into the house. Later we learned that the civil defense people had not yet figured out that they were supposed to blow the all-clear siren when the air raid alert was over.

Our quiet suburb was only seven or eight kilometers from the international airport, but the surrounding fields and hills were wilderness. The armistice line was so close that Jordanian raiders crossed almost every night. My medical responsibilities included two Yemenite villages, Bareket and Tirat Yehuda. These were settlements for Jews from Yemen who had been expelled from their home country by Muslim pogroms, airlifted to Israel by our own pilots and planes, and settled on land belonging to the state. Poverty was extreme but the newcomers bore it with patience and dignity. I was the only Western person providing medical aid—and the first woman physician my patients had ever seen. The most common injury I treated was burns, inflicted on the flesh of ailing villagers by their native healers as a means of driving out dybbuks, or evil spirits. This, so close to the airport that we could see planes passing close overhead, bearing our countrymen evacuating to London or New York.

My superiors at the health department had determined that it was too risky for me to drive to these villages alone, because of the fedayeen who would cross from Jordan, so each morning two soldiers picked me up in a jeep and provided an armed escort. These soldiers had now been returned to active duty. So I drove myself in our old Peugeot.

Every morning the newspapers said we were going to war. Then they said we weren't. This went on day after day. The state of suspense became unbearable. Every twenty-four hours that passed without a decision produced greater stress on the nation's already struggling economy, not to mention its collective sanity.

So we citizens very much wanted to hear what Prime Minister Eshkol had to say in his address to the nation. We were anxious. We were frightened. We wanted our minds set at ease, one way or the other.

A Jew's worst enemy is often himself. We think too much. Will we now second-guess ourselves into annihilation? As a physician I knew that decisions must often be made without perfect knowledge. I wanted to scream to the politicians: Do something! Make up your minds!

7.

ZAHALA

What Americans speak of as the IDF—the Israel Defense Forces—we Israelis call *Zahal*. The word is an acronym for *Zva Haganah L'Israel*. In the early 1950s the government built a colony of housing outside Tel Aviv exclusively for officers of the army. The settlement is called Zahala. My house is at 11 Joab Street. In the Bible, Joab was King David's nephew and commander of his army.

General Moshe Dayan achieved worldwide renown in 1956 with Israel's spectacular victory over Egypt in what became known as the Sinai Campaign. As chief of staff, Dayan was considered the architect of this triumph. Now, in May 1967, he has been out of the army for ten years. He is a civilian, a member of the Knesset from a small, out-of-power opposition party.

The combat arms of Israel are constituted, organized, and commanded according to a doctrine different from that of other nations. The Israel Defense Forces include as essential elements that other militaries consider unnecessary, and deliberately do without components (such as medium- or long-range bombers) that other armed forces view as indispensable. The reason is that the IDF was created for, and has evolved to wage, a very specific type of war, to be fought in a very specific place, against a very specific enemy.

In 1962, when the first French-built Mirage IIICJ fighters arrived in Israel (designated by their builders "J" for *Juif*, the French word for "Jew"), they had been modified at air force chief Ezer Weizman's insistence to suit the IAF's unique combat mission.

Gone was the rocket booster engine designed to catapult the interceptor into the stratosphere. Relegated to auxiliary use was air-to-air missile armament. Ezer and his chief test pilot, Danny Shapira, demanded guns:

two DEFA 30-millimeter cannons. Also added were racks for two 500-kilogram bombs.

Why these alterations? Because high-altitude interception is not a priority in a nation whose enemies' military runways lie within twenty-five minutes' flying time of her population centers. Our air force instead needed jets that could bomb and destroy enemy airfields, strafe armored columns and troop concentrations, and take on opposing fighters in old-fashioned dogfights in the sky.

Israel possesses none of the strategic geographical advantages of, say, the United States. Our nation does not have a 3,000-mile-wide body of water on one coast and a 5,000-mile-wide ocean on the other. She does not enjoy friendly relations with states along her borders, nor does she possess military alliances upon which she can depend.

Israel's frontiers are not borders, recognized by her neighbors and by the international community, but armistice lines, which may be declared null and void and overthrown arbitrarily at any hour.

I was military commander of the Jewish-controlled half of Jerusalem in 1948, when the Green Line was drawn, separating the infant state of Israel from her enemy Jordan. I drew the line in concord with Lieutenant Colonel Abdullah al-Tell, my counterpart from the Arab Legion. The instrument we used, a chinagraph pencil, happened to be green. Where the line chanced to pass along neighborhood streets, one side became Israeli, the other Jordanian. When the pen passed over a house, one half of that dwelling fell under the jurisdiction of the Hashemite kingdom, the other half under that of the Israeli military command. In effect the home had to be abandoned. It became, inevitably, one of scores of blockhouses and bricked-up strongpoints lining the corridor of minefields and barbed-wire entanglements that divided Jerusalem.

A strategy of defense-in-depth is not possible in a nation that is only nine miles wide at its waist and whose commercial concentrations and population centers lie within artillery range of its enemies. Offense is the only effective posture. War, if war comes, must be fought on the enemy's territory, not our own.

The IDF and IAF have been built upon the principles of speed, aggression, and audacity. An Israeli lieutenant or captain in the field does not expect the luxury of being able to appeal for instructions to higher command. He is on his own and has been trained to fight that way. "To the commander of an Israeli unit," I wrote in *Diary of the Sinai Campaign,*

I can point on a map to the Suez Canal and say: "There's your target and this is your axis of advance. Don't signal me during the fighting for more men, arms, or vehicles. All that we could allocate you've already got, and there isn't more. Keep signaling your advances. You must reach Suez in forty-eight hours." I can give this kind of order to commanders of our units because I know they are ready to assume such tasks and are capable of carrying them out.

I arrive home from visiting units of the Southern Command late on the afternoon of May 28. Prime Minister Eshkol will address the nation this evening. I have no clue what he will say. Will he announce a resolution to the crisis? Will he proclaim an accord guaranteed by the United Nations or the Great Powers? Will he declare war?

My wife, Ruth, is preparing dinner. I tell her I have spoken with our daughter, Yael, and ask about our two sons, Assi and Udi, both of whom have been mobilized with their reserve units, and about my nephews Uzi and Jonathan. Jonathan, the son of my sister Aviva, is in the navy. Uzi is the son of my brother Zorik, who was killed in the War of Independence; he is an officer in the Sayeret Matkal, Israel's special forces.

I myself have been in the field with the troops for the past five days. On Friday I visited Avraham Yoffe's division, facing Sinai, and reviewed battle plans with him and two of his brigade commanders, Colonel Yissachar "Yiska" Shadmi and Colonel Elhanan Sela. A message came for me that morning from Prime Minister Eshkol. I flew back from Beersheba and met him at the Dan Hotel in Tel Aviv. He said he wanted to form a committee, Ministerial Defense and Foreign Affairs, on which I would serve.

I refused. I will accept no "advisory" position. I insist upon a combat command. If none can be found for me, I will drive a tank or a truck. I will not permit Eshkol or his government to neutralize my voice by sidelining me into a ceremonial role.

What I hate most about the dallying and dithering of the cabinet is that they stem from lack of faith in our fighting men and commanders. Our troops are young lions. It is catastrophic in terms of spirit and morale for the nation to be overtaken by hysteria and go beating at the doors of the Powers, begging to be rescued.

At the level of state—meaning the deliberations of the prime minister and the cabinet—a clear and decisive intention must be agreed upon. This must be beyond tactical and strategic, beyond local or regional, and beyond the time frame of the present.

It must answer the question: Where does the country need to be at the end of this crisis?

Remember, we can destroy the army of Egypt to the last man and last tank, and that force will be reconstituted within eighteen months, by draft or conscription from that nation's limitless manpower and by resupply of weaponry and training from its sponsor, the Soviet Union.

Egypt and Syria are client states of the Russians, whose interests in the Middle East are in their view essential and permanent.

For us, victory, in the sense that the Allies achieved over the Axis in World War II, is not possible. We cannot defeat the Arabs. There are too many of them and their sponsor states are too powerful.

Within such limitations, then, what is possible? The prime minister and the cabinet must answer this. I despair of Eshkol because he is not thinking in these terms. In his view, the issue is "How can Israel be preserved?" This is the wrong question to ask, because it permits such an answer as "By a negotiated settlement imposed by the Powers." Such an outcome will save Israel for the moment, but it will do so at the expense of deterrence, which is the only true basis for security for a nation of 2.7 million surrounded by enemies whose numbers are greater than 120 million.

At the same time Chief of Staff Rabin, whom I respect, is thinking in penny packets, proposing to seize the Gaza Strip and use it as a bargaining chip in dealing with Nasser. Bargaining chip for what? Egypt knows that Gaza, with its quarter of a million refugees, is a nest of hornets. She wants it even less than we do.

The proper question to ask is not "How can Israel be preserved at any cost?" but "How can Israel be preserved into the future?"

To this question at this time, no reply is possible except by the sword. The enemy must be dealt such a blow that he will be deterred from striking again, or threatening to strike, for as long as possible.

Therefore our objective cannot be mere seizure of land or the swapping of territories of dubious value. It must be the destruction of the Egyptian Army, not in part and not in detail, but totally and in a straight-up fight—tank against tank, plane against plane, man against man.

There are jacks for multiple telephones in my house, from my days as army chief of staff, but only two are hooked up now, and those are manned by Ruth, between household chores and affairs of business, and whatever helpful neighbor happens to have stopped by.

I sit with my wife now for a light supper of salad, fish, and bread with olive oil. The radio on the counter is already tuned to Kol Israel, over which Levi Eshkol's speech to the nation will be broadcast, but I check it again, twice, to be sure the dial is right.

"How much longer till the prime minister speaks?" asks Ruth.

I check my watch.

"Twenty minutes."

8.

A SECOND SHOAH

In May of '67 when a reservist was called up, his car was also recruited. The army didn't have enough vehicles. I was in seventh grade then. The strangest part of that whole strange month was the way cars kept disappearing. You'd walk out each morning and the street would be emptier than it was the night before.

Haim Koren is a thirteen-year-old in the working-class neighborhood of Bat Galim in Haifa. He will earn his PhD in Middle Eastern studies from Ben-Gurion University in 1993. In 2014 he will be appointed Israel's ambassador to Egypt.

Throughout the waiting period, we listened to Kol Ha'Raam, the Voice of Thunder, out of Cairo. The station's leading announcer, respected throughout the Arab world, was Ali Ahmad Said. Said did not rant or bluster. His broadcasts were more frightening because they were delivered in a reasonable and unemotional tone. He spoke as if he were reporting the news.

"Your time is over, Jews. The experiment in nationhood that the Zionist entity has managed to sustain for nineteen years is due to expire."

Ahmad Said explained, in Hebrew with an accent, how Egyptian heavy bombers would devastate Tel Aviv and Haifa. He advised his Israeli listeners to get away while they still could. To remain was folly. "Save yourselves and your families!"

At thirteen, you are not too young to grasp the significance of events unfolding around you. Naturally you ask your parents to explain what is going on. How serious is it that every young man from our building has left for the army, or that all the taxis and buses are gone? How much should we believe of what we're hearing on the radio?

Many in our neighborhood were Holocaust survivors. Our parents never spoke of this. We children grew up knowing nothing of the Shoah. Our mothers and fathers were protecting us. We were sabras, Israel-born, brave and independent. When our parents answered our questions, their replies were confident and positive. But their voices betrayed them.

In seventh grade I already had a serious interest in Arab history and culture. I was fluent in Arabic; I read Arab newspapers and listened to Arab radio. It was clear to me that Nasser spoke not only for Egypt but for the entire Arab world. His broadcasts were greeted with as much enthusiasm in Damascus and Baghdad as they were in Cairo and Alexandria.

The qadis of Egypt's mosques had been ordered to declare jihad—holy war—against the Jews. Radio Damascus's number one song was "Cut Their Throats!" Mobs marched in the streets; thousands chanted for Israel's destruction.

Nasser preached the concentric community of the Arab world, with Egypt and himself at its epicenter. His voice called 122 million Arabs to unity and summoned them to loose their rage upon our two and a half million Jews.

How would our government respond to these threats? In Israel then, the prime minister was also the minister of defense. He commanded the army. When would Eshkol give Nasser his answer?

May 28.

I remember my mother telling me over breakfast, "Tonight Eshkol will speak. This evening the prime minister will address the nation."

In our part of the country, Levi Eshkol was revered. He was from the north, as we were. He had been a farmer and an engineer. And he had steered the state successfully through a number of crises in the economy, immigration, and agriculture.

Finally tonight Eshkol would speak. Finally Nasser and Ali Ahmad Said would get their answer.

I couldn't wait to hear.

9.

THE STUTTERING SPEECH

My first reaction was to laugh. I thought it was a joke. This couldn't really be happening.

Lieutenant Giora Romm hears Eshkol's speech at the home of his squadron commander, Major Ran Ronen, at Tel Nof Air Base, along with the other pilots of Squadron 119.

I had a friend at Kol Israel, the radio station, who told me later that the prime minister had read through the text of his speech twice in rehearsal and hadn't flubbed a word.

What happened apparently, when the program went live, was that Eshkol's aide Ady Yoffe substituted a revised version of the text at the last minute. Some of the changes were handwritten. The prime minister was taken by surprise. For a few seconds, he forgot he was sitting before an open microphone. He turned to his aide and asked, "What is this word?" We could all hear it.

Haim Koren, thirteen, is listening at home in Bat Galim with his mother and father:

He was stuttering. We could hear the prime minister stammer. The air went dead. For a moment it seemed like the whole broadcast was going to be cut off.

I thought I could hear in the background the engineer, or whoever controls such things, trying to shut down the program in midspeech.

Lieutenant Avigdor Kahalani is a tank company commander with the 7th Armored Brigade, stationed opposite Gaza in a forward position along the Egyptian frontier:

Voice is everything when you command. As a company commander in a tank battalion, you have fourteen four-man crews listening to you through their headsets. Many times in combat, when I have been frightened or unsure, I have deliberately paused to be certain that I had my voice under control. You don't want your men to hear that chicken voice.

Yael Dayan is with General Arik Sharon's headquarters on the Egyptian border:

I had driven with my friend Dov Sion from the front to Beersheba to file a story. Dov is a colonel, General Sharon's liaison with the General Staff. He and I heard the prime minister's speech on the car radio, driving back from Beersheba.

Much has been made of Eshkol's stumbling over the text. But the problem was the text itself. People were desperate for decisiveness. Instead they heard a call for patience. Wait for the Powers. Give diplomacy a chance.

I thought of the troops in the trenches listening to this mess. Some wept, I heard. The speech was a turning point. After that, the people took over. The need for decisiveness overrode all other concerns.

Itzik Barnoach listens from Burgata in the Sharon Plain, where he and his mobilized reserve unit have been training for four weeks:

I had a transistor and I said, My God, this schmuck is not only talking nonsense, he's stuttering! We were not afraid, but we were anxious. The whole world is against us, we don't know what will happen. We hoped this speech would declare war! So this was even worse. It was a disaster. A disaster.

Dr. Naomi Eilam is the wife of Major Uzi Eilam, commander of Paratroop Battalion 71:

Next day the editorials clamored for action. Either Eshkol had to go or he must cede the defense portfolio to someone else. After two interminable weeks of crisis, it was clear to all that the nation's political leadership remained paralyzed by indecision and irresolution.

BOOK TWO

EN BRERA

10.

NORSEMEN

The year 1967 was not the first time that Israel's survival had hung by a thread. Nineteen years earlier, before the nation had even declared its independence, the armies of five Arab nations—Egypt, Syria, Iraq, Jordan, and Lebanon—had massed on its borders, preparing to invade. Their intention was to wipe out the state of Israel before it could even be born.

Coleman "Collie" Goldstein is an American B-17 pilot of World War II. Shot down over France in the fall of 1943, he crash-landed safely, preserving his ten-man crew. Goldstein survived the winter, aided by the French Resistance, before crossing the Pyrénées on foot to safety.

The date was April 1948. I was at home in Philadelphia when I got a call from a guy who introduced himself as Lou Lenart. Lou told me he was a Marine fighter pilot who had flown Corsairs with Squadron VMF-323 on Okinawa and against the home islands of Japan. Lou asked me if I had been following in the newspapers the situation in the Middle East. I said I had. Did I know that the yet-to-be-born state of Israel was in mortal danger and was desperate for combat pilots to help defend it?

Lou said he had something extremely important to talk to me about, but he couldn't do it over the phone. He was in New York, he said. If he took the train down to Philly, would I meet him for a cup of coffee?

Of course, I said.

At that time, before the phone call from Lou, my day-to-day efforts were focused entirely on securing employment with a U.S. airline. I was looking for a job. I was a decorated vet, but I couldn't get on anywhere.

No one would hire a Jew. Passengers on Pan Am or TWA didn't want to hear, "This is your captain, Coleman Goldstein, speaking."

I had made up my mind to learn every skill necessary to start a career in aviation. I had my mechanic's license and my flight engineer certification. Still no one would take me.

Suddenly Lou appeared. He said he was staying at the Henry Hudson Hotel on Fifty-seventh Street in Manhattan. Apparently this was the headquarters for the Haganah and various underground organizations seeking volunteers for the armed forces of Israel. Israel, Lou stressed again, needed pilots desperately. He himself was leaving for Rome in a few days. From there, the Haganah would get him to Tel Aviv. He gave me a pitch about how the British, who were in the final days of their occupation of Palestine under a mandate from the United Nations, were giving the Arabs weapons, planes, and bombs while they were putting Jews against the wall for carrying so much as a pistol. As they say in the movies, Lou had me at hello.

I went up to the Henry Hudson, which by the way had the best martinis in the city at that time. Four-ouncers. Two weeks later Lou and I were in Rome, in a hotel on the Via Veneto with a handful of other Jewish and non-Jewish fliers, living side by side with Czech gunrunners and Russian mobsters, pimps, hookers, and Vatican smugglers shuttling ex-Nazis via secret routes called "ratlines" to haven in Argentina and Brazil.

We wore leather flight jackets and carried guns and got our meal money from a Haganah paymaster who looked like Sydney Greenstreet. It was like being in a Humphrey Bogart movie.

But this was no joke. In Palestine, the British Mandate was due to expire in a matter of weeks. Already Arab irregulars and fedayeen were cutting off roads and terrorizing Jewish farms. The armies of five Arab nations, as I said, were mobilizing to invade the new Jewish state (which still didn't have a name, and in fact hadn't yet made up its mind that it even wanted to be a state) the second it declared independence.

The Jews had a solid defense force, the Haganah, and its shock troops, the Palmach. But they had no tanks, no artillery, no weapons heavier than 88-millimeter mortars. And no air force.

The British had given the Egyptians fifty brand-new Spitfires. With fifty Spitfires, I could have conquered Eastern Europe. The English had been training and arming Arab armies since the days of Lawrence of Arabia. Iraq was a primary source of England's oil; the Anglo-French Sykes-Picot Agreement of 1916 had drawn the boundaries for the place, along with the borders of Syria, Lebanon, Transjordan, and Palestine. King Abdullah of Jordan had been hand-carried onto the throne in 1921 by British decree. His army, the Arab Legion, was British-trained and British-officered. Even now, in '48, the Legion's commander-in-chief was an English lieutenant general and its field commander an English brigadier.

Meanwhile, the Jews outside of Tel Aviv and the coastal cities were isolated in a few dozen kibbutzim scattered from Galilee to the Negev. Arab bands were cutting off the roads. It was like Fort Apache. The Jews on their farms were surrounded, under siege, with no hope of escape or resupply by road. Everything had to be flown in. But the Haganah had no planes. I mean *no* planes. Nothing.

Another American air force vet, by the name of Al Schwimmer, had made himself the visionary smuggler of surplus aircraft into Palestine. Schwimmer had set up a fake airline—Líneas Aéreas de Panama. He was keeping one step ahead of the FBI by flying the planes via South America to Africa and Europe and from there to Palestine.

Somehow Schwimmer and the Haganah got their hands on two Alaskan bush planes. They had them here in Italy. Who would fly them to Palestine? Lou and I volunteered.

The Noorduyn Norseman was made in Canada to fly in and out of the northern backcountry. It was a bush plane—a rugged, high-wing monoplane with a powerful engine and an oversized cargo bay. The Norseman was exactly what the Haganah needed. With these aircraft, supplies and ammunition could be flown in to the kibbutzim and the wounded could be taken out. Even two planes could save many lives. All Lou and I had to do was fly them from Italy to Palestine.

That was like saying that all Lindbergh had to do was fly from New York to Paris. First, the Norseman had a range of 500 miles; Rome to Tel Aviv was 1,275. With the Haganah and our copilots, we managed to outfit the Norsemen's interiors with auxiliary rubber bladder tanks. But no one knew if the extra fuel would be enough. We had no parachutes, no life vests, no rafts. No radio. My maps were from a world atlas. I didn't even carry a sandwich.

Then there was the embargo. The Western nations, led by Britain and the United States, had placed a universal blockade on arms for Israel. The British were flying patrols to interdict all shipments. The FBI was imprisoning any American caught "serving under a foreign flag." The only countries that would work with the Jews were those of the Soviet bloc, specifically Czechoslovakia, which was desperate for American dollars. We didn't dare fly overland. Even making landfall for navigational purposes was risky. Lou asked me what our protocol was for engine failure over water. I told him, "We drown."

If one of us hit the drink, the other would have to keep flying. There was nothing else he could do.

"Remember Glenn Miller, the bandleader?"

"The one who got killed in a plane crash?"

"That plane was a Norseman."

The date was May 2, 1948. I remember sitting on the tarmac at Brindisi, with no flight plans, no runway clearance—and the aircraft so overloaded with fuel (one gallon weighs six pounds) that I wasn't sure we could even get airborne. We had two other pilot volunteers with us as passengers: Milt Rubenfeld and Eddie Cohen. I had put a Haganah man at the three-quarter mark on the runway and instructed Lou to abort if his ship wasn't wheels-up by that point. This was absurd, of course. The planes would be doing over a hundred knots. There was no way to stop them short of the cliff at the end of the runway. Meanwhile, we were fighting fuel leaks and problems with the valves that switched the feed from the main tank to the auxiliaries. I'm a worrier. Lou is not. He told me, "Collie, if you think we can make it, that's good enough for me." I didn't tell Lou that I put our odds at about fifty-fifty.

The way a plane prepares for takeoff is the pilot opens the throttle to full speed while keeping the brakes locked down. When you've got your pitch right and your gauges tell you you're good to go, you release the brakes and let the craft get to speed as fast as it can. As I'm cranking up, waiting for that moment, I glance over to Lou's plane and I see him open the hatch and leap out onto the runway. What the hell! My heart practically stops, figuring he's got mechanical trouble and the whole mission will have to be scrapped. Lou scurries to the edge of the runway, kneels down, picks a fistful of wildflowers, and dashes back to the plane. I can't even yell at him because we have no radios.

Off we go.

We made it. Eleven hours staring at that single prop without a word spoken or a glimpse of land the whole way. We struck the coast north of Tel Aviv and landed in the dark on a dirt runway illuminated by fire barrels. A crowd of partygoers was cheering. I saw Lou land and spring down with the flowers in his hand. He was so wobbly with exhaustion he could barely put one foot in front of the other, but he managed to cross to the prettiest girl he could find and hand her the bouquet.

One week later, Lou was in Czechoslovakia, training on the only fighter planes the Israelis could get: the Czech version of the German Messerschmitt 109, a postwar hunk of junk that they called a *mezek,* "mule."

11.

AD HALOM

This plane was the worst piece of crap I have ever flown. It was not even an airplane. It was put together by the Czechs from mismatched parts left behind by the Nazis. The airframe was that of an Me-109 but the propeller and engine came out of a Heinkel bomber. You can't make a plane that way. But it was all we could get, so we took it.

Lou Lenart was born in Hungary in 1921. He grew up in Wilkes-Barre, Pennsylvania, and joined the U.S. Marines in 1940 because "I heard they were 'first to fight' and I wanted to kill as many Nazis as I could, as fast as I could." Lenart became a Marine fighter pilot, flying F4U Corsairs on Okinawa and against the home islands of Japan.

How bad was this plane? The true Messerschmitt's engine was a Daimler-Benz DB 605 that put out 1,850 horsepower; our Junkers Jumo power plant could barely produce 1,200. It was like sticking the motor from a farm tractor into a Lamborghini. The plane was nose-heavy, unbalanced. There was no trim tab on the rudder and the flaps had to be lowered by a single, tiny hand wheel. You couldn't slow the damn thing down. It landed at 145 knots, which was about 55 too fast. But the worst of it was the propeller.

The big paddle-blade bomber prop produced so much left-pulling torque that the first time I tried to take off, the plane ran away from me clear off the runway, through a fence, and over a cliff; I only righted the ship a few feet from crashing into the Adriatic. Meanwhile, the synchronizers for the machine guns, which fired through the oar-shaped blades of the propeller, were so difficult for the mechanics to calibrate that each time you pulled the trigger you were terrified that you'd shoot your own prop off. But nobody would sell the Jews anything, so it was this or die.

There's a phrase in Hebrew, *en brera*—"no alternative." That was us and that was Israel.

When I was growing up in Wilkes-Barre, the place was full of Polish Catholics. These kids used to kick the crap out of us, what few Jews there were, until I put together a gang and started pounding the hell out of them. I'll tell you a story about when I joined the Marines.

This was in June 1940, well before the war, but there was still a long line at the recruiting table. A Marine sergeant was sitting there signing everybody up. Each recruit stepped forward and put his papers down; the sergeant would stamp 'em without looking up. Until I came to the table.

U.S. Marine Captain Lou Lenart
and his Corsair on Okinawa, 1945.

I could see the sergeant's eyes settle on the line on the enlistment form that said, "Religion." On it, I had written, "Jewish."

All of a sudden the sergeant looked up. He hadn't looked up for any of these Catholics, but he looked up for me. He eyed me up and down. "The Marine Corps is a tough outfit," he said. "Are you sure you can make it?" I was so furious I wanted to tear this sergeant's throat out. I knew the only reason he would ask that question was because my enlistment form said I was a Jew. But I also knew that I couldn't get mad or shoot my mouth off or he might not let me join. So I stared him in the eye, as directly and as hard as I could.

"If you made it, I can make it."

That was it. He stamped my form and I moved on.

I owe the Marine Corps everything. To take a kid from a tiny village in Hungary and not only give him the chance to serve under the Stars and Stripes, but to let him become an officer and a fighter pilot—that's why I love the Marine Corps and I always will.

The war ended and I went home to Los Angeles, but I was very aware of what was going on in Europe, with the Jews who had survived the Holocaust being held up by the British in transit camps, all that *Exodus* stuff. I had wanted to fight in Europe from the start. Nobody told me the Marines were only gonna fight in the Pacific.

Anyway, one Friday night I read in the paper that a Palestinian major (in those days "Palestinian" meant someone who lived in British Mandate Palestine) was speaking at a synagogue in Hollywood. I went. He spoke; I went up to him and tried to volunteer, told him my background as a combat vet. He was wary because the FBI was all over the Jews in those days. The State Department, too. He said, "Meet me at my hotel tomorrow night. Bring your discharge and your combat citations." I went home, got my stuff, and drove to his hotel that very night. Two weeks later I was in.

Under an executive order of the War Assets Administration, a vet was entitled to buy an airplane. An ex–TWA captain named Sam Lewis, who was working with Al Schwimmer, met me and gave me five thousand bucks in hundreds. He sent me downtown to the City Center and I bought a C-46, a Curtis Commando, just like that, a big, powerful cargo plane, the kind that had flown "over the hump" from India to China. The planes were in mothballs out in the Mojave. Schwimmer had a hangar at Lockheed in Burbank with four mechanics; they got the planes in and made them flightworthy. That was Schwimmer's operation, creating an air force for Israel out of thin air. He was a genius and a visionary.

Within weeks I was in New York, working with the Haganah recruiting vets to fly for Israel. That's when I took the train down to Philly to enlist Collie Goldstein. From there we got to Europe and then flew the Norsemen to Israel. This was May 9, 1948, five days before the British Mandate was due to expire. Five Arab armies were massing on Israel's borders, ready to invade the minute the Tommies pulled out. And Israel had no fighter aircraft. Nothing that could attack the enemy. Nothing.

At the last second, six of us got sent to Czechoslovakia to pick up these bastardized Messerschmitts. The route was Cyprus-Rome-Geneva, then by train to Zurich, and finally on a Czech Airlines DC-3 to Prague, where we were stuck in a hotel for two days before we at last reached the training base. The Arab invasion was two days away.

There's no way you can learn to fly a new plane in two days, particularly a fighter, and especially this piece of junk. But again, *en brera*. No alternative.

We trained at a place called České Budějovice. Every night we got bulletins from Israel. The Arab Legion with tanks and artillery was attacking near Jerusalem. Syrian forces had crossed the Jordan. The Egyptian Army, with Spitfires, tanks, and artillery, was advancing up the coast road toward Tel Aviv. There's a kibbutz on the frontier called Yad Mordechai. Three Egyptian battalions were attacking a force of 140. Even the kibbutz women fought in the trenches, firing World War I Enfields. They held out for five days before the Egyptians stormed the place and captured it.

Our Czech training officers were wonderful guys who sped up the training as fast as they could. But we had to tell them, "You don't understand—the whole country of Israel is about to be overrun!"

May 20 we fly back. It takes four more days to get the Messerschmitts home, in crates, with the wings off, in the bellies of three of Al Schwimmer's C-46s. One of the C-46s crashes, so we lose two Messerschmitts. We're down to four. The Jewish Quarter of Jerusalem is days away from surrendering. The Arab Legion holds the fort at Latrun, cutting the capital off.

What is the Israel Air Force at this hour? David Remez is technically in charge, but who are the real pilots? Us. Me and Modi Alon and Ezer Weizman and Eddie Cohen from South Africa, none of whom has flown in combat, and a few other crazy brave guys who have flown in from around the world to try to help save the infant state of Israel.

I'm the only pilot with combat experience in fighters (Collie and a few others are combat fliers but only in bombers), so I'm picked to lead the first mission, which is going to be a surprise attack at dawn on the Egyptian air base at El Arish. Who picked El Arish? Me. I'm the senior pilot, so what I say goes. Of course, I have no idea where El Arish is. I have no idea where anything is. I know only that Egypt's Spitfires are at El Arish. Job one is to wipe those bastards out.

Finally, the mechanics bolt the Messerschmitts together. The Egyptian Army is twenty miles away, advancing up the coast road. We have no time to prep, no time to take the planes up. It's three thirty in the afternoon of Friday, May 29.

Suddenly, onto the base races a jeep carrying Shimon Avidan, the commander of the Jewish troops—two companies of the Givati Brigade—who are hanging on by their fingernails holding off the Egyptians.

"Lou, we need your planes now."

Avidan tells me his guys have blown up a section of the bridge at Ishdud, seventeen miles south of Tel Aviv. The Egyptian invasion force is seven infantry battalions, an armored battalion with artillery, antitank and antiaircraft support, and six hundred vehicles. They're held up for the moment, but as soon as they repair the bridge, there's nothing left to stop them.

I tell Avidan that my planes are hitting El Arish at dawn.

"Forget El Arish! You have to take off now and attack the Egyptians at the bridge."

I say, "No way. We haven't tried the bombs or test-fired the guns—we don't even know if these pieces of shit will fly!"

"Lou, you don't understand," Avidan says. "If the Egyptian Army crosses that bridge, they'll be in Tel Aviv tonight and that's the end of Israel."

En brera.

No alternative.

We take off. Where's the bridge? I have no clue. As I'm circling, letting the other pilots get airborne to join me in formation, my number two, Modi Alon, pulls alongside, pointing south.

The formation is me and Modi, Ezer Weizman and Eddie Cohen.

We fly for only a couple of minutes and suddenly we see 'em. The Egyptian column is miles long, choking the road, jammed up at the dry riverbed with the blocked bridge in the middle.

There is no making light of this moment. Behind us is Israel, the Jewish people hanging on by a thread. Ahead of us is the enemy, advancing to destroy everything we love.

We attack. The guns malfunction; the bomb releases balk. I look right and left and see nobody. Antiaircraft fire is ferocious. Six thousand Egyptians are putting up everything they've got. Eddie Cohen, a wonderful, brave pilot from South Africa, must have run into too much of it. His plane doesn't come back. I manage to put one 70-kilogram bomb onto a concentration of trucks and troops in the town square of Ishdud. Modi and Ezer do what they can. It's a mess. We straggle back, having inflicted minimal damage.

But the shock to the Egyptians is overwhelming. To be attacked from the air by four Messerschmitt 109s with the Star of David on the side!

That night the Givati Brigade hits the enemy from the flank. The Egyptians are thrown into disorder. Israeli intelligence intercepts this dispatch from the brigade commander to Cairo:

We were heavily attacked by
enemy aircraft and we are scattering.

The Egyptian Army deflected to the east, to link with other Arab forces besieging Jerusalem.

Tel Aviv was saved, and so was the nation.

Sometime later I got a chance to speak with several Egyptian officers who were there that day. They said that the soldiers in the column were certain that these four planes, our piece-of-crap Messerschmitts, were just the tip of the spear, that the Jews had hundreds more, poised to attack and destroy them all.

Today that spot is called Gesher Ad Halom, *gesher* meaning "bridge," *ad halom* meaning "thus far and no farther" (literally, "up to here").

Collie Goldstein:

There's a final beat to this and the Norseman story. Twenty years later, Lou is in New York waiting for a traffic light at the corner of Fifty-second and Broadway, when a good-looking woman walks up to him. "Captain Lenart?"

"Yes."

"You don't remember me, do you?"

The lady smiles and holds out her hand.

"I'm the girl you gave the bouquet of wildflowers to at that little airstrip north of Tel Aviv in 1948."

12.

FIRST SONS

The generation of the War of Independence was the generation of the first sons.

Moshe Dayan, Yigal Allon, Yitzhak Rabin, hundreds more—the home-grown sabras, born in Israel in the teens and early twenties, who rose to command in '48. I include in this company Menachem Begin and Yitzhak Sadeh, though they came to the holy land as grown men, and Arik Sharon, Uzi Narkiss, and Ezer Weizman, who were technically half a generation younger. Ben-Gurion was their father. They worshipped him.

Shimon "Katcha" Cahaner has served with every legendary formation of the IDF paratroops, from Unit 101 in the fifties through Battalion 890 during the reprisal period to the 202nd Brigade at the Mitla Pass in 1956. He was deputy commander of Paratroop Battalion 28 when it helped liberate Jerusalem in 1967.

We were the next generation. Me and Danny Matt, Meir Har-Zion, David Elazar, Aharon Davidi, Motta Gur, Raful Eitan, Shmuel Gorodish, Uzi Eilam. I could cite many, many more. These were the young fighters, some of whom had been small-unit commanders in '48 and who rose in succeeding years to command battalions and brigades. There were thou-sands of others—brothers and cousins and friends whose names no one knows aside from us and their families—who fought as bravely and gave as much or more.

Part of the generation of the first sons, the best part, gave all they had. They rest now beneath stones. You read their names on walls of marble.

Seven times in 1948 this generation tried to take Latrun, the British-built blockhouse fort that dominated the road from Tel Aviv to Jerusalem. Seven times the guns of the Arabs beat them back. The assault troops were civilians and boys and half-trained militia, without artillery or aircraft; some came to the fight straight off the ships from the transit camps in Cyprus, with numbers tattooed on their arms. They took up M1 Garands and .303 Enfields from piles collected after the round of men before them had charged and been cut down, and they ran in their turn across melon fields into machine-gun fire.

The generation of the first sons learned to fight at night. They had to, to combat the Arabs—first the thieves who raided Jewish farms to steal sheep or cattle or, later, to blow up pipelines and plant mines along roads; then later still when the marauders began calling themselves *fedayeen,* "self-sacrificers," and their objective became to drive the Jews out of Palestine once and for all.

The sons of the first generation learned to come down from the watchtowers and guard posts and to venture on foot into the darkness "beyond the wire." Sadeh taught them, and Orde Wingate, the British officer we called *HaYedid,* "the friend." At dawn the sons returned, marked by the blood of their enemies. Now, in 1948, during the War of Independence, they needed darkness even more.

Near the Ayalon Plain, where Joshua smote the Amorites, the sun rose too soon on an assault force commanded by twenty-four-year-old Arik Sharon. Arab machine gunners caught the attackers in the open. Shot through the hip, Sharon gave his men the only order he could: Save yourselves. Years later, another bullet hit him in the same hip. "But this second one I hardly felt," he said, "because I was with my comrades and not left behind."

In July 1948, Dayan took the Arab towns of Ramla and Lod with a handful of jeeps armed with .30-caliber Brownings. He became a legend. Others fought till the last bullet at Gush Etzion near Jerusalem, then fell back, watching the Arab Legion cut off the Old City and massacre every Jew they could find.

The men of the War of Independence fought in farm boots and city shoes, without ranks and without uniforms. To mount a platoon- or company-scale operation was for them the pinnacle of tactics. Battalion-scale action was beyond their capacity; when they tried, the enemy cut them to pieces.

Before these first sons had come the generations of the fathers and the grandfathers—the pioneers and the visionaries.

Ze'ev Jabotinsky was an officer in the Russian Army in World War I. His friend Joseph Trumpeldor fought at Gallipoli. There's a town in

Joseph Trumpeldor in the British
Army during World War I.

the north of Israel called Kiryat Shmona, "City of the Eight." It was named for the eight Jews who died defending Tel Chai in 1920. Trumpeldor was their leader. This was the first time bullets had flown between Arabs and Jews over the issue of land.

Trumpeldor was mortally wounded in that fight. "It is a fine thing," he said, "to die for your country." This, when there was no country except in the dreams of these few.

In 1916, at the start of World War I, Jabotinsky and Trumpeldor had worked to convince Whitehall to form a Jewish Legion to fight as a unit in the British Army. They were seeking to establish credibility for the idea of a future Jewish state. The passage that follows comes from Jabotinsky's biography, describing an evening in that year:

London, small room, dim light. Joseph Trumpeldor portrayed before me the simple, fantastic idea of the pioneer movement. Trumpeldor said:

"We need men and women who are ready for everything, everything that the land of Israel will demand. A generation that will have no private interests or habits, but be like a simple iron bar, which can be shaped to anything that is needed for the national machine.

"Is a wheel missing? I am that wheel.

"Do we lack a nail, a screw, a flywheel? Take me.

"Must we dig? I am the spade. We need a soldier? I am that soldier. Policeman, doctor, lawyer, fireman? Take me. I will do everything. I have no faith, no philosophy, no

feelings; I don't even have a name. I am the pure ideal of
service, prepared for anything. I am bound by no limits. I
know only one command: to build."

"But," I said to Trumpeldor, "there are no people like
this."

"There shall be," said he.

We are those people. The generation of the first sons, and now us,
fighting beside them and under their command.

13.

TEL SHIMRON

The first time I saw Moshe Dayan was in 1946. I was sixteen. I was a member of a youth group associated with the Haganah. The Haganah had different divisions according to age; ours was the youngest.

Zalman Shoval is an intelligence officer during the Six Day War. Later he will serve two terms as ambassador to the United States, the most recent culminating in the year 2000.

Our group took part in an overnight training exercise, with tents and sleeping gear, on a hill called Tel Shimron. Tel Shimron overlooks the village of Nahalal, where Dayan grew up. It is where he is buried today. A *tel* is a raised mound that contains in layers the sedimentary remains of previous civilizations. Joshua had defeated the king of Shimron on this site in the time of the Bible.

In the night's exercise, our party of young people was assigned to defend the camp on the hilltop. Another group, from Nahalal, was ordered to attack—not with rifles but with stones and clubs. That was how we learned to fight in those days. There were boys and girls in our group, but only boys in the attacking party. They struck at midnight. It took them about a minute and a half to conquer us.

After the fight we all gathered in high spirits around a bonfire. Dayan came forward, wearing army trousers and a sweater, with his black eye patch. He was thirty, I think, maybe thirty-one. I was riveted. So were the others. I had heard of Dayan but primarily in connection with his wound, which he had got in Lebanon five years earlier as a commando scout fighting alongside the Australians against the Vichy French.

This night Dayan was in charge of the attacking group of Haganah youth. Such training exercises provided an occasion for the Haganah leaders to become acquainted with the young people who would hold command in the future. The evenings were, as well, a way for us rising leaders to acquire exposure to the veterans and heroes under whom we would soon be serving.

None of us had met anyone like Dayan. We were used to the older generation, the grimly zealous Zionists who had immigrated mostly from Poland and Russia and who orated in a kind of lofty rhetoric that we admired but that we did not feel was our own. Here instead was a young guy like us, born here, who spoke Hebrew the way we did, with the same slang and the same rough terms that only we knew. Dayan was speaking about the future of the Jewish state, with absolute conviction that there *would* be a Jewish state. It was electrifying. Remember, this was 1946, when such an outcome was far, far from certain.

Dayan wore no emblem of rank; the Haganah had none. It was obvious, though, that he was an anointed one. He was a favorite of the Haganah leadership, including Yitzhak Sadeh, the commander of the elite Palmach. Both Dayan's father and mother stood in the senior ranks of the Labor Party; they were politicians and activists from the first families of Israel. Ben-Gurion had discovered their son and picked him out as a leader of the future.

The highlight of these night exercises was the brewing of Turkish coffee. We filled our *finjans* with cold water and heaped in spoonfuls of the rich, dark grind, then stuck the tin cups into the fire, in the least hot part so the brew would heat slowly. When the liquid just started to boil, we snatched the vessels out and gave them three sharp knocks on the ground— *bam bam bam.* Each of us put the finjan back in the coals till the coffee rose up again, which took only a few seconds, then yanked it out and poured the piping hot mud-colored liquid, with plenty of sugar, into our little cups. Nothing could have been grander or more fun.

Dayan had a younger brother Zohar, called Zorik, who had served during World War II in the Jewish Brigade of the British Army. At war's end Zorik bolted from the English and joined a clandestine Jewish outfit called "the Gang." This group had taken upon itself the business of stealing supplies and guns, even seagoing ships, in the service of helping Jews from the death camps make their way to Israel. One night this outlaw band was spiriting survivors of Bergen-Belsen across the frontier from Germany into Holland. At the crossing point, the party's passage was impeded by an entanglement of barbed wire. Zorik laid his body across this obstacle, declaring, "Let these men and women cross to freedom upon my back."

Zorik was killed fighting a Druze battalion from Syria at Ramat

Yohanan on April 14, 1948. He was twenty-two, with a young wife, Mimi, and a three-month-old son, Uzi. Moshe sent his second-in-command, Israel Gefen, who was married to Moshe's sister Aviva, to tell his and Zorik's mother Devorah the terrible news. Devorah was on the farm at Nahalal then. She was walking up the path from the little kitchen garden when she saw Gefen approaching.

Before this officer could say a word, Devorah asked, "Which one?"

The War of Independence exacted a devastating toll from the population of our infant nation. Dayan's wife, Ruth, told me that seventeen young men were lost just from her tiny village. At one point, Ruth said, preparations were being made for weddings in the houses on each side of hers. Both grooms were killed before the ceremonies could take place. Fatalities across all Israel totaled six thousand—1 percent of the population.

In November 1948 the invading Egyptian Army, whose advance had been halted south of Tel Aviv, still had not withdrawn. Instead, this force had linked with Iraqi units and elements of the Jordanian Arab Legion. The combined formation had redeployed south, to the waist of the coastal plain, where it had succeeded in establishing a belt of fortifications that effectively cut Israel in two.

The anchor of this line was a Tegart fort (so named for the British architect who designed this type of police/military stronghold, of which there were dozens throughout Mandate Palestine) called Iraq Suwedan.

Iraq Suwedan dominated the approaches to the Negev, isolating and blocking all overland access to the kibbutzim of the south. Seven times the soldiers of the Haganah had tried to take this stronghold, and seven times they had been beaten back.

14.

IRAQ SUWEDAN

There was a fort east of the Arab village of Ishdud named Iraq Suwedan. We called it "the Monster on the Hill." The British had built it and many others and gave it to the Egyptians when they pulled out in '48. This is another reason why I hate the British.

Lou Lenart, after leading the fighter mission that halted the Egyptian Army south of Tel Aviv in May 1948, became operations officer for the fledgling Israel Air Force.

When I say fort, I mean fort. The place was huge and square and tall, with gun towers and parapets and walls two meters thick with the red, white, and black Egyptian flag flying over everything. Nasser himself had commanded the place as a major. It sat smack in the middle of a plain as flat as a floor of linoleum, with not even a blade of grass that an attacking force could use as cover. The Haganah had trench works at about two thousand meters. That's where we set up, with a few trucks and cars but mostly everybody on foot. The Haganah had been attacking the fort for months. They had mounted seven assaults and been cut to pieces every time. But the place had to be taken because it blocked the roads to the south and cut Israel in half.

The Jewish commander was Yitzhak Sadeh, who had been a hero in the Russian Army. Sadeh's operations officer was twenty-six-year-old Yitzhak Rabin, who would become army chief of staff before and during the Six Day War and later prime minister. I was ops officer for the air force.

The way we were going to take the Monster was by hitting it from the air with a bomb. We had a British Beaufighter that Haganah agents had stolen from the Royal Air Force by pretending to rent it for a movie.

A Beaufighter is primarily a fighter but we had managed to rig it as a bomber, carrying a single 500-pound bomb. As operations officer, I had two jeeps with a generator and a radio. My role was ground control. The plane had a pilot and a copilot and one other flier who went along at the last minute just for fun.

If the Beaufighter could succeed in dropping the bomb in the central square of the fort, the explosion would be contained within the walls and the blast effect would be doubled or tripled. It would blow the crap out of the place. Our assault troops then had a chance of taking it.

The attack was ready to go. At the last minute a half dozen trucks rumbled up, bringing reinforcements. The men got off. They were pale and thin. They had numbers tattooed on their arms. Someone said they had spent the last two years in relocation camps—under the British, of course—in Cyprus. They had got to Israel just a week earlier and been given only a few days of military training.

They came up and were issued rifles. I will never forget their faces. They were certain they were going to die. But their eyes were shining. They had weapons in their hands. They were men.

The Beaufighter made its pass. But something went wrong on the approach. The plane hadn't gotten aligned right; it had to bank off at the last minute.

There's an axiom in every air force in the world: "One pass and go to the grass." This means that once you've lost the element of surprise, get down to ground level and run like hell.

I knew I should order the mission aborted. If the bomber attempted a second pass, the Egyptians would be waiting for it. Every gun in the fort would be firing at it and nothing else.

But we couldn't stop. The assault was ready. The men's blood was up. Sadeh waved me to go. I brought the plane around again. The guys dropped the bomb dead on target. The blast blew the hell out of the fort; our troops assaulted and overran the place.

But the Beaufighter had gotten shot up. Smoke was pouring from one of its engines. I was shouting to the pilot over the radio to turn east across the plain, to where our people were, where it was safe. But something had gone wrong with his radio. The plane turned west toward the sea. Maybe the pilot was thinking of the flat, open beach along the coast, where he could make an emergency landing. I couldn't follow him. The ground fight was just starting. Days passed before we could assemble a force and search for the aircraft.

The plane had crashed on the shore alongside the Arab village of Ishdud, which is the Israeli city of Ashdod today. We went in with six or seven trucks and jeeps, lots of guns.

Yitzhak Rabin was ops officer for the army, as I said. I was the same for the air force. The wreckage of the plane was on the beach, burned to a cinder. Our guys rousted out the whole village, including the *mukhtar*, the mayor. We gathered them in the central square, with the trucks and guns around. A Haganah intelligence officer was interrogating the mukhtar in Arabic.

The plane had been on fire when it crashed, this guy was saying. The villagers had tried to save the crew but the flames had kept them back. The Haganah officer asked what had happened to the bodies. The jackals got them, said the mukhtar. He and the villagers had tried to keep the beasts back but they couldn't. The parts of the fliers' flesh that hadn't been burned in the crash were devoured by wild animals.

While the mukhtar was reciting this bullshit, my eyes were fixed on his left wrist. He was wearing the watch that had belonged to the pilot of the Beaufighter.

I got Rabin aside, pointed out the wristwatch, and told him to burn down the village. Put a bullet in the mukhtar's head and drive all the villagers out. I pointed across the plain. The Egyptian lines are only a few hundred meters away. Let the villagers take their belongings and get out.

"I can't do that," said Rabin.

"Why not?"

I told him that was what U.S. Marines would do. We did it on Okinawa all the time. Marines wouldn't even think twice.

"Lou, collective punishment is against the Geneva Convention."

"The hell with the Geneva Convention! You think these Arabs are following the Geneva Convention? They burned our guys to death, then cut 'em up and fed 'em to their dogs—if they didn't carve 'em up first while they were still alive!"

Already I was thinking that I would have to tell the fathers and mothers of these airmen what had happened to their sons. I would lie like hell, I knew that. I would never tell them the truth of how their sons had died.

I told Rabin again: Shoot the mukhtar and burn the village.

He refused. "We are Jews. We can't do that."

Rabin was an idealist. That's what was wrong with Israel then and it's what's wrong with Israel today. The founders had suffered pogroms and persecution for so many centuries in Russia and Eastern Europe that it had become a point of honor with them that if they ever got their own country, they would not treat others with the same cruelty that they'd been treated with. You have to admire that. It's honorable. It's noble. But in war it's bullshit.

"Would Alexander hesitate to burn this village? Would Caesar?"
"Would Stalin?" said Rabin. "Would Hitler?"
He put his hand on my shoulder.
"We cannot do it, Lou. If we take such actions, we abandon every principle we are fighting for."
What could I say? Israel was Rabin's country. I was a foreigner. I couldn't force my way.

But if you ask me today whether I have any regrets in my life, I will say only one: that I didn't shoot that mukhtar right then and there, and let Rabin and the Haganah do whatever they wanted with me.

15.

UGDA SHARON

I have been with Sharon's division for four days now. Still no orders to go to war. Sharon's headquarters is at Shivta, a few kilometers from the border, though the division's positions extend west to Nitzana on the frontier. North of us, not far, lies Avraham Yoffe's division and, farther north, facing Gaza, the ugda of Israel Tal.

Yael Dayan continues her assignment with Ugda Sharon as a correspondent for the military spokesman.

What is camp like? A city. A city of sand whose roads are tire and tread tracks, whose gathering places are dugouts beneath camouflage netting, and whose buildings are vehicles—tanks, lorries, ambulances, ammunition and supply trucks, caravans and living trailers, civilian cars and buses, jeeps and command cars and half-tracks—most of which are in motion throughout the day and, to thwart detection and targeting by the enemy, must be moved and repositioned every evening.

By night our guests are gazelles and desert foxes, by day lizards and hawks. Dune lines are marked by terebinth trees, from which turpentine is extracted (*elah* in Hebrew, as in the Valley of Elah, where David slew Goliath), castor bushes, and the prickly pear cactus that we Israelis call sabra plants.

I have given up doing anything with my hair; I simply braid it and pull a desert cap down tight. The fine-powdered dust called loess coats every face. For a ladies' loo, there's a square canvas enclosure with a sign: GIRL SOLDIERS. I slept the first night in a trench, the next two on the sand alongside various half-tracks of the command group. Last night's accommodations felt like the Ritz. I stretched out across the backseat of a station wagon, a reservist's car called up in the mobilization.

This morning has started like every other. The soldiers are up and on alert before four; every engine starts, every tank, every half-track; all radio

channels are open but no one may speak. Not till the war starts. The din is
deafening, the air so acrid with diesel and petrol exhaust you have to spit
to get the taste off your tongue. The men stand ready, weapons locked and
loaded. Patrols are out. Will the Egyptians attack? By eight it is clear: not
today. The order comes to stand down. Postcards are passed out. The men
scribble notes using jeep bonnets and the flanks of tanks as writing sur-
faces. Now every vehicle and every unit moves to a different position. We
can count on the enemy learning our disposition, so we must alter it. Our
intelligence and reconnaissance units are doing the same thing to them.

Dov is my guide and mentor in all this. He's a colonel, as I said, a veteran of two wars, faculty member of the National Defense College, and
now Sharon's liaison with the General Staff. He narrates for me the ever-
evolving ballet of move and countermove by the opposing forces. The enemy has shifted a tank battalion! No, a brigade! At once the war room,
comprising a colony of communications vehicles, command boards, and
map stands, all beneath camouflage nets, counters by repositioning our
own armor. The Hebrew word for "reconnaissance outfit" is *sayeret*. The
troopers themselves are *sayerim*. Out they go, patrolling. A helicopter
lands and more maps are altered. Red is enemy, blue is friendly . . .

Sharon is very much in command and reveling in every moment. He
has welcomed me warmly despite the occasionally inharmonious history
between him and my father. The man himself: handsome in dark khaki
battle uniform, silver hair falling in a forelock; beneath a shoulder flap is
tucked the red beret of a paratrooper.

You mount to Sharon's trailer up three steps of a ladder. Inside: two
wooden benches atop which are spread blankets at night, a worktable used
as well for dining, a cupboard for paper and supplies, a desert-style wash-
stand with water drum, soap, and mirror. Sharon's kit fits into a knapsack
smaller than mine. His driver is Yoram; helicopter pilot Zeev. Asher is
operations officer; a pretty blonde named Tzipi serves tea. Among Sharon's
guests are several civilian friends; others come and go, appearing in blue
jeans and shirtsleeves, driving their own cars, being fitted in where
they can.

Dov says I must get some gear, so he helps me hunt up socks, a helmet,
boiled sweets, Hershey bars. "Always take chocolate." A sergeant asks me,
Will the cabinet give your father Southern Command? Meaning the three
divisions—Sharon's, Tal's, and Yoffe's—here on the border of Sinai. Will
Dayan be our boss? What is keeping the government from making a decision?

Radio news is reporting that Hussein of Jordan has signed, this day, a mutual defense pact with Nasser. The king flew himself in his jet Caravelle from Amman to Cairo, carrying a .357 Magnum on his hip.

Now Israel is surrounded on all sides by hostile states. Worse, Hussein has granted permission to Iraqi and Saudi troops to pass through his territory, an outrage that would have been viewed as a casus belli a week ago but is accepted now as just another dose of spit in the eye.

Kuwait, Morocco, Algeria, and Tunisia have promised troops to Nasser. We hear this on the transistor between songs on the Hit Parade.

This speech by Nasser on Radio Cairo: "If we have succeeded in restoring the situation to what it was before 1956, there is no doubt that we shall restore the situation to what it was before 1948."

Before 1948 means: no Israel.

Our troops seethe, impatient for action. "What are we waiting for?"

Danny Matt has come by, the paratroop commander. He has known my father since before I was born. I watch the officers come and go to Sharon's trailer. These men have served together under arms for most of their adult lives. When they meet, they embrace like brothers and immediately begin joking about battles fought alongside each other and wounds sustained at one another's sides. The more ghastly the recollection, the more pleasure is wrung from its recounting.

Arik and Danny speak of their friend "Katcha" Cahaner, whom I know well. One night in 1955, Katcha was so badly wounded in a reprisal operation that the medics at the field hospital pulled a blanket over his head, believing him dead. A year later, when the paratroop battalion jumped at the Mitla Pass in Sinai, Katcha was still in a medical ward, classified as 100 percent disabled. Katcha bolted from the hospital. He made his way to Mitla on army trucks and joined his comrades at the pass.

"Do you know where he is right now?" Arik asks.

"With Brigade 55, preparing for a combat jump," says Danny. "If we ever get orders."

For security reasons Dov cannot go into detail about what Sharon's division will face if it must attack, except to explain that there are two linked positions—Abu Agheila and Um Katef. The Egyptian 2nd Division holds a third bastion at Kusseima. These three "defended localities" bestride the central routes leading west into Sinai.

Our forces must break through them.

"Complexity at the top, simplicity at the bottom," Arik declares, defining in a nutshell his philosophy of command. "A commander," Sharon says, "may keep complicated schemes of battle in his head and among his staff, but when the orders reach the operational units, they must be so simple that a child can understand them. 'Go here, do this.' Nothing more complex."

Sharon's eyes light with a smile that I have seen no one resist. "Of course the Israeli soldier will make up his own mind and do whatever he wants. This is as it should be. The reason we will thrash the Egyptians is because they can't do the same. They can't improvise."

The word *balagan* is Russian-derived Hebrew for "chaos." The more I learn of the seeming disorder of this camp, the more I realize it is order within chaos.

This morning after stand-down I ride with a patrol toward Kusseima. Our jeeps draw up on a ridge across from ancient Kadesh Barnea. Here the children of Israel encamped, following the exodus from Egypt. Nasser's 2nd Division is dug in across from us now. Through binoculars I can see the enemy's armor in motion.

At night Dov drives me into Beersheba to file a report. A waitress at the officers' club brings us coffee. I ask her what day it is. She smiles. "You'd be surprised how many people ask that same question."

16.

THE UNIT

Unit 101 was formed in August 1953. It was called simply "the Unit." There were only about forty of us and we served together for only four months. But that single company established the spirit and fighting ethos of the whole Israeli Army. Arik Sharon was the Unit's commander.

Katcha Cahaner served under Arik Sharon in Unit 101. He will finish the Six Day War as second-in-command of Paratroop Battalion 28, part of the 55th Brigade, which will liberate Jerusalem.

The army's morale was in terrible shape in those days of the fifties. The Palmach, which had been the fighting heart of the Haganah and then the infant IDF, had been disbanded by Prime Minister Ben-Gurion, who believed it was too political. The Palmach was, in his words, "the Labor Party in arms." If Israel were to have a true professional defense force, this formation had to go.

But the army had nothing to replace the Palmach's warrior spirit. Our enemies quickly discovered this. Arab infiltrators began crossing the border at night. These parties would murder families in their sleep, plant mines along roads to schoolhouses, toss hand grenades into children's bedrooms.

The IDF had nothing that could stop them. Platoon- and company-sized forces would be sent across the border on night reprisal operations. Too often the fighters straggled back at dawn, carrying one or two wounded, to report that the mission had not been accomplished.

Moshe Dayan was then chief of the operations branch, the number two post in the army. He wrote:

I decided to put an end to this disgraceful situation and to the apathy of IDF Command, which accepts these despicable

*failures and the endless excuses of "we couldn't" . . . I met with
the leaders . . . and informed them that from now on, if an
officer reported that he could not complete his mission because
he was unable to overcome the enemy forces, his explanation
would not be accepted unless he had lost more than 50 percent
of his command, killed or wounded.*

Sharon was studying at Hebrew University in Jerusalem then. He was twenty-five; he had eight years of fighting behind him. He had just gotten married and he wanted a normal life.

Mordechai Maklef was chief of staff. Ben-Gurion called him in and told him he wanted a unit formed that could cross the border and make the Arabs think twice about these terror incursions. Dayan opposed the idea at first; he thought that every IDF unit should have fighting spirit, not just one elite team called in to do the dirty work. Ben-Gurion overruled him. It didn't take long before Sharon was called in and offered the job.

Sharon agreed to set up and command the new unit. But he had three demands. "First, I want to pick the men myself, with no interference from higher command. Second, the unit must have the best and most modern weapons and equipment. Third, I want to be a central part myself of all operational planning."

I had a friend named Meir Har-Zion. Dayan once called him "the finest commando soldier in the army." Har-Zion was twenty-two then; I was four months younger. Meir said to me, "Katcha, have you heard about this new commando unit? Let's go see what it's about."

So we went. That was how it worked in those days. One man vouched for another—"a friend brings a friend."

The Unit's camp was outside an abandoned Arab village called Sataf, near Jerusalem. I was serving then with the Nachal, which was a pioneer outfit. Israel was so poor in those days that the government couldn't afford to support soldiers to train, so we of the Nachal worked two weeks on a kibbutz to earn our keep, then trained as soldiers for the next two weeks.

Meir and I got to Unit 101 on a Sunday. Sharon had us and his other picked men training that day and Monday. On Tuesday night we crossed the border into Jordan, five kilometers. Do you know how far five kilometers is at night? It feels like a hundred. I was terrified. I remember at one point some Arabs popped out of nowhere. Civilians. We hit the dirt. My heart was pounding so wildly I was certain the enemy could not fail to hear it.

Two nights later we crossed into Jordan twice as far.

What did we do on these operations?

We did what had to be done.

Sharon was the best fighting officer in the IDF, then or ever, and he was just as good at intelligence. He knew everyone on both sides of the border, and when he didn't know someone, he knew someone who knew that someone. He could find out anything. If he learned, say, that a certain Arab was planning to lead a raid into Israel on Wednesday, we crossed the border Tuesday night and paid this man a visit. Or maybe Sharon acquired the identities of some gang that had shot up one of our school buses. We found them all and made sure they never crossed into Israel again.

Sharon led many of these operations himself. He would take us across the border in darkness so thick you could not see the man trekking in column in front of you. In enemy territory you never travel in a straight line. By the time we had penetrated five kilometers, we would have diverted, backtracked, and jinked so many times that none of us knew where we were going or where we had been. Sharon would call us in a whisper to gather round. "See those lights there? That's a truck moving south on Route 1 at Kilometer 106. That dark shape beneath the hill? That's the Arab Legion camp at Nebi Samuel."

Sharon knew every meter of ground, and he made us work till we knew it as well as he. He taught us to navigate without maps and without compasses. We had to know the land, period. To locate a single house in an Arab village, one house and no other, is no easy task. To get to it is even harder. Dogs bark. Sheep and goats take fright. Armed lookouts stand watch. What trail do you take to get in? By what path do you get out?

One night our patrol was ghosting along a hillside in Jordanian territory when we spotted a raiding party of fedayeen, twelve in all, moving along a wadi toward the Israeli border. We dropped to the ground silently and let them pass. I could see the muzzles of the raiders' slung rifles and the rolls of detonator wire they carried on poles between them. Sharon knew by the trail the enemy was taking that they must pass beneath a certain hill several kilometers west.

We were waiting for them when they got there.

That was Sharon. He expected greatness. He didn't have to preach it. He made you feel that the safety, the honor, the survival of the nation, and even that of the Jewish people around the world, was on your shoulders. In the Unit it was unthinkable that you could be stopped or would turn back before completing a mission. You would rather cut off your arm. If I

am creeping along a trail at night, alone or with one other soldier, and I
see five or seven of the Jordanian Arab Legion coming from the opposite
direction, I will choose death before going back to face Sharon and have
to tell him, "There were too many—there was nothing we could do."
This spirit you see today. It has spread to the whole army. This spirit
came from Sharon and no one else.

17.

BLACK ARROW

On February 25, 1955, a party of Arab fedayeen crossed the border and murdered an Israeli civilian in the town of Rehovot, about thirty kilometers north of Gaza. On the body of one of the infiltrators were found documents linking the terrorists to command elements of the Egyptian Army.

Three nights later, picked men of Israeli Paratroop Battalion 890, commanded by Arik Sharon, launched Operation Black Arrow—sometimes called the Gaza Raid—in reprisal.

Lieutenant Uzi Eilam was a platoon commander in Operation Black Arrow in 1955. He was wounded leading the assault on the Egyptian camp and awarded the Itur HaOz, Israel's second-highest decoration for valor. As a major in 1967, Eilam will command Paratroop Battalion 71 in the liberation of the Old City of Jerusalem.

A number of factors must be made clear if the significance of this action is to be understood.

First, until official documents were found in the possession of an Arab infiltrator killed in the commission of an act of murder, the Egyptian government had denied all responsibility for cross-border terrorism—despite the fact that over nine hundred such incidents had been recorded during 1954 and 1955.

The documents proved that this was a lie. Egyptian army intelligence was not only aware of these terror attacks, but was funding, arming, and training the attackers.

Second, orders for the reprisal operation came from the highest levels of the Israeli government, from David Ben-Gurion, prime minister and minister of defense, and from Moshe Dayan, chief of staff of the army.

Third, the speed of the response was calculated to leave no doubt that the blow was linked to the provocation. The reprisal came within seventy-two hours. The message was: "Strike produces counterstrike."

Fourth, the response to the Egyptian attack was directed not at randomly selected citizens or civilians, as had been the case in the initial Arab murder raid. It was not terror-for-terror. Instead, the reply was targeted at the sponsoring government entity. Because the terror attack could be traced to the Egyptian Army, Israel's response could and must be directed at this body exclusively. It had to be clear to all that our reply was mounted in direct retaliation for the murder three nights earlier—and against only those responsible for the crime.

The final factor to be understood is the tactic of reprisal itself.

Reprisal, as Dayan and Ben-Gurion conceived it, was not vengeance killing. It was not a biblical exercise in "an eye for an eye." Reprisal was a political tactic within the greater strategy whose object was the survival of the nation. As Dayan explained it in 1955, speaking with officers of the IDF:

> We could not defend every water pipeline from being blown up
> and every tree from being uprooted. We could not prevent every
> murder of a worker in an orchard or a family in their beds. But it
> was within our power to set so high a price for our blood, a
> price too high for the Arab community, the Arab army, or the
> Arab governments to think it worth paying . . . It was in our
> power to cause the Arab governments to renounce "the policy of
> strength" toward Israel by turning it into a demonstration of
> weakness.

No officer could have been better suited temperamentally or militarily to implement a policy of reprisal than Arik Sharon. Sharon was ever on the lookout for pretexts for operations. One night in 1954, near Jerusalem, a patrol of Battalion 890 got into an unplanned firefight, killed a Jordanian soldier, and brought his body back. Another commander might have been angry at the dragging home of an enemy corpse, or even employed the body by returning it with the proper chivalry as a means of reaching out with goodwill to the foe. Not Sharon. The border had been quiet for several weeks, but now, he knew, the Jordanians would be eager to seek vengeance. He instructed our company and two others, including

"D" Company under Motta Gur, to set ambushes all along the border. His aim was always to produce contact. Each skirmish or firefight was a pretext for further action—and evidence of enemy hostility that Sharon could take to the General Staff to gain authorization for even more reprisal operations.

I came to Battalion 890 the same way Katcha Cahaner and Meir Har-Zion had come to Unit 101. A friend brought me. Other comrades vouched for my abilities. "I asked the guys," Sharon told me. "They said you're all right."

That was it.

I was in.

I was assigned as a squad leader in "A" Company under Sa'adia Alkayam, whom we called Supapo, and who was already a legend in the paratroops.

Both Unit 101 and Battalion 890 were armed with different weapons than the conventional army. Each trooper was issued an American Thompson submachine gun and a commando knife. The Tommy guns used high-caliber 11.43-millimeter ammunition (.45s, like in American gangster movies), in contrast with the 9-millimeter cartridges used in Uzis. The Tommy guns were heavy—five kilograms as opposed to the Uzi's three and a half.

Company commanders in Battalion 890 were Meir Har-Zion (Supapo took over from him when he was temporarily suspended for the unauthorized revenge killings of a gang of Arabs who had raped and murdered his sister and killed her fiancé), Danny Matt, Motta Gur, and Rafael "Raful" Eitan. Every one of these officers went on to command brigades or divisions. Sharon's second-in-command, Aharon Davidi, taught me a lesson that changed forever my conception of command and my view of the role of an officer.

The night raid had begun. Our force had crossed the border. The objective was the central Egyptian army base in Gaza—a fortified encampment guarded by perimeter defenses including barbed wire, security fences, and antivehicle ditches. Approaching this camp, my unit—"A" Company under Supapo—became disoriented in the darkness. The enemy spotted us and opened fire. Supapo was killed. Alarms began blaring in the Egyptian camp; searchlights came on. All surprise had been lost. I was deputy company commander, so it was my job to take over. Half our men had been wounded; the rest were sprinting with me, under fire, for cover. We scrambled into a ditch with bullets flying everywhere. It seemed that within seconds we would all be killed.

Suddenly I looked up. There was Davidi, standing over me amid the whizzing rounds. "What has happened?" he asked. I told him that Supapo had been killed and our company was under attack.

"Well," Davidi said, as calmly as if he and I had been sipping an espresso at a café on Dizengoff Street. "What are you going to do about it?"

I said, "I'm going to continue the attack."

And I began issuing orders.

When I looked around, Davidi was gone.

I have wondered often, in the years since, if he had in fact been there at all.

The Black Arrow raid killed thirty-eight Egyptian soldiers and wounded fifty-two, an enormous number for a reprisal operation undertaken by a force of only seventy men. It humiliated Nasser in the eyes of his countrymen and those of the other Arab states for whom the Egyptian president presumed to stand as an inspirational leader. The bulk of the enemy casualties came at the hands of Danny Matt's "D" Company, the blocking force, which ambushed a convoy of reinforcements hurrying to the aid of their comrades.

The Black Arrow operation was a masterpiece of planning. It contained a number of Sharon's signature elements of misdirection and ruse, including having the party embark on trucks in civilian attire accompanied by a number of girl soldiers, singing loudly and pretending to be out for a night of fun (the females were dropped off en route) and the use of Danny Matt's ambush force as the primary killing element.

I served as Battalion 890's intelligence officer and, later, when the structure was put in place for expansion to brigade size, I continued as brigade intelligence officer. In my 2011 memoir, *Eilam's Arc,* I wrote the following:

> *I never imagined the level of schooling that awaited me, not just in intelligence, in which Sharon was a master, but in tactics and the meticulous and creative planning of military operations . . .*
>
> *Regardless of whether they were ultimately executed or canceled at the last moment, the long list of operations that Sharon planned constitutes an incomparable source of material for the study of military tactics. Each of Sharon's plans was a work of*

*craftsmanship, based on his understanding of the field, his precise
knowledge of the enemy's forces, and a wise assessment of the
strengths and weaknesses of their defenses. But in addition to the
typical military situation assessment . . . every Sharon plan had a
twist of some kind that made it special. In some cases it was the
unique way the forces were organized; in others it was a unique
route to the target or the way we went about sealing off the area
of operations from the possible intervention of external enemy
forces. Sharon was obsessive when it came to integrating variety
and innovation into planning his operations, and this enabled him
to keep surprising the enemy with new tactics every time.*

Arik Sharon, left, and Aharon Davidi,
center, during Operation Black Arrow.

Paratroop Battalion 890 and guests, November 1955. Standing left to right:
Lieutenant Meir Har-Zion, Major Arik Sharon, Lieutenant General Moshe Dayan,
Captain Danny Matt, Lieutenant Moshe Efron, Major General Asaf Simchoni;
seated left to right: Captain Aharon Davidi, Lieutenant Ya'akov Ya'akov,
Captain Raful Eitan.

I worked closely with Sharon every day and came to appreciate not
only his genius as a military tactician, but his gift for politics, which was
in evidence even then, decades before his election as prime minister. Sharon manipulated two constituencies to keep his operations going. The first
was the enemy. The second was the Israeli General Staff.

Headquarters had to approve all operations proposed by Sharon. Not
infrequently, the ministers lacked his zeal for provocation and confronta-
tion. To counter this, Sharon maintained an unofficial intelligence scheme
directed at our own political superiors that was every bit as thorough and
sophisticated, though contained entirely within his own head, as the operation he employed against infiltrators from Egypt, Syria, and Jordan.

The object of reprisal operations was, in Sharon's mind, twofold. First, such audacity provided a model of initiative and enterprise for the rest of the army. It took guts to cross the border at night and carry the fight onto the enemy's doorstep. This was "venturing outside the fence." It stood in the valorous tradition of the Haganah, of Orde Wingate's Special Night Squads, and of Yitzhak Sadeh's "Flying Squads." It was the torch from which the rest of the IDF lit the flame of boldness and resourcefulness.

Every soldier of spirit wished to serve under Sharon and to wear the red beret of the paratroopers.

Second, the policy of reprisals kept the enemy on the defensive and bought time for the fledgling Israeli nation to put down roots. Sharon called this "practical Zionism." He meant that, within the secure perimeter provided by our soldiers' enterprise, our countrymen could create "facts on the ground"—farms and cities, schools and railroads, ports and highways that would in time come to be viewed, not only by the Arabs but by the world at large, as permanent and ineradicable.

Sharon was a realist. He recognized, as did Ben-Gurion and Dayan, that the Arabs had as legitimate a claim to this land as we did, and that they possessed pride and courage and anger, against which no rejoinder existed except the sword. He often quoted the Zionist fighter and pioneer Ze'ev Jabotinsky:

> As long as the Arabs preserve a gleam of hope that they will succeed in getting rid of us, nothing in the world can cause them to relinquish this hope, precisely because they are not a rabble but a living people. And a living people will be ready to yield on such fateful issues only when they have given up all hope of getting rid of the alien settlers. Only then will the extremist groups with their slogans "No, never" lose their influence, and only then will their influence be transferred to the more moderate groups. And only then will the moderates offer suggestions for compromise. Then only will they begin bargaining with us on practical matters . . . when that happens, I am convinced that we Jews will be found ready to give them satisfactory guarantees, so that both people can live together in peace, like good neighbours.

18.

THE SPECIAL NIGHT SQUADS

This day, May 30, 1967, I am in the port city of Eilat, touring military installations. No one will let me pay for a meal. "Just keep well," says the restaurant owner at lunch, "and bring us victory."

Can I tell him I can't even get myself assigned to drive a truck?

Moshe Dayan, still lacking official authority, continues visiting forward military encampments, reviewing plans with commanders, and assessing the state of mind of the troops.

Pressure continues to build on Prime Minister Eshkol to give up his position as minister of defense. From my sources, I have learned that Menachem Begin with several colleagues of his right-wing party, Gahal, has paid a visit to Ben-Gurion last night at the former prime minister's apartment in Tel Aviv. I would have sooner expected a pack of hyenas to sit down to supper with a lion. But this shows how desperate the situation has become.

Apparently Begin appealed to the old man to join with him in an attempt to oust Eshkol entirely, replacing him at the head of a unity government with Ben-Gurion. Ben-Gurion even agreed, I am told. But Eshkol would have none of it.

Flying home from Eilat, the news is of King Hussein signing a defensive alliance with Nasser. Now Jordan is in it. Nothing can prevent war. When it comes, I fear, we shall have to fight on two fronts, even three if Syria enters the fray.

Worse, Hussein's pact with Nasser means that brigades from Iraq will be permitted by Jordan to cross its territory and even to take up positions on our border. A child can see, now, that Eshkol must give up the defense portfolio to someone who understands war. Will he? I am thinking of Ben-Gurion. The aircraft's shadow speeds over the washes and tamarisk groves of the Negev Desert that he loves so dearly.

No Jew since Moses has stood as tall as this squat, stocky Pole, or brought into being, by force of will alone, such prodigies. On my office desk sit five phone messages from him. I have answered none. I can't.

Four days ago I met privately with Ben-Gurion at the Desert Inn in Beersheba. The position he took with me is that Israel cannot defeat the Arabs without the military support of at least one superpower. I did not contest him. What purpose would it serve?

What is so frustrating and infuriating to me about the Eshkol government (and I include Ben-Gurion in this indictment, even though he is a fervent opponent of Eshkol) is that its lack of decisiveness to launch an immediate attack is setting the nation up for calamity and our brave soldiers for an ordeal of fire. Every hour that the government delays in making this inevitable decision is another hour in which our enemies grow stronger, dig in deeper, and move more troops and tanks into positions from which they can be dislodged only by the expenditure of our young men's blood.

The combat arms of Israel are a match, on ground of our choosing, for Egypt and her allies combined. But our leaders do not believe this. Eskhol doesn't. Neither does Ben-Gurion. Begin himself is simply desperate.

Ten days ago I visited Arik Sharon, with his division, at Nitzana on the Egyptian frontier. Sharon's eyes shone when he took me over the maps. "We will be bathing in the Canal in one hundred hours."

I am glad that my daughter, Yael, has been posted to the headquarters of this commander. She will see sights such as this desert has not witnessed since Napoleon.

Beyond my family, two men have influenced my life and thought more than any others. The first is Ben-Gurion. He believed in me when his contemporaries considered me too young or too intemperate and when I myself could see no farther than my shadow's fall in front of me.

I have been his army man. I have served him and argued with him and studied under him. A thousand times I have yielded to positions he has taken, which I knew were misguided or misinformed, and whose implementation I would have suffered from no other man, for the sole reason that I adored him and knew that he must be followed, right or wrong. He founded Israel. He *was* Israel. He brought the nation forth with his will and his spirit, as Moses with a staff brought forth water from the stone.

This was Ben-Gurion, for whom no honor is too exalted and no expression of love too great.

The other man was Orde Charles Wingate.

When war comes, as it surely will, tomorrow or the day after, a thousand captains and lieutenants of the Israel Defense Forces will outthink and outwit and outfight the enemy, employing (though few will realize it) principles and doctrine that were stitched into the fabric of our army by this Indian-born British officer who fell in love with us, and we with him, in Mandate Palestine three decades ago.

I am given credit far too often for founding the fighting ethos of the IDF. This spirit began with Wingate.

I met him in the summer of 1938. I was twenty-two; Wingate was thirty-five, a captain, formerly of artillery but at that time in intelligence, conducting a survey of Arab gangs and saboteur bands. He came to Tel Shimron, near my home at Nahalal, traveling in an ancient jalopy, alone save for his batman, whose services as a tea brewer or boot polisher Wingate eschewed in favor of the man's skill as a mechanic.

Wingate was a type such as only England produces. Seeking a posting in the Sudan, he rode his bicycle across Europe and traveled on foot south from Cairo. He learned his raiding skills fighting bandits in southern Sudan.

From 1936 to 1939 in Palestine was the season called by Jews the Bloody Riots and by the English the Arab Revolt. For once, the British had a use for us.

At that time the main target of the Arab gangs was the Iraq Petroleum pipeline. They would strike at night in bands of five or six, digging down to expose the pipe, which was buried only a meter or so deep. A volley of gunfire would riddle the line, soaking the sand with oil. The raiders would set it ablaze with Molotov cocktails or flaming rags wrapped around stones. The fires would burn for days. The pipeline could not be protected along its length, and patrols were useless against such tactics of hit-and-run.

Wingate proposed the creation of a force—the Special Night Squads—that would employ British officers and Jewish guides and troopers to carry the fight to the enemy. He sold the idea to General Officer Commanding Archibald Wavell, the same general who later gave his blessing to another proponent of unconventional warfare, Major Ralph Bagnold, whose Long Range Desert Group fought alongside David Stirling's SAS behind the lines against Rommel and the Afrika Korps during World War II.

Wingate was unlike any Britisher I had met. He ate onions as fruit. He carried three or four with him always, wrapped in newspaper. On a trek or sitting by the fire, he would dig into his knapsack, pull out a fresh onion, and sink his teeth into it the way anyone else would bite into an apple. He was a champion rider who could jump a fence higher than his head. He believed that Arabs feared the night and based his fighting philosophy on attacking in the dark. Raiding the gangs who preyed upon the pipeline, Wingate mounted the taillights of his vehicles up front, so the enemy couldn't tell in which direction he was moving. Reconnoitering Arab camps, he made us wear sandals bought at local markets so that our tracks would be indistinguishable from those of native shepherds. He believed patrols worthless, but ambushes indispensable. When the doctrine of the day was based on walls and guard towers, he taught us to go "outside the wire," to befriend the night, move fast and strike in ways, at hours, and from directions that the enemy least expected.

I had served as a scout for the British Army and as a commander in the Mobile Guards of their Jewish Settlement Police. I came to despise the idea of parade ground order. Wingate felt the same. "Keep your rifle clean and kill your man before he kills you." That was all he wanted of discipline.

Once, raiding a camp of Arab saboteurs, I had our men dress as British soldiers. I made them smoke English cigarettes and eat English bully beef, so they would even smell like the real thing. Wingate approved. And if you think such precautions extravagant, believe me, the Bedouin can smell an Englishman from a Jew a hundred meters away.

Wingate's family were members of a sect called the Plymouth Brethren, Old Testament Christians. He knew the Books of Moses better than any Talmudic scholar and believed in them more passionately. Wingate loved not just Israel, but the *idea* of Israel. That contemporary Jews could and would re-create the Israel of the Bible became his passion. Our young people called him *HaYedid,* "the friend."

Whenever Wingate came to Nahalal, he stayed with my family. He and I would talk all night. Wingate had drawn up plans for a Jewish army, which he imagined as a formation under British command only until the establishment of the Jewish state.

"You will need this army then," he said, "to fight the Arabs."

Wingate identified with Gideon from the Book of Judges. He loved Kibbutz Ein Harod because Gideon had fought in that place in biblical times. The first morning he came to Camp Shimron, as our young people pressed around him, I could see in his eyes that his vision for this land was identical to ours and that he would burst his heart to help us bring it into being. The principles Wingate espoused—fighting at night, the employment of stealth and surprise, taking the battle to the enemy, the use of unconventional tactics, timing, and weaponry—became the core precepts of the Haganah and later the IDF.

As chief of staff in 1954 I issued a directive that every Israeli officer in a combat berth must undergo parachute training, whether he served in a paratroop unit or not. I included myself in this order. I jumped five times. I broke my leg the last time. Arik Sharon, commander of the paratroop brigade, pinned my jump wings to my breast at the graduation ceremony. I was standing in a plaster cast.

Why did I order all IDF officers to participate in paratroop training? Because to jump, one must overcome fear. It is the closest thing to actual combat. Jumping builds esprit. To jump with your mates makes you brothers. In any army paratroopers are elite warriors.

Two nights ago a reporter asked me what Israel must do, now, at the brink of war.

I told him we must jump out of the airplane.

Our ministers cannot congregate in rooms like Talmudic scholars, parsing political and diplomatic solutions. The combat commander learns that under fire he must often make a decision, any decision, because even a wrong decision is less dangerous than none at all.

Orde Wingate was killed fighting the Japanese in Burma during World War II. He was commander of the legendary Chindits force, the 77th Indian Infantry Brigade. He died on March 24, 1944, when the Mitchell bomber on which he was returning from Burma crashed in the jungle of northeast India.

What would Israel not give now to have our old friend, and his fighting spirit, standing again at our shoulders?

19.

THE POSSIBLE
AND THE IMPOSSIBLE

On the afternoon of June 1, 1967, a demonstration of women took place outside the Labor Party headquarters at 110 Yarkon Street in Tel Aviv. The wives and mothers, many of whom were Labor stalwarts, demanded the establishment of a national unity government and the resignation of Prime Minister Eshkol as minister of defense.

"We want Dayan! Give us Dayan!"

Eshkol watched the demonstration from the windows of the party offices. He referred to the protesters later, with the humor that didn't fail him even in this hour, as "the Merry Wives of Windsor."

Shlomo Gazit took the oath of the Haganah at age sixteen in 1942. He would serve into the 1970s and 1980s, first as chief of intelligence and later as minister in charge of the territories.

This demonstration was no joke, however. The people wanted Dayan. To understand why, one must go back to 1956, to what was called in Israel Operation Kadesh but became acclaimed around the world as "the Sinai Campaign."

In four days—one hundred hours—under Dayan's leadership as chief of staff, the IDF routed the Egyptian Army and overran the Sinai Peninsula from Sharm el-Sheikh to the Suez Canal. This lightning victory humiliated Egypt's new president, Gamal Abdel Nasser, who by arming his nation with the latest Soviet weaponry, by deliberately and aggressively confronting the Western powers, Great Britain and France, and by threatening war with Israel had set himself up not only as the champion of his own people but of the entire Arab world.

To Israelis, Moshe Dayan's name became synonymous with victory.

I encountered Dayan first in 1950, when I was a very young editor of *Maarachot*, the military monthly. The paper had commissioned histories from various commanders of the War of Independence and Dayan had sent in an article about his conquest of the Arab towns of Lod and Ramla. I rejected one word in the piece as being bad Hebrew. Describing the captured armored car his forces had used, the famous "Terrible Tiger," Dayan had employed the slang term *hanamer hanora'l*. Proper Hebrew would be *hanamer hanorah*.

One afternoon, out of nowhere, a great roar came from the street entrance of our offices. "Where is this Shlomo Gazit!"

Dayan burst in, dispensing colorful language and demanding that *hanamer hanora'l* remain. His logic was, significantly, that men who had bled and died had called the vehicle by that term. If it was good enough for them, it was good enough for *Maarachot*.

Dayan won, of course.

Two years later he was promoted to chief of operations, the number two position in the army, capping what was, even by Israeli standards, a meteoric ascent for an officer only thirty-seven years old. At the time, I was the head of the office for the outgoing operations chief, General Mordechai Maklef, who was moving up to chief of staff. Maklef took me aside. "Dayan is a field commander; he knows nothing of the General Staff. Will you stick around for a month or two, Shlomo, and help him find his footing?"

I agreed. Dayan, however, did not regard my presence in such a benign light as had Maklef. To him I was a spy, left behind by the new chief of staff to keep an eye on him. Every suggestion I made, Dayan rejected. Every cause I championed, he rebuffed. By the end of two weeks, I was ready to tell him, "Either you go to hell or I do, but I cannot continue under these conditions."

Then one day we were in a meeting. Dayan was chairing it. He passed me a note. I don't remember what the meeting was about or what question he asked me, but for some reason I wrote my answer in the form of a limerick.

Dayan took the note. I could see him scan it with his one good eye. That eye became scarlet with fury. For a moment I thought Dayan would actually rise from his chair in anger. Then at once his eye grew bright with humor.

In that moment, Shlomo Gazit was moved from the impossible to the possible.

Dayan divided the world into two categories: those who were "impossible," with whom he could not work, whose presence he would not suffer;

and those who were "possible." To colleagues and subordinates in the latter class, he granted free rein and such latitude as did no other commander.

This was how Dayan ran his staff and how he directed the army. "I don't want to do anything that someone else can do."

Why waste his time? If Gazit can do it, let him. Can this problem be handled by Morele Bar-On? Let Morele do it.

Dayan saw his role as the performance of that which only he could do.

At school my classmates and I were taught that a six-foot man could see roundabout on an unobstructed plain for a distance of two or three miles. If that man were two feet taller, he could see, perhaps, for five miles.

Dayan was this second man.

His vision extended beyond others'.

In 1956 Nasser nationalized the Suez Canal. This move took the world by surprise. It enraged the British and French, whose stockholders owned the Suez Canal Company. At once these European powers determined to retake the Canal by force and to remove Nasser from power.

Secret negotiations began between Britain and France and Israel. A scheme was hatched whereby Israeli paratroopers would capture a position so close to the Canal that it threatened war with Egypt. The British and French would, for public consumption, seize upon this outrage and demand that Israel and Egypt—like bad boys in a school playground—knock off the roughhousing and retire to their corners. Egypt, of course, would refuse. Voilà! The pretext for armed intervention would have been established.

British and French troops would seize the Canal. The status quo ante would be restored.

Ah, but first: Could these Jews do the job the British and French required? Was their army up to it? Did they even have an army? Remember, Israel in 1956 had been a state for just eight years. Only eleven years had elapsed since the terminal horrors of the Holocaust.

General Maurice Challe (who in 1961 would be a leader of the failed Algerian coup against President Charles de Gaulle) represented France at the initial discussions. Dayan, who had by then been promoted to army chief of staff, led the Israeli delegation. I was the interpreter. Dayan brought in his commanders. "How long will your forces require to capture all of the Sinai Peninsula?" asked General Challe. It was clear that he anticipated a reply in terms of months.

"Seven or eight days," said Dayan.

French eyebrows rose. Can these Jews be joking? Are they mocking us? Dayan's assessment seemed ridiculously self-confident, not to say arrogant. And yet IDF commanders appeared so certain of themselves and their forces—and proffered such detailed and credible battle plans—that Challe despite his skepticism continued the deliberations. On the final morning, he put this question to the Israeli chief of staff:

"General Dayan, if your forces indeed succeed in reaching the Suez Canal, how long do you estimate they can hold it?"

What answer did General Challe expect? Forty-eight hours? A week? Clearly he was anticipating Israel calling almost at once for French or British reinforcements.

Dayan replied in Hebrew. At once, the Israeli delegation erupted in laughter.

Challe glowered.

Now came the translation:

"Three hundred and fifty years."

I saw in General Challe's eyes the same look of fury that Dayan had shown when I passed him the limerick. Then the Frenchman's expression softened. He began to laugh.

At that moment, Dayan—and the armed forces of Israel—became "possible." Within days, the Sinai Campaign had begun.

20.

SHOT DOWN IN SINAI

In Turkish there is a word, *fergal*. It means a man who owns fields. This was my grandfather, Eliezer. I am named for him. My grandfather had vineyards, apple orchards; he employed about 150 people. He was a Jewish leader in Turkey.

Major Eliezer "Cheetah" Cohen was born in Jerusalem in 1934. At the time of the Sinai Campaign in 1956, he was a twenty-two-year-old fighter pilot, flying the U.S.-built P-51 Mustang.

My grandfather was doing a good business selling fresh fruit, but it was impossible to expand because there was no refrigeration in those days and the roads and transportation were too primitive to get the produce beyond local markets. Then my grandfather got the idea to set up a factory to dry the fruit. He started selling raisins and dried apricots and apples. Pretty soon he got rich. That was around 1910, when the Ottoman Empire was still in power. Then along came World War I and the Turks lost. Everything changed. To be in business in Turkey became very difficult. Meanwhile, the British, who had won the war, had taken over Palestine and were running it as a mandate under the League of Nations.

One day my grandfather called the family together and announced: I am packing up and going to Jerusalem! Not to visit, but to live! It has been a dream of my life and now I am going to do it. Who wishes to come with me?

My grandfather built a three-story house, the biggest in all Jerusalem outside the walls. At that time, Jerusalem was only the Old City, one kilometer square. Only a few families had begun to build outside the walls. My grandfather had come to Palestine in 1918 with the whole family (my father was five at the time) and many, many friends in a big convoy.

Our house was in Sanhedria. This was a poor neighborhood then and it is still poor today. An Orthodox neighborhood. My grandfather was not Orthodox himself. He only went to shul on the Sabbath. But he wanted to live among the Orthodox. The neighborhood was called Batei Pagi.

I was born in 1934. During the preceding decades, a new phenomenon had come to the Jewish people in Palestine. This was the Hebrew language. A newspaper editor named Eliezer Ben-Yehuda had started a movement to revitalize the language spoken by Moses and King David. We are Jews! Our history is in Hebrew and we should tell it in Hebrew! In those days, many of our parents' generation spoke the languages of the Diaspora. My father spoke Turkish. My mother was from Babylonia; she spoke Bablik. I can still speak a little myself.

At six years old, in first grade, I was speaking only Hebrew. We children used to come home from school and scold our parents and grandparents: No more speaking the languages of the old countries! Now we speak only Hebrew!

I remember when I first learned of the Nazi death camps. I was nine or ten. I could not understand how so monstrous a crime could happen. I went to my uncle. "Can this be true? Why are they killing Jews? What did the Jews do wrong?"

My uncle explained to me that the Jews in Germany and Eastern Europe had done nothing wrong; the Nazis were killing them just because they were Jews.

By the time I was thirteen, I had made up my mind to become a soldier.

I'm going to be a warrior and I'm going to kill anyone who comes to harm my people, no hesitation, no conscience; they have butchered us and I am going to do the same to them. I don't give a damn about other nations; I am going to protect my own. I still talk like this. My wife nearly faints each time I do.

When I was eighteen I took the army tests and they said I qualified for flight school. Even better. I will kill more enemies from the air.

In '56 I was a twenty-two-year-old lieutenant flying P-51 Mustangs. My brother Nechemiah was fourteen. He was still at home in Jerusalem.

The Mustang was a great American plane that the Americans wouldn't sell to Israel. We got a few as war surplus and others through smuggling and illegal purchases. Later, more were acquired legitimately through Sweden.

The Mustang had all the American virtues. It was roomy, fast and powerful, and an incredible weapons platform. You felt like you were driving a Cadillac. The Mustang carried napalm, bombs, and rockets and had six .50-caliber machine guns, three on each wing.

In '56 the 202nd Paratroop Brigade under Arik Sharon captured the Mitla Pass deep in Sinai. The Egyptians began advancing armored columns to attack them. It was the air force's job to stop these forces. At the same time our own tank columns were trying to break through the Egyptian defenses at Abu Agheila and Um Katef in eastern Sinai. We had to support them too.

That was where I got shot down.

I must confess that in 1956 the Israel Air Force had not yet come into its own. Though the nation had won a monumental victory due in no small part to our efforts, still, despite many instances of skill and courage by individual pilots—well, we could have done a lot better and we knew it.

We were outnumbered and outgunned at every level. The Egyptian Air Force was all jets. We were flying propeller planes. Those jets we did have, ancient Gloster Meteors and the French-built Ouragans, were restricted primarily to close air support because they were no match for the Egyptian MiGs. The only fighters we had that were equal to these planes were one squadron of French Mystères, which were so new that we didn't have enough pilots to fly them. French and British squadrons secretly deployed to Israeli air bases. In fact, the entire air defense of the cities of Israel was given over to French squadrons.

To attack a column of tanks in a Mustang, you have to fly so low that the bottom arc made by your propeller blades passes only meters above the enemy vehicles. At that height, a guy with a pistol can knock you out of the sky. Each pass is a gunfight. You're coming in so fast and so low that the enemy vehicles go from tiny to huge in a fraction of a second. You can see the truck drivers diving out of their cabs and even the tank crews scrambling out of their hatches and running like hell for the nearest ditch. And you can see the figures of the brave men who turn toward you and make their last stand using machine guns and antiaircraft cannons and even their own rifles.

It is a terrible thing to shoot a man and see him die. A pilot does most of his killing at altitude; he can report later in the briefing room that he destroyed this many tanks or that many trucks. But down at eye level it's another story. I did not feel so sure, anymore, about my resolve to slay the enemy without conscience. No one who has killed face-to-face will ever sleep the same again.

The pass when I got shot down was against an Egyptian antiaircraft gun. I could see the muzzle flash and feel the impact of the cannon shells hitting my engine. The coolant in the power plant of a P-51 is oil. Suddenly dark goo exploded everywhere. My windshield went black. I pulled left and up. I could hear the engine sputtering. My pressure gauges plummeted to zero. I turned east and tried to gain altitude. The issue was not whether I was going to go down but how soon and where.

Later, in the sixties, when I began to fly helicopters and my brother Nechemiah had become a leader in the Sayeret Matkal, he and I did many covert operations in this same part of Sinai. He led the teams and I flew them in and out.

To this day, the content of those missions remains classified. I am not allowed to speak about them except in the most general terms.

By the mid-1960s Nechemiah along with Ehud Barak (who would later become prime minister and minister of defense) had become the commanders of the future in the Sayeret Matkal. One or the other led most of the covert insertions.

On one mission both Nechemiah and I were awarded Chief of Staff Citations for valor. That was the first time such an honor had been given to two brothers. General Rabin pinned the decorations on us himself, in his office. Not long after that, we did another night insertion that the chief of staff directed in person from a forward command post. He issued special instructions that two brothers may not fly in on the same aircraft. If something happened to us, he did not want to face our mother.

My helicopters took Nechemiah's team into Sinai at night, flying so low that the landing gear would skim the dunes from time to time. Coming back out, racing the dawn, I was plugged into the aircraft intercom when I heard my brother's voice. I got very upset. "What are you doing on this helicopter, ahuyah? You know the chief of staff expressly forbade it!"

"He said we couldn't fly in together. He didn't say anything about flying out."

Rabin debriefed the mission himself. All the pilots and Sayeret Matkal guys took part; the session went on for hours. It is an inviolable principle in the Israel Air Force that one must speak the truth in a debriefing session, even if—particularly if—it reflects negatively on himself.

I spoke up.

"General Rabin, I must report that, contrary to your instructions, my brother and I flew out of Sinai on the same aircraft."

The whole room went silent.

"Did you fly in together or out?"

"Out only."

A moment passed. "Well, I guess that's okay then. I only said you couldn't fly together going in."

Nechemiah and I burst out laughing. We couldn't stop.

Rabin glowered. "What do you find so funny, Cheetah?"

"I'm sorry, sir. What you said now is exactly what Nechemiah said on the helicopter flying out."

Our family are Sephardim. Dark skinned. This is one reason why my brother was so good on special operations. He could pass for an Arab. He knew most of the dialects, and the ones he didn't know, he picked up fast from his instructors. Most Sayeret Matkal operations are not helicopter insertions. The teams would cross the border on foot. Sometimes they went hundreds of miles deep into enemy territory, into Egypt, Jordan, Syria, even Iraq. They stole cars or rode buses. They ate in Arab restaurants, prayed in mosques. It scared me just flying in to pick them up. I can't

Photo courtesy of Amir Cohen.

Nechemiah Cohen beside his brother
Cheetah's helicopter, preparatory to a
cross-border special forces operation.
December 2, 1965.

imagine how those young guys did it, on the ground on their own, day after day, knowing that capture meant death or worse.

Nechemiah is eight years younger than I. When he was a child, it was my hope that he would not have to grow up to be a fighter. But of course he wanted to be like his father and uncles and older brothers. Nechemiah is not a big man. He is light and fast. Quiet and thoughtful, he would never boast. But in the Unit, as the Sayeret Matkal calls itself (as Unit 101 did before them), when they ran competitions for endurance, strength, and speed, Nechemiah always came in ahead of everybody else.

I crash-landed my Mustang, dead-stick, with my eyes peeking around the oil-blackened windscreen. But now on the ground I had a problem. I had broken my leg a couple of weeks earlier. When the fighting in Sinai broke out, my squadron commander at first refused to let me fly. I insisted that my leg would not be a problem. Finally he said, "Okay, Cheetah, take a Stearman up over the airfield and do two slow rolls. I'll watch you."

A slow roll is harder than a barrel roll. You need to push the rudder pedal all the way down and hold it. It takes a lot of strength. You can't do it on a bum leg.

I did it, so my squadron commander let me fly.

Now I was in the desert with a broken leg. How am I going to walk out of here when every Egyptian soldier who has seen my plane going down is racing like hell, right now, to capture me and do what they do when they get their hands on an Israeli pilot?

I hopped on one leg for about two hours, keeping within sight of a road in case I should see Israeli trucks or tanks. But everything that passed was Egyptian. I spotted an abandoned pipeline and crawled inside to hide and to get out of the sun. Late in the afternoon a couple of Egyptian trucks stopped just down the slope. I could hear the men calling to each other.

"Moshe, where's the Pepsi?" In Hebrew!

Our guys, it turned out, had captured these trucks from the Egyptians. Among the loads were cases of Pepsi-Cola, which we didn't have in Israel at the time. These soldiers apparently got a taste and liked it. But by the time I realized they were my own countrymen, they had started up the trucks and driven off.

I began walking. At least now I knew I was near my own people. Around sunset a column of IDF tanks appeared. I hopped out onto the road, waving my arms and shouting. The first tank braked at fifty meters, keeping its hatches buttoned up. I could see its coaxial machine gun traversing, stopping with its barrel zeroed right between my eyes. To my horror, I realized that I was wearing a light-colored flight suit like Egyptian pilots wore. On top of that, I am dark skinned like they are.

I began shouting in Hebrew. No one in the tank could hear me because of the distance, the noise of the engine, and the fact that their hatches were shut. Suddenly a second tank came forward. The first tank must have radioed for a superior officer. Tank number two stopped about twenty-five meters away, its gun pointed at me too.

Suddenly the commander's hatch opened. My cousin Yoav stuck his head out.

"Cheetah! What are you doing here?"

21.

THE MITLA PASS

Every paratrooper lives to make a combat jump. You get a red background patch for your uniform that you mount your jump wings on. It goes above your left breast pocket. In Israel in '67, no paratrooper had made a combat jump since the men of Battalion 890 at Mitla in 1956.

Dan Ziv is the thirty-one-year-old deputy commander of Paratroop Battalion 71. Eleven years earlier, in 1956, he was awarded the Itur HaGvura, Israel's highest decoration for valor, for his actions at the Mitla Pass in Sinai.

Let me tell you about '56. You cannot understand '67 if you don't know about '56.

This was a war, the Sinai Campaign, that lasted only one hundred hours but that put Israel on the map as a force to be reckoned with—and by the way made a worldwide hero of Moshe Dayan, who had been chief of staff and was considered the genius behind the whole show. It also was the war that humiliated Egypt's president Gamal Abdel Nasser in front of all the Arab world and by the logic of national pride and payback made the Six Day War, eleven years later, inevitable.

When you are a twenty-year-old lieutenant, you know nothing about the "big picture." The politics of whatever war you're fighting are explained to you for a few minutes in battalion and brigade briefings, and maybe you read about the international situation in the newspapers and chew it over with your friends and the other young lieutenants. But basically it's so far over your head you can't waste time worrying about it. What you are concerned with is your own piece of the puzzle.

Can I lead my men?

Can I accomplish my mission?

Can I keep my soldiers safe?

When people think of the desert, a place like Sinai, they imagine a big flat box of sand, which can be driven over anywhere you please. No. Sinai has mountains. It has impassable belts of sand. In Sinai you fight on roads, and you get through the hills and mountains only by passes.

The Mitla Pass is one of these.

Mitla is deep into Sinai, only fifty kilometers east of the Suez Canal. The plan—Dayan's plan—was to start the war not with conventional assaults along the Israel-Egypt border but to strike deep from the very start. Our paratroop battalion, 890, would jump at Mitla and seize the pass before the enemy even realized that the fight had started.

This stunt at Mitla served no real military purpose. Its aim was political. The point of having an Israeli force seize territory so close to Suez was to establish a pretext for the British and the French to invade Egypt and take back the Canal. Nasser had nationalized this previously international waterway just a few months earlier, in July 1956.

The British and French plan was to wait till we Israelis had taken Mitla, then announce to the world, "These crazy Jews and Arabs are fighting again; it's up to us powers to keep them apart, so we will invade Egypt as peacekeepers and by the way we'll kick Nasser out of the Canal."

I am only a twenty-year-old lieutenant and of course no one is telling me this plan, but if I had known, I would have said, "Wow, that is some crazy scheme!"

At that time Israel had its own reasons for going to war with Egypt, namely that Nasser had acquired huge shipments of Soviet arms via Czechoslovakia in 1955. The General Staff figured it would take Nasser three or four years to train his army up on the new tanks and planes. Then he would attack us. No nation would supply us with equivalent arms. The Americans wouldn't, the British wouldn't, the French wouldn't. Dayan believed that Israel must preempt the enemy. We had no choice but to destroy those Soviet arms before Nasser could use them against us. At the same time Ben-Gurion, who was prime minister and minister of defense, was thinking: It's good for Israel to fight alongside England and France. We can gain their respect and possibly their aid and arms in the future.

Of course, none of us at the pass had a clue about this deep thinking. It was all top secret. Even our brigade commander, Arik Sharon, knew nothing of this. If he had been told that all his paratroopers had to do was jump into Mitla and sit down, we could have broken out the cold beer and enjoyed ourselves. (Although I must say of Sharon that he would have found some excuse to overstretch the mission, no matter what orders Dayan had given him.)

We flew. We jumped. We set up defensive positions at the eastern end of the pass, at a place called the Parker Memorial. We encountered no resistance. As far as we knew, the whole Sinai Peninsula was deserted; the Egyptians didn't even know we were there.

Our jump group was in fact the advance element of a greater incursion. While we in Battalion 890 were digging in at the Mitla Pass, the rest of the brigade was speeding toward us overland, from the Israeli border, by truck and bus. We dropped at 17:00, just before dark, on October 29. The main body caught up thirty hours later.

Now we had a full paratroop brigade—almost two thousand men—on the ground, all alone at the Egyptian end of the Sinai Desert. We are a long way from Israel and a very short way from the Suez Canal.

Sharon didn't like it. The ground at the eastern end of the pass is raw, stony desert; our entrenching tools could barely scratch out a slit trench. We had no cover against air attack. A force of tanks could wipe us out in minutes.

A lot of crazy stuff went on that day among the commanders that nobody knew about till the war was over, and even then there was controversy that went on for years.

Sharon wanted to advance into the pass and take the whole thing, all thirty-two kilometers of it. If we held the western end, he reasoned, we could defend ourselves against an attack originating from Suez. Dayan said no. But he didn't explain why. The deal with the British and the French was secret. Sharon had no clue. He thought only: My guys are vulnerable; I need to take the whole pass. He appealed not to Dayan but to another general, who was chief of operations. This general gave Sharon permission to send a small reconnaissance force through the pass.

Instead Sharon sent a big recon force—two companies, under Motta Gur, on half-tracks supported by several tanks.

The pass was supposed to be deserted. The Egyptians weren't supposed to know we were there. But they did know, and they were there. They had gotten two battalions in overnight. These troops had taken the high ground and had dug into positions on both sides of the road that ran through the pass.

Gur's party got most of the way through while the Egyptians were dozing. Suddenly the enemy woke up and began firing with everything they had. They cut Gur's column in half. The rear element made a U-turn and drove like hell back to the eastern end of the pass, by the Parker Memorial. That's where I was—twenty years old, just thirty days out of my officer's course. Our commanders, Raful Eitan and Aharon Davidi, came racing up. They had been taken completely by surprise by these developments.

I knew Raful and Davidi from the original Paratroop Battalion 890, before the formation had expanded to brigade size. I had been a corporal and later a sergeant during the reprisal operations of '54 and '55. Sharon was our battalion commander. Company commanders at various times were Motta Gur, Danny Matt, Meir Har-Zion, Sa'adia Alkayam (Supapo), and Raful Eitan. My friend Katcha Cahaner was there and many others who went on to become legends in the paratroopers. Uzi Eilam was a lieutenant, Sharon's intelligence officer.

But back to Mitla. Davidi, who was a lieutenant colonel and Sharon's second-in-command, had been ordered by Sharon to direct the battle. But Davidi, like everyone else, knew nothing about the area. He didn't have any maps. He didn't know where Motta's companies were sitting or where the Egyptians were or how many men they had. He sent the recon unit forward. They captured the peaks on both sides of the pass. But the enemy was dug in below them and the recon guys couldn't see them.

I need a volunteer, said Davidi. His driver was a tough paratrooper named Yehuda Ken-Dror. Davidi told Yehuda to go forward in a jeep. I was sitting twenty meters away; I heard every word. I could see Yehuda turn white. But he jumped into his jeep and took off over the hill.

We heard heavy fire. All contact was lost with Yehuda. It turned out that he had been shot out of his jeep but had managed to dive into a ditch, where he stayed until dark before he was able to crawl back, hundreds of meters, to our lines. His mates got him to the hospital, but he was too severely wounded; he hung on for three months before he died. He was awarded the Itur HaGvura, Israel's highest decoration for valor.

Both commanders, Davidi and Raful Eitan, now turned to me.

"Now is your turn, Dan."

Now is my turn.

Okay.

But don't go by jeep, Davidi tells me. Take an armored half-track, pick five soldiers from your platoon, and now listen very carefully to your mission because I am giving you not one assignment but two. First, drive along the road and find out where the Egyptian positions are. Second, locate Motta Gur's force, find out what has happened to him and what help he needs, then take his wounded men into your half-track and get back here.

I say: "Just so I understand, my task is to drive through the Egyptian positions once, then turn around and come back through them again?"

"And keep your eyes open. Report everything you see."

What do I do? The same thing I do every time I go into battle. I raise my eyes to God Almighty. I tell him, Lord, I will be out there with five of my friends. Please look on us with your good eye.

"Dan, are you ready?"

There is my half-track. There are my guys. It is our turn now to run the gantlet.

Somehow we got through. Thirty-two kilometers, out in the open, no cover, with six hundred to seven hundred enemy soldiers shooting at us from twenty meters, a hundred meters, two hundred meters. Some things you cannot explain. No one got even a scratch.

We reached the other side. I found Motta Gur, took five of his wounded aboard the half-track. I radioed back to my company commander for permission to return. He said, "Dan, are you dead?"

I told him, "I am living like a king!"

We race back. I report to Davidi. We are under fire the whole way. Egyptian aircraft are attacking. A mortar truck blows up fifty meters from me, bullets are flying, smoke is everywhere. I'm reporting to Davidi and Raful, both of them lying prone, taking cover. I'm standing. I tell them what happened, where the Egyptians are, where Motta Gur is, how many enemy there are, everything that I can see.

"So, Dan, what do you suggest we do?"

I tell them there is only one way. We must get above the Egyptians on the mountain and root them out hand to hand, position by position.

Meanwhile, Raful is shouting at me, "Ziv, get down! Do you want to get shot! What are you standing for?"

He's a lieutenant colonel, my battalion commander, but my job is to report to Davidi, who is running the battle. I get upset. I lose my cool. "Raful, shut up, be silent, don't disturb me while I am reporting to Davidi!"

So Raful gets up and stands beside me, in the gunfire. Davidi stays put.

"Hey, my two heroes! Come over here and get your asses on the ground."

So we fought the battle. A terrible fight, all night, killing the enemy with knives and entrenching tools, hole to hole. Awful casualties, the worst ever. So many men fighting with such bravery. Not just us—the Egyptians too. Two hundred sixty dead on their side, forty-six on ours.

Horrible. Sharon's enemies in the army cried for his blood for that. But Dayan would not act against him.

Dayan was furious at Sharon. And he grieved for the losses of such elite troops, many of whom he knew by their first names. But Dayan believed that to punish an officer for acting with initiative, even such excessive initiative as Sharon had taken, would work irretrievable harm to the aggressive spirit of the Israeli Army. This was the occasion of his famous remark: "I would rather have to rein in the overeager warhorse than to prod the reluctant mule."

That was Mitla. That terrible night. After that, in four days we destroyed the Egyptian Army.

Round One had been the War of Independence, 1948.

The Sinai Campaign in 1956 was Round Two.

Now it's 1967. Nasser and the Arabs are saying to themselves: The Jews have beaten us in Round One and Round Two, but we will wipe them out for good in Round Three.

22.

LEAVING SINAI

During the Sinai Campaign of 1956, Moshe Dayan received much criticism for his frequent absences from the command center in Tel Aviv. The army chief of staff is supposed to be at headquarters running the war, people said. But Dayan believed that he could not direct events from the remote vantage of an office at General Headquarters, but must see and hear on the spot, up front with the troops.

"During such engagements," he wrote in *Diary of the Sinai Campaign*, "I like to be at the forward command post of the fighting unit; battle is after all the army's business. I do not know if the unit commander 'enjoys' finding me at his elbow, but I prefer, whenever possible, to follow the action—and if necessary even intervene in its direction—close to the scene and while it is happening, rather than read about it in a dispatch the following morning and reveal the wisdom of hindsight."

Neora Matalon-Barnoach was an eighteen-year-old lieutenant when she first went to work as secretary for Chief of Operations Moshe Dayan in 1953. Her memoir, A Good Spot on the Side, *recounts nearly three decades of service and friendship with Dayan.*

Dayan ran his operation unlike any other staff commander—in fact, unlike any commander of any kind. Entering his office on my first day of work, I was shocked at the informality of the place. There was no desk, only a campaign table covered with an army blanket and a pane of glass. Chairs were the camp type. The place looked like a field headquarters. The only thing missing was an inch of sand on the floor.

On December 6, 1953, when Dayan was promoted to chief of staff, he converted the big office, the throne room of the outgoing chief, into a conference room. He himself took the space where the administrative officer used to sit. His office was smaller than mine. The outgoing chief had been chauffeured about in a big American Lincoln. Dayan got rid of it. He drove a Plymouth.

This was the ethic that Dayan instilled into the entire army. He cared nothing for military display or spit and polish. "Our job is to produce fighters, not soldiers."

He admired the American Marine Corps in all aspects except its emphasis on the parade ground and close-order drill. On one trip to the States, Moshe was a guest in the reviewing stand at a formal military parade.

The Marines performed the complicated drill flawlessly and won excited applause. I applauded too but I couldn't help thinking it was almost an insult the way they used combat warriors as marionettes, as if they were chocolate soldiers at the opera. From the moment I started my military service I regarded foot drills, parades and lineups with skepticism bordering on hostility. The soldier was meant for war, and war does not happen in a straight line.

Dayan's physical courage was legendary in the army. Arik Sharon said of him, "He is brave to the point of insanity."

Nothing elicited Dayan's respect more than valor under fire, or inspired his love more than sacrifice for a comrade-in-arms. He could forgive anything from a fighter who seized the initiative in the face of danger. He protected Sharon after Mitla. He loved Meir Har-Zion and Katcha Cahaner. His passion was not limited to commanders of brigades and divisions. He cared as much for the lieutenants and sergeants and private soldiers.

When Dayan delegated a staff assignment, he gave his subordinates the broadest possible latitude. "I would not be assigning you this task if I did not have complete confidence that you can do a better job than I can."

He expected his officers to take the initiative, solve the problem on their own, and not come back until they had finished.

"I want to do no job myself that can be done by somebody else."

Dayan wrote all his own speeches. He would labor at his desk until he was too exhausted to continue. He would say (and I learned to say with him), "No more milk will come from this he-goat tonight."

Dayan reserved time to think, and he did his thinking alone. When he had arrived at a plan or an idea, the door to his office would open. "What do you think of this?"

The worst thing a staff member could say was, "Moshe, I agree one hundred percent." Dayan's eye would darken. "Why?" he would say. "Tell me why you agree."

Once he asked my opinion and I hesitated. "The moment you think twice before answering," he said, "our work together is over."

He liked it when people contested him. He listened. "Only a donkey," he would say, "never changes his mind."

Dayan was not a reader, except of poetry (much of which he committed to memory and recited on specific occasion), particularly the works of Natan Alterman and Rachel of Kibbutz Kinneret, Israel's unofficial poetess laureate.

What he did read was military material, particularly combat reports and intelligence analyses. He knew intimately every raid and battle from our own wars, as well as every fight from Europe and Russia and the North African desert in World War II. He could speak in detail about campaigns from the Bible, particularly those of Joshua, with whom he identified. He had walked the ground of the ancient battles meter by meter; he could explain how the Amorites utilized formations of infantry or trace, step by step, the route Jonathan employed to attack the Philistines and open the pass between the cliffs of Bozez and Seneh.

But the principles that informed Dayan's tactical doctrine came from the moderns—primarily from the Russians, the British and the Americans, and, with an irony of which he was not incognizant, the Germans.

All these factors figured prominently in the Sinai Campaign of 1956, as did two further elements: the influence of world opinion and the political self-interest of the superpowers. Another passage from *Diary of the Sinai Campaign:*

> *I stressed the point that speed was the key factor. We must end*
> *the campaign in the shortest possible time. The longer it lasts,*
> *the greater will be the political complications—pressure from the*
> *United States, the dispatch of [Russian or Communist bloc]*
> *"volunteers" to aid Egypt, and so on. It must take no longer*
> *than two weeks, at the outside, and within this period we must*
> *complete the conquest of the whole of the Sinai Peninsula.*

When the campaign ended with Israel's lightning victory, Moshe Dayan became an icon. The black eye patch, which he hated, became a symbol of a new kind of Jew. In Israel, he had become Joshua. He had stopped the sun.

But neither he nor Prime Minister Ben-Gurion could stand up, in the end, to world opinion and to the political pressure applied by the Soviet Union and the United States.

Sinai must be given back to Egypt.

The desert will be demilitarized, pledged the Soviets and Americans. UN peacekeepers will replace Israeli troops. No tanks, warplanes, or heavy weapons may be deployed between the Suez Canal and the eastern armistice line between Israel and Egypt. The Straits of Tiran shall remain open to all shipping.

The last man out of Sinai was Moshe Dayan. Watching the lowering of the Israeli flag that had flown over the municipal building in El Arish, Dayan was asked by a reporter why he had made a point of traveling to witness this dolorous event.

"IDF commanders must taste all the dishes," Dayan replied. "The bitter along with the sweet."

When we saw him next in our offices, he had no quip to offer. "What I have feared most has come to pass. Military victory has become political defeat."

The memory of this bitter reverse stuck with Moshe Dayan and affected profoundly the decisions he made during the Six Day War.

BOOK THREE

THE WAITING,
PART TWO

23.

A PLAN FOR TOTAL WAR

I was a twenty-seven-year-old captain, deputy head of Air Force Operations in late 1962, when my boss came into my office and said, "Rafi, the chief wants us to draw up a plan for total war."

Rafi Sivron is the planner of Operation Moked—"Focus"— the preemptive strike that will destroy the air force of Egypt in three hours on June 5, 1967.

In the years between 1956 and 1967 every officer in the Israel Defense Forces knew that another war with Egypt was coming. It was only a matter of time.

The Soviets under Khrushchev and later Kosygin were vigorously upgrading Nasser's air force with MiG-17s, MiG-19s, and the latest, most lethal fighter in the world, the Mach-2 MiG-21.

The Egyptians had Tupolev and Ilyushin bombers that could reach Israeli cities in under an hour. Their armored divisions were being modernized with new T-54 and T-55 tanks. And Soviet engineers had totally redesigned the Egyptian Air Force's radar and early-warning systems.

Russia and the United States had compelled our forces to give Sinai back to Egypt in 1957. The promise was that the peninsula would remain demilitarized. UN troops would man the frontiers, guaranteeing a buffer zone of two hundred kilometers between Egypt and Israel. Still, a squadron of Tupolev bombers could take off from Egyptian soil and strike Tel Aviv in thirty-five minutes. Israel was vulnerable and everyone in the IDF knew it.

In 1962 Ezer Weizman was commander of the air force. His operations chief was Yak Nevo, the legendary fighter pilot. Ezer was a brigadier general; Yak was a colonel. I was Yak's deputy. My office and his were next to each other; he and I had lunch together every day. I admired him greatly.

Now Yak was standing in my office. "Ezer wants a plan for total war, meaning against Egypt, Syria, and Jordan. The aim is to achieve complete air superiority. He wants the plan two ways—one, if we're attacked; two, if we do the attacking."

I started telling Yak how busy I was. I was still flying operational missions—in fact, I had one scheduled over Sinai this very night . . .

"Rafi, you're the planner." And he tossed me the hot potato.

That was how Operation Moked began.

"The one thing you've got is time," Yak said. "There's no rush because no one knows what the hell to do with this. Keep flying your missions and work on this when you can."

We set to work, Yak and I. We'd meet one or two hours a week, sitting outside over lunch or coffee and cigarettes. We had no assistants, no secretary, no colleagues. Nobody took notes, nobody prepared memos, we submitted nothing for approval. Will anything ever come of this? We put the odds at a hundred to one.

The overall concept was a no-brainer: a preemptive strike to knock out the enemy air forces. As far back as Lou Lenart's plan to attack the Egyptian airfield at El Arish in 1948 (with Ezer as his number three), the idea was to hit the foe by surprise and knock him out on the ground. Egypt first, because its air force was the biggest; then Jordan and Syria if we still had resources.

The next question was how? There was a powerful school of thought that believed a counterstrike would be most effective. Let the Egyptians attack us, intercept them, and shoot them down. Another said kill the pilots on the ground. Send commandos and simply gun them down. A third concept was decapitation of enemy command and control. Knock out their radar and communications.

We decided, Yak and I, to take out the enemy's runways.

Without runways, planes can't fly.

Runways became the focus. The plan had no name then. We began working on bombs and the doctrine of bombing to render a runway inoperable. This is not as easy as it sounds. It was entirely possible to score direct hits on runways with very heavy bombs and yet produce minimal damage, or damage that could be repaired quickly. Endless testing and planning went into discovering precisely what angle of attack should be taken. Bombs can skip. They can detonate a half second too soon or a tenth of a second too late.

At what angle should the bombs strike the surface of the runway? From what height should they be dropped? At what altitude should the planes pull out of their dives? Remember, the Israel Air Force had no heavy or even medium bombers. We would have to use fighters. A fighter can carry two bombs maximum. Some types can carry only one. Each bomb must count. None must be wasted.

What type of bomb would produce the greatest and most lasting destruction? Should it penetrate the runway? By how much? How many bombs per runway? Aimed at what target points?

I started talking to our intelligence people. A conflict arose at once. The way intelligence worked, I was informed, was that agents and their "assets" brought in raw data from the field; this data was then analyzed and presented to command. After that, plans were drawn.

No, I said, I need it to happen the opposite way. I will tell you what I need to know; then you go and find it out.

Oh, no. We can't do it that way.

Why not?

Because that's not the way it's done.

After many meetings I succeeded in gaining the intelligence officers' confidence. I need to know, I said, not just the geographical location of every military airfield in Egypt, Syria, and Jordan, but the physical layout of the field itself—and every potential auxiliary field. Where are the hangars, the fueling depots, the control towers, the barracks, the briefing rooms? What defenses does each field possess? Antiaircraft artillery? Where? Which squadrons are based at which fields? Of what types of aircraft are these squadrons composed? How many? Where are they parked? Protected by bunkering or revetments? Can we get at them by strafing? Will bombing be necessary?

Where do the pilots sleep? At what time do they arrive at the field each morning? When do they eat breakfast? What is their training and patrol schedule? Meteorological data. Will clouds be a problem? Ground fog? At what time of day? In what season of the year?

What time do the Egyptian pilots start each training day and what time do they finish? What are their names? What are their wives' names? What kind of cars do they drive? What routes do they take from their homes to the bases?

I need to know everything about the Egyptian Air Force's command and control. Do they even have such a thing? What are their channels of command? How do orders reach the individual squadrons? Can we compromise these networks, can we tap into them, can we destroy them?

Many issues were so elementary that they had, I realized, never been seriously examined. What is the optimum way to attack an airfield? With full squadrons? With four-ship formations? How many per field? Do we attack in waves? Do all planes attack or do some remain at altitude, providing cover? What weapons do we use to destroy enemy planes on the ground?

At the time of the IAF's acquisition of the seventy-two Mirage IIIC fighters, a passionate debate had raged on the subject of missiles versus guns. Missiles were the hot new thing. But the pilots hated them. Missiles were unreliable—they missed, they malfunctioned.

In the end, guns won.

Each Mirage got twin 30-millimeter cannons.

Piece by piece, a doctrine began to take shape.

The attack would commence with an initial bombing run whose object would be to knock out the runways. The planes would then make three strafing passes, attacking the enemy planes in their parked positions on the ground. By the time the third pass had been completed, the next wave of Israeli warplanes would have arrived on station and be commencing their bombing runs. The first wave would race for home, to rearm and refuel for the next sortie.

The genius of this concept was that one standard attack pattern could be used against any enemy field.

Through practice a specific bombing technique was determined to be optimal. The bomb runs would begin from an altitude of 6,000 feet. Angle of dive would be 35 degrees precisely, because that was the angle, calculating from the release altitude and the descending arc of the bomb in its fall, that would deliver the ordnance at the optimal angle to the target runway. Any shallower and the bomb might skip; any steeper and the plane might not be able to pull out before it flew into the zone of the bomb's explosion and debris.

Bomb release point would be 2,500 feet AGL—above ground level. Pilots would begin pulling out of their dives at 1,000 feet. At zero altitude they would execute a 270-degree turn and initiate their strafing runs. These would be performed at 450 knots or faster, preferably 550 knots, down the long axis upon which the target aircraft were parked. At a range of 900 meters the pilots would open fire with their 30-millimeter cannons. They would aim low. Rounds fired high would miss the target completely, but bullets missing low would "walk" over the target as the attacking plane continued its pass. The planes would lay down a swath of gunfire that would either strike the target aircraft directly or ricochet off the pavement or the ground into the bellies of the parked planes.

Though the plan specified three passes of strafing, the leader of each four-ship formation was permitted to make as many runs as fuel and enemy antiaircraft fire permitted within the interval of time before the succeeding four-ship formation arrived. The decision would be made by the flight leader in the moment.

Six thousand feet was the altitude at which the attack aircraft would commence their bombing runs. But how would they get to that altitude without being detected by enemy radar?

The planes must come in "on the deck"—meaning at a height of 100 feet, no higher. This meant that the leader of each four-ship formation must determine in advance, from maps or aerial photographs, a waypoint five or six kilometers short of its target and on a heading that was offset from the target by a similar distance. The reason for the offset was to help the pilots find the target when they rolled onto their backs at the peak of their climb. If their approach heading was, say, north of the target field, they knew to look south to find it.

This waypoint was called an IP, or initial point. At the IP, each pilot would "pull," or haul the stick into his belly and start his climb. The jets would ascend at a 50-degree angle under full afterburner for half a minute. At 6,000 feet the planes would invert, locate the target visually, and dive onto it.

How difficult is this? Imagine an IP. A house, a road junction, a filling station. This initial point must stand out from its surroundings. It must be unmistakable. You must be able to find it in the middle of the empty desert, say, or among the agricultural landscape of the delta, where every acre of cultivation looks exactly like every other. On top of that, you must find this IP when you're flying so low it's almost as if you're in a car, at a rate only a hundred knots slower than the speed of sound. Found it? Now pull. Remember as you enter your climb that the belly of your plane is toward the target, so you can't see. You will not know for certain that you're on target until you invert at the peak of your arc and peer up through the canopy—i.e., down at the ground. At that point the element of surprise will be gone. Alarms will be sounding. Enemy gunners will be sprinting to their antiaircraft cannons.

The primal imperative of the plan is that all planes strike their targets at the same time. If one squadron attacks early, it gives away the whole game. The enemy will scramble. His planes can get away, defend, strike back.

A timetable had to be developed.

The first problem was that our formations would be striking eleven or more airfields, each of which lay at a different distance (and thus a different flying time) from our borders. Further, the attack formations would be flying out of different bases in Israel, each one with different flying times to different targets. How could we make them all arrive at the same time?

Beyond these issues was the fact that the attacking force was composed of different types of aircraft, each of which flew at different speeds and possessed different flying capabilities. The slower Vautours and Ouragans would have to be given extra minutes to reach their targets (or be assigned targets that were closer in), so that they could arrive at the identical instant as the faster Mystères, Super Mystères, and Mirages.

Further, the attacking forces would have to take routes designed to avoid detection by enemy radar. They would have to fly "legs," to zig and zag. Yet all aircraft must arrive over their targets at precisely the same moment.

All this must be accomplished in total radio silence. Even contact with the control tower would be forbidden. En route to their targets, not a peep was permitted. If a pilot encountered an emergency and had to ditch at sea, he could not call for help or even alert his formation-mates.

Nor could the attacking forces count on knocking out the enemy in a single strike. We must plan for multiple sorties. Strike, return to base, re-arm and refuel, strike again. Seventy-two Mirages become 144 if you can turn them around fast enough. This meant training and motivating ground crews to perform at unprecedented levels of speed and skill.

How many warplanes should participate? Mirages made up 72 of Israel's fleet of 202 combat aircraft. Some would have to be held back for duty as interceptors. How many? Stationed where? To protect which population centers?

Every plane held back was a plane that could not strike the enemy. How boldly should we roll the dice? Could we attack with *every plane we had*?

The next question was time of attack. At what hour of the day would we strike? This issue produced the sharpest clash between me and Ezer Weizman, the chief of the air force.

Ezer was adamant that the attack commence at dawn. Why? Because that was how it always happened in the movies. All the great attacks in history were made at first light!

I threatened twice to quit—and once actually turned in my resignation.

First, I declared, dawn was the hour at which ground fog was most likely in the Nile delta. By eight the mist dispersed. But far more important was achieving surprise. By now our agents had acquired near total knowledge of the enemy's daily routine. The Egyptian Air Force's day began at dawn with a combat air patrol. When the formation commanders were satisfied that no enemy attack was imminent, they landed for breakfast. This was between 07:00 and 07:30. At this hour most senior commanders were en route from their homes to the air bases. The training day started with various briefings around 08:00.

I argued strenuously that the attack must come at 07:45.

Ezer would not hear of it. No argument that Yak or I could mount made a dent. The RAF attacked at dawn, and the IAF would too!

Here I must confess to implementing a stratagem. I wrote into the attack plan the stipulation that H-hour would be determined by the chief of operations *at the time of the event,* based on the latest intelligence.

By the time my plan was used, Ezer was no longer air force commander. Motti Hod had taken over.

That was how the plan dodged that bullet.

In April 1965 we began exposing the plan to senior officers and heads of departments in the air force. Everywhere response was enthusiastic. It was so positive that I began to worry.

If this many people are happy, I must have made some terrible mistake.

Danny Shapira is the Israel Air Force's chief test pilot. He will serve in six wars over five decades. In June 1967 he flies Mirages with Fighter Squadron 101:

Operation Moked could not have succeeded without the Mirage IIIC, the superb delta-wing fighter-interceptor manufactured by Dassault Aviation in France. Ezer Weizman, chief of the IAF, had acquired seventy-two of them, with the first pair arriving in April 1962 and the final complement touching down in July 1964.

Those Mirages saved Israel.

I was the IAF's chief test pilot in 1959. This was the year in which I graduated from France's Armée de l'Air test pilot school, and the year I first flew the Mirage.

At that time France was the IAF's best friend. Dassault Aviation had supplied us with Ouragans, Mystères, and Super Mystères in an era when

other nations, including Britain and the United States, would not even sell
us ammunition.

But the Mirage was the pièce de résistance. Supersecret. The French
didn't want to let me or any other foreigner near it, let alone take it up.

Ezer told them, "Danny flies or it's no deal!"

I remember Dassault's chief test pilot arriving at the embassy in Paris
to inform me that I would be flying the Mirage the next morning. The
prototype I was to take up was so new its tail number was "01." I asked
the French pilot, "Are you going to brief me on the aircraft's capabilities
and characteristics?"

He gave me a Gallic shrug. "You're a test pilot. Test it."

I was in the Mirage for thirty seconds and I fell in love. What a plane!
She was powerful, fast, incredibly responsive—a pilot's aircraft that you
flew with your fingertips. On my second flight I took her past Mach 1.5,
pulling 7 Gs. On the third I hit Mach 2.1.

Ezer was waiting the moment I landed. "Well?"

"I love it. It's made for us—but not the way the French have designed it."

Here was the problem: The French had conceived the Mirage as a
high-altitude interceptor. Like other Western powers during the Cold War,
they wanted a plane that could climb very fast to 60,000 or 70,000 feet
and shoot down invading Soviet bombers. The Mirage even had a supple-
mental rocket booster that could take it to the edge of space.

But extreme altitude is not where wars are fought in the Middle East.
The IAF needed an all-purpose aircraft that could bomb, strafe, dogfight,
even perform photo reconnaissance. Israel is not a superpower that can
afford a bomber force, a fighter force, and so on. For us, one aircraft has
to do everything.

The Mirage was that airplane, I was certain. But critical changes had
to be made.

First, the plane needed a gun.

The Mirage came with missiles only. Missiles were the hot new thing
then. The Americans had the Sidewinder, the Russians had the Atoll, the
French had the Matra. Missiles were the future, the engineers said. Push a
button and the enemy's plane explodes five miles away. Old-fashioned cannons? They were passé.

But I didn't trust missiles, and neither did our IAF pilots. Missiles were
unreliable. They could be defeated by countermeasures. Worse, missiles
are primarily air-to-air weapons. They're no match for guns at attacking
ground targets. If war with Egypt came, the IAF's primary mission would

be to knock out the enemy's air force by attacking its fields and destroying its planes on the ground.

You need cannons to strafe ground targets.

I made the French put them in.

We took the rocket engine out of the Mirage's belly and replaced it with a DEFA 30-millimeter gun pack. These tough, reliable, French-built cannons (DEFA stands for Direction des Études et Fabrications d'Armement) had proved themselves in air-to-ground action in the '56 Sinai Campaign. A 20-millimeter cannon, we pilots learned then, will not penetrate the armor of an Egyptian tank. A 30-millimeter will eat it alive.

In the end the Dassault engineers acceded to all our suggestions for modifications. The French designers watched (and learned) as we turned their high-altitude, high-glamour interceptor into a no-nonsense air-to-ground and air-to-air killing machine.

Rafi Sivron is the planner of Operation Moked:

The squadrons begin to train. When I confer with the squadron commanders, I make it clear that the master plan is written in stone, but that within each commander's sphere all decisions are his. I will plan the route to the target to avoid enemy radar; you may not take a shortcut. I will tell you what ordnance to carry and precisely where to drop it. But within two or three miles of the target, you are in charge. How you attack is up to you. You be the judge of how to deal with antiaircraft fire, the angle of the sun, and so forth. You, the leader, will make those calls.

By July '65 the master plan is ready. It has been printed, proofed, and sent to the squadron commanders, who are still not authorized to show it to anybody. But slowly the deputies, the seconds-in-command, become included; then, under heavy security, the senior pilots.

By the end of 1965, the squadrons have received individual orders folders for every target. Each squadron has its primary and secondary targets, which its pilots must know in detail. The fliers and their commanders do not need to know what part any other squadron is playing. They just have to know their own roles.

Giora Romm, twenty-two-year-old Mirage pilot:

How do you train for attacking enemy air bases? You attack your own. We ran mock operations hundreds of times against Israeli airfields.

In the Negev other training targets had been set up, with runways and even dummy planes. Life was very simple for us pilots. We trained, we slept, we trained.

I had a small room in the bachelors' barracks at Tel Nof that I shared with another pilot, Avramik Salmon—very plain, just a sink to brush your teeth in and shave. At night we watched movies and played cards. No one had a car. On the rare occasions when someone would lend us transportation, we'd drive to Gedera to a roadside dive called Auntie Leah's. Have you heard of Pancho's in the Mojave Desert, where Chuck Yeager and the other U.S. fliers from Edwards Air Force Base used to go? Leah's was the Israeli version. You sat at tables outside breathing diesel fumes from passing army trucks and tank transporters. But the steaks were good and you could get a beer as long as the place stayed open. Mainly, though, we stayed on base, trained, studied, and played poker.

We had a pilot in our squadron named Reuven Rozen, a very systematic pilot. One day he and I crossed paths outside the ops room. "Giora, I need five minutes." He took me into an empty office and handed me his map and operational notes for attacking the Egyptian airfield at Cairo West. He started reciting from memory. "Takeoff at precisely such-and-such, proceed on such-and-such heading at altitude 100 feet to such-and-such a waypoint, to be reached at such-and-such a time precisely, then new heading such-and-such to next waypoint," and so on for five minutes without stopping.

Rozen knew by heart everything that had to happen between Tel Nof and Cairo West—the headings, the time, the fuel. I mean everything. You had to. This had to be in your head with no possibility of error. To make the challenge even more interesting, 70 percent of the flight is over the Mediterranean—thus no waypoints for orientation—at an altitude so low that the slightest lapse of concentration will put you nose-first into the drink. Not to mention radio silence. No computers, no satellite guidance, no GPS—they hadn't been invented. A wristwatch, a heading, and your memory. And that was only for the specific base you were attacking. In your head you had to keep the same encyclopedic knowledge of every other base on the target list—and how to get to it, and get home, from any point over Israel or Egypt.

Rafi Sivron, planner of Operation Moked:

In the end, the plan's most dangerous foes were found not among the fliers who would have to execute it but in the individual department heads of the air force bureaucracy whose authority or fiefdoms were threatened by its existence.

At that time the Israel Air Force had one extremely rudimentary computer. This instrument was the pride of the Weapons Systems and Planning Department. The department's chief, an officer named Yoash "Chatto" Tsiddon, ran the plan through this wonder of science.

The computer said the plan would fail.

The Weapons and Planning chief called a meeting. I took my seat. Motti Hod headed our contingent. Motti was operations chief of the air force, number two under Ezer. Chatto Tsiddon had commanded Squadron 119 in its early days, as well as the test squadron. He later became a member of the Knesset. He was a person to be taken seriously. Chatto laid out his findings, backed by IBM and the science of binary calculus. Of twelve enemy bases attacked, the computer declared, only two would be knocked out. All others would remain partially, if not fully, operational.

My heart sank. I defended the program with every argument I could muster. The computer was wrong! The plan would work! The attacks would knock out every enemy base!

Chatto sat unfazed. Technology had pronounced its verdict. He would pass his assessment up the line. The plan was dead.

Motti said nothing for what seemed like a full minute. Then he leaned forward and addressed the Weapons and Planning chief.

"Chatto," he said, "do you have a better plan? Please feel free to draw up a superior operational scheme. I will be happy to review it. So will Ezer, and so will every squadron commander in the air force. But until you present such a plan, this one stays. This is the plan. No one is changing a word."

I have clashed with Motti Hod on numerous occasions. He has held me back from advancement, sought to prevent me from continuing my university studies. I never liked him and he never liked me.

But Motti saved the plan that day and he fought as its champion on dozens of other occasions. He sold Operation Moked to the squadron commanders and he shepherded it through a high command whose envy of, and competitiveness with, the air force could hardly be overstated.

It was Motti's idea to present the plan to the General Staff on a single piece of paper and to press for its inclusion in the overall war plan with as light a touch as possible. In the prewar deliberations, I don't believe the cabinet even brought it up.

And, most important of all, when the plan was put into action, Motti orchestrated it like a virtuoso.

How did the operation come to be named Moked? (A mission order has a number, but an operation has a name.)

My son Tomer had just been born. I wanted to name the plan after him. Operation Tomer. But I chanced to be having lunch with my friend Benjamin Yossiffon, a helicopter pilot who was in charge of day-to-day operations for the air force.

"You can't do that!" Benjamin said at once. "This is a plan of war. You can't name it after an innocent child."

"Well, what should I call it then?"

He suggested, "Focus."

Moked.

24.

YOUNG ROMMEL

M y brother Shmulik is commander of the 7th Armored Brigade. He's a colonel, thirty-seven years old. He has been called "Young Rommel." He likes that. My friend Yannush Ben-Gal was the brigade's chief operations officer, but he and my brother got into a fight and my brother fired him. I took Yannush's place. Not because I am a trained operations officer. I'm the only one who can get along with my brother.

Yoel Gorodish is senior operations officer of the 7th Armored Brigade.

When the Egyptians first started moving tank divisions into Sinai in mid-May of 1967, our 7th Armored Brigade was scattered in various training and operational roles across Israel. Immediately orders were issued to assemble at Revivim in the Negev. In a big country like America, to move an armored brigade would take months of planning, cost millions of dollars, and require transport by sea, air, and rail. In Israel the whole brigade was on-site in eight hours, and Shmulik was chewing out his officers for taking so long.

My brother and I had our first blowup not long after this.

Instructions had come from General Headquarters informing us that the brigade would be issued gas masks. Nasser had used poison gas in his war in Yemen; our forces would have to be prepared in case the enemy tried to use it on us. My brother ordered all beards to be shaved. The masks couldn't get a tight seal if a man had a beard.

One of our tank battalions didn't obey. They thought the order was chickenshit and they let it slide. My brother and I were in a headquarters meeting when this act of disobedience came out. The deputy commander of the offending battalion was sitting right across from Shmulik. My brother said nothing to him.

Instead he tore into me. "Why didn't Battalion 82 shave their beards? You were told to implement this order and you did not!"

When the meeting was over, I went to my brother's trailer and told him I quit. He said, "Yoel, I know it was not your fault, but this war is going to start in a matter of days and I had to get the message across without yelling at the deputy in front of every other officer."

"I don't care, Shmulik. You humiliated me. I cannot serve under these conditions."

I went back to my tent and packed up. Four in the morning, an officer came for me. "Your brother wants to speak with you." I refused to go. So Shmulik came to me, in a jeep. He ordered me to get in and drove me back to his trailer. Inside he said, "I want you to put your resignation in writing."

I told him, "This is between us as brothers. Me telling you is enough! I quit!"

"Okay," he said, "but how about if we go to mediation?"

This was where I made my mistake. I should have turned my brother down flat. Even to consider mediation showed him I was not dead-set.

"Who," I asked, "do you propose as mediator?"

"Our mother."

We both burst out laughing. Our mother is old-fashioned, very Orthodox. She would die before she would stand to see two of her children fighting.

So my brother got me to stay.

Here is how he ran the brigade:

The division speed limit was 60 kilometers per hour. Shmulik issued an order: "The 7th Brigade will go no faster than fifty-nine." So if you got caught driving sixty-one, you were in trouble two times—once with Division for exceeding sixty and once with my brother for exceeding fifty-nine.

But accidents in the brigade dropped to zero.

Whatever hour a meeting was scheduled to start, "Shmulik Time" was five minutes earlier. God help you if you didn't show up on Shmulik Time.

My brother was the best tank gunner in the division. In drills, he would kick gunners out of their seats and take over himself, then put round after round on target. He made men cry; then he would stay late and work with them personally on bore sighting and range finding. I have seen him hurl steel helmets and telephones across tables at his own officers. But against the enemy in the field he would put himself so far forward that these same officers would beg him to take greater care for his own life.

In Brigade 7, maintenance lapses were unforgivable. Uniforms had to be perfect. Even the laces of our boots had to be tied in a prescribed way, with the loose ends tucked into the boot top. Why? So that a crewman's laces will not catch on a corner when he scrambles aboard his tank. Army-issue belts could be worn with the buckle facing either way. Not in my brother's brigade. Belts must be buckled left to right only, so that if a man was wounded and you had to open his belt to apply medical aid, you knew which way to pull without thinking. Every soldier in the army was required to carry a tourniquet-type bandage. In other outfits, the man could pack this anywhere among his kit. In our brigade, the bandage was always in the left front pocket. Troops were drilled until finding and applying this bandage became second nature.

Under Shmulik, the interior of every tank had to be organized identically. Signal flags would be in the same rack, in the same order. Tanks carry

different kinds of shells for different fire missions; these must be stowed in the same place, in the same order, inside every tank. Why? Because tanks break down or get knocked out by enemy action. When a commander switched to a new tank, he had to be able to find every item he needed blindfolded. Fire orders and internal commands were likewise standardized, so that every gunner, loader, and driver could be replaced by every other if he should be wounded or killed and so that orders from any commander could be understood and obeyed without hesitation.

Under Shmulik, brigade exercises were more rigorous than combat. The men will look forward to wartime, my brother declared, because it will be easier than training.

We will operate at night and in all weathers. We will make

Colonel Shmuel Gorodish,
commander of the 7th Armored Brigade.

every mistake it is possible to make until we stop making mistakes. When our tank crews drive their vehicles into blind wadis and can't find their way out, when they get lost in the dark and their fuel tanks run dry, when they collide with each other and can't complete their missions and wind up at daylight calling for help like wayward sheep, they will learn then that filters must be changed on schedule and tracks must be tightened and maps must be read and navigation must be taught and men must act as teams and "I don't know" is not an answer to anything.

One day at the end of May, Moshe Dayan came to inspect the brigade. Dayan had no official status at that time; he had no rank and no command. A few years later, Shmulik and he had such a terrible falling-out that my brother was literally plotting to murder Dayan. But this day and this war they loved each other. My brother was Dayan's kind of soldier.

On the map Shmulik showed Dayan how the brigade would advance past Khan Younis, seize the road junction at Rafiah, and speed through the Jiradi Pass to capture the Egyptian headquarters at El Arish.

"Where do you expect resistance to be heaviest?" Dayan asked.

"I don't care," said Shmulik. "When Hativa Sheva [Brigade 7] gets through with these Egyptians, the only way you'll recognize them will be by the tracks of our tank treads imprinted on their backsides."

Dayan was not supposed to stay the night, but he did. The next morning a message came for him from Tel Aviv. As soon as Dayan read it, he went into the trailer alone with Shmulik and locked the door. The two men did not emerge for several minutes. When Dayan finally came out, he and his driver climbed straight into their jeep and drove away.

My junior operations officer was Lieutenant Yosi Ben-Hanan. Six years later as a tank battalion commander in the Yom Kippur War, he would win the Itur HaOz, the Medal of Courage, for his heroism fighting the Syrians on the Golan Heights.

Yosi, now, watched Dayan and his jeep speed away.

"Is this it?" he asked me. "Has the cabinet given Dayan supreme command?"

25.

"BECAUSE I WAS NOT AT NEBI YUSHA"

I grew up in Jerusalem, next door to the home of a young man who had been a hero of the War of Independence in 1948. His name was Yizhar Armoni. Armoni had fought in one of the war's first critical operations, an attempt to capture the British police fort of Nebi Yusha in the Upper Galilee. This fort had been given to the Arabs by the British; it dominated all access by road to the besieged kibbutzim along the Lebanese border.

Lieutenant Yosi Ben-Hanan is the twenty-two-year-old operations officer of the 7th Armored Brigade.

The Arabs holding the fort put up a furious resistance. Many of the attacking Palmach fighters were killed. The retreat of the survivors was carried out under heavy fire; Yizhar Armoni was wounded in both legs but refused to be evacuated. He stayed behind alone, for hours, with only a Bren machine gun, covering the withdrawal of his comrades. The Arabs killed him.

I was an infant then. Though the fight at Nebi Yusha had been a grim defeat for the Israeli forces, Yizhar Armoni was named one of the twelve Heroes of Israel, the highest military award for valor during the War of Independence.

If you ask me why I became a soldier, I will tell you, "Because I was not at Nebi Yusha."

I had a second hero growing up. This was Joseph Trumpeldor, who was killed by Arab forces at Tel Chai in 1920 on the eleventh day of the Hebrew month of Adar. It was Trumpeldor, mortally wounded, who declared, "It is a fine thing to die for one's country." This, almost three decades before we Jews had a country.

I was born on the eleventh of Adar, 1945. My parents named me Yosef after Yosef Trumpeldor.

Ask me why I have chosen to dedicate my life to the defense of Israel. "Because I was not at Tel Chai."

The mother of Yizhar Armoni was left bereft by her son's death, so my own mother used to let her look after me in the afternoons. I was four or five at the time. It helped Mrs. Armoni to have a young boy she could talk to and take care of.

Mrs. Armoni used to walk me down the flight of steps to the unpaved alley that had been named after her son, Yizhar Armoni Climb. She would say to me, "Do you see that big boulevard at the top of the hill, Yosi? It is named after a pioneer Zionist, Ussishkin Street. This little lane is all they gave to my son." She held my hand as we walked. "When you grow up, Yosi, you will be a fighter like my son."

My immediate superior now in June 1967 is Yoel Gorodish. He's a major, the senior operations officer of the 7th Armored Brigade. Yoel's brother Colonel Shmuel Gorodish commands the brigade.

It is a quirk of brigade command organization that the junior operations officer—i.e., me—is the one who rides up front alongside the brigade commander. The responsibilities of the senior operations officer are much weightier—among other duties, coordinating logistics and resupply for the entire brigade—so he operates primarily in the rear.

The result is that I will play a pivotal role in, and have a front-row seat for, not only the armored clashes of the brigade throughout the war but the drama of command and decision as well. Through my headset will pass most if not all orders from Gorodish to his battalion commanders and their responses to him. I will hear as well all instructions to Gorodish from higher command.

General Israel Tal commands our division. The 7th Armored Brigade is one of three under his command. The other two are the 35th Paratroop Brigade, under Colonel Raful Eitan, and the 60th Armored Brigade, commanded by Colonel Menachem "Men" Aviram, a reserve formation recently called up.

Because my position as operations officer provides me access to the latest brigade intelligence, yet I am only a lieutenant and thus approachable by all ranks, I am asked ten times an hour, "Yosi, when will the war start? Is H-hour tomorrow?"

I don't know.

"Will the government bring back Moshe Dayan?"

I don't know.

"Will they give Dayan supreme command? Will he be prime minister?"

I don't know.

Yoel Gorodish doesn't know.

Shmulik Gorodish doesn't know.

Not even General Tal knows.

I am thinking not of Dayan, but of Yizhar Armoni and Joseph Trumpeldor. If war comes, will I live up to their example? Will I serve as valiantly as they did, and give to my country all that I have?

26.

MINISTER OF DEFENSE

Colonel Dov Sion is, as I said, General Sharon's liaison with General Headquarters. He and I have not known each other well for very long, but already a strong unspoken communion is growing between us. Dov makes sure I have everything I need, including a pistol—an American .45—and deflects with a sharp look the approaches of soldiers and correspondents seeking "inside information" on the state of affairs between my father and Prime Minister Levi Eshkol.

Yael Dayan remains with Arik Sharon's division at Nitzana on the Egyptian frontier.

Supper is late in Arik's caravan on the evening of June 1. The eleven o'clock news is reporting that offers of a position have been made by Eshkol's government to my father—"an advisory role," "a consultative position in the army."

Dayan has turned them down. He will not accept a ceremonial post. He will drive a half-track, the radio quotes him as declaring, rather than serve in an ornamental capacity.

I fall asleep, missing the twelve o'clock broadcast.

When I wake, the news is on every man's lips: General Dayan has been appointed minister of defense.

"It took the arrival of 80,000 Egyptian troops in Sinai," he says for the newspapers, "to get me back into the government."

I try to stay objective about the reaction of the soldiers to my father's appointment. I can't. Overnight the mood of the army has undergone a radical transformation. I am congratulated again and again. At six thirty in the morning I phone my father at home. "I've got a new job," he says, "with a car and a secretary."

In Sharon's trailer, officers are hoisting cups of cognac before breakfast. What has changed since last night? Neither the war plans nor the commanders. The army was ready before Dayan; it is ready now. Sharon puts the feeling into words. "Now we will have war."

A profound relief and satisfaction animates all.

"See if you can get home tonight," Arik tells me. He gives me a few things for his wife, Lily. Their house is only a few blocks from ours

Moshe Dayan fields reporters' questions.

in Zahala. This is what war is like in a country as small as Israel. You leave
the front at six and you're home before eight.

My mother exclaims at my state of desert dishevelment. "Your hair!"
My father is home for an hour between meetings. We embrace. He wants
to know, How do the troops feel? How is Arik? What is the state of morale?

"Go take a bath," he says. "You'll feel human again."

My brother Assi is home, in uniform, on a three-hour pass from his
unit. My mother readies the Friday meal. The house is full of flowers and
chocolates, baskets of cheese and fruit. "Take some," says my father.

"Must you go right back?" my mother asks.

For my father the last-minute politics of appointment have apparently
been excruciating, with double-crosses and near double-crosses abounding.
Dayan takes part in no such dealings, even in his mind. "They know what I
want and where I can be found. They have my telephone number."

Dov is shy with my mother and soldier-friendly with Assi. I head for
the tub, leaving him and my father to feel each other out. Afterward I grab
packages of nuts and chocolate. I stuff my pack with clean socks and underwear, skin cream, a windbreaker. My father gives Dov a bottle of whiskey. He says little, preoccupied by a thousand urgencies and eager to get
back to the meetings that will continue long into the night. He is happy.
Reaction to his appointment has been everything he had hoped for.

For the first time my father possesses full military powers, unlike in
'56, when Ben-Gurion was both prime minister and minister of defense
and my father was chief of staff. This time he has no one over him. Responsibility rests on his shoulders alone.

Moshe Dayan is the man for the job, and now he has it. The army
waits like a coiled spring. It wants nothing but the hand to set it loose.

27.

THE ELEVENTH
COMMANDMENT

It is the night of June 1. The first meeting of the expanded cabinet is about to convene. I am thinking of David Ben-Gurion.

Moshe Dayan is now minister of defense.

"God left one commandment out of the Bible," Ben-Gurion used to say. "Perhaps the Almighty delivered this commandment to Moses but Moses forgot to bring it down from the mountain.

"That commandment is Number Eleven:

"'Be strong.'"

How many nights have I met alone with Ben-Gurion when he was prime minister and minister of defense and I was his army chief of staff? Ben-Gurion would be at the point of authorizing a military operation—a cross-border raid, say, in retaliation for the murder by Arab infiltrators of another young farmer or another Jewish family. The two of us would confer alone over the maps and the operational plans. With sober gravity Ben-Gurion would ask, "How many casualties will our forces sustain, Moshe? Can this operation succeed? Can you guarantee me that our young men will be back safely by dawn?"

No military man can offer such assurances. But I did, for his sake, to make his decision easier. He understood. Beneath all debate and discussion lay the necessity to act—and the knowledge that such actions would be accompanied by grave consequences. Ben-Gurion hated it. Each drop of blood felt extracted from his own veins.

Many times I would become impatient with him because of what I deemed his excessive preoccupation with the political repercussions of our actions. "How will the UN react? The Americans? The Russians?"

I am minister of defense now. I must think as Ben-Gurion did then. The burden will be terrible. I feel it already.

David Ben-Gurion,
first prime minister of Israel.

The first meeting of the expanded cabinet convenes, as I said, on the evening of my appointment, Thursday, June 1. Since the nation now has a unity government, those political parties that have previously been excluded except in the crisis as members of the opposition—Gahal and Rafi, my party—are represented. Menachem Begin of Gahal has a seat for the first time as a minister of the government. Gahal is an acronym for Gush Herut-Liberalim. It represents the 1965 merger of the two furthest right parties in Israel: the Herut (Freedom) Party and the Liberal Party.

In the days of the dissident paramilitary group, the Irgun Zvai Leumi, when the most radical Jewish patriots used terror to hasten the British exit from Mandate Palestine, Begin was among the most extreme. Under his command, the IZL bombed the King David Hotel on July 22, 1946, killing ninety-one people. Begin is curt, humorless, intractable. But he is without fear. He has endured political imprisonment under the Soviets, from which ordeal he emerged tougher than ever and more passionately dedicated to Jewish nationhood and to political autonomy for the Jewish people. He is a good man, possibly a great one. The nation needs men like him as much as she needs visionaries like Ben-Gurion and poets like Natan Alterman.

"To the banks of the Jordan" is Begin's party's signature. His vision is of the Israel of the Bible. He speaks passionately at this cabinet meeting, citing numerous biblical passages, to which Eshkol with good humor appends, "Amen, amen."

Begin, more than anyone, has been the engine of my appointment as minister of defense. Not out of affection or personal regard for me (I fought him, Jew against Jew, over arms smuggling in 1948), but to bring war. Days before, Begin had pulled levers for Ben-Gurion, whose bitter foe he had been for years, seeking Ben-Gurion's appointment as prime minister or minister of defense for the same reason: to produce war.

My name came next.

On Friday morning, June 2, comes the first critical meeting. It takes place at 11:30, immediately following a joint session of the General Staff and the Ministerial Defense Committee. The attendees are limited to myself and Prime Minister Levi Eshkol, Foreign Minister Abba Eban, Army Chief of Staff Yitzhak Rabin, and Yigal Allon, the former Palmach commander and current labor minister, who had been my chief rival for the post of minister of defense. Eshkol presides. He turns to me first and asks what I think the government should do.

"Attack at once. Today is Friday. If the cabinet so authorizes when it convenes on Sunday, orders can be given immediately to the commanders in the field. The war will start Monday morning."

The objective of our forces, I declare, should be the destruction of Nasser's divisions in Sinai. We should have no aims of territorial expansion, nor should we take any military action whose intent is to conquer the Gaza Strip or to take possession of the Suez Canal. The campaign will last, I estimate, between three and five days.

Against us now in Sinai are 130,000 troops, 900 tanks, and 1,100 guns. Egypt has fielded the equivalent of seven divisions. We have three.

Nasser's chief of staff, Lieutenant General Abdel Moneim Riad, has set up command headquarters in Amman. Jordan's armed forces—eleven brigades totaling 56,000 men, with 176 modern Patton and Centurion tanks—are now under his command. An Iraqi mechanized brigade, the 8th, is preparing to enter Jordan as we speak; it can be on our frontier within hours. Already two elite Egyptian commando battalions, the 33rd and the 53rd, are in place on Jordanian soil. Their role can be nothing other than to strike into the heart of Israel, possibly preemptively, to attack air bases and power and communications centers and to spread chaos and disorder. In addition, Hussein and Riad have moved forward to

Jerusalem the Imam Ali Brigade to reinforce the King Talal already in place. Both are elite, British-trained formations of the Arab Legion.

If General Riad strikes from Jordan, Israel will be facing war on two fronts. Should Syria join in with her sixteen brigades, 70,000 men, 550 tanks, and 120 aircraft, we'll be fighting on three. Our forces are not sufficient for this. Israel has barely enough men to take on Egypt alone.

These figures of enemy combatants do not include Nasser's support from the wider Arab world. Our intelligence reports a Kuwaiti armored brigade en route to Sinai. Expeditionary forces of unknown size have been promised to Egypt by Libya, Saudi Arabia, Tunisia, and Sudan. Iraqi premier Tahir Yahya has signed a mutual defense pact with Cairo. The Soviets are sending shipments of arms to Egypt and Syria, while our own allies, Britain and the United States, stall on deliveries of weapons we have already paid for. De Gaulle has cut us off entirely. Behind Nasser now stand Syria, Iraq, Kuwait, Jordan, Lebanon, Libya, Sudan, Algeria, and Yemen. King Hassan II of Morocco has dispatched a special envoy with pledges of assistance; President Habib Bourguiba has promised that an Algerian army will be permitted passage through Tunisia to fight the Zionists. Even Nasser's worst enemy, King Faisal of Saudi Arabia, has declared:

Every Arab who does not participate in this conflict will seal his fate. He will not be worthy of being called an Arab.

while Iraqi president Abdul Rahman Arif has been quoted by the BBC:

Our goal is clear—to wipe Israel off the face of the map. We shall, God willing, meet in Tel Aviv and Haifa.

And still the government dithers and dilates. The June 2 meeting adjourns without a decision. I pass June 3 in meetings from dawn till midnight. The prime minister and foreign minister continue to hang fire, waiting for the green light from the Americans.

How will this go-ahead be communicated to us? By a wink perhaps, or a nod. Our ministers scrutinize remarks by Secretary of State Dean Rusk, National Security Adviser Walt Rostow, and his brother Eugene Rostow, undersecretary of state for political affairs, as well as comments and notes from UN Ambassador Arthur Goldberg and Supreme Court Justice Abe Fortas. The parsing reaches such a state that our fellows are combing word by word through a Joseph Alsop column in *Newsweek*.

On June 4, Sunday, the cabinet convenes in the interval between two meetings of the Ministerial Defense Committee. Prime Minister Eshkol at last puts two resolutions to the vote.

The first, by me, calls for war. It requests that the government grant to the prime minister and the minister of defense the authority to choose the date and the hour for commencement of hostilities.

The second resolution, put forward by the representative of the Labor Party, calls for further delay.

In the moments before the vote, Menachem Begin crosses to me. He has sounded the cabinet members, he says. He is confident. The stalemate will be broken.

"I will next shake your hand," he says, "beside the Western Wall."

Begin is one kind of Jew. Eshkol is another. I am like neither.

My experience is founded neither in Russia nor in Europe. I am a sabra. I was born here in Israel. I know nothing of the Talmud and I don't want to know. I have no use for Yiddish. The so-called Jewish experience, which shaped my mother and father and other Diaspora Jews—the debates of the rabbis and the scholars, the interpretations of the law—to me these are angels dancing on the head of a pin. Nor do I make a religion of Zionism or socialism or the labor movement, despite all their worthy achievements.

My Bible consists of the books of the Patriarchs and the Judges. Its pages narrate the stories of Joshua and Gideon, of Saul and David and Jonathan. Say these names: Galilee, Mount Carmel, Beersheba, the Vale of Sharon. These sites are not theoretical to me. They are not a dream longed for from afar. They comprise the hills and flats that I have plowed and planted, tramped over and slumbered upon. A field at Ramat Yohanan has soaked up the last of my brother Zorik's blood. I left my own eye in the dirt across the border with Lebanon. How many thousands have given the same and more?

The treads of a half-track rend a slope that has no name and is known to no one: Up comes an arrowhead three thousand years old. Dig again. Into the sunlight emerges a shard from the era of Joshua, the handle of a vessel from which a soldier of Israel once drank. Who was that man? He was myself.

I am that man.

He shivered on watch, this fellow thirty centuries gone; he marched through the night; he defended his fields and his flocks. As a boy of fourteen I guarded our granaries at Nahalal with a weapon I had fashioned myself of an iron head and an oak shaft—a spear. When my nephew Uzi graduated first in his class in the officers' course, I presented to him, as a gift of honor, three warheads from the days of Joshua. These are not relics to me or to him. They are the weapons with which real Jews fought and died, doing what he and others will do now. No Israeli family lacks losses like ours. I am named for the first settler at Kibbutz Deganiah Alef to be killed by our enemies. Did my mother and father feel the need to tell me why they chose this name? I knew without speech, as did we all.

All the same, I am no hater of Arabs. I grew up with Bedouin herders and farmers. We have plowed together, and planted, and sat side by side in the furrows to take our noon meal.

Who is the Arab? No man makes a better friend than he. None will stand his ground with greater courage. To the Arab, honor is all. He will drain his blood for the clan and the tribe, and for the stranger he has taken in at the gate. No one laughs like an Arab, or loves his children with such tenderness; no one dances like him or worships God with greater devotion, and none is more compassionate to the weak and the helpless.

The modern world, in which the sons of Ishmael have fallen behind and become a backward people, is a nightmare of shame from which the proud Arab cannot awaken. This is the source of his violent and inextinguishable rage.

I fear Nasser not for his Soviet arms or for his brilliance as a provocateur and a brinksman, but because he has planted the standard of his ambition within this soil of wrath and shame. My people will bleed for this, but his will bleed more.

In Sinai in '56, when our armor broke through the Egyptian formations, their officers fled. Nasser's captains and colonels commandeered the fastest vehicles and bolted for the safety of the Canal. Their men, bereft of leadership, were incapable of acting on their own. They shed their shoes and took to flight.

No one is more keenly aware of this humiliation than the Arab himself, and of all Arabs, Nasser. Patriotism cannot overturn this, nor can poetry. Only the sword will serve. Who speaks for the fellah or the fedayee? The Arab intellectual is the loneliest man on earth, for he is trapped in the void between reason and faith.

The cabinet votes.

My resolution is adopted, fourteen to two.

I phone the chief of staff and inform him that the government has approved the army's operational plan.

The war will start at 07:45 tomorrow morning.

BOOK FOUR

MOKED

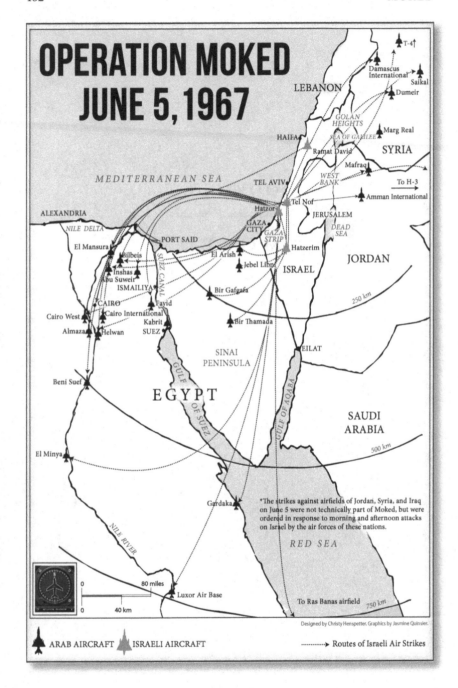

OPERATION MOKED
JUNE 5, 1967

*The strikes against airfields of Jordan, Syria, and Iraq on June 5 were not technically part of Moked, but were ordered in response to morning and afternoon attacks on Israel by the air forces of these nations.

Designed by Christy Henspetter. Graphics by Jasmine Quinsier.

▲ ARAB AIRCRAFT   ▲ ISRAELI AIRCRAFT   ·········▸ Routes of Israeli Air Strikes

28.

THE BAT SQUADRON

Major Ran Ronen commands Fighter Squadron 119:

I am the last squadron commander to enter base commander Shmuel Shefer's office. It's evening. Outside, the duty shifts are changing, technical crews heading home after the day's work. Colonel Shefer stands and takes a piece of chalk from a drawer in his desk. Without a word, he turns to the forward blackboard and writes in bold, stark strokes:

07:45

Shefer turns to face the room. No speech is necessary. The squadron commanders do not glance to one another. No one speaks a word.

The date is Sunday, June 4. Sunday in Israel is the first day of the working week, following the Sabbath on Saturday.

Shefer's briefing is as short as any I remember. Nothing of operational import needs to be said. Each squadron is as ready as it can be. Shefer stresses two elements only: surprise and secrecy.

Twelve hours remain till H-hour. No hint must be offered to the pilots. Let them go home and get some sleep. As for us commanders, nothing in our demeanor must alter. This evening's briefing will be like every other. Wives? Say nothing. Best friends? Nothing.

For the past three weeks my squadron, the Bat Squadron, has been sequestered on the base, training for nothing but the coming attack. Seven other squadrons are based here at Tel Nof, at Hatzor, and at Ramat David. Each has its own targets. Each has been drilling for nothing else.

In the evening after the day's training, I assemble the pilots of my squadron in the briefing room to go over the day's exercises and to plan for tomorrow's. I look at the faces of my young fliers—Menahem "Hemi" Shmul, who will go on in his career to make five and a half kills; Eitan Karmi, eight; Shlomo Egozi, eight; Reuven Rozen, four; Asher Snir and

Avramik Salmon, thirteen and a half each; Giora Romm, who will shoot down five MiGs in three days. I myself will finish with eight kills. Around the room sit others, many others, with whom I would gladly fly against the finest pilots in the world.

But no one in the government knows this. All is in the future. For now we are untried and unblooded. To the senior commanders of the General Staff, most of whom have made their careers in the army, going back as far as the Haganah and the Palmach, the air force is the junior wing of the defense establishment. Its effectiveness is regarded with skepticism. Who are these pilots anyway? They get the best of everything; their demands eat up the defense budget. Can we count on them? What do they do except wear Ray-Bans and eat steaks and go home each night to sleep on clean sheets?

Operation Moked, I know, is viewed by the cabinet and the prime minister as a madman's dream. A preemptive strike that will destroy the entire air force of Egypt—four hundred planes—in three hours?

Dayan, we know, has approved Moked—but based on a presentation delivered on a single sheet of paper. Does he believe the plan will work? Or does he simply see no alternative?

Two days ago, a message arrived for me from Base Commander Shefer. General Rabin's office has just phoned; the chief of staff is on his way to Tel Nof. Shefer wants me to show Rabin the squadron.

I am furious.

In my office my secretary asks where we should assemble the men. "We will assemble nothing," I tell her. "When Rabin's group arrives, I'll take them to the Standby Shack."

On every Israeli air base, four fighters are kept on intercept alert at all times. The pilots assigned to this duty wait in a rough building adjacent to the ready line. The men call this "the Villa." Inside is a coffee urn and a fridge, a 16-millimeter projector playing *To Sir, With Love* over and over, along with bunks, boards for backgammon and checkers, and a pair of threadbare couches.

The date is June 2, three days before the war. This day I have six pilots on intercept standby—one major, two captains, and three lieutenants.

I will take Rabin there. I will not warn the pilots beforehand. Let the chief of staff walk in on them.

He has come to test the air force's capacity to execute Operation Moked.

Let him test it.

Rabin's plane comes in on Runway 33 and is directed by the control tower to the standby lot. I greet him outside the Villa.

"Welcome, sir."

"Major."

I march Rabin straight into the shack. When the pilots see the chief of staff enter, they leap to their feet and snap to attention. Base commander Shefer and air force chief Motti Hod follow.

Rabin can see that I have prepared nothing. The pilots are taken totally by surprise.

"Gentlemen," I say, "the chief of staff has some questions he would like to put to you."

Rabin begins in his signature baritone. He grills the pilots about Operation Moked. I stand to the side, saying nothing.

"What airfield is your primary target?" Rabin asks the major.

"Beni Suef, sir."

"Where is Beni Suef?"

"One hundred ten kilometers south of Cairo, one hundred thirty west of the Gulf of Suez."

"What is your secondary target?"

"Inshas Air Base."

"What is the configuration of Inshas?"

The major details the locations of the runways, hangars, and fuel depots; he tells Rabin the types and number of aircraft the Egyptians have on this site, where each plane will be parked, and how he will attack them.

Rabin queries the flight leaders. He interrogates the young wingmen. "What is the distance to Cairo West? To Dumeir outside Damascus? In what formation will you attack? At what speed?"

The pilots answer everything. They are flawless.

"What weapons will you carry?"

"Two 500-kilogram bombs and two hundred fifty 30-millimeter rounds in the cannons."

With each answer Rabin's color grows stronger. He stands straighter. His voice gets deeper. He can see that these young pilots know their stuff. They do not brag. Their tone is not arrogant. They are prepared and professional.

"Can you pull off this mission, Captain?"

"Yes, sir."

"Do you have any doubts?"

"None, sir."

"You, Lieutenant?"

"None, sir."

Rabin looks from one pilot to the other. "Thank you, gentlemen."

I walk the chief of staff out to his Cessna. He will return now, I know, to report to the cabinet. What will he tell them in this critical hour?

Has he come to Tel Nof expecting, perhaps even hoping, to discover fliers who are uncertain, ill prepared, lacking in self-confidence? Has he anticipated reporting to the government that Moked will not work?

If so, the opposite has transpired. Rabin's confidence has mounted moment to moment. From a period of reported self-doubt, he has returned to himself. He has become the Rabin we all know—hero of the War of Independence, the IDF's youngest captain, youngest general, youngest chief of staff.

Beside his plane Rabin stops and turns toward me. "Thank you, Ran. Good luck!" When he shakes my hand, he holds on for an extra moment. I see in his eyes he has made up his mind.

He believes now that Israel is ready.

He believes now that we can go to war and win.

When I enter the briefing room, the pilots are horsing around as usual. I alter nothing in my tone or posture. We go over the training schedule for tomorrow. Questions arise about the fighter planes that have deployed to Tel Nof from Ramat David, Israel's northernmost air base. Is the war starting tomorrow? Ran, what's going on?

"When war starts, I will tell you. Don't worry, I will not let it happen without us."

The mission board in the ops room displays the names of the pilots and the assignments of each. I have spent hours fine-tuning this roster. My first deputy is Motti Yeshurun. During the waiting period, I have instructed him to stop me twice a day and cite at random one pilot's name from the lineup. I must be able to tell Motti exactly why I put that pilot in the slot he is in.

At H-hour tomorrow morning, four pilots from our squadron will remain at Tel Nof on intercept alert. They will not fly in the general attack. I have assigned my other deputy, Eitan Karmi, as leader of the first pair; Giora Romm will be his number two. The second pair is Avramik Salmon and Menahem Shmul. Why these four? Because they are my best dogfighters.

These two pairs from our squadron will stay behind to protect Tel

Aviv. Eight pilots from the other two Mirage squadrons are also assigned to intercept duty. Twelve planes to defend the entire country. Operation Moked will bet everything on a single roll of the dice. I send the pilots home. Darkness falls. The base grows quiet. Stepping out of the squadron building, I can see the night maintenance crews crossing to work in the blacked-out hangars and hear, in the dark across the runways, the yip-yipping of jackals and the sound of distant traffic.

These are my favorite hours. The closest thing to war, during peacetime years, is flying photo reconnaissance missions. Your plane crosses the border, penetrating deep into enemy territory. You're alone. You can't call for help. If you're detected, the enemy will scramble every interceptor for miles. And you can't even shoot back because your gun package has been replaced by a supplementary tank carrying 300 liters of fuel.

Preparing for these missions, I would hole myself up in the operations bunker and go over every detail of the coming flight. This is not like studying for exams. You are running the mission like a movie through your mind, anticipating every possible emergency, then planning and mentally rehearsing your response.

A fighter pilot accelerating down the runway on an operational mission must keep foremost in his mind one reality: At some point before his wheels touch down again, something is certain to go wrong. Will he have an engine failure? Will an unseen enemy appear? Will another plane in his formation experience a crisis of some kind? Bank on it: Something unexpected will happen. When it does, it will be followed almost always by a second emergency, and often a third, in immediate succession, each one producing a graver crisis than the one before. In such a situation, the pilot's body will exhibit all the manifestations of fear. His heart rate will soar; his flight overalls will become drenched with sweat. But his mind must remain focused. His thinking must stay clear and calm.

Why do we train? To perfect our flying skills, yes. But far more important, we practice to elevate our threshold of emotional detachment, to inculcate that state of preparedness and equilibrium that enables a pilot to function effectively under conditions of peril, urgency, and confusion.

I have sent the keyed-up pilots home at 21:00, nine in the evening, having told them nothing. Alone now except for the two pilots on standby duty and the operations monitor, I retreat to my office, turn on the lights, and crank the radio up to high volume. Down a short flight of stairs is the operations bunker. I walk down silently.

The file for Moked is in the operations safe. I dial the combination and open the door. I take the folder and slip it under my arm. Another flight of stairs takes me down to the lower briefing room. I enter, close the door, and lock it behind me. For what is surely the hundredth time, I open the file.

I prepare the briefing for tomorrow morning.

Up front in the briefing room are several blackboards suspended from the ceiling on sliders, so that the front boards cover up those to the rear. With chalk, I write out the technical details of tomorrow's operation—on the rearmost, the final lineup for the four formations of the first wave; on the next, the diagrams for the method of attack; then the comm channels, flight restrictions, safety regs, and so forth. I leave the outer board blank, concealing the boards behind it.

It never crosses my mind that we can fail or that pilots might be killed.

At 23:00 I lock the briefing room from the outside and put the keys in my pocket. I drive home in my Deux Chevaux with the canvas roof open to catch the night air. The drive is only a few minutes to our bungalow— my wife Heruta's and mine—in the upper part of the base. When the squadrons go to war, the wives and families will be evacuated. Heruta is awake. She has been packed for days. I say nothing about tomorrow and she doesn't ask.

In their bedroom are our children—Orit, eight, and Zohar, four. I tiptoe in, careful not to let the light from the hall wake them, and give each a gentle kiss. I shower, grab a bite to eat, then slip under the covers. Do I have trouble sleeping? I conk out like a child.

At 03:00 I awaken before the alarm. I shave and dress. I phone my deputy commanders. They arrive at the squadron shortly after I do. Every pilot's home or room is linked by an operations telephone. "Get them up," I say.

Within minutes, the lower briefing room is packed. There is no joking. Every eye is fixed on the blank outer blackboard. I slide it aside and give the briefing. It is all business and lasts a little over an hour.

Every pilot is present except Karmi and Romm, Salmon and Shmul. They have already left for their intercept alert stations.

I give no final emotional pep talk. "You are ready. The survival of the nation depends on you. We must succeed at any cost. *En brera.* No alternative."

Giora Romm, twenty-two-year-old Mirage pilot:

We younger pilots still cannot make the visceral connection to war. What will it be like?

Two years and three months from now my Mirage will be shot down over Egypt. I will seize the eject handle, unaware that my left arm and wrist are broken and my right leg has been shattered in a dozen places, and find myself seconds later hanging from the straps of my parachute, looking down as Egyptian farmers and field workers sprint into position below, eager to hack me to pieces with their pitchforks and hoes. By then I will know what war feels like.

Now? The idea that men will die, that wives will be made widows and children left fatherless, is beyond my comprehension. Not to mention the hell that we ourselves will soon inflict upon the enemies who have marshaled to destroy us.

Here is how clueless I am. The afternoon of June 4, a day before the war, I'm on cockpit standby with another Mirage at the end of Runway 33. All of a sudden I see a Vautour fighter-bomber land, and then another and another. On their tails is the emblem of a squadron based at Ramat David Air Base. Then Mystères from the same base begin landing. I say to myself, "Planes from Ramat David are moving here to Tel Nof—what's the story?"

Later, in the dining hall, I approach several Ramat David pilots lining up for omelets and salads. One of them, Elisha Friedman, is a friend from my flying class. "Elisha, what are you doing here?"

He says, "Giora, we are attacking Bir Gafgafa tomorrow. We were ordered south from Ramat David so we would be in range. Don't you know? There is a war tomorrow."

Lieutenant Menahem Shmul is a twenty-one-year-old fighter pilot in Squadron 119. He will fly in five wars, finish his career with five and a half kills, and go on to become, with Danny Shapira, the premier test pilot in Israel:

My father was murdered by Arabs ten days before I was born. This was in 1945, in Mandate Palestine, when he served in the Shai—an acronym for *Sherut Yediot,* "Intelligence Service"—which would later become the Mossad. My name, Menahem, is the same as his.

My father was born in Safed, the city of the Kabbalah, in northern Galilee in 1915. He spoke fluent Arabic, having grown up with many Arab friends. Following the riots of 1929 my father joined the local defense forces. He was fourteen. When the Shai was founded, around 1940, my father was recruited to work undercover. His official post was as a mounted policeman. In this capacity he was involved in a number of clashes with our Arab neighbors, including some that resulted in bloodshed.

Ten days before I was born, my mother's water broke. My father took her on his mare, Galilah—the same horse he rode on his mounted policeman's duties—to the hospital in Rehovot. Returning home that evening, he stopped by an Arab village called Na'ane. The mukhtar, or mayor, welcomed my father. This same man had secretly sent confederates to lie in wait for my father when he left the village. They ambushed him, stabbed him with knives, and dropped him alive down a deep dry well. That night and another day passed before my father was found by his comrades of the mounted service. He had bled to death in the interval.

The date was July 3, 1945.

My father's murder is not something I have dwelt upon. It seems to have happened many lifetimes ago. But this night, the night of June 5, 1967, I cannot sleep.

My father's family came to Israel in 1845. No one is even certain where

The elder Menahem Shmul on his mare Galilah, Sea of Galilee, 1943.

Photo courtesy of Menahem Shmul.

they came from, except that it was somewhere in eastern Europe. The story goes that the mother of the family, who was already a widow with three children, walked all the way, across Turkey and Syria, three years, with just a donkey.

In Tiberias there are Jews, it is said, who never left Roman Palaestina when the legions destroyed the temple in 70 CE and drove out the last Hebrews sixty-two years later. My mother's family traces its lineage to these. So when an Arab says to me, "I am a Palestinian," I tell him, "I am a Palestinian, too—and from six hundred years before the birth of Muhammad!"

Ran Ronen, our squadron commander, has a doctrine that he has drilled into our young pilots' skulls. He calls it "operational finality." What this means is: Stick to the target. Ignore all danger. Continue the attack. At all costs, do what you have been sent to do.

A fighter pilot cannot think about his own safety. Personal survival is not among my top five priorities, except as it bears upon my ability to keep flying sorties and to continue inflicting damage upon the enemy.

Dvekut baMesima.

Adherence to the mission.

What you worry about are the little things, the simple mistakes that are so easy to make and so difficult to recover from.

The air force debriefings after Moked revealed that not every attack formation found its target on the first try. There's a well-known story of one flight leader who pulled, climbed to 6,000 feet, rolled onto his back, and saw . . . nothing.

What did he do? He retraced his steps. He led his formation back to their final waypoint and picked up where he left off. The leader did it over. This time it worked. He struck the target and blew the hell out of it.

No pilot will fault another for a failure of navigation in circumstances so extreme. It happens. But I will buy drinks all night long for any formation leader who has the balls and the presence of mind to regroup and get it right.

Major Ran Ronen, Squadron 119 commander:

06:15. The sun is up but it's still too early to board the planes. I drive to the hangars to check one last time with the technical crews. I love ground crews, and I make my pilots treat them with respect and care. They are more nervous than we are. They fly with us, in a sense that the non-airman cannot understand, and they die with us, too. As I enter the hangar where my plane waits, a sergeant stands alone in a shaft of sunlight, eyes closed, facing toward Jerusalem in his morning prayer, with his *tallit* shawl over his shoulders atop his uniform.

My aircraft this morning is Mirage No. 58. Beneath its fuselage hang two 500-kilogram bombs—more than a thousand pounds each. We have two missiles, Israeli-made Shafrirs, but we will strafe and fight air-to-air primarily with our twin 30-millimeter cannons. The belts hold 250 rounds, 125 for each gun. The technical officer and his ground crew have been working on the aircraft and its systems all night. I go over all details with the ground crew. Check the flight equipment, rescue gear, communications sets, and my pistol, including an extra clip.

06:45.

You mount to the cockpit of a Mirage from the left side up a seven-step ladder. At the top of the ladder you place the heel of your left palm on the steel upper rim of the windscreen and your right palm on the headrest at the back of your ejection seat. Securing yourself on these points, you swing your legs in, straddling the control stick, and slide your weight down into the seat. The shoulder harness has a strap that goes over each shoulder to secure you to the ejection seat. You are wearing your flight overalls, your rescue belt, and your G suit. The throttle is on your left, a hand grip atop a short shaft that slides in a fore-to-aft track. Push it forward to apply power. To light the afterburner, twist the grip outboard as you push it forward. A pilot will say "Push it up" when he means "Go faster."

There are two radios in a Mirage. Red is the squadron channel, green the controller's. You talk to your pilots on one, to ground control on the other. Both are on now, but we may not touch them. Strict radio silence will be maintained all the way to the targets. We will not even talk to the tower.

Up front on the windscreen is the gunsight with its pipper. A switch toggles the targeting setting between air-to-air and air-to-ground. On the weapons panel, ordnance switches arm the bombs and cannons. All are pointed down now: off. Atop the grip end of the control stick is the "pickle" button—it looks like a pickle—for releasing bombs and firing missiles. You flip the mechanism with your thumb. Squeeze a trigger on the stick with your forefinger to fire the guns.

We are below ground level now, in a secure hangar. A ramp leads up and out through the big sliding doors and along lanes between revetments to the runways. I cinch the straps of my shoulder harness tight, helped by the crew chief, who hands me my helmet. Back at the squadron office, the combat operations officer has given me a note with the updated takeoff time. Because of radio silence, any last-minute changes must be communicated in person or by note.

Ready.

Close the canopy and push the starter button; the engine's RPMs climb and the red lights come on, one after the other. A ground crewman disconnects external power and signs, "Ready to roll." I nudge the throttle forward but the plane doesn't budge. The bombs and fuel tanks make it heavy. I apply more power. Here we go, slowly up the ramp and out into the sun.

Rafi Sivron is the planner of Operation Moked:

Air force headquarters is sited in the Kirya military campus in Tel Aviv. The operations bunker underground is called "the Pit." I have been down these steps a thousand times but never on a morning like this.

Here is Moshe Dayan in the seat that is normally mine. Next to him sits Chief of Staff Yitzhak Rabin. Operations chief Ezer Weizman is two seats over, beside Yak Nevo, and down front, alone at the central map table, sits Motti Hod, commander of the air force.

My watch reads 07:07. I can recite from memory which squadrons are still on the ground awaiting their takeoff times and which are already in the air, departing from which Israeli bases, commencing their routes to which enemy bases in Egypt and Sinai, to arrive on the dot of 07:45. But here in the Pit we can confirm nothing. The only thing coming from the radio speakers is static. A ruse to foil Egyptian surveillance has been put into play. Aircraft of the IAF's flight school have been sent up, within Israeli airspace, with their radios set to the frequencies normally used by the operational squadrons. We can hear the training pilots now, doing their best imitations of a workday morning.

In the Pit, no one jokes. The women in uniform stand silently beside the situation table. The scene looks like a World War II movie. The female soldiers use long-handled pointers to nudge the little airplane markers, each one representing a four-ship formation, across the map toward their targets. But they are guessing, too. Until the attacks begin and radio silence is broken, we can know nothing.

Am I nervous? I am human. But my faith in the plan is total.

The only issue is detection. Will Jordan's British-built radar station on Mount Ajlun pick up our formations skimming at altitudes of 100 feet and less over the Mediterranean? If so, will they know what they're seeing? Will they convey this to Egyptian Air Force headquarters? Will Egypt's controllers believe them when and if they do?

Will mischance befall our formations once they enter Egyptian airspace? I have designed the approach routes to avoid enemy radar, and the planes, of course, are flying so low that nothing electronic is likely to pick them up. But will they be spotted by eye, over the desert or the marshland of the delta, perhaps, by some alert young officer manning an observation post?

Ran Ronen commands Mirage Squadron 119:

I am first to the takeoff holding point. Aircraft are taxiing in an intricate choreography, executed in absolute radio silence. I check my watch. The note that the combat manager handed me says we have seven minutes till takeoff.

Odd.

That seems a long time.

Here come my numbers two, three, and four—Shlomo Egozi, Eliezer "Layzik" Prigat, Asher Snir—taxiing into place.

I glance to the combat operations officer's note with its updated time.

Six minutes to takeoff.

At the far end of the runway I see a four-ship formation of Vautour fighter-bombers from Ramat David Air Base. They will take off right after us.

The first Vautour begins to move. What's wrong? Why is he starting out of order? The Vautour leader advances onto the runway, gaining speed. His three formation-mates follow.

The bunch of schmucks! They've got the time wrong. They're taking off out of order!

I can't alert the tower. Radio silence is sacred.

Then it hits me.

They're not the schmucks—I am.

I stare at the combat operations officer's note, the one that was updated and handed to me back at the squadron.

My watch reads 07:24.

Out loud I calculate: "Flying time to target: twenty-six minutes. We must be over the target at 07:45 exactly."

I look back at the note.

Its time is five minutes late.

My heart is hammering. The instant the last Vautour passes, I power onto the runway, full afterburner, accelerating like a madman. Here come my formation-mates behind me. Do they know what has happened? No matter. I know.

I am banking toward Palmachim on the coast. Treetop level. To my left, the formation cuts the corner, catching up with me.

Planned speed is 420 knots—seven miles a minute. I push it up to 480. Eight miles a minute.

"Keep cool and think straight."

We cannot be late over the target. The enemy will have time to scramble. The whole war could be lost.

Over the Mediterranean now. Convoys of IAF warplanes hug the surface, streaking as if on highways toward Egypt. How will my formation get through this traffic jam? Go over? We can't. Enemy radar will pick us up.

Pass under.

There's no other way.

In moments like this, your body is shitting bricks but your head must stay cool and focused. Glance to your gauges? You can't. Every ounce of concentration is required to keep glued to the horizon, flying parallel to the surface of the sea. You "take a photo." A fraction of a second. Check your heading. Click. Check your watch. Click.

We pass under a four-ship formation of Mystères.

There is no navigation system in a Mirage. The only computer is between my ears, and it is crunching numbers furiously. The route over water is in three legs, which we navigate using only time, heading, and speed. Each five minutes at 480 knots gains us a minute over the planned speed of 420. We are burning fuel like crazy, but there is no alternative. By twenty-five minutes, we should have recovered all lost time.

We fly in combat formation, leader up front, wingman on the right, numbers two and three left and slightly to the rear. Asher Snir is my number four. He will tell me later we are flying so tight to the surface of the Mediterranean that we kick up a wake.

The slower planes are heading for targets closer in. My formation's target, Inshas Air Base, is farther away, adjacent to the capital, Cairo.

Now: beneath a four-ship formation of Ouragans.

We pass under another of Super Mystères.

Eleven minutes into the flight. We have made up three and a half minutes. Is our heading correct? We should cross the coast at Bardawill Lagoon.

There it is.

I have flown half a hundred reconnaissance missions over the delta. These will save us now.

The coast. We're over land now. Throttle forward to 540. We've made up most of the time. Canals and power lines whip beneath us. Farmers heading to the fields. They wave, thinking we're Egyptians.

The Nile delta is full of little towns, all alike.

I'm looking for Fakos.

Five hundred forty knots equals 270 meters per second. We are riding a rocket sled at the height of a clothesline.

You pick waypoints that are unmistakable. A gas station, a junction of canals. Farm country will fool you. Low spots will flood, lagoons will drain. Below us: rows of palms. Are these the trees I've picked as an IP? Roofs of mud-brick houses boom into view and vanish beneath the nose of the plane.

Fakos!

07:44.

We're on time.

Switches armed. Gunsights on air-to-ground.

Ten seconds to "pull."

Now: Tug the stick into your belly, throttle up to full afterburner, 50-degree climb, the heavily loaded plane hesitates for a second; then the acceleration plasters you into the seat, the altimeter spins clockwise wildly. Your muscles tense inside the G suit; the gauge climbs through two, three, four but you have no time to look. Approaching 6,000 feet, you start gently to roll onto your back.

Inverted, I see Cairo ahead. Inshas is one of the fields defending the capital. There it is!

First destroy the main runway. Two bombs, 500 kilograms each. The first pair of Mirages will aim for a point two-thirds of the way down the runway; the second pair goes for one-third.

Clouds obscure the field, but we can still see. Turn now. Line up on the runway. Don't overturn. When a four-ship formation dives onto a target, the planes go in order: one, two, three, four. Radio silence is no longer necessary. "One, in," says the leader. Two in, three in, four in, each pilot repeats.

My nose is down now, I'm diving at 35 degrees exactly, put the green dot on the target and lead it. I guide the stick gently, looking all the time to the altitude. Twenty-seven hundred, wait a bit, feel the pickle button on the stick; wait a little longer, you are dropping more than a ton, the plane is going to get very light when you release. Now. Pull at one thousand, eyes all around, watch for triple-A. You're pulling out of your dive and breaking hard, pulling heavy Gs, with antiaircraft fire zinging all around you.

"One, out."

At 100 feet put the plane over and turn hard, full military power. A Mirage puts up a lovely scream in that moment. You are flying at 550 knots, lower than the roofs of the hangars, dodging power lines, searching for your number two while you line up for the second pass. Where are the parked MiGs? Take a photo with your eyes. You're on the radio nonstop to your formation-mates: Watch out for that power line, I'll take the last four, you take the next four. Behind you, you see and feel the bombs detonating.

What is my state of mind? Am I calm? Hell no. I am focused to a pitch of intensity that only a lion feels in a charge or an eagle in a dive upon its prey.

"Two, out."

"Three, out."

"Four, out."

Switch to guns.

Bombs off, cannons on.

We are in a wide loop now at 550 knots, one Mirage after another, turning through 270 degrees as we pull to a thousand feet.

The Egyptian method of antiaircraft defense is not to shoot at each plane as it passes above their positions (we're moving too fast for their guns to follow) but to erect a "curtain" of cannon fire through which our planes must pass. Climbing now to commence our first strafing run, we can see this curtain. Our four planes must dive through it.

Beyond the antiaircraft fire waits our target: Egyptian MiGs on the ground. Because Inshas Air Base protects Cairo, it has the most planes and the best. Forty MiG-21s. A prize beyond reckoning.

As we dive we can see the enemy pilots scrambling. Men are racing toward their planes. On the flight line, pilots are strapping into their cockpits.

"There they are. We have caught them. Make every pass count."

The MiG-21s are parked beside the runway in sets of four. Line them up in your gunsights. Put your pipper just below the first plane. At 900 meters, squeeze. The 30-millimeter cannon fires twenty rounds per second. You can feel the bullets as they go. The swath of gunfire rakes the parked planes. I see blooms of flame, fireballs of blinding intensity, as I pull a tight 270-degree turn directly above and come back to attack again from a new angle.

Two passes.

Three.

The antiaircraft fire is more intense than I had expected. But we are here. I see MiG-21s still intact on the tarmac. This chance may never come again, not just to get the planes but to get the pilots in the cockpits as well.

I take our four ships through another pass and another. Five strafing runs. The plan calls for three, but I have made up my mind to keep attacking until I hear the next wave of Israeli planes commencing their bombing run.

Every antiaircraft gun on the field is firing at us. Speed is our only protection. Each pilot is turning as fast and tight as the aircraft can handle. Pull to a thousand, find the line that puts you on the axis of the parked MiGs, then plant your pipper and tear them up.

On the squadron channel I hear the next formation overhead, going into its dive.

08:02. My four are all safe.

We climb and head for home. As we reach altitude we can see, across the delta, dense columns of black smoke rising from the other airfields that have been hit by other squadrons in the first wave. Though I have believed heart and soul in Moked, the sight is beyond anything I have hoped for. The plan works! We are doing it!

Stay alert.

Don't be too happy.

Other MiGs may have scrambled; now is the most dangerous hour.

I am not thinking of my family, nor of my children, nor the air force, nor even the Jewish people. Only the mission. Concentrate. Do it. Do it well. Don't let elation erode your focus.

We climb. Fires can be seen all over the delta. Cairo West. Abu Suweir. Fayid, Kabrit, Beni Suef. All the attacks of all the squadrons.

We streak east for home. Somewhere below us, poised on the Egyptian frontier, three Israeli ground divisions are waiting for the order to attack. I cannot let myself think about them. My concern is only to land, refuel and rearm, strike again.

Yael Dayan remains with the command group of Arik Sharon's division on the Israel-Egypt frontier:

07:00. Sharon's tanks start moving toward the border. "I want to be," says Arik, "on the last inch that is Israel."

The fight that is coming today and tonight, Sharon says, will be the most complex ground operation any Israeli force has ever attempted. But his eyes are shining. "We are going to win a war."

By 08:00 the entire division has moved up to the border.

Last night Dov told me to pack what I'll need for Sinai. I grab a bottle of whiskey, chocolate, writing paper, a change of uniform, and a Bible. "Don't forget toilet paper."

Sharon is on the phone to his wife, Lily. "Be calm, kiss the children for me, don't worry, shalom shalom shalom." His car, a Studebaker Lark, waits with its driver.

At 08:15 comes the attack code.

Sadin Adom.

"Red Sheet."

All division communication channels are switched open. Arik takes the mike. "*Nua, nua!*" he orders. "Move, move!"

South, our tanks descend from the hills above the frontier. Arik peers through binoculars. "Here we go—we are firing!"

Captain Ori Orr commands the Recon Company of the 7th Armored Brigade:

I pass swiftly among the jeeps and half-tracks. Camouflage netting is being pulled off. Every engine fires up.

"This is it. We've rehearsed, we're ready. Do what you know how to do."

Our job is to lead. The brigade's tanks will follow. Behind them will come General Tal's command group. But we in Recon will cross the border before any.

We will be the first.

Miriam Lamm is pilot Giora Romm's fiancée and a sergeant with General Tal's command group:

I'm with General Tal's mobile HQ, boarding our coder/decoders' half-track. All around, vehicles are belching petrol and diesel plumes. I'm at my console, which is just a typewriter and a teleprinter, a bench, carbon paper, and mimeograph sheets. We're moving.

I send a quick prayer for my Giora. Where is he now? In his Mirage over some enemy airfield?

My lofty Giora. Fly safe! Do what you must!

Giora Romm, Mirage pilot in Squadron 119:

08:05. I am still on the ground at Tel Nof. Assigned to intercept standby. Eitan Karmi is my number one; we are the first pair. Salmon and Shmul are the second.

We have been in our cockpits since before dawn. Days ago, our squadron commander, Ran Ronen, took our four names out of the attack formations and put them on the mission board as air defense. This is terribly disappointing on the one hand, since we will not be part of the attack, but on the other it is the highest of compliments. It means that in Ran's mind we are his best dogfight pilots. Fliers will donate a kidney to get into such a group.

We feel the weight of that responsibility. It's not something one speaks about. We have all heard Nasser's threats. We know what the Egyptians will do to our country and to our families if we cannot stop them.

We sit in our cockpits—helmets on, canopies up. You can't piss or even scratch your ass. We watch the squadrons take off. The burners light, lifting the planes, heavily loaded with bombs and fuel. The four-ship formations form up and bank west with the sun behind them, turning hard and low. On the ground we can listen only to the tower radio, with its fake chatter to fool Egyptian electronic surveillance. We don't speak. Radio silence is holy.

I try not to think of Miriam. A pilot must stay in the present, particularly when he may receive at any moment the order to scramble. But I am human. Where is she? With Tal's division, I know, but I have no idea where. In the IDF, security is taken so seriously that I have no idea of my fiancée's whereabouts, nor she of mine. Be safe, that's my only prayer.

As I'm thinking this, I'm watching a four-ship formation of Vautour fighter-bombers taxiing. The lead plane has its air brakes extended. What the hell? These are panels on the fuselage used to slow the aircraft for landing. Does the pilot know? Retract the brakes, man! Your plane will never get airborne! It will crash at the end of the runway with all its ordnance and fuel!

This calamity-in-the-making unspools before the pilots and controllers in slow motion. In our cockpits, in the tower, every eye is riveted. We can't warn the pilot. We can't violate radio silence. There's no choice. We will watch someone kill himself before keying a microphone button.

At the last instant, the pilot realizes his error. His air brakes retract. He takes off.

Thank you, brother! You almost gave me a heart attack!

07:20.

07:35.

At 07:45 the planes of the attack formations will be over their targets. Here on the runway at Tel Nof, ground crewmen scamper out to us from the squadron building, handing scribbled notes up to our cockpits. Beni Suef is burning, twenty MiGs hit on the ground. Kabrit is toast. Bir Gafgafa: both runways destroyed.

The Egyptian Air Force will not be coming to attack Israel. We interceptors are not needed. My shoulders sag beneath the rescue harness. Here is the most momentous hour in the history of my country, for which I have trained every waking moment of my life—and I am nailed to the dirt, contributing nothing.

Rafi Sivron is in the air force bunker, the Pit, in Tel Aviv:

People said later that it was not a Six Day War but a Three Hour War, meaning the critical clash was over once Moked had destroyed the Egyptian Air Force on the ground. Others called it a Seven Minute War, as the first surprise blow did the bulk of the damage.

For me, it is a Minus-One Minute War.

I have feared only detection. If the first wave can reach their attack points without being discovered by enemy radar, then nothing can prevent the total destruction of the Egyptian Air Force.

From before dawn, I have been working in Combined Operations, one floor above the Pit. There is much other work to do. At 07:45 I creep into the command center, in time to hear the radios of the attacking squadrons come alive from over their targets.

Dayan stands and embraces Rabin. Ezer claps the chief of staff's back. Everyone is shaking everyone else's hand. I'm standing to the side with another officer. I tell him, "The war is over."

It isn't, of course. Ask the paratroopers. Ask the men in the tanks. At that exact moment, they are getting their orders to advance. Seven untouched Egyptian divisions wait in Sinai, against our three. Eight other Arab nations are moving troops into readiness.

At the big map table in the Pit, my boss, Motti Hod, must have felt his heart start again after sitting frozen all night and all morning. Give him credit. He made Moked happen. He presided over it, he protected it, he championed it, and he sits at its controls now like a maestro conducting a symphony.

Give Ezer Weizman credit. In the face of massive political resistance, of doubt and scorn and disbelief, he rammed through the purchase from Dassault France of seventy-two Mirage IIICs, without which the IAF could not have dreamed of this hour. It was Ezer who charged Yak Nevo and me with developing this plan for total war.

I watch Motti at the map table. No one pounds his back or breaks open a bottle. Motti is working.

What exactly is he doing? In English his function would be defined in two words: command and control. In Hebrew we have three. This constitutes an extremely significant distinction. "Command" in Hebrew is *pikud*. "Control" is *bakara*. The third term, which does not exist in English, is *shlita*.

What is command? A squadron commander in the air commands his formation as Ran Ronen, say, commands his attack on Inshas. He directs the action of his four-ship formation on-site.

Then there is control. The controller's station is on the ground. He is at headquarters, say, or manning a radar console in the field. Observing his screens, he can tell the planes in the air, "Listen, you are not on your proper heading," or, "Look out—there are MiGs approaching you from the east."

Neither of these capacities is enough. The squadron leader in the air (or even by radio from the ground) cannot make decisions whose basis is wider than what he can see or know. He does not possess the big picture, such as which other units are in the area, which additional operations are in progress, how the current operation is unfolding. Likewise, the controller on the ground sees only part of the picture. He can assist the flight leader in the air. He can transmit critical information. But he can't call the shots. He possesses neither the perspective nor the authority.

What is needed is a third locus. This is *shlita*.

The officer with shlita possesses both the big picture and the authority to direct the overall action.

A helicopter squadron commander, for example, may transmit the following in distress: "We're taking heavy fire from the landing zone. Do we land or not?" You, the controller possessing shlita, can make that decision. "Hold on," you can say. "I'm sending you some strike aircraft."

And you are not suggesting; you are ordering. The helicopters will wait; the strike aircraft will rush to the rescue. That is shlita. You are employing this power, which is beyond "command" and "control."

This is what Motti Hod is doing now.

Moked is a symphony. Motti wields the baton.

An additional crisis will arise within two hours, one that will supersede even Motti's shlita.

Jordan's air force will attack Israel. King Hussein's fighters will strike Netanya and go after our air base at Ramat David. The question then becomes: Do we strike back, and, if so, how and where and with what levels of force? What will be the consequences of such a decision?

Motti will not be able to make this call. It lies beyond his rank and station.

He will turn to Moshe Dayan.

Dayan, as minister of defense, must assess the consequences of retaliating against Jordan. He must answer the question: Is King Hussein attacking in earnest or is he simply "making a demonstration" to satisfy Nasser and his Arab allies?

If the former, what are the strategic implications? Hussein has 176 new Patton tanks in two brigades, the 40th and the 60th. Against this force, Israel has only ancient Shermans and a few light AMXs, manned by reservists. Jordan's Arab Legion is the best-trained enemy force in the Middle East. In addition, Hussein has two crack battalions of Egyptian commandos poised on our border, with additional formations of Iraqi armor and air moving up.

If we strike Jordan in retaliation for her attack on us, how will the other Arab nations react? Will the act bring Syria in, opening a *third* front? How will the Russians, Syria's sponsor state, respond? The Americans? The UN?

Strike or not? The decision must be made, but Motti can't make it; it is beyond his level of authority. Prime Minister Eshkol has the authority, but he is not a military man; he lacks the knowledge and experience.

Only Dayan can make this decision.

Giora Romm:

Waiting on the runway, our planes carry no bombs. We are in intercept configuration. Suddenly, orders come from the tower: Scramble!

Our pair—my leader, Eitan Karmi, and I—are ordered to Abu Suweir, an airfield near Ismailiya at the northern end of the Suez Canal.

We close the canopies and start the engines. The tower is telling us that Egyptian MiGs are attacking an Israeli formation; we are to fly to our comrades' aid. This is ridiculous. It is twenty minutes to Abu Suweir. No dogfight takes twenty minutes. But these are our orders.

We're in the aircraft, we have our mission, let's go!

I have never been out of Israeli airspace. I am a geographic virgin. So this is exciting, just nearing the border. Karmi and I climb through 15,000 feet. No need to "hug the deck" anymore to avoid enemy radar; the Egyptians know we are coming.

As our two-ship formation crosses the frontier above Gaza, my leader tests his guns, firing a short burst. The cannon shells have a self-exploding mechanism so they will not hit the ground. But Karmi forgets to tell me. All of a sudden at 20,000 feet I see black air bursts before me. I say to myself, What the hell—we have just crossed the border and already the Egyptians are shooting at us!

Sinai. Wow. I have never been over this desert before. I feel like Magellan, like Marco Polo. This is unknown territory to me. I have seen the Sinai Peninsula a thousand times on a map; I've flown over it ten thousand times in my mind. But I have never looked down from the cockpit of a Mirage and beheld this incredible expanse.

In a few minutes: Suez. The Suez Canal, for which Verdi wrote *Aida*. I, Giora Romm, twenty-two years old, am at 25,000 feet flying over the Canal. There are the Bitter Lakes; there is Ismailiya . . .

But I am not here as a tourist. I came here on a mission.

The GCI—ground control—takes us to Abu Suweir. Descending through 10,000 feet, we can see the mess that the first wave of Israeli planes has made of the place. Columns of black smoke rise from all over the delta. Everywhere buildings and airplanes are blazing. I say to myself, Boy, our guys really did it.

Abu Suweir has a unique characteristic. The planes are parked in "eights," meaning circular driveways, one adjacent to the other, to form what looks like a numeral 8. We start to descend, Karmi and I, and suddenly there is a MiG-21 taxiing. I have never seen this before. I go after him the way a child reaches out for a toy. I'm on his tail when Karmi, my leader, who is closing from 90 degrees, says, "Don't touch him." What? Okay. I follow orders.

Karmi goes in and shoots the MiG. He gets the kill.

My kill.

I have only moments to feel the sickening feeling in my belly and then

a formation of Mirages from Ramat David appears; they are attacking
Abu Suweir and right behind them are two MiG-21s.

I go to full afterburner and in seconds I am behind the first MiG. I fire
a burst and nothing happens—the only time this has ever happened to me.
I don't panic. I say to myself, Go closer. A hundred sixty meters. On the
gunsight, there is a circle we call "the diamond." When a MiG-21's wing-
span fits in that circle, the range is exactly 160 meters. I fire a short burst,
a third of a second, and he immediately blows. I break fast, look back, the
plane is a ball of flame. Now I see a second MiG. I line him up in my gunsights and put a burst into him. He explodes too.

At once everything has become very simple.

I say to myself, This is my role. This is what I was sent here to do. I am
not concerned with the outcome of the war. I have just shot down two
MiGs!

Let Moshe Dayan worry about the fate of Israel. My job is to shoot
down MiGs and I am doing that.

One more thing. Theory works. The "death burst" works. What we
have envisioned and practiced and trained for . . . it works. Put your gunsights on a MiG-21 two hundred meters in front of you, squeeze the trigger, and the MiG explodes.

Theory works.

As I'm passing over the second MiG, I spot a third one, running west
away from me. I'm thinking, Should I shoot him down, too? Hello! You
are Giora Romm, twenty-two years old, who was in the Boy Scouts only
months ago. Don't be such a greedy pilot!

I go after him with an air-to-air missile. You're supposed to listen for
the tone in your earphones, which tells you the missile has locked onto the
target. But I pull the trigger too soon. I miss.

Okay.

Let him go.

By now my leader is gone. He has turned for home, low on fuel.

I arrive back at Tel Nof by myself (Karmi has had to make a no-fuel
landing at Hatzerim, fifty kilometers closer) with enough fuel to do a victory roll over the field. I say to myself, Your leader is a much more experienced pilot than you; this is your first operational mission, in which both
you and he started with 3,500 liters of fuel but he has had to land at another field while you have gotten home with 500 liters to spare, which is a
tremendous difference, considering you and he have flown the identical

Giora Romm in 1983 with sons
Assaf and Yuval.

distance. In addition, that extra juice could have been the difference between life and death, between completing the mission and not completing
it, if other MiGs had jumped us or if we had had to fight our way out of
trouble. More than that, Giora, within the battle at Abu Suweir, you
fought with greater focus and were more cool and economical than he.

This gives me tremendous confidence.

I have landed now. The ground crew takes my helmet, they are putting
me on their shoulders. I am not sweating or tired. I'm kind of blasé. Another day at the office. A driver takes me back to the squadron. Yeah, I
shot down two MiGs, here is my gun camera, what is the next mission?

The ops room is the heart of the squadron. There is the mission board,
with the names of the pilots and their next assignments. It's also where the
gossip is. The war gossip. The only thing I am interested in is getting refueled and rearmed and back into the air as soon as possible. I want to fly.
War is fun. War is fun! You take off, shoot down one or two MiGs, then
go back and do it again.

Ran Ronen, Squadron 119 commander:

Now the missions are coming thick and fast. I fly to Inshas at 07:45, to Abu Suweir at 10:30, Gardaka at 12:30, then Cairo International at 16:30. The ground crews work like the Indy 500. Watching them, I think, By God, I actually feel sorry for these Egyptians.

Arnon Levushin is the youngest pilot in Squadron 119:

We are attacking Cairo West. I'm number four in the formation. I'm so new that I have been certified as operational only two weeks earlier.

I'm into the dive, 2,500 feet AGL, the runway is wide, wide, wide in my sights, I execute the release—but I fail to hold the trigger down long enough.

Only one bomb drops.

I grew up on Kibbutz Kfar Menachem. This is a very spartan kibbutz. The ethic was no waste, hard work for all, everyone pitches in. At twelve, my job was to graze the sheep. I had 250 animals that I moved from pasture to pasture. On one trail you had to cross a railroad track. One day, when the flock was half over, I heard the train whistle. It takes three or four minutes to get that many animals across a railroad track. I could see the train approaching fast. One of my friends' fathers, who happened to be driving a tractor nearby, had leapt off and was sprinting toward the tracks, waving his red shirt, trying to get the engineer's attention. I could hear the brakes on the train screeching, but it was clear there was no way it could stop in time.

I found that I was very cool. Despite the train's approach, I continued thinking clearly and calmly. I stayed beside the track. I drove half the flock forward out of the train's way and the other half rearward, where they would not be hurt. I saved the sheep.

That may seem like a small thing, but it was not. A task of serious responsibility had been entrusted to me at a very young age, and I had handled it. This was recognized on the kibbutz.

In the psychometric tests for flight school, there is an exercise in which you trace a pencil line across the paper, zigging and zagging through a series of mazes. But the pencil is not held in your hand; instead it is mounted on a drawing machine that you operate using two controls, one horizontal and one vertical. I could do this with ease.

In another test, a page of a book is shown to you for a few seconds—a complex schematic with drawings, graphs, and text. When the test administrator shuts the book, you report what you remember. I remembered everything.

In flight school I struggled at first because I was small and not particularly verbal. Twice they almost washed me out. But the chief sociologist championed my cause. "This kid tested off the charts. We must be patient until he finds himself."

In a Mirage, when your bombs drop, you feel it because the aircraft gets very light all of a sudden. But it's hard to tell if you've dropped one bomb or both, particularly if you're brand new to the aircraft and you are executing the release during your first time in combat.

I glance to my indicator. I've still got one bomb. This is worse than the sheep on the railroad track. With one bomb still hanging, my cannons won't fire. This is part of the safety systems of the Mirage. The bombs are carried under the fuselage; each one has its detonator fuse protruding from the front. The 30-millimeter cannons are forward of this. When you fire the cannons, the spent shell casings come streaming back past the bombs at 400 or 500 miles per hour. The safety system is designed so that, if for any reason the bombs are still in place under the fuselage, the cannons won't fire.

So I can't strafe. Meanwhile, the other three Mirages in my formation have gone into their strafing runs. They are blasting the hell out of the Tupolev-16s on the ground. What can I do? I pull to altitude, wait for the second strafing pass to finish and my formation-mates to get out of the way. Now I drop my second bomb. Antiaircraft fire is coming from everywhere and all of it is aimed at me because I'm all alone, high and exposed, and the gunners now know exactly what I'm trying to do and where I am heading. I'm not panicking; my mind is clear. I'm embarrassed. I'm no big talker on the radio but now I have shut up completely.

Finally I get into the strafing pattern. But I'm so late, and the smoke is so thick from the Egyptian bombers burning beside the runways, that I can't see a thing. No targets. This nightmare is never-ending.

I'm thinking, Okay, what's Plan B? What other damage can I do? I see a building. The biggest building on the base. Oh, boy. I fly straight at it at 100 feet and blow the hell out of it.

Back at Tel Nof, we're debriefing fast; ground crews are bringing up rearmed and refueled planes. We're getting our second mission briefing. There's just time to take a piss, tell a few stories, then run for the aircraft. But first I have to see what building I shot up at Cairo West. I'm hoping it's something good. That will redeem a small measure of honor. I find the base layout in the ops room. What did I shoot up? Was it intel, a major fuel depot, the base HQ?

The motor pool!

That is like destroying the room that contains the urinals.

Now I feel even more humiliated.

Second mission: Gardaka. Ran Ronen is the leader. It's past noon and we are over the base. Surprise is gone. The Egyptians are waiting for us.

I had thought the antiaircraft fire was bad at Cairo West, but it is nothing compared to what we're seeing now. This is real triple-A. It looks like a lid has been placed over the runways, a lid of angry, red fire. I can see muzzle flashes from what look like fifty different guns. Worse, Gardaka is wide open, a broad desert plateau with no trees, no tall buildings, nothing to disrupt the triple-A gunners' lines of sight.

"One, in." This is Ran, diving into that murderous crossfire.

"Two, in."

That's me. I can see the triple-A "stepping up." The next black burst will get me, I'm certain.

"Three, in."

"Four, in."

Somehow we survive. We put our bombs on target. Gardaka is one of the fields that Egyptian planes have fled to from the other fields. Reuven Rozen is our number three; Buki Kenan is number four. Buki normally has a high voice. Suddenly we hear it even higher:

"*Migim! Migim!*" "MiGs, MiGs!"

I have never actually seen a MiG in the air. But I am reacting like every other fighter pilot: First my head is doing a one-eighty to locate any plane on my tail; second, I am red-hot to shoot one of these bastards down.

"How many?"

"Four."

It is as if the sky has exploded. Planes are zooming in all directions. Forget about our strafing passes. Almost before I can think, I see one explosion. Ran has shot down a MiG-19.

Buki is chasing another.

I've got one myself. He is in my sights. Suddenly he breaks hard and runs. His afterburner lights. A MiG-19 can do 600 knots, but a Mirage can hit 700. I light my burner. Over the radio I hear Ran:

"Two, hurry up! MiG on your tail!"

Ran is behind me, going after a MiG that is going after me. Everything leaves my mind except the plane I'm chasing. I have forgotten Gardaka, the mission, the whole war.

I want my MiG.

He runs like hell but my plane is faster. The MiG-19 has a very distinctive fuselage, shaped like a cigar. I'm closing in, my pipper is almost on his tail. Over the radio I hear Ran shoot down the MiG behind me. Suddenly my MiG breaks! MiG-19s can turn very, very sharp. I will overshoot him! He'll get away!

I put my nose up and do a "yo-yo." My MiG is losing speed fast in his turn, too tight for me to follow. He is pulling a lot of Gs. But I am losing speed faster by going straight up. This is good. I turn above him. I can see his head on a swivel, looking for me. I come down on him like a hawk and squeeze the trigger. No flames. No explosion. What the hell? I know my guns have fired.

Then I see his parachute.

I am redeemed.

Squadron commander Ran Ronen, returning from Gardaka:

The red radio in a Mirage is the squadron channel; green is ground control. Ten minutes after hitting Gardaka, on the way home, the green comes alive with an emergency transmission: "Any airborne formation with suitable ordnance and fuel to reach Amman, notify me immediately!"

Amman? Jordan! Has King Hussein entered the war?

I can speak in the clear to my formation leaders; we know each other's voices as if we were brothers. "Who's in the air with bombs?"

Avramik Salmon responds that he's on his way to Gardaka.

I ask: "Where are you?"

"South of Eilat."

I tell him my formation has destroyed Gardaka. We have wiped out the runways, shot down three MiGs, and watched another plunge in the chaos into a bomb crater on the runway.

"Switch to the GCI's channel, tell him you can attack Amman."

Menahem Shmul is in Salmon's formation, approaching Gardaka:

We're at 25,000 feet, descending to attack Gardaka. The war has been raging for hours now; there's no need anymore to fly below the radar approaching a target. My formation is Salmon number one, Omri Hoffman two, Jacob Agassi three. I'm number four.

Suddenly Ran comes on the air. He tells us his formation has hit the base and wiped it out. Forget Gardaka. Call the GCI.

You're going to Amman.

Amman? This is big news—it means Jordan has entered the war.

But we have no maps to Amman. We've studied the base. We know it by heart. But Amman is not on the Moked target sheet. The only fields we have maps for are Egyptian. We have nothing for Jordan.

"Two, have you got a map? Three? Four?"

Nothing.

We're blank.

Wait! Our survival maps.

I dig mine out from the survival kit under the ejection seat. The booklet is in a waterproof wrapper. On the cover is an illustration that includes Eilat and Amman. We're over Eilat now.

"One, this is four. I've got it."

"Got what?"

"I see Amman on the survival map."

Ran Ronen:

This is why you as squadron commander must put so much thought into the composition of a four-ship formation. It's not just chemistry. Each player must complement the others. He must fill gaps.

Shmul is number four in Salmon's formation. Four sounds like the least important, the last car in the train. But four has its special role. Everything is in front of him; he can see the whole formation. This gives number four a unique perspective. He is the backstop.

So when numbers one, two, and three are all saying they've got no chart to Amman, it's Shmul in the caboose who remembers the survival map.

Menahem Shmul:

The genius of Moked is that it is modular. We attack like wolves, meaning we know the pattern, we know the sequence. The alpha wolf only has to tilt his tail and every beast in the pack knows what to do.

The basic pattern is bomb, strafe, strafe, strafe. Come in low, pull to six thousand, put your bombs on the runway, then go after the parked planes, three passes in a 270-degree cloverleaf pattern. *Sha'yish* is left-right-left. *Yishai* is right-left-right.

Salmon calls yishai and in we go, attacking Amman. The elite warplanes of the Royal Jordanian Air Force are Hawker Hunters—British

Courtesy of Jacob Agassi and Menahem Shmul.

Lieutenant Colonel Jacob Agassi, left, and
Lieutenant Menahem Shmul, June 8, 1967.

built, fast, very maneuverable. They have just returned from strikes against
Israel. They are parked like ducks in a row, being refueled and rearmed.

When you strafe, you come in fast, with the afterburner if you need it.
This is what keeps you safe from triple-A. Start shooting at 900 meters.
The distance goes by fast at 550 knots. Aim low so you can see the bullets
strike. Walk them up over the parked planes. On the first pass, note your
targets for the second. The 30-millimeter cannon does not have a high rate
of fire, but the bullets are big. They do the job. Every wolf gets his share.

I am not literally thinking about my father. In the moment there is no time.
But under every pass sits the knowledge that I am attacking the people who
murdered him ten days before I was born. I have waited my whole life for this.

Three days from now, Jordan's King Hussein will appear on television in a news conference, fighting back tears as he speaks of his beloved Hawker Hunters being massacred on the ground. I will think, I wish you had more Hunters, Hussein, so we could have massacred more of them.

I am here to kill everybody.

Landing back at Tel Nof, I don't want to waste even a minute to debrief. "Give me the next mission! Let's go! Darkness is coming!"

Giora Romm:

Each time we land to refuel and rearm, the briefings get shorter. We are told the target field, that's enough. Besides, the missions keep changing. By now every pilot knows how successful the first attacks have been. We have destroyed 198 Egyptian planes in the first wave, 101 more in the second. Eight Israeli squadrons have hit seventeen Egyptian bases. Incredible. But the more we get, the more we want.

Jordan has joined the war now. Our planes have wiped out her two primary fields, Amman and Mafraq. At Amman we destroyed every single plane. One of our Mystères even made two passes on King Hussein's office, the first with rockets, the second with guns. Fortunately for Hussein, he was not there. At Mafraq, the only building left standing was the mess hall. I was patrolling the Sinai border through all this, a total waste of time that left me so furious and frustrated I was shaking.

Finally in the afternoon: a bombing mission! To Syria. Now she too has entered the war. Ran is supposed to lead our formation, but he gets called out of his cockpit at the last moment by air force chief Motti Hod. We won't learn why till later. It seems a number of MiGs have survived this morning's attacks on Egypt's military fields; they have escaped to Cairo International, the capital's civilian airport, and are hiding now under the wings of commercial airliners. Only Ran has a cool enough head to be entrusted to nail the MiGs without touching the civilian jets.

(Which he does, by the way.)

But our formation has lost him as its leader. Ran's second deputy, Eitan Karmi—my leader from the first sortie this morning—takes over. Our formation is Karmi number one, Asher Snir two, Layzik Prigat three, and me four. Our target is a field called T-4 in Syria.

T-4 is at the fourth station along the Tapline oil pipeline, near a city called Tadmour. We must cross all of Jordan to get there.

The idea that suddenly you can fly all over the Middle East—this is great! I cannot get enough of it.

Menahem Shmul:

The third mission is briefed to be Cairo West. But as we're on our way to the planes, the tower changes the target to a base called Saikal in Syria. We know the place. It's not far over the border, so no fuel problems. Oded Sagee is number one, Reuven Rozen two, Udi Shelach three. I'm always number four because I'm the youngest.

But between Gedera and the Sea of Galilee, the controller comes on the air with a second target change: We're rerouted to T-4.

This is a mystery field to us. We haven't briefed on it. We have no maps. We don't know where it is, except that it's a long way. Plus we're flying right on the deck to avoid detection by Syrian radar, so we can't navigate by landmarks. We need headings. Meanwhile, our number two, Reuven Rozen, has had to drop out because his afterburner won't light. Now there are only three of us.

Where the hell are we going? This is serious.

Suddenly I remember that there's another four-ship from our squadron with orders to attack T-4. I chanced to hear them talking when we were on the way to the planes. Ran was supposed to lead this formation, but he got called away to a more sensitive mission. Karmi has taken over, with Asher, Giora, and Prigat.

They're ahead of us.

They can tell us where to go.

I inform my leader, who has not heard about this. I take my plane up to 10,000 feet, alone, to get line-of-sight radio reception. I'm thinking: T-4, man! Syria, Jordan, everybody is getting into this war!

I raise Karmi, commanding the other four-ship formation, who tells me to get to Beit She'an, take such-and-such heading to Sheikh Maskin; he gives me two more headings and minutes on each. I scribble it all and drop back down to my formation.

We're over Syria now, 420 knots, at what the books call zero altitude but is actually about 100 feet. You see camels, gazelles, Bedouin camps; the landscape is an ancient volcanic plateau. Austere, raw, magnificent. It's beautiful to be up here seeing this.

Smoke ahead. Our target: T-4. We can hear over the radio Karmi's formation attacking the field. Karmi, Giora, Prigat, and Snir. I know three of them, if not all four, are demons for dogfighting. They are doing their patterns and they start to talk about MiGs. MiGs are chasing them and they are chasing MiGs.

Giora Romm:

I hear the call come in from Shmul. Shmul is a wild man, very smart, an animal in any kind of fight. Give him credit: It took tremendous presence of mind, when his formation got the change-order to attack T-4, to remember that another four-ship from Squadron 119 was heading to that same target—and to radio ahead to get the routing.

So now we know four Mirages from our squadron are behind us. This is good and bad. Good because it means together we will give T-4 a real pasting. Bad because now there is more competition for killing MiGs.

Since Karmi stole that MiG-21 from me this morning at Abu Suweir, I have resolved that such an outrage will never happen again. I will not give away my candy. Now over T-4 we see three or four MiGs loitering but in a nonthreatening posture, so we ignore them and go into the attack. I have made up my mind that I am going to make all three strafing passes no matter what. Asher Snir can't wait. As soon as the bombing pass is finished, he flies the coop and starts fighting with a MiG. Prigat and I come out of the third strafing pass with a MiG-21 behind us. Now I have two problems. One, to shoot down the MiG; two, to make sure that no one else gets him before I can. I tell Prigat, "There's a MiG behind you—break!" I drop my fuel tanks and turn after the MiG.

Suddenly Shmul and his formation appear. They are only three, not four. Shmul is an incredibly courageous flier. He later became a famous test pilot. He sees the MiG, pulls his nose out of the bombing run, puts his pipper on the MiG in a very sloppy way, and fires a burst. At this instant, his engine goes out!

He's got a compressor stall.

I say to myself, Shmul is a POW. He has lost all power, and the geometry is such that the MiG is now behind him. He will get Shmul on a plate. The MiG looks at Shmul and shoots at him in a very unprofessional manner. I'm thinking, What a bunch of schmucks!

Shmul is shouting over the air that he has a compressor stall, the MiG is shooting at him, and I'm coming back on the MiG and I get him in the first burst. But he doesn't explode. Maybe I didn't hit the fuel tank. Smoke is pouring from the MiG; he's dropping fast and starting to spin. I'm following him down because in all the Battle of Britain books that I read as a kid, you don't get credit for a kill unless you see the plane hit the ground. Meanwhile, Shmul has gotten his engine restarted. My MiG plows into the dirt east of the runway. Shmul is now going into his interrupted bombing run. He's okay, he says. He is back in business.

Menahem Shmul:

We're in the attack, very low, just starting to pull, when here comes a MiG-21 directly above. He doesn't see us. I decide to go after him. My afterburner is on, I line the MiG up and pull the trigger, but my sights are still on air-to-ground for the bombing run. The MiG keeps flying, but I don't. My engine stalls and shuts down.

The Mirage engine is notoriously prone to compressor stalls under certain conditions and I have put my plane in exactly that position, not to mention failing to switch my sights from air-to-ground to air-to-air. This is the first MiG I have seen in my gunsight and I'm so excited, I am fucking up big time. (To my relief, after I land, the engine's fuel control will be found to be faulty.)

Under my fuselage are two 500-kilogram bombs and two tanks of fuel; I'm 450 kilometers from home, over the Syrian desert, and I have no engine. In emergency moments you always go to the basics. Over the radio I report: "Number four, lost engine." Silence for a moment. Then Karmi comes on: "So relight it."

I'm trying! I jettison my tanks, punching the button wildly. I'm in a dive, 90 degrees to the ground, when the engine relights and my heart starts beating again. I have to go very low to gain speed, so that now I'm north of the target, by myself. Sagee and Shelach are attacking. Giora takes the MiG behind me (there are two) and Asher Snir, a little later, shoots down the other. These are the first MiGs that I've seen in my life.

How much adrenaline is in my bloodstream? I'm so jacked up from the MiG that I missed, my engine flaming out, and barely pulling out of a 90-degree dive that I can hardly breathe. My indicator says I've still got my bombs. Okay, let's use 'em. I climb above the runway and go in. Our practice is to pickle at 2,500 feet above ground level, meaning drop the bombs and begin to pull out of the dive at that altitude. You don't want to wait any longer or the exploding bombs will get you, not to mention you will plant yourself face-first into the deck.

Here we go. The altimeter passes 3,500, which is still pretty high, but the runway is growing wider and wider in my windscreen and I'm getting the terrible feeling that something is wrong. Suddenly I realize the pickle figure is based on sea level, the approximate reading for the airfields in Egypt. But we are at T-4 on the Syrian plateau; its altitude may be as high as 2,500 feet. All this goes through my mind in a fraction of a second.

I drop my ordnance at 800 feet AGL—way, way too low. The ground is coming up very fast; I pull out at impossibly high Gs and am saved only by the fact that my bombs are on delayed fuses, so they don't explode as my plane passes directly over the impact points. My gun camera is on or no one will believe later how low I am. A MiG-21 is taxiing. I'm at the same height as he. I kick the rudder, set the nose, and squeeze the trigger. He explodes. I pull and get out.

I'm all by myself now and out of sequence. I turn to come back. Three MiGs are sitting ducks alongside the runway. The other planes in my formation are strafing right to left; I'm coming back left to right. Again I feel something wrong. I start to turn at 500 knots and I see another Mirage so close I can make out the bolts on its aluminum skin. It's our number three, Udi Shelach. He correctly goes left, following the yishai pattern he has called. I'm going the wrong way! Our planes are going to collide. I turn wildly, just barely missing him, in a more than 90-degree bank at zero altitude. He is not even aware I'm near. I recover, heading dead-on at a Syrian hangar. What the hell—I shoot it up, pull out, and continue my attack.

Meanwhile, Giora and Asher have gotten their MiGs. Karmi, Prigat, Snir, and my formation-mates are heading home; Giora, who always has fuel left, is sweeping the site, looking for another MiG to tangle with. I complete my three strafing runs and follow him home, a few minutes behind.

What a balagan! But, unprofessional as it was, we have found the field and destroyed it. I wiped out a hangar and two MiGs on the ground. And I'm alive and I've still got my plane.

My paramount crime is losing "battle picture." This is a sin, a black mark that must be regarded with the utmost seriousness. Throughout the attack I have maintained awareness of where I am in relation to the field, the ground target. But I have lost track of the other Mirages. A pilot can never do this. He must keep the battle picture in his mind at all times, even when he's inverted or out of pattern. He must know where his formation-mates are and what they are doing. If they are in a strafing pattern, he must know whether it's sha'yish or yishai and where each of them is within the pattern.

I have lost this completely.

Ran Ronen, squadron commander:

The fighting day is over, it's eleven o'clock at night. I'm alone in the bunker, going over the film from the gun cameras. I will watch the footage from every plane in the squadron and from every sortie. Details count.

Has one of my pilots broken formation, run off on his own due to excess excitement, anger, or confusion? I must see how every four-ship formation has flown, and each pilot. Today already we have had two moments where I had to step in.

Between the second and third missions I came out of my office onto the balcony and there is Asher Snir, alone, standing with his face to the wall. He is crying.

"Asher, what's wrong?"

He says he has just learned that his dear friend Yoram Harpaz has been killed, shot down by an Israeli Hawk missile when his plane strayed into secure airspace over the nuclear reactor at Dimona.

"Come with me." I take him into my office and close the door. Asher is twenty-three, handsome as Montgomery Clift. He will finish his career with thirteen and a half kills, tied with Avramik Salmon for second all-time on the list of Israeli aces. He could have been chief of the air force if cancer had not killed him at forty-four, a brigadier general.

"Asher, this is war."

He is trying to get ahold of himself.

"Friends will die. We cannot think about this now."

"Yes, Ran."

"We'll mourn later. Next week. Next month. But not now. Do you understand?"

Asher straightens.

"Yes, Ran."

I stand up. So does he.

"You and I may die today, this afternoon. We know this. We accept it."

I put my hand on his shoulder.

"I'm sorry, Ran. It won't happen again."

During that same break, I'm in the operations room, configuring the formation for the Gardaka mission. I put my name on the board as leader. One of my deputies, Eitan Karmi, reacts.

"You are taking all the plum shots for yourself, Ran." He says this in front of the other pilots.

I tell him to follow me into my office.

Karmi is a friend, an outstanding pilot; in his career he will shoot down eight enemy planes in air-to-air combat, putting him in the all-time top twenty in the IAF. And he is a leader. But what he has just done cannot be allowed to stand.

"Change out of your flight suit," I tell him. "You are not flying any more with this squadron. Change out and go home."

I brief the Gardaka mission. When I come out onto the balcony, Karmi is waiting for me. "What are you doing here?" I say. "I told you to leave the squadron. Go home."

As I'm taxiing I see his Volkswagen pull out of the lot.

Back from Gardaka two hours later, I have got two MiGs, Levushin has downed another, a fourth crashed, and we destroyed the base. As I'm crossing to the squadron, I see Karmi. "Ran, can I talk to you?"

"Of course. We are friends."

In my office, Karmi apologizes. He was wrong, he says; he should never have spoken to me that way and certainly not in front of the others. Please, he asks, let me fly.

I take his hand. "All right, you are back with us. From this moment forget the past. We will discuss this when the war is over." I give him a mission to T-4 in Syria.

I'm thinking of this now, watching the film from Oded Sagee's formation, which hit T-4 right after Karmi's. On the screen I see a row of parked MiGs being strafed and in the background a huge hangar. Suddenly from the right-hand edge of the frame a Mirage drops out of nowhere, moving like a bullet, completely out of pattern. It booms past the hangar, standing on its ear at zero altitude, nearly colliding with another Mirage.

Now it is Shmul in my office. That was his plane. I have had him hauled out of bed. It's after midnight. I show him the film and ask him if he carries a service pistol.

"I do."

"Then take it out and kill yourself. I need that airplane. If you are going to commit suicide, do it in a way that doesn't cost this squadron your own plane and whoever else you're going to crash into."

I tell him he is grounded.

Menahem Shmul:

Ran is telling me I will not fly anymore. The war is over for me. I know he is right. What I did is inexcusable. But I also know there is no way I am going to let him ground me. This cannot happen. I cannot let it.

I glance to the closed door. "May I speak?"

"Of course."

I tell him about my father. This is no excuse, I know. I screwed up. But only because I wanted so badly to destroy the enemy. I will control myself tomorrow, Ran. You will never have a problem with me again.

Ran Ronen:

He is sitting across from me, this young guy, redheaded, brave as a lion, the kind of flier every squadron commander dreams about.

"Goddammit, do you think I can let you fly like that? You almost killed yourself and Shelach!"

"I fucked up," he says. "I fucked up big."

Get out of here, I tell him. Let me think about this.

From Shmul I am learning a very important lesson. You must know your pilots. I had believed that a squadron commander could know his men as fliers only. Now Shmul tells me of his father, whom he never saw, never knew, murdered by Arabs ten days before he was born. He grew up with this.

You have to know what drives your people.

Ran Ronen in 1976 as a brigadier general.

Menahem Shmul:

Ran comes out after the longest five minutes of my life. "You can continue to fly," he says. He tells me he will keep me with him in every formation tomorrow. "If you so much as fart crooked, I will know."

I thank him and swear again that I will keep myself under control. I will fly for him like no one has ever flown.

"And forget about the pistol," Ran says. "You don't have to kill yourself."

BOOK FIVE

SINAI

29.

SADIN ADOM

My jeep is speeding along a dirt track with broad, barren fields on each side. No people, no houses. We have crossed the border. The war has started.

Yosi Ben-Hanan is operations officer of the 7th Armored Brigade. He is twenty-two years old, a lieutenant.

Less than an hour earlier we saw Israeli warplanes streaking overhead on their way to attack the enemy. Every man in the brigade is on his feet; every tank and half-track is alive—engine running, radio channels open. Finally at 08:15 comes the go-code:

Sadin Adom.

"Red Sheet."

We are rolling. Up ahead is the 1st Platoon of the brigade's Recon Company, led by Lieutenant Yossi Elgamis. His jeeps are leading Battalion 79, consisting of American-built M48A Patton tanks. I'm with the brigade headquarters right behind.

One imagines that crossing a border in the Middle East is a big deal, with massive fortifications and guns and minefields. But here there is nothing. The frontier consists only of a sign that says STOP and a shallow furrow scraped by a bulldozer.

So far there is no fighting and no resistance. Ahead, we know, wait two enemy divisions: the 20th, called "the Palestinian" because it is composed largely of refugee militia from the Gaza Strip, and the 7th, a regular formation of the Egyptian Army. What can we expect from these? The irregulars of the Palestinian Division could be hidden anywhere. They may be wearing uniforms or they may be dressed like civilians. They will fire Kalashnikovs and machine guns, mortars and rocket launchers from houses and hedgerows. The tanks, artillery, and antitank gunners of the

7th Division will be manning prepared positions along the main road that leads from the Gaza Strip to El Arish.

El Arish is the Egyptian 7th Division's headquarters.

Our immediate objective is the road junction at Rafiah. From there the brigade will turn west toward El Arish. Then the real war will begin. At least that's what we're expecting. Our brigade command group consists of two tanks, the command half-track, the air force liaison jeep, and several others in support.

I'm in my own jeep with my driver, Joshua Gaist. A lieutenant is not supposed to rate a jeep and driver, but because my billet is that of a captain, an exception has been made. Suddenly the radio crackles:

"Screwdriver, this is Twenty. Where are you?"

Screwdriver is the call sign for any operations officer. Twenty is the brigade commander, Shmuel Gorodish.

"I'm coming in a minute!"

I tell Joshua to keep behind the brigade commander's half-track and be careful. All my stuff and his is in back—canned meat, cigarettes, underwear, sleeping gear. I don't want to lose this. We never know when we'll need it.

The 7th Armored Brigade's Recon Company crossing the border.

Lieutenant Eli Rikovitz is the twenty-year-old commander of the 3rd Platoon of the Recon Company of the 7th Armored Brigade:

We're moving at 20 kilometers per hour down a two-lane track that is off the edge of our maps. Plans have changed so frequently that the maps can't keep up with them.

Two days ago, our company was slated to cross the border near Kerem Shalom, leading the brigade's tanks straight north toward Rafiah Junction—a route that would have taken us head-on into heavy fortifications manned by Stalin tanks of the Egyptian 11th Brigade. Stalins are the World War II monsters with 122-millimeter cannons.

Last night those orders were changed. We have shifted positions to a featureless place called Gvulot Junction, where desert roads 232 and 222 meet, about seven kilometers from the border. Instead of going north, we are making a wide "right hook" to the east, bypassing the Stalin tanks.

This is no small relief.

The Israeli concept of armored warfare is blitzkrieg. Why hurl ourselves against the dug-in enemy? Go around. Hit him from a direction he doesn't expect, or bypass him entirely.

Our route now runs through a couple of small villages, then into the bigger town of Khan Younis. From there we will strike Rafiah Junction from the north, from behind. I have stuck a piece of white medical tape to my dashboard.

Abasan el-Kabir

Khan Younis

Rafiah Junction

Sheikh Zouaid

Jiradi Pass

El Arish

This is it. This is where we are going.

Zvika Kornblit is a twenty-year-old jeep commander in Eli Rikovitz's platoon:

We have been training for three weeks here, near the very spot where we will go to war, but now that we are moving, my legs are shaking. It is a serious thing, crossing a border. Your knees understand this.

We are not in Israel now. We are in Egypt.

Itzhak Kissilov is a nineteen-year-old trooper in Lieutenant Yossi Elgamis's 1st platoon:

Battalion 79 trails us. Patton tanks. We are leading them in our jeeps and half-track. A half-track is open-topped, like a farm truck. I'm up front with our lieutenant, Yossi Elgamis. The guys in back sit and stand. It's loud. My friend Pinhas Yaakov is shouting up to Yossi. "Is this war yet?"

"What?"

"When does it get to be war?"

Yaakov wants to know when he can start shooting. All around is nothing but fields of stubble and in front of us the impoverished village of Abasan el-Kabir.

Yossi shouts back: "When someone shoots at you, Yaakov, I give you permission to shoot back."

Menachem Shoval is a nineteen-year-old trooper in Lieutenant Eli Rikovitz's platoon:

In those days at the main recruitment center, certain elite outfits were allowed to set up their own recruiting tables, with veteran sergeants seated behind, trolling for "good fish." At the Recon table sat a sergeant named Moti Shoval—the same last name as mine. He asked my name. I said, "Shoval." He said, "You're in."

We laughed, but then I did get in.

In my jeep now are Lieutenant Shaul Groag, an outstanding navigator and fighter who commands all four jeeps in our platoon; David Cameron, an American, driving; and me, in the backseat with the radio.

When you are a simple soldier, which I am, you know nothing. We only have one map—Shaul has it—and it is 1:100,000. Terrible. Yet our job is to lead the tanks. We're supposed to know exactly where we are at all times.

Already we've passed through two Arab settlements. The civilians
have locked themselves indoors, out of harm's way.

Our officers have told us over and over that in a battle of breakthrough,
the first day is the most important. We must use these hours as if the survival of our nation depends upon it. We must break through the enemy at all costs.

Yosi Ben-Hanan, 7th Armored Brigade operations officer:

General Israel Tal commands our division. I will tell you a story about
him, to show you what kind of man he is.

A couple of years after the war I had left the army and gone to New
York City, to *Life* magazine. My dream was to become a photojournalist.
I had a letter of introduction from Bernice Schutzer, the widow of legendary *Life* photographer Paul Schutzer, who was killed in Gaza on the first
day of the Six Day War.

Sure enough, *Life* offered me a job. But when I left the editor's office
and got back out on the sidewalk, I started to have a bad feeling. I put a
dime in a pay phone and called home to Israel. I phoned Talik—this is
General Tal's nickname—collect.

He took the call.

"Yosi, what are you doing in a place like New York? *Life* magazine?
Are you crazy? You should not be taking pictures of others. They should
be taking pictures of you!"

Talik told me to come back to the army. This was where I belonged.
He would make a place for me where I could do what I did best.

"Yosi, I am going to give you the address of the Israeli Defense Mission
in Manhattan. It is thirty blocks south of where you are. Start walking
now. When you get to the mission, an envelope with a thousand dollars in
cash will be waiting for you. Use the money to fly home. Pay me back
when you can. Oh, and one last thing: Lay over for a few days in London
and Paris on the way. Have as much fun as you can, Yosi, because I am
going to work you very hard when you get home."

That is Talik.

Yesterday he gave a speech to the officers of the division. This was not
General Patton mounting to a big stage. Talik is a little guy, but when he stands
in front of a tank you know he can take it apart blindfolded and put it back
together piece by piece. Tal has commanded the armored corps since 1964.

Talik speaks. What he says will be repeated thousands of times over the ensuing years. His speech will be quoted and excerpted in military journals and academies of war around the world.

Tal tells us that our battle plans are excellent and that he feels confident that we know them down to the smallest detail. But tomorrow when the war begins, those fine plans will fly out the window. Nothing, Tal says, will happen according to those plans. The lines of assault will change; the direction of the enemy's movements will change. Everything will change. This is the way things work in war. But, Talik says:

> One thing must take place exactly as in the plans: the principle
> upon which these plans were made. Every man will attack.
> Every unit will push forward as fast as it can. Pay no attention
> to your flanks. Give no thought to resupply. If you lose nine
> tanks out of ten, keep advancing with the tenth. Stop for
> nothing.

Other nations can afford to lose the first battle, Talik says, and still recover and carry the day. This will not work for Israel. If we fail in the

General Israel Tal.

initial clash, our nation will be overrun. The fate of the war on the ground rests with what we in our division do tomorrow. The survival of our country depends upon us.

Now I'm going to tell you something very severe. En brera. No alternative. The battle tomorrow will be life and death. Each man will assault to the end, taking no account of casualties. There will be no retreat. No halt, no hesitation. Only forward assault.

Talik points on the map to El Arish, the main base of the Egyptian 7th Division. Tomorrow, he says, when things go wrong, remember this only:

El Arish.

"Keep moving toward El Arish. Get there at any cost. I will meet you there and shake your hand."

Dov "Dubi" Tevet is a nineteen-year-old trooper in Eli Rikovitz's Recon platoon:

In the days preparing ourselves for the war, Eli and I ran many scouting surveys along the border, picking crossing points for the tanks. Under those early plans, the tanks needed us in Recon because the penetration points were on side roads and dirt tracks. The tanks would get lost without our jeeps to lead them.

But now that the real war has started, the tanks are advancing on main roads. They don't need us for that.

But our Recon jeeps are still driving out front. It's insane. A jeep is a sitting duck, with the men riding in it exposed to fire from all directions.

Boaz Amitai is a twenty-year-old second lieutenant, second-in-command of the 1st Platoon of the Recon Company under Lieutenant Yossi Elgamis. He commands the platoon's four jeeps:

The first village we come to after crossing the border is Abasan el-Kabir. My jeep is up front, with our three others following. We haven't taken any fire yet. In fact, Arab kids on the way have been waving to us.

My driver, Uri Zand, has a transistor radio. We have heard Dayan announcing the onset of hostilities. We're hearing music. Maybe war is not so bad.

Up ahead: An irrigation ditch blocks the road, a big one—too deep and too wide for the jeeps to cross.

"Boaz!" Yossi Elgamis, our platoon commander, pulls alongside in his half-track. "Find a way around for the jeeps. I'll take the lead."

Yossi goes ahead. With its caterpillar treads, a half-track takes such obstacles in stride.

Of all the great guys in our company, Yossi is the best. When we were training at Camp Nathan before the war, he and Eli Rikovitz and I used to go into Beersheba after the day's drills to a place named Morris's for steaks and Nesher beer in the big liter bottles. Yossi made us take off our lieutenants' insignia so we wouldn't spoil the fun for the sergeants and privates.

Captain Ori Orr is the twenty-eight-year-old commander of the Recon Company. He has three platoons under him— Yossi Elgamis's, Eli Rikovitz's, and Amos Ayalon's:

Your mind starts working feverishly when the order comes, "Go." You are the commander. You feel everyone's eyes on the back of your neck.

My vehicle is what they call a command half-track. The command vehicle is the one with multiple radios. We have three. An operator mans these sets, but I can hear all channels, too. I have a microphone and a headset, which I don't wear because I want to hear what is happening all around as well. One radio links us to the tank battalion we are leading. Another connects us to brigade commander Shmuel Gorodish via his operations officer, Yosi Ben-Hanan. The third, a surplus American GRC, puts me through to my own guys in their jeeps and half-tracks.

The mission of the Recon Company is to locate the enemy and to lead the tanks. We are their eyes and ears. But in a fast-moving advance, if we run into resistance, Recon can wind up biting off more than it can chew.

We're up front. If we run into enemy fire, will we delay the advance by sending back for heavier forces? Sometimes you can't. You have to attack. But our Recon vehicles have no armor, no heavy weapons. We are not shock troops.

I am thinking this when I hear over the company channel, "Commander down! Commander down!"

Boaz Amitai, second-in-command of 1st Platoon:

Yossi Elgamis has been shot in the head. A burst of machine-gun fire. Just as Yossi's half-track entered the village of Abasan el-Kabir.

I'm in my jeep. Bullets are striking the sand all around me. It's like a movie. The sense of unreality is hypnotic. Rifle and machine-gun fire deafens us, but it doesn't seem real. I can't assimilate it.

It occurs to me, with lethargic slowness, that I am second-in-command of this platoon. Our leader has been shot. I have to take action.

At once I snap awake.

Yossi's driver has reversed out of the kill zone. The half-track has found cover behind a building. My jeep speeds up. Fire continues, close and intense. I approach from the rear of the half-track. Yossi lies on his back in the vehicle bed with Itzhak Kissilov and Shmuel Beilis from Yossi's half-track command team supporting him.

One look is all it takes to know Yossi's wound is very bad. I am thinking of the ditch at the entrance to the village. Because of that ditch, Yossi went ahead. Otherwise it would be me who was in line for that bullet.

Lieutenant Yossi Elgamis.

I call to Kissilov: "Where is the fire coming from?"

"What?" When Yossi was shot, he fell on top of Kissilov. I can see Yossi's blood all over the front of Kissilov's uniform.

"The shooter that got Yossi! Where is he?"

Kissilov points ahead. A mosque. A minaret tower.

We have three tanks with us. We are not supposed to fire on civilian buildings. I get on the radio to the tanks' commander.

"See that tower?"

He says yes.

"Blow it down."

He does.

All of a sudden, war has become real.

Yosi Ben-Hanan, 7th Brigade operations officer:

Over the radio, we're hearing that Yossi Elgamis has been killed. He is a friend and a critical component of the assault—Ori Orr's deputy, second-in-command of the entire Recon Company.

A terrible thing has happened here, too. A few thousand meters over the border, our column of tanks and trucks has come under mortar fire. Vehicles began hitting their brakes. Joshua, my jeep driver, was run over by the tank behind him.

He has been killed.

I'm at the front of the column with Shmuel Gorodish, the brigade commander, when this happens. My post is on Gorodish's left in the command half-track. We hear frantic cries over the radio. A jeep has caught fire. Looking back, I can see the smoke.

I realize it is my jeep. It is Joshua.

This, I realize with sudden and searing pain, is how things happen in war. Dear friends are lost not only to hostile fire, as with Yossi Elgamis, but to mishaps, accidents, crazy stuff that has nothing to do with shooting the enemy or being shot by him.

What will I tell Joshua's mother?

There is no time to feel or to think. A thousand other urgencies press on me. "Where is Kahalani?" Gorodish asks. "Has Battalion 79 reached Khan Younis?"

It's my job as operations officer to know where every unit is, to feed their reports to Gorodish, and to relay his orders to them.

*Lieutenant Avigdor Kahalani is a tank company com-
mander in Battalion 79 of the 7th Armored Brigade:*

I'm in the lead tank on a back road approaching Khan Younis, following Yossi Elgamis's Recon team. Enemy machine-gun fire is making chips
of paint dance off my hull and turret. Suddenly the road narrows, hem-
ming our column between massive prickly pear hedges. I order my driver
to break out. As he does, I hear a deafening roar and the tank bellies to a
stop. A tread chain has come off. We have thrown a track.

A dozen tanks jam up behind me. What a balagan! I am mortified with
shame.

I leave my tank and take the tank behind me. Two kilometers later,
outside Khan Younis, the same thing happens. The second tank has blown
a chain, too! I am beside myself.

I take a third tank—my deputy Daniel Tzefoni's.

I'm so furious I could chew through a steel tread. I want to be first into
Khan Younis. My company must break through before all others! I am
cursing in Arabic (Hebrew is notoriously deficient in profanity), using
words even I didn't know I knew.

*Lieutenant Eli Rikovitz commands the Recon Company's
3rd Platoon:*

The idea of attacking Khan Younis is not to capture the place. All we
want is to run a right hook and loop back south to attack Rafiah Junction
from the rear. From Rafiah, the main road leads to El Arish.

El Arish is our target.

Khan Younis is only a bump on the way.

Lieutenant Avigdor Kahalani, tank company commander:

We have entered Khan Younis. Machine-gun and antitank fire is coming from everywhere.

Tanks are not meant to fight in an urban setting without armored
infantry to spot the enemy and make them keep their heads down.
To protect ourselves we are firing our machine guns over each other's
flanks.

Suddenly in the center of town an Israeli tank materializes on my right, with other tanks of our "C" Company right behind. The platoon commander tells me his company commander, Benzi Carmeli, has been shot. Benzi is in the tank now, gravely wounded.

I must take the lead with my "B" Company.

Eli Rikovitz, Recon platoon commander:

From the outskirts I can see the Patton tanks of Battalion 79 entering Khan Younis and vanishing amid clouds of smoke and dust. I don't know why they're going in. The town means nothing.

I turn left, bypassing Khan Younis. My platoon is leading the tanks— British-built Centurions—of Battalion 82. The commander of Battalion 82 is Gabi Amir. With him is the deputy brigade commander, Lieutenant Colonel Barouch Harel, nicknamed "Pinko." Pinko is in the lead, right behind me. Over the radio I'm telling him to follow my platoon's dust.

Looking back, I must say it is a hell of a sight.

Behind me in the clear morning air are at least thirty Centurion tanks. The column stretches back half a kilometer. It is one giant cloud of alkali. Every time the dust parts, another two tanks emerge. In between are various command cars, jeeps and half-tracks, and intelligence and air liaison vehicles, all bristling with antennas. In the lead, my platoon has four jeeps, two half-tracks, and three tanks. As we pull away from Khan Younis, another half dozen Pattons from Battalion 79 rumble into view and roll into the town.

A big part of war is spectacle. What are these Egyptians thinking when they see all this armor steaming directly at them? Even I am impressed.

Gabi Gazit is a twenty-year-old trooper in the Recon platoon of Lieutenant Amos Ayalon:

My half-track is rolling beside the CJ-5 jeep driven by my friend Benzi Nissenbaum. We're two thousand meters across the border now and starting to hear mortars and small-arms fire. Benzi's jeep looks a lot safer to me than this big, rumbling half-track.

"Benzi, let's trade vehicles!"

He grins and shows me his middle finger.

There are eleven of us in this half-track. The first thing that soldiers

A column of half-tracks in the desert.

do, boarding such a vehicle, is to tie their haversacks, bedding, and web gear over the kit rails that run along both flanks. They do this to add a layer of protection against enemy fire. There's a joke about a half-track's armor. It doesn't stop bullets coming in; it just lets them rattle around inside for a while. With the packs and the gear, the men hope, they will be shielded at least from flame or shrapnel. Every little bit helps.

Our half-tracks are U.S. Army M-3s from World War II. Good vehicles, tough and reliable. A half-track has tires up front and a lightweight caterpillar track in back. It will cross sand and gravel and, with a skilled driver, can zip along wadis—dry riverbeds in the desert—as if they were paved roads. On asphalt, a half-track will do 50 kilometers per hour. In the desert, that is supersonic. Troops on foot in the desert are dead troops. They can do nothing except wait to die.

Half-tracks unfortunately are targets. That's why I want to trade with Benzi.

His speedy little jeep looks awfully good to me.

Avigdor Kahalani, tank company commander:

In the center of Khan Younis, the road forks. Where's the road to Rafiah? I'm navigating on instinct. I have no map. I forgot it in the first tank.

Then I remember the railroad—the old Ottoman line that runs from Alexandria to Damascus. The railroad runs through El Arish. If we can find the tracks, we can follow them out of this hellish town.

A tank turret is high up. You can see. I spot date palms and a line of dunes indicating the Mediterranean coast. Telegraph poles! Train tracks!

I order my driver forward.

We're back in business.

Eli Rikovitz, Recon platoon commander:

Our objective now is Rafiah Junction. We have run a right hook via Khan Younis, avoiding the Egyptian Stalin tanks to the south. We are coming at Rafiah from the north. My headset crackles:

"Five, this is Twenty. Where are you?"

"Twenty" is Shmuel Gorodish, the brigade commander. "Five" means our Recon Company commander. That's Ori.

Gorodish gives the map code for the UN camp north of Rafiah Junction. He is almost there, he says. Ori answers that he is coming fast.

Ori Orr, Recon Company commander:

Rafiah Junction is a crossroads built up into what the manuals call a "fortified encampment." How fortified, we don't know. There's a ridge that commands the main road west to El Arish. If I were the Egyptians, I would defend this with everything I've got.

We know the Egyptian 7th Division is present, but Intelligence can't tell us where because the enemy shifts positions every night after dark. We know the foe has two infantry brigades. He has tanks. He has artillery. He has antitank guns.

The antitank guns are more dangerous to us in Recon than the tanks because they won't be saving their ammunition to take on heavier targets. They would love to nail our jeeps and half-tracks. The antitank guns will be dug in low, only a foot or two off the ground, in hedges of castor bushes and prickly pear. We have trained to spot them. It's impossible. Not even their muzzles will be visible.

Boaz Amitai now leads the Recon Company's 1st Platoon:

I can hear Ori and Eli over the company channel. They have reached the UN camp on the way to Rafiah Junction. Gorodish, the brigade commander, is already there. This is why they call him "Young Rommel." If he were any farther forward, he would be shaking hands with the Egyptians.

The camp is where a detachment of UN peacekeepers stayed before Nasser kicked them out on May 17. The site is directly north of Rafiah Junction. Gorodish has pulled up at this vantage to scope the place before he advances into the open.

Ori Orr, Recon Company commander:

We are peering through binoculars at Rafiah Junction—me, Gorodish, Ben-Hanan, others. I've got Eli on the company channel. He's not far, coming from Khan Younis, leading Pinko and tanks of Battalion 82.

Gorodish's vehicles have pulled up beneath the water tower of the abandoned UN camp. On the radio Eli confirms the report that Yossi

Elgamis has been shot in the head entering Abasan el-Kabir. Eli has this as fact from Boaz Amitai, who has taken over Yossi's platoon. Eli doesn't know if Yossi is dead or wounded.

I have no time to think about it.

The situation before us is this:

Our tanks are behind us, some close, others strung out over kilometers. It will take half an hour to bring them up into an attack formation, issue orders, assault the junction.

Most of my Recon Company is here.

We are ready now.

Do we wait for the big guns or go forward now with our peashooters?

I know Gorodish well. I served under him as a tank company commander before I took over the Recon Company. Gorodish is thirty-seven, impatient, aggressive, without fear. He is from a religious family, where all that zeal has gone into ambition. He would attack hell itself if he could get clearance.

"What do you think, Ori?"

Through the binoculars I can make out castor bushes and low scrub-covered dunes. Dark lines could be trenches, but we're too far away to tell. I can see the ridge that commands the main road to El Arish. A division could be hidden on it or behind it. Beside Gorodish, Yosi Ben-Hanan is on the radio to tank Battalion 79. The lead company is Avigdor Kahalani's. I know him well, too. He is young and even more aggressive than Gorodish. But his tanks are still a good distance away.

With another brigade commander, you might say wait. Not with Gorodish. Momentum is everything. We must break through.

"Let's go."

Avigdor Kahalani, tank company commander:

My tank is the first of Battalion 79 to reach the abandoned UN camp north of Rafiah Junction. Some tanks of Battalion 82 are already there. I can hear antitank guns and mortars ahead, an all-out battle. I see brigade commander Gorodish and his operations officer, my friend Yosi Ben-Hanan, with the command vehicles beneath the water tower.

I'm shouting from the open hatch of my turret, "Where are the Egyptians?"

Gorodish gestures with both arms. He's telling me that the enemy trenches run north-south, on the ridge at the road junction to the southwest.

I respond by gesturing the same way. I understand.

I signal my tanks—I have twenty or more by now—to follow me into the attack.

I understand that Ori Orr's Recon troopers are ahead of us, pushing south toward Rafiah Junction.

Photo by Yosi Ben-Hanan.

Lieutenant Avigdor Kahalani gesturing to Colonel Shmuel Gorodish, approaching Rafiah Junction. In the lower turret is Kahalani's friend and deputy company commander Lieutenant Daniel Tzefoni. He will be killed several hours later on the way to the Jiradi Pass.

30.

"FOLLOW ME!"

Eli Rikovitz, Recon platoon commander:

I'm in my command half-track, pushing west from the UN compound into an area of dunes. Behind me are the tanks of Battalion 82. In thirty seconds we'll turn south and advance to assault Rafiah Junction. Ori Orr and Amos Ayalon's platoon will attack parallel to us, but on the paved road from the UN compound.

I've got Pinko's command half-track on the radio. "We're turning south," I tell him. "Turn behind us."

But he doesn't turn.

The tanks keep going west, toward the sea, away from the junction! What the hell? I have no time to screw with them.

We turn without them.

Gabi Gazit is a Recon trooper in Lieutenant Amos Ayalon's platoon:

I'm in the back of the lead half-track on the paved road. There are eleven of us, swaying and bouncing. Mortar rounds are coming in, a barrage targeting the road. Rafiah Junction is ahead somewhere but we can't see it yet.

My friend Eliyahu Goshen stands on my right in the back of the half-track. A big guy, like a tree. The mortar rounds start dropping closer. I hate to admit such a thing but I edge a little nearer to this tree.

Ori Orr, Recon Company commander:

Amos Ayalon leads our 2nd Platoon from his command half-track. I command the company from my own half-track, right behind him. We're on the paved road that leads to the junction. Eli's platoon is about a kilometer to the right, in the dunes. His platoon and ours will attack in parallel. But attack what?

Menachem Shoval, Recon trooper in Eli Rikovitz's platoon:

Our four jeeps are bogging down in the dunes. David Cameron may have gotten his license in America, but he is a lousy driver. Shaul Groag, our lieutenant, tells me to get Eli on the radio and tell him we're all balled up.

Eli Rikovitz, Recon platoon commander:

I've got three half-tracks and three tanks. We're in the dunes, still more than a kilometer north of Rafiah Junction. Battalion 82's tanks have vanished completely.

Shaul Groag commands our platoon's four jeeps. He radios me to report that all four are bogged in the dunes.

"Shaul, take the jeeps back to the paved road. Follow Ori. I'll meet you at the junction."

Moki Yishby is a nineteen-year-old trooper in Amos Ayalon's Recon platoon:

I'm driving a jeep. Yaakov Yarkoni is my lieutenant, a great guy and a good friend, beside me in the commander's seat. He commands all four jeeps in our platoon. We hear gunfire ahead.

I glance to Yarkoni. We're on the road behind Ori Orr—dunes on the right, low scrub on the left.

Yarkoni gestures ahead. "Go!"

Eli Rikovitz, Recon platoon commander:

We're under fire from Egyptian trenches on the right. I'm returning fire with the .50-caliber machine gun when our half-track's right front tire hits a mine. The world becomes bright yellow; I go deaf. The floorboard kicks me upward like a diving board. The half-track rises straight up, hangs for a moment, then crashes straight down on its front wheels.

All seven of us are flung out onto the sand. Miraculously, no one is hurt.

Machine-gun and rifle fire is coming from ahead and from the right.

I shout to my men, "Find another vehicle and keep going!"

I sprint rearward, under fire, toward one of our tanks. A tank has radios. I must have radios to command the platoon and to keep in contact with Ori.

Dubi Tevet, Recon trooper in Eli Rikovitz's platoon:

I'm in the dunes in one of Shaul Groag's four jeeps. We're trying to get back to the paved road to join the attack behind Ori and Amos's platoon. The enemy has seen us and is opening up with everything they've got.

I can see Israeli tanks on the right. One is hit and burning. As I look, a second tank takes a hit. Flames leap from its engine compartment; hatches pop open, the crew piles out.

Shaul waves our four jeeps forward. We have to help the men in the tanks.

Moki Yishby, Recon jeep commander in Amos Ayalon's platoon:

Are we attacking? If we are, it is becoming a serious balagan. I'm driving Yarkoni's jeep. Shells are falling all around us. We stick to the paved road, following Ori and Amos.

We still can't see the enemy.

"Straight, Moki!" Yarkoni, beside me, points ahead. "There!"

Ori Orr, Recon Company commander:

Eli's half-track has hit a mine. So has another half-track. I don't know this yet. Eli's platoon is attacking parallel to ours, on the right, in the dunes. I'm on the paved road, moving fast toward the junction.

The Egyptians' fire from the right is getting heavier and heavier. We're catching hell from their dug-in tanks, from mortars and machine guns, and, most lethal of all, from their antitank guns. If we keep going on the road, we're all dead.

There's no way but to assault the trenches. I give the order:

"Turn right and attack!"

My half-track leads. We push twenty meters into the dunes and we hit a mine, too! The half-track doesn't blow up; it just tilts onto its side, grinds into the sand, and spills all seven of us out, amazingly unhurt. I leap onto Amos's half-track and keep leading the assault.

No way can we slow down the attack.

Gabi Gazit, Recon trooper:

I'm in the third half-track, close behind Ori's and Amos's. Mortar shells are falling. My friend Benzi Nissenbaum is driving his jeep a few meters behind us when a shell explodes beside him. Benzi cries out, "Ay!" From my position atop the half-track I can see a red stain on his trouser leg. We stop the half-track.

"Benzi, trade places with me! The medic is here in the half-track—he'll take care of your wound."

There are eleven of us in the half-track, including our lieutenant, Shlomo Kenigsbuch, and my big, tall friend Eliyahu Goshen.

Benzi won't leave his jeep. He feels safer there than in the big-target half-track. We're negotiating, Benzi and I, across the space between the vehicles.

"Send the medic to me," Benzi insists.

"I promise I'll give the jeep back."

"Swear to me, Gabi. I'm not getting into that half-track and have you run off with the jeep."

"Benzi, I swear. Just switch till you're treated."

Benzi agrees. He crosses to the half-track packed with ten of our friends. I scamper to the jeep that had been Benzi's and pull away, just a few meters.

That instant, an Egyptian shell hits the half-track.

Ori Orr, Recon Company commander:

Over the radio I hear that one of our half-tracks has been hit. Half-tracks run on gasoline. The men are sitting on top of the tanks of fuel.

We can't stop now under heavy fire.

There is no alternative but to attack and keep attacking.

Moki Yishby, Recon jeep commander:

I hear Ori on the radio: "Turn right and attack." We do. Yarkoni in the commander's seat is pointing ahead, shouting, "Go!" I see a trench. Dark shapes peek from it.

We start up a dune. It feels like the whole world is shooting at us.

Yarkoni leaps out of the jeep and charges at the trenches. We are so close now we can see the Egyptians' faces. Yarkoni's Uzi is firing but everything is so loud you can't hear.

Suddenly Yarkoni goes down.

Ori Orr, Recon Company commander:

As commander you can shout "Follow me!" and charge at the enemy, but how do you know your men will follow?

The answer is that you don't even think such a thought. You know they will. They are bound to you tighter than brothers, stronger than blood.

Eli Rikovitz, Recon platoon commander:

To say we are brave to charge into enemy fire is nonsense. If we stay where we are, we will all be killed. We must get at the enemy. There is no other choice.

Moki Yishby, Recon jeep commander:

Yarkoni is the first one into the trenches. He gets shot by a wounded Egyptian who had been lying facedown and then sprang up.

At the other end, Eli and his platoon are racing forward on foot. There is no way to describe such a sight. Up and down the enemy trench line, our guys are running, firing, leaping down.

My platoon commander, Amos Ayalon, has jumped down from his half-track. He races to Yarkoni. "Help me, Moki!" Together we lift Yarkoni onto a stretcher and set the stretcher into the mounts on the jeep. Bullets are chewing into the dashboard.

I race in the jeep across the dunes, steering with one hand and hanging on to Yarkoni and the stretcher with the other. A shell lands beside us; the stretcher goes flying. I stop and somehow get it first, then Yarkoni, back

Lieutenant Yaakov Yarkoni.

onto the jeep. Half of the stretcher extends forward over the hood; the other half is beside me, above the seat.

Somehow we reach the paved road. Yarkoni is begging for water. I spot a jerry can on the ground and jump from my seat to grab it. Bullets blow it out of my hand.

I spring back into the jeep. "Yarkoni, are you all right?"

His eyes are still open. He's making a sound like, "Ay, ay."

Years later, when Prime Minister Rabin was shot by an assassin, his driver said on TV that Rabin was making that same desperate sighing sound. When I heard that, it took me back to Yarkoni.

Zvika Kornblit, Recon jeep commander:

I'm with the first vehicles to reach Lieutenant Kenigsbuch's half-track. God, what a sight! A pile of corpses that once were our friends. They are burned black, on fire, smoking.

My friend Avraham Galenti, the driver of the half-track, is trying to help Kenigsbuch out of the vehicle. Kenigsbuch is still alive. He pleads with Galenti, "Kill me! I can't go on living the way I look!" The skin of his arms is hanging down like a pair of black curtains.

Galenti cries, "No one is killing anybody! I'm getting you out of here!"

Eli Rikovitz, Recon platoon commander:

We're in the Egyptian trenches, running and shooting down the line, when we hear fire from .50-caliber Brownings and 105-millimeter cannons behind us.

It's the Centurion tanks of Battalion 82.
They have finally decided to join the party.

Ori Orr, Recon Company commander:

The Egyptians are running away. They fling their rifles, haul themselves out of the trenches, and beat it out of there as fast as they can.

From the junction we can hear the crack and scream of our Centuri-

Moki Yishby.

ons' cannons. Their 105-millimeter main guns sound distinctly different from the Patton tanks' 90-millimeter cannons.

Moki Yishby, Recon jeep commander:

I arrive at our blown-up half-track. The horror is beyond anything I could have imagined.

Corpses sprawl around the blackened vehicle. My good friend Eliyahu Goshen is lying on his back on the road. A huge guy, like a horse. He has shrunk down to four feet. The fire has consumed him. He has become the size of a child. My great friend is lying there naked, on the road, black, totally burned up.

Half-tracks run on gasoline. The vehicle has gone up like a bomb, incinerating all our guys in it.

Dubi Tevet, Recon trooper:

You can carry only one man in a jeep if he's seriously burned, two if they're okay. The field hospital is not too far back. I see Moki speed past in his jeep, carrying Yarkoni and two others.

Moki Yishby, Recon jeep commander:

We get Lieutenant Kenigsbuch into my jeep. His shirt is off. The skin is hanging from his arms in sheets. He is screaming such screams. I never knew a human being could cry out in such agony. His soul is burned.

I load the jeep with two more wounded friends.

At the field hospital I see another trooper from the half-track, Shmuel Hacham, whom we call "Borvil." Every centimeter of his body is burned, but he is still alive. I can recognize him. He is one of my best friends.

I sit beside Borvil's stretcher. He says, "I am so ugly now, Moki, not even birds will look at me."

Ori Orr, Recon Company commander:

Let no one call these Egyptians cowards. Who knows what their officers have told them? They had believed their positions unassailable behind minefields. Now suddenly these crazy Jews are racing at them on foot, firing and jumping from their armored vehicles down into the trenches.

Eli Rikovitz, Recon platoon commander:

The Egyptian tanks are dug in behind the infantry trenches. Their crews are abandoning them. We pull up and stare, astonished, as the enemy soldiers flee on foot, west toward Sheikh Zouaid, the next village.

When the figures for the fight at Rafiah Junction are finally tallied up, the Egyptians will have lost forty tanks and two thousand men dead or wounded.

Lieutenant Boaz Amitai now commands the Recon Company's 1st Platoon:

Our platoon, Yossi Elgamis's, arrives at Rafiah Junction not long after the fight. My friend Shaul Groag, who is Eli's first lieutenant, is rounding everybody up. He's wearing an Australian bush hat that he has found somewhere. People have scattered in all directions, some aiding the wounded, others just out of their minds with grief and anguish.

I see Gabi Gazit being evacuated, his face smashed to a pulp and blood soaking one of his trouser legs. "His jeep hit a mine," somebody says.

Shaul is shouting to me to rally at the junction.

Two friends, Shlomo Oren and Haim Fenikel, have saved Gabi. Sergeant Fenikel will himself be killed only a few minutes later.

Fenikel had been shot during the assault and picked up for evacuation by a support vehicle. Suddenly the crew realized they were in the middle of a minefield. Fenikel dismounted, wounded as he was, and cleared a path all the way back to the road. Just as he returned to the vehicle, a shell hit it dead-on.

For this my friend was awarded posthumously the Itur HaOz, Israel's second-highest decoration for valor.

Haim Fenikel.

Forty-five years later, I see his face as clearly as I did then.

Menachem Shoval, Recon trooper:

My jeep is one of the last two up after the fight. The first thing I see is Ori's half-track—recognizable by its commander's flag—on its side with its burned treads. Ori and Eli are reorganizing the company at the junction. The tanks of Battalion 82 are rolling past, fast, heading west on the road to Sheikh Zouaid and El Arish.

Menachem Shoval.

We pass the other half-track, the one that Kenigsbuch and all our other friends had been in.

We don't ask who is wounded and who is dead. We don't want to know. Seeing such a sight, you can't let yourself think. You must continue. You have a mission; you have to go on.

Lieutenant Boaz Amitai, Recon platoon commander:

When we passed Kenigsbuch's half-track, I didn't even realize it was one of ours. The metal had been consumed. Nothing that was inside that inferno could have survived.

Ori Orr, Recon Company commander:

We have lost many men and vehicles. I don't know the count, and I have no time to think about it. Our mission is to lead. We must keep moving.

I reconfigure the three platoons into two. A process that would take ten minutes in training takes only seconds now. "You go here, you go there."

The Centurion tanks of Battalion 82 are speeding past us toward the next village, Sheikh Zouaid. We must catch up with them and get ahead.

Our mission is to lead.

Eli Rikovitz, Recon platoon commander:

In such a moment, the part of yourself that feels grief must be switched off. You are thinking only of the mission. The tanks of Battalion 82 have passed us. It is our job to lead them. We must catch up and do our job. The tanks need us; the mission needs us.

It is like this for all soldiers in all wars. It must be, or they could not keep on.

31.

THE WILDERNESS OF ZIN

"Cheetah" Cohen commands Squadron 124, twenty-four Sikorsky S-58 helicopters:

I'm at Ashkelon on the coast south of Tel Aviv when an emergency call comes in: "Mass casualties near Gaza City." I get on the air, asking which of my pilots is nearest the evacuation site. Reuven Levy answers: "Citrus Leader, this is Lemon Leader. I can go."

My younger brother Nechemiah is somewhere near the Gaza Strip, a captain with the 35th Paratroop Brigade, but it does not occur to me that this medevac call could be for him. He is too good a soldier. Too smart. Nothing has touched Nechemiah. Nothing can.

What has happened, though I will not know this for another six days, is that my brother's half-track has been hit by a 122-millimeter shell from a Stalin tank. He is up front in the lead vehicle of a force of forty half-tracks. The Stalins are hidden in orange groves. Thirty-six paratroopers are killed and sixty wounded in this action, the single worst casualty evacuation emergency in IDF history.

My brother has been killed instantly. My pilot, Reuven Levy, arriving to evacuate the wounded, has been ordered by an officer on-site to tell me nothing about Nechemiah's death.

I am Israel's primary helicopter squadron commander.

I am needed.

Danny Matt commands the 80th Paratroop Brigade, part of General Sharon's division:

Our division is a hundred kilometers south of General Tal's. Tal's forces have been in action since this morning; ours are preparing urgently to attack tonight. We will go against the Egyptian 2nd Infantry Division—80 guns, 90 tanks, 16,000 men.

Where are my helicopters? Cheetah Cohen's squadron of Sikorsky S-58s is slated to carry my paratroopers into the fight tonight.

Where are they?

My paratroopers are brought up to the assembly area in civilian buses. Their boots have not yet touched the ground and already we're in a crisis.

The landing zone we have planned to use tonight has become untenable. Bad luck: A formation of Egyptian tanks has shifted position and now occupies an adjacent sector.

I will not wait for General Sharon to provide an alternative plan.

I will draw up my own now.

Sharon and I go back to 1953 and earlier. We know each other so well we speak in a kind of code. He is, in my opinion, the greatest field commander the IDF has ever produced or ever will produce. What he performs this night at Um Katef and Abu Agheila will be called "a masterpiece of war."

My family is from Poland. In World War I, my father served in the army of the Austro-Hungarian Empire. He got out to Palestine in the 1930s. He lost his father and brothers, seventy family members, in the death camps.

Before the Six Day War, I was asked by a journalist if I thought Israel would win. I said yes. The reporter asked why. "Because if we lose, what our enemies will do to us will make Auschwitz look like a summer resort."

When I grew up, if you had finished elementary school, you were considered an educated person. Tenth grade meant highly educated. If you had graduated from high school, you were an intellectual.

In our generation, you began to make your way at fourteen. You joined the Haganah or the Palmach or the Lehi. You carried messages or smuggled pistols and explosives. The Haganah sent me to serve in the British Army, the Jewish Brigade, in World War II. I have fought in every war of Israel from 1946 to 1982. In my body are over a meter of surgical stitches from wounds suffered in combat.

This night, June 5, 1967, my men and I will undertake an operation that no force, including the Americans in Vietnam, has ever attempted: the insertion of a paratroop brigade by helicopter, in darkness, behind enemy lines.

Yael Dayan is also with General Sharon's division on the Egyptian border:

When Sharon speaks to the paratroopers, his voice alters. These are his boys. He knows the first name of almost every man. He himself still wears the red boots of the airborne units, though he now commands an armored division.

The advance to the border has paused while buses bring up the infantry and the paratroopers. The column extends back for miles. I donate a cigarette to a sergeant, who asks me if there is any rivalry between Sharon and my father. What can I tell him? They are the two commanders who beyond all others have shaped the doctrine and fighting spirit of the Israel Defense Forces. But there can be no competition between them. Arik and my father are almost a generation apart. When Sharon was a major, Dayan was chief of staff. What they share as military professionals and as men (and what unites them with virtually every officer in the army) is an idea of the land.

When for thousands of years the Jewish people were separated from this land, they yearned for it. Their prayers invoked it. The land dwelt within them, in dreams and songs and in a hunger so deep that no words existed to convey it. Their rabbis and scholars prepared the people emotionally and morally to return to this land, but when the nation had achieved this repatriation in fact, the reality was for many too much to take in. They preferred the dream. Even our anthem, "Hatikva"—The Hope—sings not of realities achieved but of visions hoped for in the future.

This is not my father's way. It is not Sharon's. Nor are they unique in this regard. For their two generations, and mine as well, the land is here, now; it is ours and always has been. Beside the road from Tel Aviv to Jerusalem lies a melon field in which Sharon nearly bled to death in 1948, shot through the hip by a Jordanian gunner. From those slopes can be seen the Ayalon Valley

Sun, stand still over Gibeon,
Moon, stop over Ayalon Valley

where Joshua defeated the Amorites 3,500 years ago. In Sharon's mind this victory happened yesterday. He is fighting the same battle today. No interval of centuries separates the tanks of the Egyptians, who would grind our nation to dust, from the war chariots of the Pharaohs, from whom the children of Israel escaped, over this same wilderness through which our armored columns advance this noon, east to west instead of west to east.

My father has spearpoints and pottery shards from the era of Joshua, dug from those very battlegrounds. Yesterday I drove forward with the jeeps of the Reconnaissance Company to the site of Kadesh Barnea. Upon those slopes the Hebrew tribes encamped in their flight across the wilderness of Zin. From here Moses sent spies into the land of Canaan. Here the Edomite king refused Moses's request for passage. Here the god of the Israelites ordained the southern border of the lands he pledged to the children of Abraham. And here He told Moses that he would not be permitted to enter the Promised Land.

> Because ye have believed me not, to sanctify me in the eyes
> of the children of Israel, therefore ye shall not bring this
> congregation into the land which I have given them.

I am not religious. Neither is Sharon. My father has never even had a bar mitzvah. But he and Sharon have stepped straight from that era of patriarchal scripture, as have Gavish and Tal and Yoffe, and thousands of others in this army.

They are farmers and warriors. Not children of the book but of the plow and the sword. War has called them from their families and from the land. But to the land they will return with joy. When my father dies, we will not bury him beneath some monument or national tomb, but at home on the hill above Nahalal, which is a small village even today, where he grew and learned to read and ride and shoot.

32.

CASUALTIES OF WAR

The first casualty reports have come in from the Gaza Strip. Do I read them? What commander does not? On a list of twenty names, I will know ten.

> *Moshe Dayan, minister of defense, directs the conduct of the war.*

One name in particular breaks my heart.

Nechemiah Cohen, killed in the first hour attacking dug-in Stalin tanks somewhere between Kerem Shalom and Rafiah Junction.

Nechemiah is the most decorated soldier in the Israeli Army. Only twenty-four years old, he had been temporarily transferred from the elite Sayeret Matkal and given command of a company in Raful Eitan's 35th Paratroop Brigade to prepare him to lead larger formations when "the Unit" expands to battalion or possibly brigade size. Nechemiah's brother Uri is a much decorated armor officer. The eldest of the family, Cheetah, is the best helicopter commander in Israel.

A second, happier report follows. This is the tally of enemy planes destroyed in the first two waves of air attacks.

Eleven Egyptian bases have been hit in the first strike. IAF squadrons have destroyed 198 enemy aircraft, 9 in aerial combat, the remainder on the ground. Six airfields were put out of action, sixteen radar stations destroyed. Our losses: eight planes, five pilots killed, two captured, three injured.

Our second wave has destroyed 107 more Egyptian planes at fourteen fields. Before noon Israeli warplanes will have wiped out 286 of Egypt's 420 combat aircraft and put out of commission thirteen airfields and twenty-three radar and antiaircraft sites. By day's end, the toll of enemy aircraft destroyed—including planes from Jordan, Syria, and Iraq—will reach 402.

The weight of one great stone, but only one, has rolled off my heart.

I am handed now the casualty reports from the 7th Armored Brigade's fight at Rafiah Junction. I have to scan the sheet twice to be certain I have read it right, so devastating are the totals.

The proverb says that the only truly happy men are wounded men. This is nonsense. The wounded are the most miserable of men.

I was shot in the face, the night of June 8, 1941, in Lebanon north of the Litani River. Our ten-man party was the forward element of an Australian division advancing against the Vichy French. The main body had been held up and could not reach us to bring aid. We had to hold out all night on our own.

I remember my comrades bearing me to safety. They laid me on the ground, seeking to make me comfortable. Of what does a wounded man think? I thought of my young wife, whom I loved more than life, and of my baby daughter. I had lost an eye. Half my face felt as if it had been shot away. Would I live? Would I be a cripple? How would I care for my bride and child? How could I continue to serve my country?

The wounded soldier understands a thing that others do not. He understands the earth. He has become more intimate with it than with any element in his life. This is how you die, he understands. The earth accepts your blood. A scrap of ground no wider than your hips will hold you.

My brother Zorik died in a field at Ramat Yohanan, April 14, 1948, seven years after I was shot in Lebanon. His blood drained into a furrow. We could not retrieve his body for three days, so continuous was the fighting.

The identities of the young men who fell at Rafiah will be known within a few hours. Shall we honor them alongside Zorik and the thousands of others who have fallen defending the Jewish nation in this century? No. To me these soldiers' names stand as well with those who fought beside Joshua and Gideon, with Saul and Jonathan and David.

We will weep for them tomorrow.

Now more immediate business presses upon us.

I am handed transcripts of broadcasts recorded this morning from Radio Cairo. The first transcript boasts of the destruction of forty Israeli warplanes. An hour later a second report inflates the figure to fifty-two. Then sixty-one. Then seventy-seven.

I instruct our public information officers to hold back the true totals, which are one-tenth of Nasser's vaunting tally.

Let Arab pride and vanity serve our purposes.

A few minutes into the war, Intelligence intercepts a telephone communication from King Hussein's chief aide, Colonel Mashour Haditha al-Jazy, informing the king that Israeli armor has crossed the border into Egypt. An hour later orders in code arrive from Egypt's chief military commander, Field Marshal Abdel Hakim Amer, instructing General Abdel Moneim Riad, assistant chief of staff of the United Arab Command and the commander on the ground in Jordan, to "open a new front, according to plan."

A subsequent call from Nasser will urge King Hussein to attack Israel with all the strength he possesses. "Seize all the territory you can before the Russians and the Americans impose a cease-fire."

Against us in Sinai are six Egyptian divisions and two near-division-size task forces: the 20th and the 7th Divisions in the north between Rafiah and El Arish, the 2nd at Abu Agheila/Um Katef, backed by the 3rd between Jebel Libni and Bir Hamma, with the elite 4th Armored Division to their rear at Bir Gafgafa. The 6th Mechanized Division, supported by the 1st Armored Brigade with 100 T-34s and T-54s, is at El Thamad, opposite Kuntilla. Joining it, east of Bir Hassna, is the 9,000-man, 200-tank Shazli Force. This formation was pulled out of Rafiah and moved south in response to the movement of an Israeli "phantom division," the 29th, made up of mock tanks and dummied-up jeeps. In all, the enemy has in Sinai eighteen infantry brigades, one paratroop brigade, six armored and two mechanized brigades, plus four special forces battalions.

We need every tank and every gun to deal with these.

If Jordan enters the war, Israel will be compelled to fight on two fronts. I will have to pull forces from Sinai and send them to defend Jewish Jerusalem and the eastern frontier. Jordan's forces, as I have noted, include 176 new M48 Patton tanks in two armored brigades, the 40th and the 60th, the latter commanded by King Hussein's cousin Sherif Zeid Chaker and deployed at the southern end of the Jordan Valley, within immediate range of Jerusalem. Against these, the IDF has only two reserve brigades equipped with ancient Shermans and light AMXs. In addition, Hussein has in and near Jerusalem the crack Imam Ali and King Talal infantry brigades, the elite formations of the Arab Legion.

Beyond that, Egypt has deployed to Jordan two commando battalions, the 33rd and the 53rd, not to mention a mechanized brigade crossing now from Iraq, as well as promised air and ground forces from Syria and Saudi Arabia.

What does Israel have on the chessboard to throw against these? I see only one piece, a newly formed reserve paratroop brigade, the 55th.

But this formation is slated to jump tonight at El Arish, to support Tal's and Gorodish's advance. We can't redeploy it. El Arish is critical.

We have nothing else.

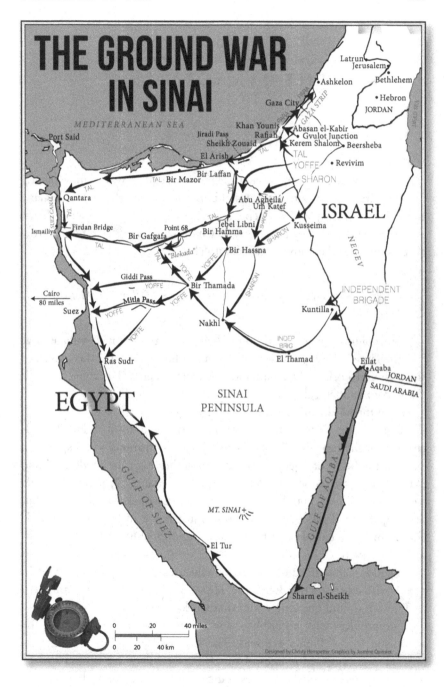

THE GROUND WAR IN SINAI

33.

THE JIRADI PASS

The war we are fighting is what the manuals call a "war of movement." Its principles are the principles of blitzkrieg: Break through the enemy and drive as quickly and as deeply as you can into his rear. Such a thrust may not literally destroy the enemy's men or armaments, but it will throw his command and communications into chaos.

Yosi Ben-Hanan is operations officer of the 7th Armored Brigade.

Our columns have pulled up in Sheikh Zouaid, the next village after Rafiah. Time is 13:20, a little more than five hours since the day started. I am with Gorodish in the command half-track when orders come from division commander Tal:

Hold the advance, stop where you are.

The column pulls into a dusty square fronting an abandoned headquarters of the Egyptian 7th Division. Gorodish dismounts and spreads a map on the hood of a jeep. Around him gather his commanders—Ehud Elad of tank Battalion 79, Gabi Amir of Battalion 82, deputy brigade commander Pinko Harel, with Lieutenant Colonel Zvika Lederman, the brigade intelligence officer (who has just flown in from the École de Guerre in Paris, called back for the war), and Ori Orr of the Reconnaissance Company.

Avigdor Kahalani rumbles up, my wild friend, leading his company in a tank with a cannon that won't fire. He sends his deputy, Lieutenant Daniel Tzefoni, to find one with a gun that works.

The problem with rapid blitz-type penetrations is that they leave the advancing forces' flanks exposed. The bypassed enemy may counterattack. He may cut off the lines of supply. The enemy's left-behind strongpoints may become pockets of resistance that must be mopped up.

This is what has happened behind our advance. Paratroop Brigade 35, an elite regular-army formation, has run into unexpectedly strong resistance back in the Gaza Strip. In addition, forces of the Egyptian 20th Division have begun shelling Israeli kibbutzim along the border. General Tal has ordered our brigade to respond.

Gorodish decides to send all the tanks of Battalion 79. He wants Ori Orr to take a platoon from Recon and lead them.

"Ori, do you know where you're going?"

"I always know where I'm going."

Gorodish is aware of how badly the Recon Company has been mauled at Rafiah Junction.

"Be careful."

Menachem Shoval, Recon trooper:

Where I am, we don't know anything about Ori and the tanks of Battalion 79 getting sent back. All we know is we are going forward.

Our platoon, Eli's, has been ordered to lead Battalion 82 west through the fortified Jiradi Pass to El Arish.

7th Armored Brigade commander Colonel Shmuel Gorodish, bareheaded, with Gabi Amir, right, commander of Tank Battalion 82, at Sheikh Zouaid.

At the village of Sheikh Zouaid my lieutenant, Shaul Groag, takes a new jeep—his third so far today. The others keep getting blown up.

We have new men, too. Guys from various shot-up vehicles and support teams have come forward, refusing any role except a fighting one. Our operations sergeant, Benzi Zur, takes over driving for Shaul, with Yoram Abolnik taking my radio seat in back. Our sergeant major, Haim Lavi, whom we call Etzioni, leaves his support post and piles onto the jeep I've been moved to. It's him, me, and David Cameron now.

Our jeeps follow Eli, heading for the Jiradi Pass.

Eli Rikovitz, Recon platoon commander:

We have caught up now with the tanks that passed us at Rafiah Junction. We're out front again. Time is around 14:00. We're leading the tanks of Battalion 82 as fast as we can toward El Arish.

I don't like the formation our vehicles are in. It's too exposed. I'm leading in my own jeep, with our whole platoon—three jeeps and a half-track—right behind.

Lieutenant Eli Rikovitz.

It's crazy for all of our defenseless Recon vehicles to be forward of the tanks. The pass we're approaching is reported to be heavily defended. It's ten kilometers long and could be a gantlet of fire the whole way.

I drop back and pull alongside Shaul's jeep. I tell him and the men in the other vehicles to let the tanks pass and then fall in behind them. I'll take the lead myself, ahead of the tanks, with my own jeep and Zvika Kornblit's.

By moving Shaul and the others back, I'm trying to protect them. Let the tanks go ahead. Shaul and his guys will be safer behind them.

Dubi Tevet, Recon trooper:

Crazy things happen in war, and the craziest of all happens now.

I'm up front, driving Eli's second jeep, ahead of the tanks as we enter the Jiradi. The pass is one ten-kilometer ambush. The Egyptians have tanks dug in on the reverse slopes of the dunes flanking the roadway. They have antitank guns in dugouts smack alongside the road. The slopes themselves are honeycombed with fighting positions for machine guns and bazookas. Trenches are reinforced concrete, full of soldiers. Artillery batteries line the hillsides.

Into this we roll in our defenseless jeeps.

Egyptian defensive positions near Sheikh Zouaid.
Note the dug-in tank beneath camouflage netting.

Nobody shoots at us.

In fact we see soldiers waving to us. They think we're their own guys.

Our two CJ-5s—Eli's and Zvika's—lead thirty tanks at full speed and nobody fires a shot at us.

We pass like kings, like kings on a carpet.

Eli Rikovitz, Recon platoon commander:

The road is lined with burning Egyptian vehicles, knocked out by air strikes just a few minutes earlier. So the enemy knows we're coming.

We've gotten here so fast, the Egyptians can't believe we're not their own men.

Menachem Shoval, Recon trooper:

Our group is in back now. We've lost sight of Eli's and Zvika's jeeps. They're up front, leading the tanks. They're at least a kilometer ahead of us.

From my perch in the back of Etzioni's jeep I'm trying to get a picture of the situation. I'm young but I'm not stupid. I can read a map; I understand the mission. I'm trying, like every soldier, to grasp the connection between what I know we're trying to do and what is actually happening.

Between Eli's jeeps and ours are two companies of tanks—between twenty and thirty in all. Eli's jeeps are deep into the Jiradi Pass. Our group in back hasn't even reached the start.

The topography of the land is changing. We're on a narrow road twisting between dunes. The Mediterranean is farther away on our right, out of sight. You can feel the desert coming. The country is starting to look like what you expect Sinai to look like.

Is that the Jiradi ahead? Maybe Shaul knows. He's our lieutenant. He's got the radios and the maps.

The road climbs to a rise, then starts down a long slope to the left before leveling out and swinging back to the right. Shaul has stopped our vehicles at the crest. Our vehicles come up and stop. Shaul is peering ahead through binoculars. Ahead we can see, even with the naked eye, many Egyptian troops dug in on the slopes and within concrete pillboxes. Through glasses enemy tanks are visible, dozens of them, hull down, along the ridgeline to the left, two kilometers ahead. What should we do?

It's a moment like the pause at the top of a roller coaster. On the one hand, the road ahead looks absolutely peaceful. From radio reports we know that Eli, Zvika, and the tanks from Battalion 82 are speeding through, untouched. Maybe we can do the same.

On the other hand, we can see the enemy dug in in bunkers and trenches, looking as menacing as Normandy on D-day in World War II.

Here on the high ground, we can still find cover. But the moment we start down the slope, our unarmored vehicles will be in the open, funneled between minefields. There will be no place to hide.

Shaul decides to go forward. He leads in the first jeep, with Benzi Zur driving and Yoram Abolnik in back. They start down the slope. The jeep gets no more than a few meters when a shell hits it.

The blast is huge and deafening. The shell—maybe artillery, maybe a tank round—has hit Shaul's jeep dead-on. Smoke blankets everything. Where the vehicle had been is now only smoke. I'm right behind. I had started the day with Shaul. I had been in his jeep. I stare at the dark, billowing smoke. Part of me refuses to believe this is happening. Then the smoke starts to clear.

I see the jeep with no people. There's no one there. The jeep is sitting there, miraculously intact, but no one is in it. I'm thinking, Hey, my friends have jumped clear! They got out in time! Then the smoke clears a little more.

I see three half corpses sitting in the jeep. The shell has passed at the height of the driver, shearing all three in half. This is right before my eyes. My friends, my commander.

This is the picture I am carrying with me. Of my friends being there and then not being there. It is horrible.

A second shell explodes, directly above us. The blast tears open part of our jeep and shreds Etzioni's left arm. He is half a meter from me, in the front seat. Amazingly, he stays cool. He gets out of the jeep, with his half-torn-off arm, calling for our medic, and starts walking back to the vehicles coming up behind, looking to warn others to stay back.

A barrage has begun. Egyptian artillery is firing air bursts, shells that explode five or ten meters above you, blowing shrapnel in all directions.

In the army you are drilled never to leave a weapon, never to abandon a working vehicle. I get the jeep out of there. I am so young I don't even have a driver's license.

We find cover on the reverse slope behind the crest of the road. A mob of vehicles has piled up there. Everyone is diving into ditches.

Lieutenant Shaul Groag.

Shaul's cut-in-half body and those of Benzi Zur and Yoram Abolnik remain half a hundred meters down the road, still in the seats of their jeep.

Eli Rikovitz, Recon platoon commander:

Our brigade is now divided. It is split in half. But up front, we don't know it. We are alone in two jeeps, ahead of everybody, leading the tanks of Battalion 82.

The Egyptians alongside the road have woken up.

Our jeeps—mine and Zvika's—are now nine-tenths of the way through the Jiradi Pass. We have entered the palm groves that mark the approach to El Arish. The Egyptians are firing at us from both sides of the road. Uri Zand is my driver. I see his foot flatten the accelerator. Our jeep feels as if it is crawling.

Egyptian soldiers are firing from prepared positions behind sandbags at the bases of the palm trees. They are so close we can see their mustaches and their wide, dark eyes. At one point three Egyptian soldiers, the crew of a heavy Goryunov machine gun, line me up in their sights. I see the gunner pull the trigger. My entire body stiffens, waiting to feel the impact of the bullets.

His gun jams.

I turn my jeep's .30-caliber Browning and pull the trigger.

My gun jams too.

I shout to Zvika in the jeep behind: "Hit them!"

He does.

Behind us, our tanks have buttoned up their hatches. Up front, we in the jeeps are totally exposed. A stitch of bullets shreds my dashboard. At the wheel, Uri cries out and collapses forward. He has been hit in the left side. We can't stop or we'll be killed. Uri swears he can still drive. I reach around behind him and stick my fist into his ragged, wet wound to plug the hole.

I plant my left foot on top of Uri's right foot and press on the accelerator, doing everything to get out of the kill zone.

Yosi Ben-Hanan, 7th Armored Brigade operations officer:

In the command party, we have no idea that the Jiradi Pass has suddenly become blocked.

I'm with Gorodish in a jeep, racing toward the beginning of the pass from the village of Sheikh Zouaid. The most recent report says that the tanks of Battalion 82 have cruised through untouched.

Suddenly, as we speed forward, our command party is flagged down by a sergeant from Recon. He steps into the road, holding up both hands. I know him. His name is Moti Shoval.

If you want to know what makes the IDF the force it is, here is an answer:

A sergeant stops the brigade commander leading all the tanks of an armored battalion and thinks nothing of it.

Kahalani is here with his tanks. So is Ehud Elad, commander of Tank Battalion 79. Gorodish grabs his binoculars and moves forward to assess the situation.

This is what "leading from the front" means. In other armies the brigade commander might be fifteen kilometers to the rear, trying to make decisions based on maps, intelligence dispatches, and conflicting reports from his officers on the radio.

Patton tanks of Battalion 79 near the Jiradi Pass.

Gorodish is right here. He can see with his own eyes the Egyptian positions on the dunes above the road. He can see the minefields and the trenches and feel the concussion of the air bursts overhead.

More tanks from Kahalani's company come up. Ehud Elad is standing in the turret of his own tank. His operations officer, Amram Mitzna, pulls alongside in a half-track.

There is no question that Gorodish will order Battalion 79 to attack. The only issues are in what manner, against what positions, and how soon.

Avigdor Kahalani, tank company commander:

I'm peering through binoculars, straight into the setting sun. Ahead is a broad, shallow valley: the Jiradi Pass. I'm trying to spot the entrenched Egyptian tanks but I can't see a thing with the sun in my eyes. My gunner is named Rafi Berterer. "Can you see anything through your scope, Rafi?"

Rafi says he can see trenches ahead, but no tanks. I'm just starting to lower myself from the turret to look through Rafi's gunsight when the tank takes a blow, as if from a titanic hammer.

I crash from the turret into the waist of the tank. The interior fills with smoke and flame. For a second I'm paralyzed. I feel pain, as if a steel shaft has been driven between my shoulder blades.

"We've been hit!" I call. "Jump out!"

My only thought is, Don't scream. The commander, before all else, must lead his men. If you are hurt or frightened, your soldiers must not know it. You cannot let them hear that chicken voice.

The interior has become solid flame. I reach for the grip handles above me, to haul myself up into the turret. My arms will not pull me up. I fall back. The fire is inside my lungs. I try again and fall again. I realize that my legs are pinned.

It's true what they say about your life flashing before you. Mine does now. Still I try one last time.

It works. I'm up into the turret. At this point I can no longer control my voice. I cry for my mother and hurl myself clear of the flaming tank.

Moti Shoval, Recon sergeant:

I am standing right there when Kahalani's tank takes a direct hit.

Six years from now, in the Yom Kippur War, Kahalani with a handful of tanks will hold off more than a hundred Syrian tanks in the Valley of Tears on the Golan Heights. He will be awarded the Itur HaGvura, Israel's highest decoration for valor, and become a legend in the armored corps.

Now he is consumed by flame.

We can see Kahalani spill out of the turret and plunge to the sand. He is naked except for his belt and his boots. Everything else has been incinerated. His face and legs are black. The skin is hanging off his arms in great sheets.

Three of our Recon guys—Nadav Ilan, Tani Geva, and Amitai Heiman—race down the slope to help Kahalani and the tank.

Avigdor Kahalani, tank company commander:

I am rolling in the sand, trying to put the fire out. My friend Daniel Tzefoni and the crew are still in the tank. I can hear myself screaming, but it sounds like the voice belongs to somebody else. I want to get out of my body. My body is on fire.

I begin running. Soldiers stare in shock. One tank almost runs me over.

I see Ehud Elad, my battalion commander, in the cupola of his tank. "Kahalani, what happened?" He stares at me dumbfounded.

I race past him.

Boaz Amitai, Recon platoon commander:

Suddenly Ehud Elad's tank gets hit. He is standing, exposed in the turret. The explosion consumes him.

Another round hits Mitzna's half-track. Men are rushing to pull him out. In moments we have lost a battalion commander, his operations officer, and a brave young company commander. Every leader we have is going down!

Photo by Yosi Ben-Hanan.

Lieutenant Colonel Ehud Elad, center, commander of Tank Battalion 79, half an hour before he was killed by an Egyptian shell at the entrance to the Jiradi Pass. The watch in the foreground reading 14:55 is on the wrist of Lieutenant Colonel Barouch "Pinko" Harel, deputy commander of the 7th Armored Brigade.

Ori Orr, Recon Company commander:

Nowhere in the manual does it say that Recon's job is to evacuate the wounded. Our role is to lead the tanks. But we have the jeeps. We have the nimble, sure-footed vehicles that can carry burned and maimed men. Our guys are rushing to help the wounded.

Tani Geva, Recon trooper:

To pull the crew out of a burning tank, a man must go in face-first. He reaches in with his hands and arms. The tank crewmen are screaming in pain and out of their minds with fear. The interior burns like a furnace. High-explosive shells are cooking, half a meter from their face.

When you witness this, when you do it yourself, you cannot believe it.

In war soldiers perform feats of valor of which they never, before they do them, believed themselves capable.

34.

MASTERPIECE OF WAR

Cheetah Cohen commands Helicopter Squadron 124:

I have just landed at Nitzana, four in the afternoon, first day of the war. Sharon's division will assault Um Katef tonight. My helicopters will carry Danny Matt's paratroopers into the fight.

An hour ago I was at our squadron's forward base at Ashkelon on the coast. My helicopters were scattered all over Sinai, Gaza, and the West Bank, rescuing downed fliers and evacuating wounded soldiers.

Suddenly a call comes in for me from Rafi Har-Lev at Air Force Operations. "Cheetah, I'm giving you two orders. One, take your helicopters to Arik Sharon, and, two, I'm giving you no more orders. Do whatever Arik tells you."

In peacetime it would take all day to assemble and move a helicopter squadron. Now we do it in three minutes. I get into the air and open the squadron channel. "Whoever can hear me, relay my orders to whoever can't."

Now here we are, above Sharon's division. I'm at 3,000 feet, looking down on ten thousand men and hundreds of buses, trucks, tanks, half-tracks, artillery pieces. Sharon's forces are spread out over thirty kilometers. Where is Danny Matt? I've got him on the radio but I can't see him amid the massive sprawl below.

"Danny, hold down your transmit button."

On my instrument panel the radio compass has a needle that indicates the source direction of an incoming transmission. I'm following that needle across the encampment.

There's Danny!

I set the helicopter down next to a column of mobilized civilian buses.

"Cheetah, where have you been?"

Like I was supposed to be here a month ago.

"I am here, Danny. I brought the party!"

Colonel Danny Matt commands Paratroop Brigade 80, part of Ugda Sharon:

I love Cheetah. He and his brothers Uri and Nechemiah comprise one of the leading military families in Israel. He is a fearless flier who will take his helicopters anywhere, anytime, against anybody.

But now we've got a real problem.

The landing zone for which my plans have been drawn was supposed to be on the left flank, the south, of the Egyptian defenses at Um Katef. With my deputies I have worked out the insertion plan for this LZ, or landing zone, down to the meter and the minute. Now at the eleventh hour the enemy has moved a force of tanks into that area.

Where else can we land? No one knows. Time is 16:00. I must have a brigade of paratroopers on the ground in the middle of the Egyptian defenses within four hours.

Cheetah's helicopters are landing. We need twenty-four. I count seven.

"Cheetah, where are the rest of your birds?"

"Don't worry, Danny. They'll be here."

Cheetah Cohen:

Danny and I go back forever. I was flying P-51 Mustangs in support of his paratroopers at the Mitla Pass in '56. He knows my brother Uri in the armored corps and has been a champion for my younger brother Nechemiah in the Sayeret Matkal. At the command levels of the IDF you will hear over and over the names of the same acclaimed officers, all of whom trained under Arik Sharon: Meir Har-Zion, Katcha Cahaner, Aharon Davidi, Raful Eitan, Uzi Eilam, Motta Gur.

And Danny.

Danny Matt:

I have picked a new landing zone. The site is identified as Point 181 on the code map. It's on the right of the Egyptian artillery instead of the left. Intelligence is reporting that a force of our own tanks has just seized the adjacent ground.

I'm drawing the new plan in chalk on the hood of a jeep and explaining the changeover to my deputies and battalion commanders.

Cheetah is watching me scribble. He thinks he has entered chaos, a world-class balagan. But my plans are meticulous. Each team of ten paratroopers knows which helicopter it must board in the takeoff sequence, and each man knows his place in that team. He knows what he must do the instant his helicopter touches down and he knows his part in the overall assault plan. I have worked out the force structure down to the final detail.

Improvisation is not a wild scramble at the last minute. You are not pulling plans out of thin air. Improvisation is the payoff of scrupulous preparation and drill.

Don't worry, Cheetah. You are witnessing no balagan. I am simply transposing our plan from the old landing zone to the new one.

Cheetah Cohen:

Yes, yes, but what new one? Point 181 is just a spot on the map. To locate it is like flying over the ocean saying, "Go to Wave 181."

Off we go. I must find the site in advance of tonight's assault and mark it with illumination beacons. Otherwise we will never find it in the dark, when we return, ferrying Danny's paratroopers.

It's 16:45. I'm banking in a ravine between dunes, so low that the rotor blast is kicking up clouds of sand. We're flying directly into the setting sun. I'm thinking, My P-51 Mustang was shot down not far from here in '56.

We pick a spot. The pathfinders want me to get as close to the target as possible, so Danny's paratroopers don't have to trek for hours through deep sand.

You mark a landing zone with a beacon called a "trapeze." This is a three-sided square made of lights, with one open end. The pathfinders plant this in the sand. The lights are powered by batteries and are shielded around their circumference by panels so that they cannot be seen from the side. The lamps point directly up. They are visible only from the air. The open side of the trapeze points downwind. The helicopters enter from this side, so they can land into the wind.

The pathfinders put down three trapezes. My helicopters will come in formations of three, dropping ten paratroopers from each aircraft—thirty paratroopers at a time.

Danny Matt:

A combat commander under Arik Sharon is granted broad independence of action. Sharon tells you what to do but not how to do it.

I will have my deputy inform him of the changes we've made to the plans. But as long as these alterations don't affect other operational elements in Sharon's design, I won't bother him personally.

I know how Sharon thinks: If I don't hear from Danny, that means everything is okay. If there is a problem, Danny will contact me.

Major Eliezer "Cheetah" Cohen,
commander of Helicopter Squadron 124.

Cheetah Cohen:

Danny will tell you that he and I never spoke in person with Sharon, but I remember the moment clearly.

In we went, to Sharon's trailer. Wherever Sharon is, a meal is always cooking.

"Come in, Danny! Come in, Cheetah! Do you want something to eat? Coffee? Cheetah, can your helicopters take Danny's guys and put them behind the Egyptian artillery? Danny, from the landing zone you and your paratroopers will cross the dunes and destroy the Egyptian batteries from the rear. Got it, Cheetah? Okay, Danny? Good luck!"

That's it. In and out. We never even got our coffee.

Danny Matt:

Sinai is a war of roads. Armored columns cannot negotiate the mountains and the belts of sand. To win in the Sinai Peninsula you must command the arteries of transport.

The road we will seize tonight is the one that runs from Abu Agheila to the Suez Canal. The primary fortifications protecting this locality are centered upon a ridge called Um Katef.

The Egyptian defenses at Um Katef are based on the British design, overlaid with the Soviet.

The English believed in "boxes." A box is a rectangle of desert, often many kilometers across, which has been built up artificially into an obstacle. A box will contain minefields and extensive barriers of barbed wire. Vehicle passage will be impeded by berms, antitank ditches, "hedgehogs," "dragon's teeth," and other obstacles. Infantry, antitank forces, and self-propelled "tank killers" will further strengthen these boxes, while behind them by ten, twenty, even thirty kilometers will wait a mobile reserve of tanks, antitank guns, and self-propelled artillery.

Each box is sited to support all others in its strategic vicinity. Lanes between boxes will be covered by artillery and reachable easily by the tanks in reserve. This is the British system, developed by her generals Wavell, Auchinleck, Alexander, and Montgomery in the North African desert during World War II. These officers and others passed this wisdom on to their clients, the Egyptians.

On top of this, Soviet engineers have overlaid the Russian system. Russian doctrine is linear. Its principle is defense in depth. You can recognize a Soviet position from the air by its multiple trench lines, one behind the other. In the rear of the first three trench lines is the artillery.

Russians love artillery. The Soviet doctrine evolved from defense of the homeland against the Nazis. The concept is one of attrition.

At Um Katef, Soviet engineers have built three successive trench lines of reinforced concrete, extending from impassable dunes on one side to similar obstacles on the other. Each trench line is separated from the other by three hundred meters.

Four kilometers behind these first three trenches, the Soviets have constructed a fourth trench line, backed by a tank regiment with sixty-six T-34s and a battalion of twenty-two SU-100 self-propelled guns. Between this rearmost trench and the first three are the main Egyptian artillery batteries.

These batteries are our objective.

Tonight my paratroopers will attack these guns.

The Egyptian position is constituted of between five and seven battalions—approximately eighty artillery pieces—arrayed in line, facing to the front. Minefields and antitank ditches protect all forward-facing approaches, as do the three trench lines manned by infantry armed with antitank guns, bazookas, rifles, and machine guns.

How will Sharon attack these?

I have sat with him in enough planning groups to know exactly how his mind works.

First, he will regard as good fortune the fact that enemy doctrine has concentrated so many troops and so much firepower in one position. "We can kill them more easily when they have brought themselves together in one place."

Second, he will ask himself, "How can I attack this locality in a way that its defenders will least expect and to which they will be least capable of responding in the confusion of the moment?"

One of Sharon's principles of planning is "complexity at the top, simplicity at the bottom." This means he keeps the big, complicated symphony to himself. He understands it, and no one else has to.

Cheetah and I—and all other subordinate commanders—just have to play our violins.

Of course, the rest of the plan, held in Sharon's head (and on a jumble of chinagraph-marked code maps), is more complicated than Beethoven's Ninth. Sharon has already this afternoon sent a battalion of Centurion tanks under Lieutenant Colonel Natan "Natke" Nir (reinforced by infantry, mortars, and combat engineers) in a flanking movement to the north, across dunes that the enemy believes impassable to heavy armor. It has taken the tanks two tries, but they are now in a position to cut off Egyptian reinforcements from the north—and to strike at Um Katef from the flank and rear. At the same time, Yaakov Aknin's 213th Artillery Regiment is waiting for dark to lay down what will be the heaviest barrage any force of Israeli gunners has ever fired. The three battalions of Kuti Adam's 99th Infantry Brigade will assault the first echelon of trench lines from the flank, after they have hiked ten kilometers in the dark to get into position. Combat engineers will clear lanes through the Egyptian minefields. Immediately the tanks of Motke Zippori's 14th Armored Brigade, minus Natke Nir's Centurions, will assault the enemy.

The overriding concept is one that has characterized Sharon's planning since the days when he commanded Unit 101. This is the concept of the *tachboulah*.

A tachboulah is a ruse, a stratagem.

Sharon loves to tell his young officers, "It's all there in Proverbs 24:6":

By a tachboulah shalt thou wage war.

General Ariel "Arik" Sharon in 1969 as chief
of Southern Command.

I have studied the campaigns of Caesar and Alexander, Hannibal and Napoleon. Believe me, when Sharon one day joins them, they will save a place for him at the sand table. And they will all listen when he speaks. A tachboulah, however, is more than just a feint or misdirection. It is greater than simply achieving the element of surprise. The intent of a tachboulah is to compel the enemy to respond, in the moment, under conditions of chaos, *in a way that he is not prepared for.*

Sharon loves to tell this story:

"We captured some Egyptians once after our guys had overrun their heavily fortified position in a matter of minutes. Then later we took a bunch of Syrians prisoner in another fight. We put the Syrians in together with the Egyptians. The Syrians were giving hell to the Egyptians. 'How could you let a bunch of Israelis overrun you in a matter of minutes?' 'These Jews,' said the Egyptians, 'they don't attack by the book.'"

That, Sharon would say, is the tachboulah.

"The Egyptian soldier is tough and brave when he knows what is expected of him. But make him improvise in the heat of the moment and he is lost."

In tonight's plan are many tachboulot. If all goes well, Sharon will play them in sequence. Each combat arm—artillery, infantry, engineers, armor, helicopters, paratroopers—will arrive in coordination with every other, so that tachboulah follows tachboulah.

Cheetah Cohen:

My helicopters have all arrived, seventeen out of twenty-four. The other seven are evacuating wounded from Gaza, Rafiah, and the Jiradi.

We will take Danny's paratroopers into the landing zone thirty at a time. Three helicopters, ten men in each. It's like a train. The trains of Cheetah. Three Sikorsky S-58s, followed at one-minute intervals by three more, with another three after that. In the LZ, the three trapezes are in place. Each bird will set down in its own trapeze. In and out in sixty seconds.

Danny Matt:

At the last minute the brigade rabbi shows up with an armload of prayer cards. He's passing them out to the guys. You'd be surprised how many tough-nut paratroopers scurry over to grab one.

My intelligence officer is Yigal Talmi, the son of Emma Talmi, one of the pioneer Zionists and a noted atheist. He passes me now, tucking a prayer card into his shirt pocket. "Yigal, what if your mother should see you doing that?"

"Danny, this is no time to piss off the Big Guy."

Yael Dayan:

22:30. Sharon stands beside Yaakov Aknin, his artillery commander. "Let the earth shake," says Arik.

Our guns open fire. They will shoot six thousand shells in twenty minutes, the heaviest barrage IDF gunners have ever fired. I have never been this close to batteries of 105-millimeter and 155-millimeter howitzers. The gunner yanks the lanyard and the whole cannon becomes airborne. Men with earplugs press their palms against their heads and brace themselves as if expecting to be blown off their feet. They nearly are. They labor like devils in hell. Our force has six battalions in all, including field guns, heavy 160-millimeter mortars, and medium guns.

"Shake, it shall," says Aknin.

But the unhappy fact, as Dov has explained to me, is that our guns are small-bore alongside the mighty Soviet hardware employed by the Egyptians. Though our cannons have been moved forward as far as they can go, taking advantage of the approach of darkness, their range remains too limited to reach the mass of the enemy's artillery. Nasser's batteries sit safe, beyond our reach. We are shelling only the Egyptians' minefields and the infantry hunkered in the three forward trenches.

Arik's answer to the distant enemy batteries is to attack them with Danny Matt's paratroopers, flown in behind the lines by Cheetah Cohen's helicopters.

This has never been done before. Not by the Americans, not by the Russians, not by us.

When I ask Dov, "Will it work?" he answers with a phrase I am becoming familiar with.

"It will have to."

Cheetah Cohen:

The Egyptian big guns are firing. Airborne in the helicopters we can feel them. The line of batteries is four or five kilometers across. The ascending shells light the sky. I can read my gauges by their illumination. It's like daylight.

"My God, Cheetah," my copilot, Moshe Carmeli, says through the headset. "Have you ever seen anything like this?"

"No one has seen anything like this!"

We're skimming the sand at 80 kilometers per hour.

The battle rages five kilometers to our left. I am not a religious man, but I am praying like mad: Let me find those trapezes!

Danny Matt:

I land in the second group of three helicopters. My deputy, Lieutenant Colonel Shmulik Pressburger, is already moving off into the dunes to the south with thirty paratroopers.

You may ask, How does an officer know in which direction to march? Is it by map? By compass heading?

These are not necessary tonight. The Egyptian batteries paint a swath of fire in the sky. A blind man could follow it. Even in the troughs of the dunes, we can feel the walloping whoosh and hear the scream of the ascending shells.

What will go wrong? Something always does.

First is the direction of the dunes. Dunes run in a specific direction, depending on how the prevailing winds have piled the sand. In two strides we learn that these bastards are running against us. It's like swimming upstream—two steps forward, one step back. By the end of my career, I will have served for fifty years, in six wars, three of them in Sinai. Never will I labor as I do this night.

For many of our young troopers, this is their first experience of combat. A lieutenant tells me he has instructed his men to bring twice as much ammunition as they think they will need and twice as much water. This weight now becomes hell in the soft sand.

It will take us from eight till midnight to cross the four kilometers that separate us from the Egyptian batteries.

Cheetah Cohen:

The train of helicopters takes a different route out from the one it took in. We're flying a great circle around the battlefield, if you can call it flying when the birds are so low that sand is collecting on the decks of the cargo bays and so close to the walls of ravines that the tips of the rotors are abraded by the flying grit. The air force has rules against this. I have rules against this.

Tonight we are breaking all of these rules.

We touch down by the lamps of the trapezes. The paratroopers leap to the earth from the right side of the helicopter, single file, in darkness, into a storm of rotor blast and howling driven sand, with two more helicopters touching down simultaneously, all without landing lights and all with tail rotors, invisible to the paratroopers in the dark, waiting to liquefy their skulls if they don't dash away in the prescribed manner.

The insertion goes on for an hour and a half before Danny calls it off when shells from the Egyptian artillery begin to fall dangerously close to the landing zone.

Danny Matt:

We have reached the Egyptian positions. The enemy has between five and seven battalions, each constituted of three batteries of four guns apiece, along with whatever supplementary firepower he has been able to bring up. The line stretches out of sight, between three and five kilometers long. The sight of the big guns is spectacular. The barrels are glowing orange, so furiously have the cannons been firing.

We attack the closest batteries first.

Artillerymen are not trained to defend their posts by themselves. Special infantry squads are detailed to do this. The gunners' role is only to fire their cannons. In their minds, the enemy is miles away. When they see my paratroopers suddenly rushing upon them from the rear, out of the darkness, slinging grenades and firing automatic weapons, they don't know what to do.

I have a photo in my possession to this day of Egyptian infantry shot dead on their trucks. The soldiers had no time even to get to their defensive posts. We took them completely by surprise.

My paratroopers have carried explosive charges to blow up the cannons. But after we attack the first few batteries, the enemy artillery stops firing. The gunners along the rest of the line run away.

The three battalions of Kuti Adam's infantry are attacking the Egyptians' first three trenches from the flank, supported by Motke Zippori's brigade of M50 and M51 Shermans. Egyptian defenders are the three infantry battalions of the 12th Infantry Brigade, 2nd Infantry Division.

The Egyptians have about ninety tanks arrayed in the Soviet defensive posture. Zippori's armored brigade gets into a furious firefight with them. Our IDF tanks are equipped with powerful projector spotlights, which they use to locate and sight upon the enemy. My guys are caught in the middle. We are getting shot at by our own soldiers. At one point it gets so crazy that some commander—it might even have been me, I can't remember—simply orders all Israeli tanks to cease firing. When they obey, we can see which tanks belong to us and which to the enemy.

Natke Nir's Centurions attack now too.

Our work is done. My paratroopers withdraw to the flank, in a formation shaped like the Hebrew letter *het,* a three-sided square with the wounded in the middle. We start back through the dunes.

Egyptian soldiers are running away in the same direction. They're moving a lot faster than we are.

Cheetah Cohen:

I have landed back at Sharon's camp. It's past midnight. The landing zone for the helicopters is half a kilometer clear of all troop or vehicle concentrations. From this site, my crews and I have an unobstructed view to the west, toward the enemy positions.

Here is what we see:

The sky, which had been lit up like daylight by the firing of the Egyptian artillery, now goes black, one section at a time.

I'm standing on a rise with the other pilots, copilots, and aircrew. As we watch, the right side of the line goes dark; then the middle; then the whole line. It's a rolling blackout, like a city when the power fails in one neighborhood after another. The only lights remaining on the battlefield are the searchlights of our IDF tanks, darting this way and that like the site of a movie premiere in Hollywood.

Arik gives me a kiss. "Cheetah, I love you!"

He needs no report from his commanders to know how the battle is going.

35.

BAD NIGHT IN EL ARISH

Eli Rikovitz, Recon platoon commander:

We have reached El Arish. Night has fallen. The tanks of Battalion 82 have seized the crossroads east of town and set up in a circle, cannons facing out. They have been firing for hours.

My driver Uri's wound is bad. Worse has happened to Zvika. He has been run over by a tank.

Dubi Tevet, Recon jeep driver:

Uri has been shot through the hip. The hole is as big as my fist. Zvika's extremity is ten times worse. When we captured the crossroads, Zvika positioned his jeep behind one of our tanks to protect it from Egyptian fire. Suddenly the tank began moving in reverse. The driver couldn't see Zvika's jeep behind him.

Zvika Kornblit, Recon jeep commander:

I was folded up inside the jeep. The last thing I saw was the tank track passing over my head. I was sure I was going to die.

Moshe Perry, Recon jeep driver:

Dubi and I got Zvika out. We had to peel him out of the mangled steel. He was nothing but a mass of flesh, dismembered.

Zvika Kornblit, Recon jeep commander:

I try to feel my face, to see if I still have a face, if I still exist. My hip is broken, I have five fractures including my spine, not one rib remains unbroken, my right arm is shattered.

Dubi Tevet, Recon jeep driver:

We in Recon have been trained in first aid, but we are not medics. Has Zvika's spine been crushed? What of his internal organs? How can we help him?

Ori Orr, Recon Company commander:

Eli has informed me over the radio of what has happened to Uri and Zvika. The only good news is in the big picture. The brigade now has most of a battalion of tanks at El Arish.

This is beyond the army's dreams. In our most optimistic projections we could not have imagined reaching our objective before tomorrow. A pitched battle was anticipated to capture the airfield at El Arish and the big Egyptian base. An entire paratroop brigade, the 55th, is set to jump tonight to help us.

Instead the Egyptians are withdrawing.

The tanks of Kahalani's company and others have attacked the enemy's positions at the east end of the Jiradi Pass. Our division's other tank brigade, the 60th, has gotten behind the foe to the south. As the Egyptians pull back, I myself make the dash through the pass, with Amos and Boaz and others from Amos's platoon. Our vehicles get through just before midnight.

We're here.

We have found Eli.

Dubi Tevet, Recon jeep driver:

This night is the longest of my life. I believe it will never end. The main body of Battalion 82 has captured the road junction at the east entrance to El Arish. I am here, within the circle of our tanks, tending to the wounds of Uri Zand and Zvika Kornblit, my friends.

Behind us, the pass remains cut off. We are alone. Ori has gotten through with our fast Recon jeeps, but the rest of the brigade is stuck at the east end.

We wait here at El Arish with our wounded friends. We have no doctors, no medics. We have run out of morphine.

Boaz Amitai, Recon platoon commander:

It's one in the morning. Gorodish and half the brigade are still back at the entrance to the Jiradi. Over the brigade radio net, we can hear him ordering Infantry Battalion 9 forward to clear the Egyptian trenches that flank the pass. These positions must be taken so that our trucks with fuel and water and ammunition can get through to resupply us and so that Gorodish and the rest of the brigade can come up.

Ori's brother is in Battalion 9. It's a good outfit; they will do the job.

Ori Orr, Recon Company commander:

The way you think in war is not the way you think in peace. Your mind must remain on the mission. This is not always possible when you have lost so many friends.

Our company has been leading the brigade for eighteen hours now without a break. We have fought through two enemy infantry brigades and one tank brigade. The ordeal shows on our faces. I do not need retrospect to see this. I see it now.

I am looking across the darkness at Eli, Amos, and Boaz. Amos stands, lighting a cigarette. Eli and Boaz sit in the sand with their backs against the tires of one of our jeeps. Are they thinking of Rafiah? Are they, like me, seeking to tally up the numbers of friends we have lost?

"How long," Eli asks, "since we started this morning?"

Amos says he can't remember.

"A lifetime," says Boaz.

Eli Rikovitz:

The nature of warfare is stupidity, and advancing under fire in open vehicles must be near the pinnacle of this. A mortar round that hits a half-track will kill every man in it. An antitank round will burn them all to death. When an artillery shell or a round from a tank's main gun hits an unarmored vehicle, it leaves nothing but smoking metal and boots with no feet in them.

The farther you advance under fire, I am beginning to learn, the more items you lose. First you lose your equipment and your bedding. It falls off or gets shot up or burned up. You lose your ammo next. You shoot it up or hand it off to others who need it more. You lose your bearings. You lose communication, you lose vision, you lose hearing. You lose parts of your own body. You lose your men. You lose your connection to reality, you lose your composure, you lose your sanity.

The one thing you must never lose is your will to complete the mission.

Boaz Amitai:

No one can sleep. We try, under blankets in the seats of our jeeps. I'm thinking of my father, Eliezer, who commands a reserve infantry brigade defending Jewish Jerusalem. Is he all right? Is he worrying about me? The worst, this night, is sitting up with Eli and Ori. We have acquired now a pretty good idea of how many friends we've lost. You can't think about it. You can't let yourself.

Ori tries to buck us up by reminding us that not all are necessarily dead; some may only be wounded. But we have all seen Kenigsbuch's half-track at Rafiah. I myself put blankets over the bodies of Shaul and Benzi and Yoram, cut in half in their jeep at the start of the Jiradi.

No one was brave enough to lift them out.

Ori Orr:

I have been strong all day. Being in command, you have no choice. But now, as I sit in the cold dark with Eli and Amos and Boaz, the part of my mind that I have turned off comes back awake. How many men have we lost? Eight? Ten? More? And others wounded. In one day.

Two more days like this and we will have no one left.

Dubi Tevet:

Boaz Amitai is one of our lieutenants. He comes by to say he has been ordered by Ori to take two jeeps back across the Jiradi to link up with the brigade's resupply vehicles. It's 03:30. When Boaz reaches the far side of the pass, he will lead the trucks back to us with fuel and water and rations and ammunition.

Brigade knows we have wounded here. Eli has radioed back four times. The medics are trying to get an ambulance up or even a helicopter when daylight comes.

Uri and Zvika suffer without a word. Will help ever arrive? I have given up searching the darkness for headlights.

Boaz Amitai:

The pass is ten kilometers long. Every meter seems like it's on fire. The asphalt has melted from tanks burned and crews incinerated.

You try not to think morbid thoughts.

Why am I still above the earth when so many friends, who are better men than I, have been taken beneath it? Why them? Why not me?

I am not religious. I don't think the way a religious person thinks. But now, driving across these ten kilometers of hell, I feel the presence of the Angel of Death.

"You," he says to one man. "I shall take you now."

To another: "You wait. I will come for you later."

It is a terrible feeling.

Eli Rikovitz:

At 04:30 Boaz comes back, leading the first vehicles of the supply echelon. At first light a helicopter medevacs Zvika and Uri to Soroka Hospital in Beersheba.

The tanks start to line up for the petrol tankers. At dawn we get into a firefight at the airfield with some retreating Egyptians and Boaz gets shot in the right thigh. He's okay. The wound is his ticket out.

Gorodish is here now. The whole brigade has reached El Arish. A paratroop force from Brigade 35 is ordered to push west toward Suez along the coast road. We, with the tanks, will drive south into the desert toward Bir Laffan and Jebel Libni. The Egyptian 3rd Division is there.

It's interesting to observe how the campaign evolves. The army has no official plans to advance beyond El Arish. Yet events dictate that it must.

If we check our advance here, Egyptian command may rally. Right now they are reeling. Their officers are fleeing, leaving their men to fend for themselves.

We have to keep attacking.

We have to keep advancing west.

Yosi Ben-Hanan, 7th Armored Brigade operations officer:

The operational maps of the 7th Armored Brigade end at El Arish. I know because I drew them. There are no arrows pointing beyond.

But El Arish is only the doorstep of Sinai. It's nothing. Nowhere. Over half of Nasser's armor remains untouched in the inner desert—the 3rd and 6th Divisions, the Shazli Force, and the elite 4th Armored Division.

Are there plans to take Jebel Libni? No. Has an attack program been drawn up for Bir Gafgafa? Never. The Suez Canal? In our brigade it hasn't even been mentioned.

But, plans or no, we must keep attacking. The logic of events demands it.

This is my first experience of war, as opposed to exchanges of fire, such as the brigade has participated in on the Golan Heights over the past couple of years.

The real thing is beyond anything I could have imagined. Not only the "little picture" of events on the ground—who lives and who dies, for what

Collection of Yosi Ben-Hanan.

Lieutenant Yosi Ben-Hanan,
7th Armored Brigade operations officer.

reasons of chance or necessity—but the way the process plays out on the level of armies and nations.

Certain principles have become clear.

Blitzkrieg works.

War of movement works.

In little more than twenty-four hours of fighting, the Egyptian 7th and 20th Divisions have essentially ceased to exist. Thousands of enemy vehicles have been destroyed, hundreds more captured intact. Fifteen hundred Egyptian soldiers have been killed, while thousands more flee on foot into the desert.

El Arish, where we are now, is a big, powerful base with a town and an airfield. Yet it has fallen without a siege and with only a short, fierce firefight.

This is amazing to me.

When historians write of this war, they will draw maps with assault arrows and lines of advance; they will speak of how the commanders planned this, the generals schemed that. And this will be true, as far as it goes.

The missing element is the momentum of events.

Gorodish understands this. He could see, back at the entrance to the Jiradi—even while one indispensable battalion commander, Ehud Elad, had been killed, and an equally brilliant company commander, Avigdor Kahalani, had been nearly incinerated—Gorodish could see, and declare aloud, that we could not stop here or at El Arish. Our force could not cease from advancing. And that nothing could or would stop us short of the Suez Canal.

Yoel Gorodish, senior operations officer of the 7th Armored Brigade:

Gorodish is a *shochet*—a kosher butcher. My brother learned the trade when he was fifteen. The shochet is a respected position in any Jewish community. In some smaller congregations, the rabbi and the shochet are the same man.

Now this shochet, Shmuel Gorodish, has become "Young Rommel." The carcass he is carving is that of the Egyptian Army.

BOOK SIX

JERUSALEM

36.

A THOUSANDTH OF A POUND

When I was five years old, I visited Jerusalem for the first time. I cannot express the magnitude of this occasion. The journey was for me the first time out of the little kibbutz, the first time to ride in a car or a bus, the first time I ever sat down to a meal at a real table in a real dining room.

Captain Yoram Zamosh commands "A" Company in Major Uzi Eilam's Battalion 71 of Paratroop Brigade 55.

For half a year my sisters and I had prepared for this monumental event. An untutored boy—myself—must be taught the proper way to shine his shoes and tame his cowlick, to hold a spoon and fork. We were going to the great city! I had to know how to behave like a gentleman.

We traveled—my parents, my two sisters, and I—by a very old bus to Tel Aviv, to the central station, then by a slightly newer bus to Ramla, and from there up to Jerusalem. We were going for Passover to my uncle's house in Jaffa Street. The total distance of the trip was not even a hundred kilometers, but it felt to me like girdling the globe.

We had a wonderful seder, and I received the gift of a coin worth two mills. A mill equaled one-thousandth of a Palestinian pound. This was to me a treasure beyond imagining.

The year was 1946. The British had instituted a curfew because of violence threatened by the Irgun and other dissident Jewish groups. Directly beneath the windows of my uncle's house was a post manned by British paratroopers with their red berets and pompoms. I sat for hours on a little balcony behind this position, watching the soldiers, fascinated.

Suddenly my coin slipped out of my hand!

It fell down among the British sandbags!

Though such an act was absolutely forbidden, I ran down the stairs to the military position. A big Scottish officer with a red mustache and blue eyes helped me find my coin. The paratroopers gave me chocolates and sat me behind a machine gun with a beret on my head. Half an hour later I was returned to my uncle, who immediately put all my identification details in a pouch around my neck so I would not get lost again.

The next day we went to the Kotel. The Western Wall. Over sixty-five years later, I have forgotten nothing. The political state of affairs was vividly clear to me, even as a child—how poor we Jews were, and how small and powerless compared to the mighty British.

The Arabs were not the enemy then. They were under the imperial thumb, just as we were. But Jerusalem was a Jewish city—*the* Jewish city. I felt keenly that this Wall, these stones, belonged to us by right and justice, but we had yet no power to possess them.

To be in this place with my parents was an overwhelming emotional experience, for them as well as for me, because as a child on the kibbutz you were raised not with your mother and father but with the other children. You lived in the children's house. You saw your parents perhaps on the Sabbath or for holidays, but the rest of the time you were apart. So this trip was indelible to me for that reason as well.

I remember several years later traveling to Jerusalem on my own. I was sixteen years old the first time, setting out from the kibbutz on foot, trekking from early in the morning, seventy kilometers, carrying only a wrinkled old 1:100,000 gas station map and a few sandwiches, arriving at Ein Kerem just as the setting sun turned the white stones of the city to gold.

The Jordanians held the Old City then. The year was 1958. A Jew could no longer visit the Kotel or get anywhere near it. I made this trip many times. The pilgrims would go to Har Zion—Mount Zion—near to the Old City but outside the walls. There was a flight of stairs that mounted to a lookout platform from which, on tiptoe, you could peer in the direction of the Western Wall, which was hundreds of meters away. You were warned not to point your finger because Jordanian snipers might mistake it for a rifle and shoot at you. I went to Mount Zion at every visit, as well as up to the roof of Notre Dame Hospice, another vantage point from which one could look out over the rooftops of the Old City.

You could not see the wall from either position. Only a grove of poplars was visible, which stood somewhere nearby, on the Temple Mount, above the wall. Only the tops of these trees could be glimpsed. At that time I was outwardly observant, as you had to be on a religious kibbutz such as mine, but I wasn't a particularly strong believer. Still, to see those poplars, only a glimpse of their crowns, was worth walking all day or all my life.

I served as a paratrooper in the regular army from 1960 to 1966, first as a corporal, then a lieutenant, finally as a company commander, before being released into the reserves. The army was forming a new reserve paratroop brigade, the 55th. My good friend Moshe Stempel had been appointed second-in-command; he brought me into the unit as a company commander. It was Moshe Stempel who formed the brigade, not Motta Gur, though Motta came to command it.

We had our first brigade exercise at Arad near the Dead Sea in April of '67, just two months before the war. Rain fell in torrents day after day, but we were young paratroopers; nothing could faze us. Practically everyone in the paratroops was a kibbutznik, most from the north, very secular, guys who had never said a prayer or even wanted to. My kibbutz was in the south, not far from Arad. I took all my friends from the brigade there, to meet my mom and to show them we weren't all crazy on a religious kibbutz. My mother made home-cooked meals for everyone. To her, they were her sons. She could not do enough for them.

37.

A PARATROOPER'S
WET DREAM

Every paratrooper's fantasy is to make a combat jump. You get a red border for your jump wings. But I will tell you the truth and you can believe it: There never was a paratrooper who wasn't secretly relieved—even Arik Sharon himself—when he learned that a jump under fire had been postponed or canceled.

> *Lieutenant Zeev Barkai is the twenty-three-year-old operations officer of Paratroop Battalion 71.*

We're at Givat Brenner now, a kibbutz near Tel Nof Air Base. It's Monday morning, the first day of the war. The men have been divided into jump groups and given their jump numbers and jump bags. In the bag are your weapon and your gear. You jump with the bag suspended between your knees.

Givat Brenner is citrus orchards. The entire brigade, all three battalions, is camped here among the groves. All morning we have been hearing and seeing Israeli warplanes take off from Tel Nof. They come screaming past the treetops in formations of four—Mirages and Vautours and other types that I don't recognize. No one tells us anything. The only news we have is from our transistor radios, and that news is all bad.

Radio Cairo is reporting that IAF fighter jets are attacking Egyptian bases in Sinai and across the Canal. According to the Egyptians, seventy Israeli warplanes have already been shot down. This is a calamity. Our air force has only, what, two hundred planes?

Wait, a new report: Eighty Israeli aircraft have been shot down. No, ninety. Can this be true? Radio Israel is mum. All reports are boilerplate. Blah blah heavy fighting, blah blah great struggle.

Our parachutes have arrived. At Tel Nof the planes are warming up—the Nords and Dakotas from which we will jump tonight at El Arish. One battalion, 66, has already left for the field to board the aircraft.

Our battalion is 71. Uzi Eilam is our commander. My job as operations officer is to stay glued to his shoulder, so I am privy to the latest news, which continues to be nothing. Not even Uzi knows what's going on.

We jumped two days ago, Saturday, a brigade-strength rehearsal at Ashkelon on the coast. Jumping is always a mess, even under ideal circumstances. Men break their legs. Wind scatters the formation; companies and platoons become separated. No one has good memories of jumping at the Mitla Pass in '56.

Tonight we will jump at El Arish in Sinai. Only the officers know this. Uzi will tell the men this morning. He has already made one speech about treating prisoners properly and refraining from looting.

At 10:05 an air force sergeant from Tel Nof pedals up to our camp on a bicycle. "Cairo West is ashes," he tells us. This is apparently an Egyptian airfield. We've never heard of it. The bicycle sergeant tells us not to believe a word we hear over Nasser's radio. It's all bullshit. Propaganda. The IAF has blown the hell out of eleven Egyptian airfields and is rearming and refueling to do it again. The sergeant promises to come back with more news as soon as he gets it.

Someone asks why we're not hearing this over Radio Israel. The brass is holding the news back, says the sergeant, because we want the Egyptians to keep lying. If the UN believes Nasser is winning, they will not intervene to force a cease-fire, and if the Russians believe it, they won't send their own troops to help Nasser.

"Cheer up, guys. The way things are going, you might not have to jump at all."

Paratroopers have their own crazy way of thinking. Two minutes ago we were all pissing in our pants about jumping tonight at El Arish. The Egyptians have a division or more there, with modern Soviet T-54 and T-55 tanks as well as the huge World War II Stalins and powerful SU-100 tank destroyers. Paratroopers travel light. What can we do against such armament when the heaviest stuff we'll have will be a few air-dropped jeeps and a handful of bazookas and 106-millimeter recoilless rifles?

That was two minutes ago.

Now, with news of the air force's success, our fears have flipped over. Now we're afraid we'll be left out of the war entirely.

No combat jump.

No El Arish.

The trucks arrive to take back our parachutes. Morale plunges further.

Wait! Here comes the bicycle sergeant with more news of the air force's successes.

"Go to hell!" our men are shouting. "Get outta here!"

"What's the matter with you guys?"

Our company commanders cluster around Uzi, the battalion commander, along with officers and senior noncommissioned officers from the other two battalions, 28 and 66.

Apparently the El Arish jump really has been scratched. Our guys in Sinai are advancing so fast they don't need us anymore.

"What does this mean, Uzi? Will we miss out on the whole show?"

Uzi reassures the officers. "We'll get something good—don't worry."

He has just spoken to Colonel Motta Gur, our brigade commander. Motta, Uzi swears, is on fire for action. He is lobbying the generals right now. Motta will not let us be left out. He will get us something good.

38.

"WHAT ARE YOU DOING IN JERUSALEM?"

I was filling my car with petrol when the shells started falling. I had a business meeting in Jerusalem at noon, but I had arrived early, so I decided to stop and fill up at a gas station I knew on a street near the King David Hotel. All of a sudden the shooting started. My watch read 11:15. Shells were exploding in the streets. Men and boys sprinted for cover. In the lane a policeman was shot by a Jordanian sniper firing from the Old City walls.

Ruth Dayan is Moshe Dayan's wife. She and her husband have been married since 1935 and have three grown children. Sons Assi and Udi have been mobilized and are serving now with their reserve units. Daughter Yael is with Arik Sharon's headquarters in Sinai.

I had no idea there was going to be a war today. How was I to know? At breakfast my husband said nothing. He was fooling me just as he had misled the reporters from the *New York Times* and the *Daily Mail* and even young Winston Churchill, grandson of the great Winston, and his father, Randolph, who had flown from London to Israel as journalists, eager to cover the apocalypse. Winston asked Moshe yesterday, man to man, how soon he anticipated the outbreak of hostilities. Should he and his father return to England or was war imminent?

"Nothing will happen for at least two weeks, if it happens at all," said my husband.

So Winston and Randolph Churchill went home.

Of course, Moshe knew the war was starting. He had given the orders!

Now here I am, crouching below the window line in the petrol station office while bullets are whizzing past outside. The phones are still working. I'm trying to reach my sister Reumah. I'm the only woman in the garage; the men are all lying flat on the floor. I'm not afraid. I can see hill-sides burning above the neighborhood of Yemin Moshe, but the Jordanian shelling does not seem furious, as it would if it were meant to precede an imminent assault. The rhythm of the explosions feels random, as if King Hussein's artillerymen are firing at whatever targets strike their fancy—if in fact they are aiming at all.

When I get through to my husband's office, he reacts with shock and surprise. "What in the world are you doing in Jerusalem?"

"I told you this morning I had a business appointment."

Well, he says, you can't come back by the main road; it's under artil-lery bombardment. He will be driving up to Jerusalem himself, Moshe says, to be sworn in as minister of defense. Well, I say, shells are landing close by; I'm heading to the King David Hotel before this whole block blows up.

To understand Jerusalem you must grasp its geography. The city is high. One goes "up to" Jerusalem. The Old City measures one square ki-lometer. It is surrounded by walls of rugged Jerusalem stone that look ancient enough to have been set in place by David or Solomon but in fact were erected by the Ottoman emperor Suleiman the Magnificent in the 1500s.

Jerusalem was King David's capital. He attacked and conquered the city around 1000 BCE, selecting the site because it was the one part of the kingdom that belonged to no tribe of Israel. All could convene here in peace. David brought the Ark of the Covenant here. His son Solomon built the Great Temple, where the ark resided within the Holy of Ho-lies. Mount Zion lies just outside the Old City walls, David's Tower just within.

The Old City has been identified as the site of the biblical Mount Mo-riah, upon which God commanded Abraham to sacrifice his son Isaac, and where an angel stayed that terrible blade. Canaanites and Israelites have held this city, as have Assyrians and Persians, Babylonians and Ro-mans and Hasmoneans, Byzantines, Mamelukes, Turks, and Crusaders. The Ottomans ruled for centuries, before the British succeeded them un-der the Mandate of the League of Nations.

Seven great gates (some name as many as eleven) give entry to the Old City, of which the most famous are the Zion Gate, the Jaffa Gate, the Da-mascus Gate, and the Lion's Gate.

Within the Old City walls lies Judaism's holiest site, the Western Wall and the ruins of Solomon's Temple. Christians presenting baptismal certificates may enter the Old City during certain holy seasons via the Mandelbaum Gate, the lone diplomatic accessway between Arab East Jerusalem and our own West Jerusalem. But the way is barred to Jews at all times.

The Jewish Quarter was razed by the Jordanians when they captured the Old City in 1948. All of its nearly sixty synagogues were destroyed or desecrated and its inhabitants killed or driven out. No Jew may enter, to pray before or even to glimpse the Wailing Wall.

Sites sacred to Christians and Muslims lie within and without the walls of the ancient city. The Lion's Gate Road leads directly into the Via Dolorosa, whose stones Jesus of Nazareth trod, bearing the cross upon which he would be crucified. The Church of the Holy Sepulchre lies footsteps away. It was built, so legend declares, on Golgotha itself, the Hill of the Skull. A slab inside the church is said to be the very one upon which Jesus's body was laid after the crucifixion.

Immediately east of the Old City walls, in a hollow of the Kidron Valley, lies the Garden of Gethsemane, where Jesus was betrayed in his final hours. Above this, at the summit of the city, towers the Temple Mount, upon which stand the Dome of the Rock, third holiest site in Islam, and the Al-Aqsa Mosque. The prophet Muhammad is said to have ascended to heaven from this spot.

Around these ancient quarters, the contemporary city has grown up.

Jordanian cannons are firing now from the collar of hills to the east, whose southernmost eminence is the Mount of Olives, which dominates the Old City and Jewish Jerusalem.

The Knesset, Israel's parliament, is sited here, in West Jerusalem. This is where Moshe will be sworn in. He will be driving up from the Kirya in Tel Aviv, from General Headquarters.

My husband and I know the city well. In 1948, immediately after the War of Independence, Prime Minister Ben-Gurion appointed Moshe military commander of Jerusalem. If you look at the cease-fire maps, you will see his initials, "M.D.," next to the Green Line. My husband drew these, with his counterpart of the Arab Legion, Lieutenant Colonel Abdullah al-Tell, with whom we both became good friends. The agreement, signed in November 1948, was called the "absolute and sincere cease-fire."

My own family goes back for decades in Jerusalem. My mother was the first woman driver in the Jewish city, in the 1920s. She had a Morris Minor that she drove every winter to Lebanon to ski.

My mother ran the first Arab-Jewish kindergarten in Jerusalem. We lived then in the Talbiya neighborhood near the Dormition Abbey, upon whose site the Last Supper is said to have taken place. My parents attended the London School of Economics. They spoke six languages and were socialists to the bone.

My husband and I met and fell in love on the moshav—the cooperative farming village—at Nahalal. I was a student at the village's excellent agricultural school. One time I was assigned to the milking in the dairy's quarantine shed—just me, alone at three in the morning with twelve sick cows who kicked violently each time I tried to approach. I confess I sat down and cried. Suddenly Moshe appeared. He had come to help me. This he did, sweetly and masterfully. Many nights he and I would hose down the cowsheds, standing in rubber boots beneath the light of a single lantern. I thought, Life does not get any happier than this! One morning I made a decision. I said to myself, Why am I getting up early to milk the community's cows? Why don't I get up early and milk the Dayans' cows instead?

After that, Moshe and I were never apart.

This is how a nation is built. We young people could see it then. We are creating a new kind of Jew and a new species of community—one couple, one family, one village at a time.

When the shelling slackens I make my way to the King David Hotel, where I leave my car. Teddy Kollek is Jewish Jerusalem's young mayor. He escorts me to city hall, very calm and unruffled, and from there across the slope to the Knesset. My husband will send soldiers to have my car driven home.

At the Knesset, Moshe is waiting, directing the war via multiple military radios and telephones. The swearing-in cannot begin. Prime Minister Eshkol has not yet arrived.

Two of my husband's most frequently used words are "moron" and "idiot." He does not direct these now toward the PM (who is in my opinion a good man and an extremely able leader, worn down, alas, by ill health and the terrible pressures of his office), but rather at himself, for agreeing to this ridiculous ceremonial trek in the hour of our nation's gravest and most immediate peril.

I tell Moshe the details of the shelling and of my taking shelter in the petrol station. He laughs and puts his arm around me. "Someone give Ruth a combat badge!"

39.

JERUSALEM OF GOLD

When word arrives that our brigade is being sent up to Jerusalem, I think, Dammit! That is my reaction and everyone else's, though in stronger language.

Sergeant Moshe Milo is Captain Yoram Zamosh's radioman and good friend in "A" Company of Paratroop Battalion 71.

We are paratroopers. We are the elite. Now, we're thinking, the generals are exiling us to some meaningless security assignment, protecting the city that the Jordanians will never be reckless enough to attack. We will sit on our hands and miss the war completely.

In Israel in '67 the army is too poor to have its own trucks for troop transport. We must use civilian vehicles, called up under the mobilization plan. Israel's national public transportation company is called Egged. That's what our brigade gets—the same Egged buses that take tourists sightseeing, and even city buses and school buses, with the same civilian drivers.

Five buses have been assigned to us in "A" Company. It takes a hundred or a hundred twenty to transport the full brigade. Our driver is a famous soccer player named Yehoshua "Shia" Glazer. He's an old guy, forty years old. He becomes like our father.

Each paratrooper is assigned a seat on a bus. That seat will be his for as long as the war lasts. I scratch my initials into the metal plate in front of mine. We have had the same buses and the same drivers for the whole three weeks of the waiting period.

Now here they are again, our familiar Egged buses, pulling up to the orchard at Givat Brenner. And here we are again, lining up to board them to be driven up to Jerusalem instead of jumping at night from Nords and Dakotas over Sinai. This is embarrassing. We feel frustrated.

We will not get our combat jump.

We will not get a red border for our jump wings.

Captain Yoram Zamosh, "A" Company commander:

The company commanders have been called together and sent up to Jerusalem ahead of the men and the buses. Time is four or four thirty in the afternoon. The idea is to get up to the city in daylight, so the commanders can assess the situation on the ground and come up with a plan of action.

We're in jeeps, a convoy of about twenty. I'm with Dan Ziv, the deputy battalion commander, and Uzi Eilat, commander of "B" Company. There's no ceremony to the departure. We throw our stuff in the back of the jeep and take off.

Dan Ziv is a head shorter than I and about ten years older. He is a bona fide hero of Israel, holder of the Itur HaGvura, the nation's highest decoration for valor, for his actions at the Mitla Pass in 1956. Uzi Eilat is just as tough, a farmer from Beit Hashita, a kibbutz up north around Mount Gilboa.

I'm not a hero at all. My aim is to do my job and keep my men safe. That will be glory enough for me, if I can achieve it.

Our convoy travels on back roads through Tsomet Nahson to Hartuv and from there to Sha'ar HaGai. Jerusalem is about sixty kilometers from Tel Nof. You cross the coastal plain and climb into the hills. We take the bypass roads because the Jordanians have mortars and artillery in the hills along the main highway. This is the shape of our country according to the 1948 armistice. From Tel Aviv, Jerusalem lies at the end of a narrow corridor that can be brought under enemy fire along its entire length.

The road we're on is narrow, one lane each way. Traffic is moving in one direction only, up to Jerusalem. Tanks from a reserve brigade—ancient Shermans, no match for the new Jordanian Pattons—shoulder our jeeps off the pavement. It's a mess, a slow-crawling jam of jeeps and command cars, tenders, ambulances, fuel tankers, and ammunition trucks.

I know the soldiers in my company are angry and frustrated at getting sent to what they believe will be old man's duty, manning defensive positions far, far away from the real fighting in the Sinai Desert. My feeling is the opposite.

Jerusalem!

Can this be the hour, after two thousand years?

Will we be the ones?

Meir Shalit is a nineteen-year-old sergeant in Paratroop Battalion 71:

My kibbutz is a place called Grofit. In Israel in '67, saying you come from Grofit is like saying your home is on the moon. Grofit is a patch of palms and melons deep in the Arava wilderness on the way to Eilat. One paved road runs from Beersheba, 190 kilometers. There's a phrase in Hebrew, *Sof haolam smolah*—"Go to the end of the world, then turn left." That's my home.

Seventeen guys from Grofit are paratroopers in Battalion 71. We are nineteen, twenty years old. One is twenty-one. He's the old man. On the kibbutz there is only one phone. No newspapers. We know nothing. A jeep drives up from Eilat and tells us, "Be ready, you will be mobilized soon." Then we hear that a bus is coming. We gather in the square in the evening with our girlfriends. No weapons, no equipment, just shirts and shorts.

Suddenly here is the bus and we are on it. No one tells us where we're going. I have half a minute to clutch my sweetheart, Malka, who will later become my wife. She's crying. "Take a bus to Tel Aviv," I tell her. "Tell my mother that my battalion has been called up and that I am fine."

My mother too has no phone. It is 1967.

Now, a few weeks later, our seventeen guys and a few hundred others are on a different bus, this time bound for Jerusalem. You would think a Jew would know all about Jerusalem, but I am as ignorant as a turnip. The Wailing Wall is there? Don't pull my leg. Mount Moriah? Tell me again, did something important happen there?

There is a popular song now called "Jerusalem of Gold." The radio plays it every twenty minutes. Some of the guys on the bus are singing it now. It seems to mean a lot to them.

On the buses we are jammed shoulder to shoulder with our packs and weapons and equipment. The little Uzi submachine guns are not too bad, but the bazookas and radios and, worse, the bangalore torpedoes and demolition charges fill every centimeter of space. It's hot. The road is terrible.

A bangalore torpedo is a device for blowing up barbed-wire entanglements and clearing paths through minefields. A bangalore is basically an iron pipe, about a meter and a half long, packed with explosives. In combat, our engineers, or just regular paratroopers like us, will slide the bangalores forward along the ground under the tangles of concertina wire, prime the detonator, then scramble back out of the way. If a barrier of barbed wire is too wide for a single bangalore to reach from front to back, two or more can be sleeved together to make one long charge that will, theoretically, do the job.

Do we even need bangalores? What is our mission? Why are we even going to Jerusalem? In the buses we are interrogating one another, as if each expects the guy next to him to know more than he does.

We are the blind leading the blind.

Yoram Zamosh, "A" Company commander:

At Latrun, halfway to Jerusalem, our convoy starts receiving mortar fire. A truck in front of our jeep takes a direct hit and blows sky-high, a big, powerful blast that fills the air with dust and smoke and sends men diving into ditches and medics rushing forward to help the wounded. All of a sudden it feels like war. It smells like war.

In Abu Ghosh, Israeli tanks in the street begin shooting to the north, toward Kiryat Anavim, Ma'ale HaHamisha, and Givat Har Adar—Radar Hill. I check my watch. It's 17:30, five thirty in the afternoon. We're in the outskirts of the city now. Streets are empty. You see fires here and there, shells land randomly, ambulances appear out of the smoke, followed or led by police cars. We come to a gas station on Malkei Israel Street. Two small boys in T-shirts are sitting on a little hill of sand. "What are you doing here?" we ask. "We want to see the war." They're the only ones on the street.

Schneller Camp is the headquarters of the Jerusalem Brigade, the reserve infantry force charged with the defense of the city. Wounded men are being carried on stretchers out of the gate. Someone says that Jordanian artillery has zeroed in on the compound; it's too dangerous for us to enter.

I run into my friend Amos Ne'eman, a kibbutznik from Beit Hashita. He's the operations officer of the Jerusalem Brigade. He gives us a few maps (we have none) and directs us to a nearby rooftop in the Batei Pagi neighborhood. "You'll be able to see from there."

"See what?"

"Whatever you can."

Sergeant Moshe Milo, Captain Zamosh's radioman:

Some in the buses think it is silly to sing "Jerusalem of Gold," and I would have agreed with them two hours ago. But now we are here. The setting sun is reflecting off the white stones of the city. I am thinking of a story of Rabbi Akiva.

When Rabbi Akiva and his wife were very young, before he was even a rabbi, they were so poor that they had to sleep in a barn. (This was 1,900 years ago, in the first century CE.) One morning when Rabbi Akiva awoke, the sun's rays chanced to glisten upon a few stalks of straw that had caught in his wife's hair, shining like gold. Rabbi Akiva was deeply in love with his bride. He felt ashamed that their straits were such that they must take shelter under a roof beside sheep and goats.

"One day," he promised, "I will get you a Jerusalem of gold."

For centuries Jews have wondered what Rabbi Akiva meant. What was a "Jerusalem of gold"? Some kind of jewelry? The meaning could not be literal. How could he give his bride a city of gold?

Here is what I think. I think the word "Jerusalem" signified to Rabbi Akiva something unattainable, a great prize, like paradise, the ultimate crown and gift of love.

Who are we, paratroopers on this bus, to speak, or even to think, of such matters? But in many ways that is what Jerusalem means to us too, even if we seldom give it thought and cannot put it into words.

Jerusalem is not a capital of wealth or empire. It is sited upon no river or harbor or overland trade route. It is not a hub of finance or commerce. Fashion or the arts have no place here. Jerusalem possesses no natural resources. Its location is of minimal strategic value. It is not London or Paris, Moscow or New York.

Jerusalem is a city of the spirit, a capital of the soul.

Let us make pilgrimage there, you and I, just once in our lifetimes. The wretched and the weary, the bereft and the broken in spirit: Let these tread Jerusalem's stones for one moment only, and, behold, each and every is made whole.

This is the Jerusalem Rabbi Akiva meant when he promised it, of gold, to the bride he worshipped. This, too, I believe, is what the poet William Blake sought to communicate in his poem, which became even for the English an anthem of the spirit:

> I will not cease from Mental Fight,
> Nor shall my Sword sleep in my hand:
> Till we have built Jerusalem,
> In England's green and pleasant Land.

In Hebrew, *har* means "mountain." Overlooking Jerusalem on Har HaTsofim, Mount Scopus, is a Jewish enclave surrounded on three sides by territory occupied by the Jordanians. The site contains the original Hadassah Hospital and several buildings of Hebrew University. The 1948 armistice safeguards this precinct, which is manned by a detachment of about a hundred twenty Israelis—eighty-five police and thirty-three civilians. Every two weeks the garrison is relieved and food and supplies are brought in, protected by a UN convoy. I have been among the soldiers (we had to dress as police officers, to adhere to the armistice) to man this outpost.

From Mount Scopus you look out over Jerusalem. You can see the Old City. On watch, I used to stand at a certain elevated vantage, searching with my eyes for the poplar grove that stands above the Western Wall. My name is Moshe, and I felt like Moses on Mount Nevo: I could see the Promised Land but would never be permitted to enter.

That is Jerusalem to every Jew. The Old City stands as the highest aspiration, the soul center of the people. Jerusalem is that which is longed for, dreamed of, prayed for—yet something that you believe you will never see and never touch. For two thousand years others have held this place. Babylonians, Persians, Romans, Hasmoneans, Byzantines, Muslims, Crusaders, Mamelukes, Ottomans, the British—for two millennia they have ruled this capital, which is sacred to our nation.

Sergeant Moshe Milo.

Where were we throughout these centuries?

Driven across oceans, scattered in Diaspora among the lands of strangers who hated us—exiled, outcast, subject to inquisitions, purges, pogroms. Laws are passed by barons and senators of our host nations, by whose edict we are forbidden to own land or property, to study or enter the learned professions, to govern ourselves, to marry. "Passion plays" are performed, in which the agony of our hosts' avatars are experienced as ecstasies by the faithful. At the heart of these rituals resides a devil, and the devil is us: the Jew.

Depicted as a rat, a parasite, subhuman, grotesque; rendered with horns and cloven hooves; portrayed as eaters of babies, vampires sucking blood in satanic rituals; vilified, calumniated, made infamous, and all from this lone ground: the fact that we possess no state, no home, no country, as every other people on earth.

We have a nation now at last. A Jewish state exists. Our country holds half of Jerusalem. But it is the vacant half, the barren half, the half that excludes the Old City and our people's most sacred sites. This I think on Mount Scopus, manning my post above Israel's ancient capital. I think that the exile of the Jews has not yet come to an end.

Now here we are, paratroopers on buses.

What is our mission? We don't know. Why do we hasten to Jerusalem? No one has told us. Yet each man, in his heart, cannot but feel and ask:

Can deliverance for David's city be at hand? Is this the hour at last?

No one dares speak or even think this, so we sing "Jerusalem of Gold."

I am not the only one who must hide tears.

40.

THE MOMENTUM OF EVENTS

By my orders issued this afternoon, June 5, Paratroop Brigade 55 has been detached as an element of Ugda Tal. I have canceled the combat jump that had been planned for tonight at El Arish in Sinai.

The 55th Brigade has been reassigned to the defense of Jewish West Jerusalem. Brigade commander Motta Gur and his senior officers are on their way to the city at this moment, traveling from Tel Nof in a convoy of jeeps. Their instructions are to assess the tactical situation and report back to the General Staff as soon as possible with their conclusions and plans of action.

Moshe Dayan is minister of defense.

I hate the sending of troops to Jerusalem. The act is the issue of the recklessness of one man: Jordan's King Hussein. I know Hussein well. He is not a rash leader, nor as a rule imprudent or irresponsible. But his throne rides upon the tiger's back. To preserve it he has had to put his head into the tiger's mouth.

The tiger is not Egypt. It is the anti-Israel fervor of Hussein's own people. Two-thirds of Jordan's population are Palestinian Arabs, displaced from their homes during the War of Independence in 1948. Nasser's general Riad now commands Jordan's armed forces. Hussein has ceded this power to him. He has had to, to quell his own mob. When Hussein returned from Cairo six days ago, having concluded with Egypt an alliance of war, the crowd swamped his limousine in joy and lifted the vehicle physically off the ground.

This morning Hussein's air force has attacked Israel. His long-range artillery has loosed barrages aimed at our air base at Ramat David; shells have fallen in civilian neighborhoods of Tel Aviv. Hussein's batteries continue to bombard Jewish West Jerusalem. By day's end his artillery will have fired six thousand rounds into the city. The king himself at 09:30

over Radio Amman has denounced "Zionist aggression" and declared that "the hour of revenge has come."

These actions of Hussein could be discounted, possibly, as the "making of a demonstration" to satisfy his Arab allies. But not the king's—or General Riad's—moves on the ground in Jerusalem. Troops of the Arab Legion have seized Jebel Mukaber, the high ground in southern Jerusalem upon which sits Government House, which had been the British high commissioner's residence in Mandate Palestine and which now serves as headquarters for UNTSO, the United Nations Truce Supervising Organization. This site is critical because it dominates the road to Bethlehem and Hebron, Jordanian cities in the West Bank from which Arab reinforcements—Hussein's two brigades of Patton tanks, not to mention the Iraqi brigades that may have entered Jordan from the east—may advance. Jordanian troops are reported advancing as well on the Israeli enclave on Mount Scopus.

I have ordered reserve forces forward to dislodge the Legionnaires from Government House and to seize all strategic road junctions by which enemy columns may approach Mount Scopus from the north. I have been compelled as well to send armored columns toward Jenin in the northern West Bank to silence Jordan's guns firing into the cities of our coastal plain. These actions must be taken. There is no alternative. But we are playing with fire. The last thing Israel's overtaxed forces need at this hour is the opening of a second front in the east.

What, in the end, is the job of the minister of defense?

Not the planning of war, nor of any individual battle. Long before I assumed my post, these designs were in place. I direct no clashes on the ground or in the air. My role as an emblem of national decisiveness was critical for morale in the three or four days prior to commencement of hostilities. But that need has now largely passed.

What task, then, am I called to perform?

I must manage the war, yes. But beyond that and indivisible from it, my task is to see beyond the curvature of the earth. My charge is to discern and to direct for the nation's advantage, so much as this is possible, the momentum of events.

The army wants all of Sinai. It wants to see its tanks on the eastern bank of the Suez Canal. This is one element of the momentum of events. A second element is evolving even now along our eastern front: the clash with Hussein and Jordan.

This day in Jerusalem, taking shelter from enemy shells in a broom closet beneath the Knesset, Menachem Begin has begun pressing for an assault on the Old City. The regional commander, General Uzi Narkiss, has approached me already with this ambition. Even the army's chief rabbi, Shlomo Goren, is quoting scripture:

> In the same day the Lord made a covenant with Abraham,
> saying, Unto thy seed have I given this land, from the river
> of Egypt unto the great river, the river Euphrates . . .

There is a phrase in Hebrew, *Eretz Israel HaShlema*. It means "Greater Israel"—biblical Israel, the land that God gave to Abraham, to Moses, to the Twelve Tribes.

Israel's current borders are, in the view of the champions of this cause, but a poor and shameful shadow of Eretz Israel HaShlema. The nation holds only half of our ancient capital Jerusalem. Judea and Samaria languish under Arab rule. Our holiest sites, the Western Wall and the Tomb of the Patriarchs, remain in enemy hands, where no Jew may tread, let alone worship.

The passion of the Jewish people to reclaim these prizes is a primary and perilous component of the logic of events.

Can I contain it?

In the academies of war, students are instructed in the tactical level, the operational level, and the strategic level. Beyond these, ministers manipulate the political level, the diplomatic level, the international level.

I must contend with all these, and the levels beyond.

The critical component is time. The future. It is fair for Gavish or Tal or Sharon to declare, "Take all of Sinai" and "Seize the Canal." This is the fighting commander's charge, to exploit success, to capitalize upon advantage.

Nor do I contest the legitimacy of the passion of Begin and Narkiss and Goren for the liberation of the Old City of Jerusalem. I share this dream myself. What Jew doesn't?

But someone must consider the effect of these acts, should they be accomplished—not only today but tomorrow, next week, and not only here, in this theater, the Middle East, but in Moscow and Washington, in the political capitals of the world. Nor may I in my deliberations leave out the centers of finance, of oil and energy, of trade by sea and air.

We in Israel do not contend against only one opponent or do battle upon merely one field. Behind Egypt and Syria stands the Soviet Union, which fears for its influence and prestige not only in the Middle East but also in other quarters of the globe. A reverse in our theater may overturn Russia's positions in Africa or Southeast Asia. Heaven only knows what debate is taking place now in the Politburo and the Kremlin.

At the antipodal pole from the Soviet Union stands the United States, whose objects and concerns, high-minded in the main, are even more dangerous for our vulnerable nation on account of their unintended and unforeseeable consequences.

Beyond these actors looms world opinion, the unpredictable and unknowable passions of the global audience, which may rally this day on behalf of the underdog Jews, then turn, tomorrow, and demand from us retrenchment and retreat.

Like a wildfire on a mountain, events create their own logic. When I was a boy I fought such conflagrations. I watched my sheep bolt and saw my goats break their necks in mad rushes over precipices.

Eshkol, now, believes in the army. Abba Eban has turned hawk too. Events have captured both of them. Menachem Begin recounts with passion the story of a fellow convict under the Soviets, an atheist and internationalist his whole life who, at the point of death aboard a prison train bound for Siberia, beseeched Begin and others to sing for him Israel's anthem, "Hatikva."

The land.

Eretz Israel HaShlema.

Of all our nation's ministers and commanders, Begin represents the most passionate articulation of this vision of return and reconquest. His blood is on fire with it. I cannot say he is wrong. But his fervor, seized upon by others of our people, will, I fear, unchecked by me, produce catastrophe in the end.

41.

NIGHT ANIMALS

I know Jerusalem well. After the Sinai Campaign in 1956 I served for three months as second-in-command to the legendary paratrooper Meir Har-Zion, with a battalion of commandos assigned to guard the city. Our soldiers manned posts along the Green Line. Wherever there was an Israeli position, a Jordanian post sat across from it. We got to know the Arab Legionnaires. We exchanged news with them across the barbed wire, the minefields, and the sandbagged barricades.

Major Uzi Eilam commands Battalion 71 of Paratroop Brigade 55.

I lived in Jerusalem again a few years later, on a break from service. I was an engineering student. My wife, Naomi, was finishing medical school. We lived in a small apartment at 18 Hapalmach Street in Rehavia.

Naomi and I were a young couple, without children at that time, and with very little money. We spent most Saturdays walking and exploring the city. It was a happy time. I must confess, however, that during those romantic perambulations I kept one eye out, as any Israeli officer would, for the tactical implications presented by the high ground and the low, the layouts of the streets and intersections, and the placement of man-made obstacles and fortifications.

I doubt that any officer in Brigade 55 knows Jerusalem as intimately as I.

Now, in the convoy of jeeps hastening up to the city, I am searching my memory for likely breakthrough points and potential lines of advance. Mortar rounds are falling when we reach Schneller Camp, headquarters of the local reserve brigade. Choking smoke fills the streets. From the operations officer of this formation we battalion and company commanders get a quick briefing and a few poor maps. Then Motta Gur, our brigade commander, pulls us aside, to a narrow street clear of the shelling, and lays out the concept of attack. He has worked this out in his head on the drive up to the city.

"Will we assault the Old City?" one commander asks.

"No!" is Motta's emphatic reply. "Our task for now is, first, to relieve the garrison of 120 Israeli soldiers who are surrounded on Mount Scopus, and, second, to seize positions in East Jerusalem from which we can defend the city if the enemy brings up tanks and troops from the Jordan Valley."

In other words, we must break through the Jordanian border defenses and capture the strategic ground east of the Old City.

The brigade, Motta says, will mount an assault across the Green Line—the 1948 armistice boundary between Israel and Jordan—along a sector demarcated on the north by Ammunition Hill and the Jordanian Police School, in the center by the neighborhoods of Sheikh Jerrah and Wadi Joz, and in the south by the American Colony and the Rockefeller Museum.

We are three battalion commanders—myself commanding Battalion 71, Yossi Yoffe leading Battalion 66, and Yossi Fratkin in charge of Battalion 28. Motta gives us an hour to prepare a plan for his approval. The buses carrying the soldiers of the brigade are on the way from Givat Brenner now. We will attack tonight, as soon as the men can be brought up and moved into position.

Each of the brigade's three battalions is given a specific objective in this night's operation. Battalion 66 will seize Ammunition Hill and the Jordanian Police School, then assault across the high ground to liberate the Israeli enclave on Mount Scopus.

My battalion, 71, will advance through the Arab neighborhoods of Sheikh Jerrah and Wadi Joz, "cleaning" these of enemy defenders and positions of resistance. We will move into positions from which the battalion will be able to assault the Augusta Victoria Ridge, adjacent to Mount Scopus, when and if such orders shall be issued.

Battalion 28 will break through the Jordanian defenses immediately after my battalion (our role is to clear the way for them), advancing on our right. These troops will neutralize enemy defenses in the quarter of the American Colony and the Rockefeller Museum. Together with our battalion they will seize the road junction beneath the northwest corner of the Old City walls and hold it, should the site be attacked, as is anticipated, by enemy reinforcements of armor and infantry advancing from the south and east.

The brigade will have a handful of ancient Sherman tanks in support and possibly a bit of artillery. We will have our own mortars. Motta says he may even be able to scare us up a few half-tracks to use as ambulances. No further mention is made of the Old City.

Though Brigade 55 is a reserve formation, and a newly constituted one at that, it possesses no shortage of proven commanders and heroes stretching back to the days of Unit 101 and earlier. Meir Har-Zion has joined his friend Micha Kapusta, who has brought his recon company from Sinai, volunteering to serve in any capacity. Katcha Cahaner commands a company in Battalion 28; five minutes into the fighting he will replace the battalion's fallen deputy commander, finishing the war in that post. My own second-in-command, Dan Ziv, is a holder of Israel's highest decoration for valor from the battle at the Mitla Pass in '56. Our brigade commander, Motta Gur, has led companies in Unit 101 and Battalion 890 under Arik Sharon. He fought at Mitla as well. I myself have a Medal of Courage, the Itur HaOz, from Operation Black Arrow. I have served as well for a year as Sharon's intelligence officer in Battalion 890. Many of Brigade 55's company and platoon commanders have trained under and served alongside Dayan, Sharon, and Rabin, as well as Uzi Narkiss, Aharon Davidi, Raful Eitan, Dado Elazar, and other legendary combat commanders.

But no one has assaulted a city. None has fought house to house in a locality of this scale. And no one has thrown together a plan of attack in sixty minutes, then put it into action, at night, with virtually no supporting armor or heavy weapons, in an urban environment that is a maze and a mystery to most of his men.

And that city is Jerusalem.

Sites sacred to three great religions intrude upon every potential axis of advance. As a battalion commander leading more than five hundred men, every one of whose lives is precious to me, this means one thing: I and my paratroopers will be constrained tactically in ways unimaginable in any other urban environment. The enemy may fire upon us from the Garden of Gethsemane. May we return fire upon this holy precinct? My soldiers may be shelled from positions adjacent to the Dome of the Rock or the Al-Aqsa Mosque. Our mortar batteries may be called upon to return fire on sites contiguous to the Church of the Holy Sepulchre. How can we do this? What degree of force may we bring to bear?

Every officer is aware of these excruciating constrictions. That we may be compelled by the religious and historical inviolability of the battleground to place our men's lives in jeopardy is a prospect none of us even wants to think about.

Zeev Barkai is a twenty-three-year-old lieutenant, operations officer of Paratroop Battalion 71:

Who knows the city? I certainly don't. What is the American Colony? Where is Sheikh Jerrah? Augusta Victoria and the Mount of Olives are just names to me. And I'm Uzi's operations officer! I'm supposed not only to know this stuff but be able to explain it to the guys who will be fighting in these places only a couple of hours from now.

We're on a rooftop. Shells are dropping randomly. Three hours ago we were rigging our jump gear, preparing to drop by parachute into the Sinai Desert. Now we're in Jerusalem.

"Have you seen the maps?"

Uzi Eilat comes up to me. He's our "B" Company commander, a tough kibbutznik, twenty-six years old, from Beit Hashita near Mount Gilboa.

"I haven't seen a damn thing."

"There's one the size of a napkin, and a few blurry aerial photos. That's it."

Eilat tells me he has it from an unimpeachable source that the Jerusalem Brigade has an office full of beautiful maps, maps they've been developing for years for just this moment.

"How can we get them?"

He laughs and shakes his head.

The building whose roof we're on is called a *shikun*. It was designed to be part living quarters, part blockhouse. The walls on the Jordanian side are triple thick; gunports have been cut into the roofline. Families live in the apartments below. In fact, mothers are shuttling back and forth in the street right now, bringing our paratroopers hot tea and cakes. Shells keep falling. When they hit a building, they punch sharp holes, making a boom like thunder. When a round lands in the street, it explodes with a fierce, sharp bang that rings and rebounds between the walls of the stone buildings. Sniper and machine-gun fire is constant enough to make you keep your head down, but 90 percent of it seems aimed at nothing.

I cross the roof, looking for Yoram Zamosh, our "A" Company commander. He's a religious guy. He knows the city.

I find him with his radioman, Moshe Milo. Zamosh gives me a quick orientation, kneeling and drawing a map in the stone grit of the rooftop.

"Think of the city as the English letter 'D.'"

His finger traces a vertical stroke.

"This is the Green Line. It divides the city. Israelis on the left—the west—Jordanians on the right."

East of the vertical stroke Zamosh draws a curved line, swelling outward like the bulge in a "D." This line represents the collar of hills that dominate the city. Mount Scopus at the top, Augusta Victoria Ridge in the middle, the Mount of Olives at the bottom.

The Jordanians hold all three.

Our brigade will have to take this high ground, Zamosh says—the Mount Scopus enclave first, because that's where 120 of our people are cut off and surrounded.

At the southern end of the curved line, Zamosh sketches a rough square. This is the Old City. That's where the Western Wall is, and a lot of other religious stuff that he hasn't got time to tell me about.

The Old City is held by the Arab Legion.

That, I do know.

But Zamosh's finger-drawn map helps. I'm starting to get a picture.

Uzi Eilat commands "B" Company of Battalion 71:

It's afternoon but the streets are already dark. Smoke. Thick, choking stuff. Our operations officer, Zeev Barkai, points out the cars parked along the curb. Every tire is flat, every window shattered from shrapnel. We and the other company commanders confer with our battalion commander, Uzi Eilam, in the shelter of a wall.

Uzi says the plan is to attack East Jerusalem, but nobody yet knows how or where. I ask when. "Soon," Uzi says. He has to run to meet with Motta Gur, our brigade commander. Get up on a rooftop, he tells us, and see what you can see.

I don't know the city. The landmarks mean nothing to me. We have to spring from rooftop to rooftop because the Jordanian snipers keep finding us. Someone says we may assault the Mandelbaum Gate. I don't know what that is.

Yoram Zamosh commands "A" Company:

When I came home to the kibbutz in '66 after six years of army service, I got married. My wife and I were very happy. We worked hard; we were planning a family. The army, of course, is very secular; after six years of life in the barracks and the field, I confess I had lost quite a bit of my spiritual focus. This did not go unnoticed in a religious community like mine, Kibbutz Yavne. One day several of the elders approached me. "Zamosh, it is time for you to start taking yourself seriously. Winter is here; there is no work in the fields. Take six months and go study in the yeshiva."

There was an excellent religious academy right next door to Kibbutz Yavne, but I didn't want to commute from home. I wanted to live and study full-time. I will do as you suggest, I told the elders, but it must be in Jerusalem.

I enrolled in Yeshiva Mercaz HaRav Kook. *HaRav Kook* means the academy of the legendary Rabbi Abraham Isaac Kook, the first Ashkenazi chief rabbi of modern Israel, who died in 1935 and was succeeded by his son, Zvi Yehuda Kook. To say you did your studies under either of these rabbis is like saying you sat at the feet of the Pope in Vatican City. The experience changed my life in every way. What had been to me the shiny but superficial surface of a sea became the great depths of an ocean.

In the evenings after studies, I used to lead groups of students exploring the streets of the Holy City. I got in trouble for this. In the yeshiva you are supposed to study Torah and nothing else. The case was brought to Rabbi Kook. He considered my nightly rambles and approved them. "To walk in Jerusalem," he declared, "is to study Torah."

So I know the city. I have hiked every street.

Beit HaKerem is a quarter at the western edge. From our rooftop reconnaissance posts along the Green Line we officers drive back west now, in the jeeps, five kilometers clear of the city center and the shelling. The soldiers have come up from Givat Brenner. The buses pour into Beit Ha-Kerem's central square.

It's safe here, a good marshaling place, well back from the Jordanian artillery. I find my men. Our battalion commander, Uzi Eilam, catches me for a moment. He has made up his plan of attack, he says, and now must get it approved by Motta Gur, who commands our brigade.

On the first rooftop, forty-five minutes ago, I got the chance to speak with Uzi aside. I have made this request: If the battalion gets the green light to enter the Old City, will he let "A" Company go first? Will he let my company lead the way into King David's capital?

Uzi has promised that he will check with Motta.

Uzi Eilat commands "B" Company of Battalion 71:

It's dark now. Our battalion commander, Uzi Eilam, runs a short, very focused commanders' meeting in a tiny apartment with the civilian family present. The mother and daughters bring us coffee and sandwiches. In the streets the people's morale is very low. Everyone is hunkered in shelters. They fear for us and for themselves. But no one leaves.

Zamosh has gotten into his head the idea that our brigade may get orders to enter the Old City. This is very important to him. Me? I couldn't care less. I am thinking of one thing only:

I have now seventy soldiers alive and in one piece. I want to come back with seventy soldiers in the same state.

I don't give a damn about the Old City.

Uzi shows us a map of Jerusalem. It's the only one he has. He passes out several fuzzy aerial photos. As hard as I squint, I can make sense of none of these.

I'm a kibbutznik from the north, from the Valley of Jezreel. What do I know of Jerusalem? As a commander you know only two things: what higher command wants your men to do, and what they actually *can* do.

The whole city is under blackout. We huddle under a single lightbulb. Uzi explains his plan. The street the battalion will marshal on is called *Shmuel Hanavi.* Samuel the Prophet Street.

"Where is it?" I ask.

"Go up the street till you get to the orchard."

"Which orchard?"

"You'll know it when you see it."

With that, I go out to the buses to brief my soldiers. I tell them that I have served with Uzi Eilam for six years. In every operation, he has picked "B" Company to go first.

"Understand?"

One more thing. Motta has given Uzi and the other battalion commanders the option of holding off the assault till morning, when the brigade will have air support.

The commanders have elected not to wait.

We will go now.

We are night animals.

42.

SAMUEL THE
PROPHET STREET

No streets feel as dark as those of a city under blackout in war. Our drivers grope through the maze of lanes and alleys, at the pace of a walking man, behind headlamps painted blue and narrowed to slits. Already buses are getting lost.

Uzi Eilam commands Paratroop Battalion 71.

We are moving forward to Samuel the Prophet Street. I know an alley there, called Gemul. On a night ten years ago, when I served as deputy to Meir Har-Zion, we set an ambush on that site to protect a supply convoy heading toward Mount Scopus.

Gemul, tonight, will be our breakthrough point.

Why have I chosen this site? It's obscure. Out of the way. The last place anyone would pick to cross. The march-up is safe. A line of buildings protects the approach both from enemy fire and, more important, from observation.

There are adjacent lanes in which our companies can marshal before descending the slope into no-man's-land. Gemul Alley is broad enough for us to advance in force but defined enough to keep our column from straying off the axis of advance.

H-hour is forty minutes from now. With luck we can get the men into position in fifteen or twenty minutes.

I have presented two plans to Motta. The first is a frontal assault on the Mandelbaum Gate. There is a phrase in Hebrew, *hafooch al hafooch*. It means "upside down of upside down." In baseball, a pitcher in a situation that demands a curve ball may choose in fact to throw a curve ball, figuring that the batter will never expect him to do something so obvious.

This is the logic of *hafooch al hafooch*.

My battalion could assault Mandelbaum, the most heavily fortified post in the city, figuring the Jordanians would never believe we would do such a crazy thing.

Motta smiles when I suggest this.

"Uzi, that is too clever by half."

So here we are, on Samuel the Prophet Street.

Dan Ziv is my second-in-command. He is the best and most experienced soldier in the battalion. With such an officer, one has no need to issue instructions in detail. I tell Dan what needs to be done. He will figure out the best way to do it.

I shuttle back up the hill to the soldiers materializing out of the darkness. The men move swiftly, crouched and silent, into the shadows of the lanes beneath the buildings. None of us has experienced this type of fighting before. The battalion has had only one day of training in urban combat, and I had to argue strenuously with brigade staff to get us those few hours, appropriating a vacant school complex in the Ben Shemen Youth Village to run my soldiers through house-to-house and close-quarters fighting drills.

As the men find their places within their platoons and companies, I speak individually and collectively to my officers. Such good men! Dan Ziv, Zeev Barkai, Uzi Eilat, Moshe Peled, Yoram Zamosh, many more. I find Zamosh with his 1st Platoon commander, Yair Levanon. "Do your men understand what they must do?"

Levanon points east into the dark. "Go that way and don't stop till we reach Amman." He and Zamosh are ready. I rap them warmly on the shoulders.

Against all probability, a respectable plan has taken shape. It's simple. Its demands lie within the battalion's capabilities. On paper it should work.

But we all know what happens to paper, and to plans.

Dan Ziv is deputy commander of Paratroop Battalion 71:

At midnight Uzi tells me to pick the precise breakthrough point. I take my two radiomen and go down the slope of Gemul Alley. Samuel the Prophet Street is behind and above us, with the first men of our battalion and part of Battalion 28 coming up and finding their way into the shadows in the lanes and the side streets.

A hundred meters down the slope our party strikes barbed wire. Staked entanglements and coils of concertina wire stretch across a shallow basin about 150 meters wide and 200 meters deep. Twenty years of paper and trash have piled up in this junkyard. It's a mess. Mined, no doubt. Fire from half a dozen Jordanian positions pops and zings over our heads.

I pick a spot and sit down.

War is not like a John Wayne movie. Sometimes the best thing is just to stop, hold still, watch, and listen. After twenty minutes, with heavy fire continuing the whole time, I get the picture.

The Jordanians have machine-gun emplacements on the roofs of buildings and in sandbagged positions on upper and lower floors. They are firing from ground positions and from basement slits. But no one is shooting at us here at the base of Gemul Alley. They can't see us. For whatever reason, the Jordanians are not covering this low point. Nor do they realize that our battalions have moved into position above on Samuel the Prophet Street. The enemy is firing randomly, to keep his courage up and so that his officers will not yell at him for doing nothing.

This spot is a good one.

It will be our breakthrough point.

An advance party will use bangalore torpedoes to blow a path through the wire and to set off any mines. Then our battalion and Battalion 28 will pour through.

It can work.

If our column of paratroopers can cross this valley quickly, at a run, we can get past the enemy's forward defenses. We can get behind him before he realizes we have even broken through.

Uzi Eilat, "B" Company commander:

We can't find the bangalore torpedoes. What the hell? In the dark, two of our buses have taken wrong turns. They're lost. All our bangalores are on those buses.

Dan Ziv has come back up the hill. Two Sherman tanks have arrived to reinforce us. Dan chases them away. If the Jordanians see or hear the Shermans, they'll know that this is our crossing point.

My guys are scrounging bangalores from the other companies. Finally, when we get six or seven, the lost buses arrive, except for one or two teams. If I believed in God, I would thank him. We are ready.

*Shai Hermesh is a twenty-three-year-old bazooka man in
Yoram Zamosh's "A" Company:*

I'm in one of the lost teams. We're still lost.

Every platoon in an Israeli paratroop company has a "weapons element" in addition to the combat soldiers: two bazooka men (gunner and
loader), three mortarmen with a light 52-millimeter tube, and three men
with the bangalores.

Our team was ordered into the first buses because our heavy weapons
will be needed to support the initial breakthrough. That's how we got lost.
The column of buses came under mortar fire. Two went forward; the others went back. Now we're separated.

We're on the street. Seven of us. Heavy mortar fire continues to rain
down, scaring the hell out of us. The streets are pitch black. We're lost. We
have no officer, no map. None of us knows his way around Jerusalem.

Our job, we know, is to support the breakthrough. But we don't know
where we are, we don't know where the breakthrough point is, and we
don't know how to get there.

Meir Shalit, nineteen-year-old sergeant in "B" Company:

One of the buses is still missing. It might have gotten hit by mortar
fire; nobody knows.

I'm in the third bangalore team in Uzi Eilat's company. We're safe.
We've reached the assembly point for the assault. A bangalore torpedo
team consists of three men—two with the bangalores, one with a Belgian
FN light machine gun to cover them.

The first two teams will blow the wire; my team is the reserve. "Push
the bangalore under the wire, activate the fuse, run like hell."

Uzi Eilam, battalion commander:

My plan calls for "B" Company, Uzi Eilat's, to breach the wire. The
next company will race through and take positions facing right and left.
Their job will be to protect the flanks. After them, the main body of our
battalion—with Battalion 28 immediately behind—will move through as
fast as it can, penetrating the Jordanian defenses as deep as possible.

A couple of hundred meters east of the breakthrough point lies the
Nablus Road, called on some maps Shechem Road (the ancient name for

the city of Nablus). The Nablus Road is our first objective. When we strike this thoroughfare, which runs north and south, half the battalion will turn right—south—and move as quickly as possible to seize the neighborhood of the American Colony and, beyond it, the Rockefeller Museum. The other companies will continue forward, east, through the neighborhood of Wadi Joz. A wadi is a dry riverbed; Jordanian mortars are firing from somewhere down in the wadi. We will eliminate them, capture the entire quarter, and take up positions at the base of the slope facing the collar of hills made up of Mount Scopus, the Augusta Victoria Ridge, and the Mount of Olives.

To our left, north by several hundred meters, lies Ammunition Hill and the Jordanian Police School. Battalion 66 will assault these positions. We don't know now, and won't learn till the sun rises tomorrow, that the fight for these positions will be the bloodiest and most brutal of the war.

Dan Ziv, deputy battalion commander:

Eilat's company is first down the slope. They will blow the wire. Eilat is solid and smart, without fear. Zeev Barkai has come up, our operations officer, young, another good fighter. And we have Benny Ron, too, Uzi's friend, another strong hand who is not even part of the battalion but has bolted from his own desk-bound unit to be with us in this fight.

The teams with the bangalore torpedoes scoot ahead. They will slide the explosives under the wire. Behind them in single file crouch the paratroopers—fifty that I can see, a few hundred more above them—along the slope. They're scared, yawning.

I remind the men up front of what every soldier knows: In a breakthrough, the first ten minutes are everything.

See the Jordanian machine guns?

See the houses they're shooting from?

Get through, get behind them, hit them from the direction they least expect.

Benny Ron has joined Battalion 71 from an administrative outfit:

I'm not even part of the battalion. My unit is research and development, an office job. When the war orders come on June 5, I tell my boss there's no way I'm going to be kept out of combat.

I bolt to Uzi. "Can you give me a job?"

Uzi and I have been friends forever. He says, "Sure, Benny. Let me think up a title for you."

That's the way it works in this army. Old-timers from a battalion, retired guys—they just show up. They can't stand not to be part of it. Others fly in from the States, from England, from South Africa. "Put me to work!"

Uzi assigns me to Dan Ziv's team, to help organize the breakthrough. You can learn a lot watching a soldier like Ziv. He did not win his Medal of Valor for nothing. Ziv's body language projects fearlessness. It says to the young troopers, "I am in no hurry. Watch me do my job. Do yours the same way."

The neighborhood we're in is called Sheikh Jerrah. Houses are sparse. Jewish families live up top on Samuel the Prophet Street; Arab neighborhoods spread downhill across the wire. Arab houses are built high, with thick walls, like forts. The top story is where the sons in the family will live when they take wives. You can tell an Arab house because the rooftop is flat and unfinished.

02:25. H-hour. Mortar and machine-gun fire opens up along the whole line. Powerful projectors mounted on rooftops light up the city, seeking targets for the artillery. Eilat's men creep forward, ignite the bangalores.

Nothing happens.

Duds.

Our guys behind are cursing.

"What's the holdup, guys?"

"What are you idiots doing?"

Our mortars have set up their firing pits a kilometer north, in the neighborhood of Sanhedria. Gideon Bikel is the weapons officer. Dan Ziv has given him orders to blanket no-man's-land with fire, to make the Jordanians keep their heads down.

Amid the dust and smoke, Eilat's bangalore teams try again to blow the wire. This time the charges detonate, only the wire rises straight up in a big, tangled mass and lands right back where it started from!

Somehow we get it cleared.

The paratroopers stumble down the slope and into the gap. We go too. There's some kind of industrial yard a couple of hundred meters ahead. A brick factory, we'll learn later. The enemy has at least one heavy machine gun in there, maybe two. North of the brick factory, invisible now in the dust and smoke, squats a bastion that our fellows will come to call the House of Death.

43.

THE HOUSE OF DEATH

The battalion has broken through. I am heading on foot back to the casualty collection center. Our command group, with one company, has reached the Nablus Road. But there are problems in the rear. They must be dealt with before we can move forward.

Uzi Eilam, Battalion 71 commander:

Our medical officer, Dr. Igal Ginat, has commandeered a house and made it into a triage center. He and his medics have been overrun with casualties. At the breakthrough point, as our men of Battalion 71 moved forward to dash through the wire, soldiers of Battalion 28 advanced into their places behind them. Suddenly a barrage from a battery of Jordanian 81-millimeter mortars began. Rounds fell directly upon the concentration of troops. Sixty-four men were wounded and killed, a catastrophe in a battalion of only about five hundred men. Dr. Ginat and his medics stayed at the breakthrough point for an hour, getting the wounded men treated and evacuated. Now he has come forward across the wire into Jordanian territory. He and his team have set up a medical station in a yard adjoining an Arab house and in several rooms inside. On the ground I see prone forms, motionless. Blankets cover their bodies and faces. Boots, protruding, are paratrooper red.

In combat there is no time for grief. A commander must act. He must project decisiveness and certainty. No matter how grim the situation, he must act as if it is under control. If your soldiers read fear on your face or discern irresolution in your posture, you have failed them.

I thank Dr. Ginat and his medics. I commend them on their extraordinary efforts. The worst is over, I assure them. Our lead companies have reached the Nablus Road. Elements of Battalion 28 have joined us. The enemy is on the run. Our combined force is moving forward.

The combat commander must be an actor sometimes. This is war. You must use everything. Everything.

Dan Ziv, deputy battalion commander:

When I call my soldiers to me, I explain how this type of fighting feels to the enemy. I want to ease my young men's fears. They must understand that the Arab Legionnaires are scared, too. "I would not trade places with them. They are done for and they know it."

I make my young paratroopers hear me:

Where are the Jordanians? They are in houses. On roofs. In basements. Do you think these positions are impregnable? The night is dark. The enemy can't see a thing. This house he is using as a machine-gun emplacement? People live in this house! It is not a bunker or a pillbox that he has built and cleared fields of fire for. It is not designed to fight from. The enemy defender has had to move the family out, find a window where he can put his gun. Invariably the weapon covers only a portion of the field. He and his team are surrounded by blind spots, dead ground, and approach angles that attackers can use to get at them.

The enemy knows he is a sitting duck. If the walls of his house are thick, he is blind and deaf. If they are thin, our small-arms fire will rip through them. For sure these civilian hideouts are no protection against a heavy machine gun or a bazooka or a 106-millimeter recoilless rifle.

What is the enemy hoping for? His fondest wish is to hold off these crazy Jews for even a few minutes, then pack up and get the hell out, because he knows if he stays too long, twenty guys with red boots will be pounding down the steps to his burrow, coming at him from all sides, from the roof, from the house next door, and the next thing he knows, a hand grenade will be rolling across the floor and stopping between his knees. Time always works against the defender. The enemy is waiting to be killed and he knows it.

Uzi Eilam, Battalion 71 commander:

In battle you must always go forward. Has a seam opened? Run through it. Don't stop at ten meters; keep going for a hundred. The deeper you thrust into the enemy's rear, the more you disorient him and the more you sap his fighting spirit. The foe may be brave, he may be well trained, he may be led by officers of courage. But when he hears your men's voices on his right and left and in his rear, he will grab his kit and flee.

At the same time, you may not press forward so recklessly that you leave your rear exposed and vulnerable to counterattack. The commander must keep moving among his fighting elements. Go to the spot. Feel the ground. The more you move, the more you see your soldiers and the more they see you.

Are my officers conducting the fight wisely? Are they in control? Are they aggressive? Do they have a picture of the field and of their own and others' positions on it?

Sometimes, issuing instructions to your soldiers, you see that adrenaline and fear are so strong in them that they can't hear your words, they can't understand your meaning.

Keep your questions simple.

"Where is your commanding officer?"

"From which direction is the enemy fire coming?"

Make your orders even simpler.

"Go there."

"Do that."

In battle, soldiers hide. Officers hide. They are afraid. They don't want to be killed. Someone has ordered them to capture a certain house. But they have seen six of their friends enter that house and none has come out. So they make themselves invisible.

This is how an advance stalls. An officer is not willingly acting the coward; he's trying to gather himself for a minute, to collect his men and his thoughts. But sixty seconds becomes twenty minutes and pretty soon two hours have passed and that house is still killing your men.

You have to go there. You must find the officer on-site. When he sees you, he will act. If he cannot, you must replace him. Right then.

The commander has graver responsibilities than any man in the battalion. He has to acquire and hold in his mind a picture of the entire field. He must know where he is, where each of his companies are, where all elements of the enemy are, and how that dynamic is changing and evolving.

You are receiving reports from runners, from radio operators. A problem persists here; an opportunity has opened up there. You are holding the battle picture in your mind, not in three dimensions but four. The fourth is time.

What you cling to is initiative. Your forces are attacking. They are

dictating the action. What you fear most is an enemy counterattack, because it shows that the foe's spirit is strong. Your struggle, remember, is
not with your enemy's men or his positions but with his fighting spirit.
That is why we break through, why we rush into the foe's rear: to sow
terror and confusion, to disrupt his rehearsed schemes, to compel him to
decide and to act amid fear and chaos.

At the medical station, I learn that one of my company commanders
has been wounded. Where is his deputy? Missing. What has happened to
his soldiers? No one knows.

Zeev Barkai, my operations officer, is with me. I know now, from radio reports and from firsthand accounts, that two enemy strongpoints in
our rear have not been reduced. They are still killing our soldiers. One is
being called by our men the House with the Burnt Roof. The other, the
House of Death.

My watch reads 03:20. We must be past the Nablus Road by sunrise.
I assign Barkai to take care of the House with the Burnt Roof. He takes
several men, including our intelligence officer, Barry Hazzak, and Gideon
Bikel, our mortar platoon commander.

Zeev Barkai is operations officer of Battalion 71:

I am trying to find the House with the Burnt Roof. As our party nears
a thoroughfare—which could be the Nablus Road, but who the hell knows—
out of the darkness comes a column of paratroopers from Battalion 28. I
recognize the commander. He's a friend from Kibbutz Deganiah Alef, near
my home. He has been wounded. His head is bandaged.

"Barkai?"

"Nachshon, are you okay?" My friend's name is Nachshon Ben-
Hamidar. His father was the principal of my elementary school.

I radio to Uzi, alerting him that a column from Battalion 28 is in his
rear. The last thing our guys want is to start shooting at each other.

"Nachshon, how would you like to help me clear a house of Jordanian
snipers?"

He laughs. "Good luck, Barkai!"

And he leads his guys away down the road.

Before my group advances another fifty meters a grenade explodes out
of nowhere. Bikel is hit. Barry and I carry him, lifting from under his
shoulders, back to the casualty collection center.

This is the insanity of fighting at night in a place with buildings and roads. You cannot have an imagination. If you do, you'll be paralyzed with fear, because every window and shadow may hold your death. No one has told me the problem with the enemy strongpoints in our rear. It's not hard to figure out, though. Men get scared. Their buddies have been killed entering a house and they don't want to go back in.

What's screwing everything up is that the enemy has pulled out of his original defensive positions and taken cover in various civilian houses. These new posts are no longer operating as pillboxes or fighting positions. They're just four or five Legionnaires trying to survive. This makes them very dangerous. You don't know where they are or when they'll hit you. You pass along an alley and suddenly the man in front of you falls dead.

We drop Bikel off with Dr. Ginat and start across an open space toward an area of dark buildings. I have Barry, with Bikel's radioman, plus my own operations sergeant, Leizer Lavi. Suddenly voices call from the shadows.

"Barkai! Barkai! Help us!"

The men are from one of our companies. As battalion operations officer, I have little contact with individual troopers, so I don't recognize anyone. But they know me. They're begging me to take over, to lead them.

"There's a house back there . . ."

"We attacked it . . ."

"Two of our friends got shot on the stairwell . . ."

"They're still there, Barkai!"

This is not an easy thing to hear. The men are racked with anguish. Soldiers, without someone to command them, often cannot organize themselves to act, even though they know they must and they wish desperately to do so. But as soon as someone gives shape to their problem and puts forth a solution, they respond with will and courage.

I can see the house. Its roof is not burnt.

This is not my assignment. It is not the task Uzi has set for me. But I am an officer. What comes before me, I must act on. I cannot pass up a wounded man or turn aside from an emergency.

I organize the men quickly. I will get to the House with the Burnt Roof later.

We attack this other house with rifles, machine guns, antitank guns, and hand grenades. I and two others scramble up the staircase where our two men have been shot. We get them out. They're alive. One is David Giladi, whom I don't know but who, it is clear from the men's concern, is a favorite among his platoon. He has been shot in the head.

The staircase is slick with blood. I cannot believe that men can bleed out so much and still be alive. We have no stretcher. We break down two wooden doors and carry the men on these.

As we're stumbling toward the casualty collection center, my radio-man asks if I'm okay.

"Of course. Why?"

"Your back."

My shirt apparently is dark with blood. I remember a grenade explod-ing earlier and feeling a sensation like needles striking my back.

It's nothing.

I'm fine.

The firefight continues around the House of Death. My party has not been able to overrun the place. But we have got our wounded men out, and I have organized the soldiers to keep the building under fire without letup. Dawn is coming. The enemy will either be killed or run away.

Moshe Peled is deputy commander of "C" Company:

What is our advance like? Little wars. We are fighting little wars all over the field. A house, a bunker, a machine-gun position. Each one is a war that is fought by a platoon, a section, sometimes just three or four men. What keeps them together? They are friends—simple as that.

In American movies you see the typical squad of GIs and dogfaces: the wisecracking guy from Brooklyn, the corn-fed kid from Kansas, the hand-some lieutenant from Tennessee. They fight as one. But when the war is over, each man, no matter how close he has been to his buddies, will go home to his town or farm or city. He will never see his friends again.

It's not like that in Israel. My officers, my men, I have known them my whole life. I will call them friends till I die. We will fight this war together, as we have fought the one before that and we will fight the one after that, all in this same battalion, this same company.

When I call to a man, "Assault that house from the north side," I do not call him "corporal" or "sergeant." He is Mickey. He is Avi.

Shai Hermesh, bazooka man in "A" Company:

Finally our "lost patrol" has found somebody. A Recon team is leading us toward the breakthrough point.

Hurry! We feel desperate to help our friends, who are under fire and need our heavy weapons.

The hours have been a nightmare. Bazooka and mortarmen are supposed to be issued light weapons to defend themselves with—Uzis or at least Webley pistols. You can't protect yourself against an Arab Legion patrol with a bazooka. But we have nothing. The army is so poor.

"Don't worry," a sergeant told me three days ago at the supply depot. "You'll find plenty of weapons on the ground once the killing starts."

Meir Shalit, nineteen-year-old sergeant in "B" Company:

03:40. Our company has formed up on a road. Which road? I don't know. Heading where? I have no clue.

I'm still carrying my bangalore torpedo. Why? Because I can't find anyone to give it to and if I throw it away I will get in trouble. Where are we? Two minutes ago some guy from "C" Company moved past and said in an excited voice, "Look up there—that's Mount Scopus." I suddenly realized we're in Jerusalem. I'd forgotten completely. This is how dumb you can get.

My job now is messenger for Lieutenant Menachem Reineets, Uzi Eilat's second-in-command. I'm supposed to run with dispatches. Carrying my bangalore torpedo.

We advance along the road, step by cautious step, in two columns, one on each shoulder, weapons facing outward, with a wide interval between men. It's still dark. Mortar shells are dropping, making sharp, hard bangs; machine-gun and sniper fire comes from scattered directions.

I have learned one thing from this, my first experience of war: Leaders are everything.

Individually, we soldiers may be brave. Collectively, we may make up a skilled, well-trained unit. But without a strong hand to guide us, we balk and freeze. We become confused and surrender initiative.

I can see Uzi Eilat up front, leading the column. This is Israeli style: The company commander goes first. Is this crazy? He makes himself a prime target for a sniper. But by his presence, in the lead, we in the column are made strong.

I know nothing. I can see nothing. But if Uzi tells me, "Do this," I will do it.

Uzi Eilam, Battalion 71 commander:

We have reached "the Springboard," or the place that the men are calling by that name. It's a wide spot, with a gas station, at a junction on the Nablus Road. From here I can see the field. To my right the road runs south toward the Rockefeller Museum. Good. The junction beneath the museum is one of our objectives. I have sent Uzi Eilat's company forward to seize it. This force is not actually Eilat's company, but elements of "B," "C," and "A," with no small smattering of paratroopers from Battalion 28 who have gotten separated from their units and have latched onto any formation speaking Hebrew and wearing red boots.

To my left, in the first glimmers of daylight (which works against us because it will help the Jordanian gunners see us) I can make out the western terminus of the dry riverbed of Wadi Joz. The Jordanian mortars are down there somewhere. I have sent a force, and will send another if I have to, to locate this position and destroy it. Once that post has been silenced, half the danger to the battalion will be over.

A residential street, also called Wadi Joz, parallels the ravine. I will take a company myself—Yoram Zamosh's "A" Company—and advance down this axis. This street will take us to the forward edge of our other objective: an imaginary line facing the high ground of Augusta Victoria Ridge.

Ten minutes ago, I had to lead my own command group to knock out a sniper. This is insanity. But there was no alternative. We were under fire; it would have consumed minutes to organize another group to do the job. When we finished with the first position, a second machine gun opened up on us from another house. We had to take care of that one, too.

This is how the struggle is playing out in all quarters. Each company, each platoon, each squad is fighting its own war.

Zeev Barkai, operations officer:

The sky is getting light. We have brought the wounded men from the House of Death to the medical station. Bodies of paratroopers lie in a row on the ground, covered by blankets. A pile of no-longer-needed weapons grows beside them.

The casualty collection station is in the home of an Arab family. The owners remain, scared to death, though our guys are treating them with great courtesy. I ask the father's permission to enter the kitchen for a drink of water. "Go in," he says in Hebrew.

In the kitchen I come face-to-face with my reflection in a mirror. Can that be me? I'm so pale! My shirt is soaked with blood. On a whim I decide this will be my lucky shirt. I will not take it off till the war is over.

A joke pops into my head. The one about the officer who deliberately wears a red shirt into battle so that if he gets wounded the blood will not show. Then he gets into a particularly terrifying firefight. At the height of the action, he looks down at himself and shouts to his sergeant, "Bring me my brown trousers!"

Dan Ziv, deputy battalion commander:

I believe in being stupid. You have to be stupid in war because if you were smart you would never do what you need to do to survive. That's why being young is so important in soldiers. When you're young, you don't know the horrible things that can happen to the human body and the human mind.

At Mitla in '56 I drove down a road and they gave me a medal. Was I brave? I was stupid. I am not so stupid anymore and not so brave, either. But here and now I know one thing: I have three recoilless-rifle jeeps with their crews and I must get them to the junction of Sultan Suleiman Street and the Jericho Road, beneath the Rockefeller Museum, where the northeast corner of the Old City walls juts out. And I must get them there before full daylight.

What is a recoilless rifle? It's the poor man's Sherman tank.

The rifle itself is just a tube, like a big bazooka. It's too heavy for one man to carry. You need a jeep. A recoilless rifle fires a 106-millimeter shell that will blow the third story off a three-story building or the turret off a Patton tank. Already this night our recoilless rifles have taken out three positions of enemy machine guns.

The problem with a 106 mounted on a jeep is it makes an irresistible target. On the training range, a recoilless rifle crew sights carefully (this is done by firing a .50-caliber tracer round, as a marker, from a barrel that is calibrated to be precisely parallel to the recoilless cannon's barrel), then fires the actual 106 round. In combat if you did that, you and the crew would be dead five seconds after the enemy spotted you. So what we do is dash the jeep into position, leap off and take cover, make sure we haven't been spotted, then spring back out onto the jeep, sight quickly, fire, and get the hell out.

The reason these recoilless rifle jeeps are needed at the intersection of

Sultan Suleiman Street and the Jericho Road is to stop any Jordanian tanks that might be coming from the east and south, from the Jordan Valley, to reinforce their Arab brothers. The topography of Jerusalem is such that the enemy can advance along this one road only.

We must get our 106s in position to fire down that road. We won't last long, slugging it out with Arab Legion tanks and their British-trained crews, but maybe we can knock out the first one or two and jam up the road with their wrecked hulks.

Zeev Barkai, battalion operations officer:

I have found the House with the Burnt Roof. This was my original assignment from Uzi, what seems like two days ago but was actually only ninety minutes. Dawn is coming; the sky is starting to get brighter. I have lost Bikel to wounds. My other guys—Barry and my operations sergeant and Bikel's radioman—have gotten lost along the way.

It's just me as I creep up behind the house.

The heavy machine gun in the house has stopped firing. At this moment I hear nothing.

Suddenly I see soldiers, paratroopers from Battalion 28, in several shallow trenches only a few meters behind the house. I recognize one. He's from Beit Hashita. Years later, he will be elected mayor of the town next to mine. "What are you guys doing here?"

No one answers.

I know what they're doing. They're keeping alive.

I tell them they're coming with me into the house. But when I look, the rear door is solid iron. "Look at this! How the hell are we gonna get in?"

"You wanna get in?" says the future mayor. And he screws a rifle grenade onto the end of his rifle and blows the hell out of the door.

"Follow me!" I shout and dash into the house.

No one follows.

Two Arab Legionnaires pop from a doorway. It's like an American Western. We all go for our guns. I win. I don't even stop to look. I sprint up the stairs to the room with the machine gun.

The soldiers out back have not budged.

The upstairs room is charred black and reeking of smoke. The roof and one whole wall are gone. I think, Dan Ziv's guys must have knocked this post out with their recoilless guns. That's why our guys are calling this the House with the Burnt Roof.

Outside, the paratroopers from Battalion 28 look relieved to see me emerge in one piece. They ask what they should do. I point them toward the front, or where I imagine the front is now.

You have to understand how soldiers are. The Jordanians inside the house were not about to shoot it out with the Israelis outside, and neither were the Israelis about to burst in and start a war with the Jordanians. Why should they? They might get killed.

A smart soldier, if he has not been ordered to go inside a house, won't go. He will get ready, he will clean his rifle, he will take cover. Until an officer comes along and tells him to do it.

Shai Hermesh, bazooka man in "A" Company:

Finally we have caught up with our company. For hours I have had no thought except to find my commander and dear friend, Yoram Zamosh. A bazooka man does not fight on his own. You don't say, Oh, look there, let me shoot at that machine-gun nest. Your commander directs you. Your job is to serve him.

On Wadi Joz Street, a Ford three-ton truck suddenly appears, packed with Arab Legion soldiers. Zamosh points and shouts, "Shai, shoot!" What am I thinking? Nothing. There is the enemy. Hit him. I barely feel the rocket blasting from the tube.

A second truck appears.

"Shoot again!" shouts Zamosh.

Uzi Eilam, battalion commander:

The last big fights of the night take place in Wadi Joz. In the first one, two truckloads of Arab Legion soldiers have descended from their positions on the Augusta Victoria Ridge, attempting to counterattack along Wadi Joz Street. One of Zamosh's young bazooka men, Shai Hermesh, who will later become a distinguished member of the Knesset, fires a rocket into the first truck's engine, killing a number of enemy soldiers and stopping both vehicles in their tracks. Zamosh's troopers have finished off the rest in an hour-long firefight.

The other shoot-out occurs in the wadi itself. A squad led by Lieutenant Arye Dvir, whom his men call "Kooshie," comes upon a burial cave in the wall of the dry riverbed. Arab women and children have taken shelter inside. They are terrified, begging the paratroopers not to shoot.

Kooshie comes forward to help. A Jordanian soldier stands up from behind the women and shoots Kooshie through the cervical spine. He drops, permanently paralyzed.

Yoram Zamosh, "A" Company commander:

A bluff overlooks the dry riverbed of Wadi Joz. I put four MAGs at the brink. A MAG is a Belgian-made light machine gun. Our gunners fire box after box of ammo, covering Kooshie and his platoon.

We can feel the fury of the night beginning to ebb.

Just after dawn, a few minutes before the fight with the Jordanian soldiers on the two trucks, one of our heavy weapons teams, which had been lost, catches up with us. My friend Shai Hermesh is the bazooka man. We embrace, he and I, so relieved to see each other alive. Shai's face is white. I see he is holding back tears.

"Zamosh, I just came from the casualty collection station. Someone directed us there, saying we would find discarded weapons that we could take so we could defend ourselves . . ."

Shai struggles to control his emotions.

"What a terrible sight, Zamosh! On the ground . . . a line of blankets . . . twenty, maybe more. Red boots were sticking out from under the blankets. Beside these was a pile of helmets and Uzis and FNs. 'Help yourself,' said the medic.

"Zamosh, I couldn't make myself take a weapon. Not from our men who had been killed. So many! Zamosh, there were so many!"

I see that Shai has gotten a rifle from somewhere.

"Are you all right, Shai?"

"Yes . . ." He clutches my arm to steady himself. "But I never want to see such a sight again."

Our battalion has gotten off easy. Most of the dead paratroopers that Shai saw were from Battalion 66, from the night-long carnage on Ammunition Hill. Shai could not know that when he saw them. It will be days before any of us learns the true tally.

Our battalion commander's plan has worked. Uzi has picked a smart place to make the breakthrough, and we soldiers have crossed no-man's-land fast enough to get behind the Jordanian defensive positions before the enemy could inflict heavy damage. The sun is up. Most of the Arab Legionnaires have melted away, to save themselves.

Our sister battalions have not been so lucky.

Battalion 28 has suffered terribly in the initial mortar barrage on Samuel the Prophet Street. Their companies, advancing toward the Rockefeller Museum, have lost many more in an ambush after taking a wrong turn in the dark between the Nablus Road and Saladin Street. Even now most of the battalion is pinned down by enemy fire from the Old City walls.

In daylight, above Wadi Joz, I am standing with my radioman, Moshe Milo, when we see Yossi Yoffe, the commander of Battalion 66, come up to our battalion commander, Uzi Eilam. Yoffe's face is black from burns and dirt. He speaks privately to Uzi. From the two commanders' grim postures it is clear that each is asking the other about their battalion's respective casualties. How many men have you lost this night?

Battalion 66's sector of responsibility was immediately north of ours. Their assignment was to assault the Jordanian Police School and the enemy positions atop Ammunition Hill. We in Battalion 71 will not learn till evening of the hand-to-hand struggle for that objective and of the terrible slaughter that went on for hours in those trenches.

Moshe and I can't hear what Yoffe says to Uzi. We're too far away. But we see the color drain from our commander's cheeks. Uzi's head bows. He covers his face with his hands.

44.

THE LEGACY OF EMPIRE

Hussein will lose Jerusalem now. Our paratroopers will complete the conquest of the eastern half of the city. It is only a matter of time.

Moshe Dayan is minister of defense.

This day has started for me at 07:45 with the issuing of instructions to Chief of Staff Rabin for the continuation of operations on the Sinai front. "Complete the conquest of the Gaza Strip. Clear the El Arish axis. Advance west but remain ten kilometers short of the Canal. Prepare to attack southward to Kusseima." Now, at last, I have a few minutes to turn to Jerusalem.

Why has King Hussein entered the war? A message was sent to him from Prime Minister Eshkol on the first morning of the war, several messages, in fact, pledging that if Jordan undertook no hostile action against Israel, Israel would take none against her. These notes were not sent out of personal regard for Hussein, though Eshkol surely feels this, as do I. They were dispatched out of Israeli self-interest. Contending with Nasser's divisions in Sinai strains the IDF's resources to capacity; the last thing we need is a second front against Hussein.

The king understands this. He understands as well that Israel's forces, taxed as they may be at this hour, are still sufficient to rout him and every tank and gun he possesses. His air force has already been reduced to wreckage. If he presses his aggression, he will lose his army and probably all of the West Bank.

Yet Hussein has struck.

This is the Middle East. We are all shackled to lines drawn on maps by the British and the French, with the assent of the Russians, in the waning months of World War I.

Hussein's Jordan is a made-up nation. It was created out of whole cloth (as Transjordan first, in 1921) by the imperial powers, to serve their own interests. Jordan's borders reflect no tribal or political reality. Iraq is another fiction, patched together out of three Ottoman satrapies. Arabia's borders are similarly arbitrary, as are Syria's and Lebanon's.

And of course our own.

Hussein is mistrusted by the Egyptians, despised by the Syrians, and tolerated for the most part by his own people. Of what blood are the Jordanians? A third are of Bedouin stock, kin of Hussein's grandfather and the Hashemite order. The other two-thirds are Palestinian Arabs—refugees, many of them, from our War of Independence. In the sleeves of their galabiyas nest the keys to the homes they lost when the Arab Legion attacked infant Israel in '48 and they, the villagers and farmers, fled across the Jordan, awaiting the victory and the return that never came.

Atop this incendiary mix perches Hussein.

He has made common cause with his enemy Nasser, whom he now calls brother. What scenarios must have played out in the king's mind as he and his counselors sought a solution during the days leading up to war? Victory allied with Nasser would produce what? A second Holocaust across all Israel, with Jordan's Palestinian masses running riot? The

King Hussein of Jordan addresses the international press, June 7, 1967.

Egyptian dictator, flush with triumph, establishing a pan-Arab state with himself at the head? Armed intervention by the United States and the Soviet Union? A nuclear clash between the superpowers? World War III?

This, for Hussein, is the cheeriest scenario. What of the others?

If Jordan holds aloof from the fight and Egypt loses, Nasser will denounce Hussein as a traitor to the Arab cause; the Palestinians will revolt, joined perhaps by the army. Hussein will be deposed, if not murdered outright, along with his family. The government will be replaced by rule of the generals or the PLO, the Palestinian Liberation Organization.

If Jordan holds aloof and the Arabs win, Nasser will not even have to call for Hussein's deposition. The king will be dead already at the hands of his own people, or decamped to exile with the royal family to Paris or the Potomac, while Nasser's army rolls across the Negev and seizes Amman.

The prospects are nearly as grim under the fourth scenario.

If Hussein allies himself with Nasser and Israel wins, the king loses Jerusalem and probably the West Bank. He has a chance of retaining his throne, however, perhaps even a shred of personal honor. This, clearly, is why Hussein has placed his army under Egyptian command. He will be blamed for defeat, should it come. There is no escaping that. But he can point the finger at others in the wake of vanquishment and be believed by some.

But a catastrophe of honor stands at the core of such a decision. This is the loss of the holy places. For centuries Hashemite monarchs have accounted themselves guardians of Islam, though they have lost care of her two holiest places, Mecca and Medina, to the Saudis. Hussein's branch of the family yet retains defense of Jerusalem's jewels, the Dome of the Rock and the Al-Aqsa Mosque. Here is the foundation upon which much of the king's political legitimacy is based.

Hussein will lose these sacred sites now.

It will not surprise me, should that hour come, if the king takes his own life.

But the gravest peril of such an outcome falls not upon Hussein, but upon me. The fatal hazard is not to Jordan, but to Israel.

With the success of the paratroopers' preliminary assault, and that of our Harel and Jerusalem Brigades and other units, sealing three of the four overland approaches to the city, the possibility—I almost said "inevitability"—now exists of an Israeli Jerusalem.

I am in the city now. With the regional commanders I have made a dash in a military convoy to Mount Scopus, our toehold on the heights that ring the eastern extremity. Hussein's Arab Legion still holds the Augusta Victoria Ridge and the Mount of Olives. It still holds the Old City. Shall we take it?

The momentum of events builds to this. By this I mean the blood shed this night and this day by our paratroopers and by the soldiers of the Jerusalem and Harel Brigades; the emotion of the nation as it realizes not only that it will not be destroyed by its enemies, as it feared so desperately less than forty-eight hours ago, but that its forces may prevail in unprecedented measure; and the pure military necessity of seizing all enemy-held positions that may aid the foe in bringing up additional troops and tanks with the intention of dislodging our forces from the gains they have already achieved.

Dwarfing these elements, of course, is the final component: the millennial opportunity of taking back from our enemies the Jewish people's most sacred site, the Western Wall. Two thousand years of exile cry out for this. I wish to bring it about no less than my countrymen. What is the alternative? Do I wish to be remembered as the commander who stood at the threshold of the greatest feat of arms in Jewish history and refused to let his brothers consummate it?

Yet I cannot give my approval.

Ministers and generals may be aflame to enact their agendas. I don't blame them. In their place I would feel the same. But my role is to see beyond the immediate elation that such an outcome would produce.

I am haunted by Sinai, 1957. I remember ultimatums from Moscow and less bellicose but equally insistent communiqués from the White House and Whitehall and the Quai d'Orsay. I remember cables between Prime Minister Ben-Gurion and Secretary-General Dag Hammarskjöld and diplomatic prose dispatched beneath the letterhead of the United Nations. Translation: That prize, which you Jews have won by the blood of your sons, must be restored to those who burn for your destruction and who daily arm and rearm toward that end. In the name of regional stability. In the name of reason. In the name of peace.

I understand the position of the United States and of the United Nations. I even understand the Soviets. I don't want World War III any more than they do.

Capturing Sinai and being forced to abandon it was, for Israel, like amputating a limb. To endure the same in Jerusalem would be unthinkable.

This is what I fear.

How will the Arab world react to the presence of Israeli paratroopers on the Temple Mount or the sight of Jewish half-tracks in the square before the Dome of the Rock? Will the other nations of Islam take arms, backed by the Soviets, while the United States, France, and Britain stand aside? What will two hundred million Muslims do when they behold on their television screens the flag of Israel flying over the Al-Aqsa Mosque?

If we enter the Old City, our paratroopers will be fighting house to house along the Via Dolorosa. How will the Vatican respond to that? Where Christian pilgrims tread the Stations of the Cross, our soldiers will be advancing street by street, room by room, with the enemy resisting by means of booby traps and snipers and ambushes, a real dirty business. I cannot authorize artillery or air strikes anywhere near the holy sites, and the Old City holds nothing but holy sites.

What is the alternative? Can I tell Motta Gur's brave paratroopers, nineteen-year-olds straight from the kibbutz, that they may not fire upon that church in whose upper story the enemy has emplaced a Goryunov machine gun? Or that they are forbidden to return fire upon that mosque from whose minaret tower Arab snipers are cutting down their brothers?

I must back our paratroopers. I will join them myself. Then what? How will three hundred million Roman Catholics respond when Israeli mortar rounds tear holes in the roof of the Church of the Holy Sepulchre or Jewish machine guns shred the shrine where Jesus presided over the Last Supper?

Hussein himself will be desperate to preserve his honor in the eyes of the Arab world. At the last gasp, what will stop him from blowing up the Dome of the Rock and blaming it on the Jews? Such an act need not even be ordered by Cairo or Amman. It will take only one desperate patriot, one fanatic willing to act on his own.

Whom will the world blame then?

What will be the consequences for Israel and the future?

I hate myself for even thinking such thoughts. I would give ten years of my life to be in Sinai with Sharon and Gorodish, shouting, "Follow me!" Yet someone must take care for such prospects.

What, then, is my plan? What alternative do I propose?

Capture the heights that surround Jerusalem. Cut off the Old City. Seize Augusta Victoria Ridge. Take the Mount of Olives. Let our air force finish destroying Jordanian and Iraqi armor attempting to come up via the

Jordan Valley. Set a ring of Israeli steel around the Old City. Leave one avenue of escape for the Arab Legion to slip away by night.

Preserve the holy sites.

Let the city fall by itself.

This is my alternative.

So I say no to Narkiss, and no to Eshkol and Eban and Begin and to Motta Gur and to everyone.

You cannot have the Old City.

Not yet.

45.

THE CHICKEN FRICASSEE HOUSE

My men have found me an excellent command post. It's in a house on Wadi Joz Street, home to an affluent Arab family. The building is four stories, abutting the dry wadi and the slope that ascends to the Augusta Victoria Ridge. From my windows on the second floor I can see the whole valley.

Uzi Eilam commands Paratroop Battalion 71.

Morning and afternoon have come and gone. We know now the extent of casualties suffered by the brigade last night. Battalion 66 has lost thirty-six men on Ammunition Hill. Such a number is beyond tears. Yossi Fratkin's Battalion 28 has suffered heavily, too. But both have seized their objectives, and so have we.

My command group has taken special care to be respectful of the Arab family whose home we now occupy. Our team uses only two rooms. I have given orders that no man is to touch any item of property or to speak to a member of the family, particularly the women, except as he would address his own mother and sisters.

The date is now June 6, the second day of the war. At 16:00 the battalion commanders and their staffs meet with Motta Gur, the brigade commander, in a courtyard of the Rockefeller Museum. The place is still under fire from Arab Legionnaires atop the Old City walls. In fact, Battalion 28 is pinned down on several terraces.

We receive the order to capture the Augusta Victoria Ridge and the Mount of Olives this night. The assignment is given to my battalion. The formation will be reinforced by two special companies, one from our own brigade and another belonging to Danny Matt's paratroop brigade, though Danny himself is still in Sinai with his other two battalions. We will have tanks in support, Motta informs us, as well as mortars and artillery.

The reason this task has been given to my battalion is that we have suffered the fewest casualties so far.

The commanders have assembled in a courtyard on the western side of the museum. Already I have in mind the basic concept for the assault. I will present the plan to Motta as soon as I work out the particulars.

As I'm concentrating on this, I feel a hand on my shoulder. Rabbi Shlomo Goren appears. Rabbi Goren is the chief religious officer of the IDF. He is dressed in red paratroop boots and combat fatigues. To call Rabbi Goren larger than life would be an understatement. He is a paratrooper. A general. He wears a beard worthy of an Old Testament patriarch, with politics to match.

We talk. Rabbi Goren tells me that his mother is buried in the Jewish cemetery on the Mount of Olives. I make him a promise. If Battalion 71 succeeds in capturing the site, I will walk with him personally and find the stone of his mother. Rabbi Goren says nothing about the Old City. No one does. The idea of capturing the Western Wall or the Temple Mount remains beyond the scale of our hopes or our imagination.

The only person who brings the subject up is my "A" Company commander, Yoram Zamosh. I ask Motta again about Zamosh's request of last night. If the brigade should receive orders to liberate the Old City, will Motta permit Zamosh's men to lead the way?

Again Motta approves, without a moment's hesitation.

Uzi Eilat, "B" Company commander:

It is no accident that our battalion has suffered the fewest casualties. This is Uzi's doing. He will never speak of this. He is too modest. But the men know. We know.

Soldiers love a commander who takes care for their lives. I have heard Uzi faulted, with good cause, for putting his own life at risk, chasing after snipers not once but twice during the night. I have seen him in his jeep racing from position to position along Wadi Joz Street, exposing himself repeatedly to enemy fire. Uzi will own up to this, I am sure. But such courage is why we will all walk through fire for him.

Tonight? The battalion is spread out in groups of five and ten, in combat posts along the valley floor facing the ridge of Augusta Victoria. The slope ascends above us. Open ground with very little cover—olive groves, a few scattered buildings, and one odd hotel called the Palace.

The ridge takes its name from the Augusta Victoria Hospital, which

sits big and wide on the summit. It was built by Kaiser Wilhelm, somebody tells me, in the early years of this century. The Jordanians have held
this ground since 1948. They have had nineteen years to string wire, sow
mines, and build bunkers. They are on the Mount of Olives, too. Assault-
ing that one will be even worse.

How do foot soldiers attack a hill?

I can think of only one way.

Meir Shalit, sergeant in "B" Company:

The assault has been postponed. Thank God.

The word is being passed right now.

We had been organized into assault elements. It was going to be another night attack. Tanks were supposed to lead the way this time. Suddenly out of the darkness we begin hearing a ferocious firefight several
hundred meters behind us and to our right, beneath the Old City walls.

No one knows what is happening. Runners are dashing to the various
assault elements; radio transmissions are coming in from Brigade:

Stand down from assault positions.

Prepare defensive posts.

Get ready to be attacked.

Yoram Zamosh, "A" Company commander:

What has happened is one of those fiascos that occur in war when a
complicated operation is initiated in darkness. A company of Sherman
tanks has been assigned to support, in fact to lead, our battalion's assault
up the hill. But the vehicles come from two separate units whose radios are
not compatible. A jerry-rigged system has been hastily thrown together.

The tanks have assembled out of sight of the enemy in a courtyard of
the Rockefeller Museum. They are supposed to descend into the valley
between our Israeli positions and the rising slope that leads to the Augusta
Victoria Ridge. From there they will lead the attack by advancing up a
street called Shmuel Ben Adaya.

In "A" Company we are ready to go. Our orders are to follow the jeeps
of the Sayeret, the Reconnaissance Company under Micha Kapusta. They
will advance immediately after the tanks.

But in the darkness, under heavy fire, the lead tank has taken a wrong turn. Instead of going left then right onto Ben Adaya Street, which leads up the ridge, it has turned immediately right onto the Jericho Road, which runs parallel to and directly beneath the eastern wall of the Old City. The other tanks have followed. Now they are trapped. Arab Legionnaires atop the wall are pouring small-arms and antitank fire onto them, point-blank.

One tank, we will hear later, has become stuck atop the narrow bridge that crosses between the Garden of Gethsemane and the Church of Jehoshaphat. The tank is under relentless fire from the Old City walls. The driver hears an order from his commander to advance. His turret is pointing forward, along the road that leads safely off the bridge, but he does not realize in the darkness and confusion that the tank itself is oriented sideways. When he advances the throttle, the tank plunges off the precipice. A Sherman tank weighs thirty-two tons. This mass flips over in midair and crashes upside down into the dry wadi below. Miraculously, the crew survives. This is just the beginning of the chaos.

The struggle goes on for hours. When the tanks make their mistake and turn onto the Jericho Road, the heroes of the sayeret, Meir Har-Zion and Micha Kapusta and others, understand the peril immediately. They leap into their jeeps and chase the tanks, to bring them back. They themselves become caught in the cross fire. Before the night ends, they will lose five dear friends, killed.

Our battalion's orders are to hold in place at the line of departure. We can hear the firefight, around the corner from our positions beneath the Rockefeller Museum. The men of the Reconnaissance Company, reinforced by elements of Battalion 28, continue under heavy fire to recover and evacuate the wounded and dead from the Jericho Road.

In the midst of this struggle Motta Gur, our brigade commander, receives a dispatch from army intelligence informing him that a column of Jordanian Patton tanks (for which our ancient Shermans are no match) is hastening up from the Jordan Valley toward the city.

This is why Motta has called off the assault on Augusta Victoria and why he has ordered our battalion and Battalion 28 to prepare positions for defense.

Uzi Eilam, Battalion 71 commander:

Plans have changed again. Apparently the report of Jordanian tanks approaching is false. We won't have to hold off an attack by enemy armor.

The assault up Augusta Victoria Ridge is back on. We will attack in daylight, tomorrow morning.

All night I shuttle between my battalion's positions along Wadi Joz and Motta's command post in the Rockefeller Museum. I have not slept in forty hours. If I've eaten, I can't remember when. Most of my soldiers are in the same situation. I have issued orders permitting our men to break into stores in the Arab neighborhoods they occupy. They may seize, however, only what is necessary for a meal, nothing more.

Our companies will spend the remaining hours of darkness preparing to resume our interrupted assault, this time at dawn, in broad daylight, upon the enemy's positions atop the Augusta Victoria Ridge.

Meir Shalit, sergeant, "B" Company:

You wouldn't think it would be cold in June. It is freezing. We have coffee and smokes but you can't strike a match because of snipers, and if you do, you have to stay deep in a hole when you drag on the cigarette.

We have been ordered not to take shelter in any house that has civilians in it. It's amazing how many people are still here. Arab families. They're all scared shitless, of course. Hey, how do you think I feel?

It sounds nuts but I still don't know where I am. To our right a few hundred meters the rescue operation for our tanks is still going on. But soldiers only care about their own problems. No one's shooting at us, so we're okay. We are five guys in an improvised fighting position in the open ground floor of a three-story Arab house. I have found a pile of construction debris and carved out a nice snoozing spot. The only problem is it's so cold I can't sleep. I've still got the bangalore torpedo from last night. Each time I try to dump it, someone catches me and won't let me do it.

Zeev Barkai, battalion operations officer:

You need to understand how soldiers think. When they are scared, they go to sleep. It's a defense mechanism. They want to wake up and find that everything is okay, the danger has passed.

So I keep moving among our positions, making sure everyone knows what's going on. Of course, I know nothing, either. I make it up.

Soldiers don't care what they are told, as long as they are told something.

Yoram Zamosh, "A" Company commander:

We have found a spot to settle down and wait for morning, near the four-story Arab house where Uzi has set up his command post. My radioman, Moshe Milo, has found some flat pita bread, which he shares out, with jam from the few C-ration cans that our men have brought with them.

Sleep is out of the question for me. I must be alert if events break or if I am needed by Uzi. But I can at least rest my back against a wall. As I do so, I feel the lump tucked into my web gear just above my hips.

An Israeli flag.

Late yesterday, when the officers of the battalion had first reached the city and were scrambling from rooftop to rooftop, trying to gain an understanding of the topography, we—Uzi's command group, joined by the company commanders—gathered beneath the apartment of a local family, at 10 Beit HaKerem Street, in the cramped basement shelter. The family's name was Cohen. The mother and two daughters brought us hot tea and cakes. They let us use their telephone, which was still working.

The family was frightened but excited, too. Would war really come to Jerusalem? Would Israeli forces be given permission to advance upon the Old City? At one point the grandmother of the family, who was past eighty years old, left the room. Her daughter told Uzi and the rest of us that she, the grandmother, had lived with her husband for many years in the Old City, in the Jewish Quarter, before the Jordanians captured it in '48. Her husband had since passed on. The grandmother had lived here, in the tiny apartment next door, ever since.

Uzi was explaining his plan of attack to us. He was stressing the importance of the first few minutes. We must break through the initial Jordanian resistance at all costs. I was mentally formulating an attack plan for my own company when the grandmother, Mrs. Cohen, returned from the next-door apartment and came up behind me. I was seated. She was standing directly over me.

"Take this," she said.

Into my hands she placed a flag of Israel.

"This I have kept," the grandmother said, "since my husband and I were driven from our home. It flew last in the Old City."

The lady wept.

To this day I feel her tears upon my back.

I folded the flag and tucked it into my web gear. I promised Mrs. Cohen that if Brigade 55 should be given orders to liberate the Old City, her flag would be the first to fly over its holy stones.

No one took particular notice of this exchange.

Then, at the door, as we commanders were leaving to return to our companies, my friend Moshe Stempel caught my arm. He had overheard the conversation between me and the elder Mrs. Cohen. He had heard my promise. Stempel was number two in the brigade, second-in-command to Motta Gur. It was Stempel who had built the brigade, less than a year ago, and he who had gotten me my post in it.

"Zamosh, do you have it safe?"

"What?"

"The flag."

Stempel had the chest of a bull, with wrists and forearms like iron. I could feel his strong, thick fingers probing into the web gear at the small of my back. "Make sure it will not fall out."

He pushed the flag deeper into my harness.

Now, on the second night, my radioman, Moshe Milo, takes a seat in the dirt beside me.

"Zamosh, do you still have the flag?"

I pat the spot to let him know, but I can see in his eyes he wants to be absolutely sure. I roll away so he can see. Again I feel fingers, not as powerful as Stempel's but just as fervent, pressing the flag into place even more securely.

Uzi Eilam, Battalion 71 commander:

Sometime past two in the morning, I get back to the Arab house that is serving as our battalion command post. I have been at the brigade CP all day, except for several hours making the rounds of our companies' positions. My operations sergeant is named Leizer Lavi. He stops me as I enter the two rooms in which our command group has crowded itself. "Uzi, the lady has something she wants to give you."

"The lady?"

"The owner of this house. She has been waiting all night for you to get back."

I remove my helmet and wipe the grime from my face and hands. The lady enters carrying a lacquered tray. On it sits a covered dish, silverware rolled inside a linen napkin, a china cup and saucer, and a small pot of coffee. The dish is chicken fricassee. The lady has prepared it for me her-self, she says, knowing that I have probably not eaten in many hours. This is not a moment like in the movies. Our hostess knows only a word or two of Hebrew. She simply lifts the cover to show me the dish, then sets the tray down on a table and, with a gesture of gratitude for the consideration our soldiers have shown to her family, she takes her leave.

I have had many wonderful meals in my life, but none has ever been more welcome or tasted more delicious than that simple plate of chicken fricassee.

46.

AUGUSTA VICTORIA

The world of a green soldier compared to that of an experienced one can be imagined by visualizing concentric circles. The rookie's circle ends inside his own helmet. That's as far as he can see or think. If he's unusually clearheaded, the circle may extend to the man in front of him, maybe even to his full squad.

Dan Ziv is deputy commander of Battalion 71.

The veteran, on the other hand, sees the whole field. He has been under fire enough times to know what incoming rounds sound like and to tell when all that noise is heading toward something other than himself. He has learned to conserve energy. He's alert but he is not filled with fear.

It's morning, June 7, the third day of the war. We're climbing the hill toward Augusta Victoria. Motta Gur's tanks are ahead, in column, on Shmuel Ben Adaya Street. Our air force has been pounding the hell out of the ridgeline for over an hour.

I can see, looking ahead up the slope, that Motta's tanks are not under fire. They have almost reached the summit of the ridge, where the Jordanian positions are supposed to be. But no one is shooting at them. I am at the base of the slope, several hundred meters behind the tanks, with my crews and the recoilless rifle jeeps. Benny Ron is beside me.

"There's nothing up there, Benny."

We're supposed to let the tanks reach the summit before we expose our vehicles to fire.

"It's clear—let's go."

Zeev Barkai, Battalion 71 operations officer:

Believe me, the idea that we will capture the Old City has entered no one's mind. Our axis of assault is, in fact, *away from* the Old City.

A collar of hills dominates the Old City from the east—Mount Scopus, Augusta Victoria Ridge, and the Mount of Olives. Battalion 66 occupies Mount Scopus. Their brave paratroopers captured it after hellish fighting last night on Ammunition Hill. We in Battalion 71 are attacking Augusta Victoria. When we link up with Battalion 66, our combined force will turn south and assault the Mount of Olives.

The only reason I understand this is because I'm Uzi's operations officer, so I get to stand next to him when he explains this. Down the line, the paratroopers know only that we're going up the hill.

Meir Shalit, sergeant, "B" Company:

The summit might as well be Mount Everest, it's so far above us. I can't see it. None of us can. It's on fire, the peak, and obscured by thick black smoke from the aerial bombardment. Heavy machine guns are hammering the Jordanian trenches. Our 81-millimeter mortars, and some bigger ones,

Paratroopers of Battalion 71 advancing toward Augusta Victoria Ridge.

are putting a barrage dead on top of the Jordanian positions, or at least on the site where we have been told the Jordanian positions are. We are three paratroop companies advancing upslope, on foot, through the tall grass. The hillside is an olive grove. We're walking between and under the trees.

In the middle of the flat stands a white, bullet-pocked five-story building with PALACE HOTEL in big letters in English across the roof. What a hotel is doing among olive trees in a destitute Arab neighborhood in East Jerusalem, I have no idea. The whole scene is like a crazy movie. I'm exhausted. Everyone's exhausted. I can't believe I'm still humping this bangalore torpedo along with all my other gear. I'm less afraid of getting killed than of embarrassing myself by collapsing from fatigue three-quarters of the way up the hill.

Uzi Eilam, Battalion 71 commander:

Can it be that the Jordanian forces have withdrawn? We are taking no fire. Could the enemy have pulled out during the night?

I am with my soldiers, mounting the slope between the olive trees. A few minutes ago I could see Motta's tanks advancing in column up the road to the summit. They have moved now from sight. I hear no firing of tank cannons.

Zeev Barkai tramps on my left. My two radiomen are on my right. Uzi Eilat's "B" Company is climbing the hill ahead of us. My friend Benny Ron is supposed to be with Dan Ziv in the rear with the recoilless rifle jeeps, but now I hear over the radio that he and Dan are climbing the road in the trail of Motta's tanks.

"Zeev, the summit positions have been abandoned."

"I don't know. I hear fire."

Yoram Zamosh, "A" Company commander:

Uzi has left my company in reserve. We remain at the foot of the slope. The Rockefeller Museum is directly behind and above us. Behind and to the right is the northeast corner of the Old City walls.

Uzi has left us behind because he thinks our battalion may get orders to enter the Old City. I have asked him, if it should be within his powers, to let "A" Company be the first to enter.

Moshe Milo, Zamosh's radioman:

There's a famous photo of Motta Gur and his command group on top of the Mount of Olives, overlooking the Old City. The picture records the moment when Gur issued the order to the 55th Brigade to advance to the Lion's Gate and to enter and capture Old Jerusalem. The order is famous because Gur issued it "in the clear," meaning he felt the moment was so historic that he did not use code names for the brigade units; he spoke in plain Hebrew for all the world to hear.

We in "A" Company missed this moment completely. We were monitoring our battalion's advance up the Augusta Victoria Ridge. We had two radios, mine and another soldier's, but we were on the company and battalion nets, not the brigade net.

We never heard the historic order.

Instructions authorized by the General Staff at that time were to seize the collar of hills—Mount Scopus, Augusta Victoria, and the Mount of Olives—and hold those positions. Moshe Dayan, we knew, had been saying, No, no, no, I won't let you take the Old City.

On the Mount of Olives, Motta Gur gives the order to enter the Old City. Gur, seated, is bareheaded. Standing, center, is deputy brigade commander Moshe Stempel.

Suddenly a radio call came from Uzi to Zamosh: "Proceed to the Lion's Gate. Go now! We have orders to enter the Old City."

What has happened, though none of us will learn this for days, is that shortly before dawn Menachem Begin has telephoned Dayan in a state of extreme emotion, informing him that the UN Security Council is at that hour preparing to declare a cease-fire. All combatant forces will be ordered to halt in place.

If this happens, says Begin, the Old City, the Western Wall, and the Temple Mount will remain in Arab hands. We cannot let that happen!

Still Dayan refuses to give the green light. He continues to fear the outrage of the world community if the holy places are destroyed or damaged by Israeli military action.

Finally our own brigade's on-site reports, relayed to the minister of defense from the summit of Augusta Victoria Ridge, confirm that Jordanian forces have, except for odd or stray elements, withdrawn.

Dayan issues the order to enter the Old City.

The signal goes from him via Deputy Chief of Staff Haim Bar-Lev to Uzi Narkiss, commander of all Jerusalem area forces, who relays the order to Motta Gur, the paratroop brigade commander, who in turn instructs his battalion commanders—first among them our Uzi Eilam—to execute this historic command.

There is a curious footnote to this moment. The military code word

Paratroopers of Battalion 71 reach the summit of Augusta Victoria.

for the Lion's Gate was "Vietnam." Strictly speaking, Uzi's directive to us should have been "Enter Vietnam" instead of "Enter the Lion's Gate."

But Uzi was caught up in the emotion himself. Like Motta, he issued his order in the clear.

Meir Shalit, sergeant, "B" Company:

We have reached the summit of Augusta Victoria. The Jordanians have taken off. The place is burnt black. The ground reeks of petrol. For hundreds of meters the earth is charred.

I've still got my bangalore. I can't believe how tired I am.

Benny Ron is with Dan Ziv atop Augusta Victoria Ridge:

At the summit a tragic volley of fire erupts. An enemy sniper? Our own guys from Battalion 66? No one knows. A beloved company commander of Battalion 66, Giora Ashkenazi, has been hit and killed, minutes before his brothers-in-arms enter the Lion's Gate.

Meir Shalit, sergeant, "B" Company:

From the summit of Augusta Victoria, I can see our companies moving down off the hill toward the gates of the Old City. Tanks, half-tracks, and command cars are descending the road from the Mount of Olives. It's not a mad rush. The enemy still mans the city walls. The fight is far from over.

For the first time I can actually see the Old City. It looks like something out of Hollywood or the Bible, which I suppose it actually is. Big, thick walls, ten meters high, with fortress parapets on top. You can see the Arab Legionnaires up there.

I'm thinking, How the hell are we gonna break into that?

47.

FOUGAS

We are told that Jordanian and Iraqi tank brigades are advancing on Jerusalem from the east and that our own armor cannot get there in time to stop them. "You pilots are the last line of defense."

Zvi "Kantor" Kanor is the youngest pilot in the IAF.

I was born June 11, 1947. I am not yet twenty. The Israeli system for training pilots is different from that of most air forces. In America you go to college first. By the time you're flying operationally, you're twenty-four or twenty-five years old. You're married. You have children.

In Israel you go to flight training straight out of high school. It's a great system.

Think about it. You're young, single, you have no kids. No fear. You're too dumb to know what fear is.

Our squadron has been created for the onetime emergency of the war. Air force command has thrown it together in the three weeks prior to the outbreak of hostilities. The squadron is made up of retired pilots, reserve fliers from El Al, and nine of us straight out of flight school. The air force has about fifty Fouga Magisters, the planes we trained on in flight school. It will make twenty-four into warplanes.

We are twenty-four pilots.

This is it.

We are going to war.

I have graduated from flight school only three months earlier. I have not even been assigned to a squadron; I'm still in OTU, Operational Training Unit. I have only six weeks of training instead of the required four months. I cannot be certified as operational.

Suddenly Nasser is closing the Straits of Tiran. War has become inevitable. What can the air force do with us young pilots? *En brera.* No alternative. I and my fellow recent graduates are sent back to the only plane we know how to fly: the Fouga Magister. Now we must learn to fly it in combat. That is like telling an intern who has just finished medical school, "Here, perform brain surgery."

We train at Beersheba. There are no living quarters for us at Hatzerim Air Base; the place is still under construction. We are put up in a hotel instead: Neot Midbar—the "Desert Oasis."

Beersheba today is the capital of the Negev. Then it was a one-horse town without the horse. The place is dark because of blackouts and empty because everyone has been called up for the war—everyone except the girls who flock to the hotel each night because there is nothing else to do and nowhere else to go. We pilots train all day, learning to fly in formation, to attack armored columns, to use our rockets, and to fly very, very low. If you flew that low in flight school, they would put you in jail.

The Fouga has no night flying capability, so when the sun goes down, we pilots are free. Our commanders—three regular air force officers—are no-nonsense types. They remain on base, preparing for tomorrow's training. The rest of us head down the dirt road to the Desert Oasis.

None of us young guys has a car. We ride with the old-timers. These fellows are like James Bond to us. They are thirty, thirty-five years old. World travelers, El Al captains and first officers. They have danced at the Plaza Hotel in New York; they have dined at the George Cinq in Paris. They steal girls from us. They make us pay for drinks. But they also take us under their wings.

We ask, Is war coming? Bank on it, our mentors declare. Keep close to us and do what we do.

The Fouga Magister is a forerunner of the American A-10 Warthog, which is a heavy, lumbering bucket designed for close air support of ground troops. The joke is that you train a Warthog pilot by making him sit in a garbage can while you throw rocks at him.

The Fouga has no bombs and only a peashooter 5.62-millimeter gun. It had no weapons panel at all until the flight mechanics cobbled one together a few days before the war. The Fouga's armament is 2.75-inch rockets. That is ridiculously small. The original U.S. version was called a Mighty Mouse.

The Fouga has no targeting system. The gunsight is a cross on the windscreen. All targeting calculations must be done in your head. You have to eyeball your dive angle and "play the wind" like a kicker in soccer.

To attack a column of enemy tanks, you approach at zero altitude, pull up about three kilometers out, climb to 1,500 feet (which takes forever because of the weight of the rockets), then line up on your target and go in. No chatter on the radio; the channels must be kept open for emergencies. You go in very shallow. No need to dive, because you aren't dropping bombs.

The Fouga has eight rockets. You fire four at a time, in salvos, aiming the whole volley at a single tank. What are your chances of hitting it? At 400 meters: zero. At 200, you can't miss.

If you tell this to pilots today, they will think you are crazy or lying. Two hundred meters? The tank is so big in your windscreen you can see the seams of the welds on the turrets.

How low do you fly to attack a column of tanks? The Fouga has two fuel tanks, one at the tip of each wing. The third day, near Jericho, I hit one of my tanks on the ground. You are so young you think nothing of this. You have a mission and you will do anything—anything—to accomplish it.

On the first day I lost my leader. Ground fire killed him. Speed is what protects you from antiaircraft fire, and the Fouga has no speed. We were over the Jiradi Pass in Sinai. We had just finished attacking a radar station near El Arish. All four planes in our formation had been hit by triple-A flying over the pass the first time, though without serious damage. Now we were heading home along the same route—a big mistake. We went through another barrage of ground fire. I saw my leader slump in his cockpit. His head fell to one side. I was right alongside as his plane yawed and dived into the ground.

How did this affect me? I didn't panic in the moment or react with grief in the aftermath. But I flew like a crazy person for the rest of the war.

You attack a column of tanks in a formation of four, with the first pair a kilometer ahead of the second. The lead pair aims for the front of the column; the second pair takes the rear. The object is to pile up wrecks at each end, trapping the vehicles in the middle.

Military columns are of mixed composition. Trucks and jeeps and command cars are interspersed among the tanks. Tank crews are trained to maintain an interval ahead and behind; they keep their vehicles dispersed. You have two passes before you use up your rockets. You must pick out two tanks and kill them. You can't waste precious ordnance on anything less.

We say that Fougas are slow, lumbering, and ancient. They are. But to the men in the tanks being attacked, the planes surely feel as if they're screaming out of the heavens at supersonic speed. Below us, we can see the crewmen scrambling out of their hatches and diving into ditches on the side of the road. The Jordanian Pattons, like ours, carry their shells in the turrets. The turrets are not armored on top. Put a salvo of rockets into them and they go up like cases of dynamite. The turret—all of it— blows straight into the sky.

When an attack from the air knocks out the front and rear tanks of a column, the crews of the vehicles trapped in the middle become stricken with panic. How brave must a man be to see vehicles exploding in front of him and behind—and then get back into his own tank? He doesn't know that we have only one Fouga squadron with only twenty-four planes. He doesn't know that these aircraft are only trainers, flown by balding airline pilots and boys who still do not shave. To him we bring death from the skies, and he has no friendly warplanes to protect him.

After the war, we pilots drove in jeeps with the infantry to see the roads and highways that we had attacked. The ground soldiers could not stop thanking us. They took us from tank carcass to tank carcass. They could not believe that we had done all this damage with training planes from the flight school.

Let me, then, put in a word for the Fouga Magisters, these planes with the funny name. History has passed them over, even within the chronicles of the Israel Air Force. Because our squadron was temporary, because its planes and pilots scattered to other duties immediately after the war, we have had no place to plant our standard. Squadron 147 has no headquarters, no historian, no oral tradition like other squadrons that flew then and are still flying today. We have only a number, and even that has been relegated to mothballs.

Beyond that, much of our work was done out of sight even of those whose lives we saved. The Jordanian and Iraqi columns we destroyed were advancing up from the Jordan Valley. The troops and inhabitants of Jerusalem never saw them. We blew the enemy's tanks up before they reached the top of the hill.

In five days our squadron lost a fourth of its pilots. We started the war with twenty-four and finished with eighteen.

The plodding, unglamorous Fougas broke the Jordanian and Iraqi advance upon Jerusalem. They saved the city and the troops in it, and they produced victory in the West Bank.

48.

THE WESTERN WALL

O ur orders are to enter the Old City via the Lion's Gate. The Lion's Gate is in the city wall on the eastern side.

Yoram Zamosh commands "A" Company of Paratroop Battalion 71.

One of the legends of Jerusalem is that, of the forty or more times over the centuries that the city has fallen, the invading host has always come out of the north. Jeremiah 1: "Out of the north, an evil comes."

Only twice in three thousand years has Jerusalem been conquered from a different direction—once by King David, and now by us.

Uzi has left my company in reserve near the Rockefeller Museum, while the battalion's other companies have assaulted the Augusta Victoria Ridge. His purpose is to place "A" Company in position to get to the Lion's Gate quickly, in the event that General Headquarters gives the go-ahead to enter the Old City. Uzi has left two half-tracks with me, the only vehicles of any weight that the battalion possesses, to help if we need to force our entry or, once inside, to fight house to house.

"A" Company starts down the Jericho Road directly beneath the Old City walls, the same road where the terrible tank battle of the night before has taken place. I am expecting the same fierce resistance. The Arab Legionnaires fought well and hard last night. These British-trained troops of the elite King Talal Brigade displayed daring, imagination, and professionalism. Parties sallied out from the city walls, taking the fight to our soldiers and exploiting the darkness and the confusion. Give the Jordanians credit. They stopped our entire night attack on Augusta Victoria.

Nor am I the only officer who regards this moment with apprehension. A radio call comes to me now from Motta Gur's operations officer, Uzi Frumer, whom I know well, ordering "A" Company not to assault the

Lion's Gate until he, Motta, can send tanks down from the Mount of Olives to reinforce us.

The Lion's Gate is approached uphill via a narrow walled lane, the Lion's Gate Road. The passage is enclosed along its entire length. Above on both sides rise thick stone walls, five to ten meters high. The lane is between a hundred and a hundred fifty meters long. There's a thick, metal-sheathed gate at the upper end. No cover. Men and vehicles advancing up the lane have no place to hide.

I hold my company back on the main road, at the turn of the Lion's Gate Road, waiting for Motta's tanks. One appears—a Sherman with a 90-millimeter cannon. At the rear of the tank is an intercom telephone in a covered compartment. I dash to this and grab the receiver. The tank commander can hear me now. I identify myself as the paratroop company commander and tell him I have a fire order for him.

"Put three shells into the gate."

The tank fires once and blows the right-hand door off its hinges.

A new Mercedes bus squats on the right side of the lane.

"Hit the bus, too." It might be booby-trapped or rigged with explosives.

The tank's cannon booms again, setting the bus ablaze.

My watch says 9:45. "A" Company starts forward. The bus is cooking like an inferno. My men advance one step at a time, hugging the wall, with their fingers on the triggers of their Uzis, FNs, and MAGs. I'm shouting to them to be ready to sling hand grenades if we receive fire from the gate or the walls. Another group of paratroopers hurries into the lane behind me. I recognize Katcha Cahaner from Battalion 28. My own soldiers are about thirty meters from the gate, when suddenly Motta Gur's half-track appears in the lane from behind us. It speeds forward toward the Lion's Gate!

Motta races past me, very excited, passes the tank, passes Katcha, and accelerates up the lane to the gate. He drives through. I'm dumbfounded. Motta is the brigade commander. How can he so recklessly risk his life?

At this instant Uzi Eilam, my own battalion commander, rushes up to me.

"Zamosh, what are you waiting for? Go on! Go in!"

Motta's half-track is well through the gate now. We hear no enemy fire. "Go on!" says Uzi.

"A" Company pours through.

Inside the Lion's Gate is a small court. On the left and slightly uphill I can see the Gate of the Tribes, which leads to the Temple Mount. Straight ahead lies the Via Dolorosa. Uzi has ordered me to secure this lane, which snakes away into the center of the Old City. A Jordanian counterattack could come from here. I send the two half-tracks forward with a force of men to seal this approach.

Motta's half-track is rumbling through the Gate of the Tribes. My whole company follows. A hundred thoughts race through my mind. Foremost is this:

Across the Temple Mount, no farther than a few hundred meters, waits the Western Wall.

Sergeant Moshe Milo is Captain Zamosh's radioman:

We are running behind Motta's half-track. We pass through the Gate of the Tribes. Inside: the yellow tents of the Arab Legion. The defenders' camp. We stride past Land Rovers and weapons carriers, stacks of ammunition boxes, cases of combat rations. We are expecting barbed wire and mines, blockaded passages, ambushes. But the Jordanians are nowhere to be seen.

We sweep up the slope in a skirmish line. The place is vast and open. Buildings on the right have apparently been used as quarters and command posts by the Jordanians. Zamosh sends men to clear and secure this area, including Avremale Shechter, who is his friend from childhood and our company runner.

The rest of the company hurries ahead, taking long strides, following Motta's half-track and spreading out on both flanks.

Avremale Shechter, sergeant, "A" Company:

Jordanian soldiers are very British. Their footpaths are bordered by neat rows of whitewashed stones. The Arab Legion offices when I enter are tidy and orderly. I see flags and notice boards, uniforms on hangers, wellorganized desks. I grab the scarlet pennant of Jordan's Battalion 8 and keep it for forty years.

Yoram Zamosh, "A" Company commander:

I can see the Dome of the Rock ahead. We have crossed at least three hundred meters, maybe more, from the Gate of the Tribes.

The whole summit is an army camp—tents and latrines, field kitchens, mortar emplacements. Protection of this holy site has been entrusted to Battalion 8, one of three battalions of Jordan's elite King Talal Brigade. Since King Abdullah was assassinated in this spot in 1951, only this formation has been entrusted with the defense of the Temple Mount.

At least fifty vehicles are parked in good order, many under canvas covers—Land Rovers, water and fuel tankers, ammunition and supply trucks. Sporadic gunfire comes from lanes inside the city. Ahead in the plaza we see soldiers, and some civilians, scurrying across the open space. Their intent is clearly not hostile. Some are in pajamas. They may be military men who have cast off their uniforms to escape into the civilian crowd.

I pass the order to my men to fire on no one unless fired on first.

Suddenly Moshe Stempel appears. He pounds my back in jubilation. Stempel, as I said earlier, is deputy battalion commander. He falls in with us now, sweeping up the steps and onto the broad open square on the summit of the Temple Mount.

Motta Gur has dismounted from his half-track. Stempel hurries to him. They embrace. Stempel is a head shorter than I and built like a block of stone. To see him clutch Motta is almost comical. The golden dome rises behind them. The Al-Aqsa Mosque is visible a little farther on. The

On the Temple Mount, paratroopers of Battalion 71's "A" Company advance toward the Dome of the Rock.

sense of the moment is not of victory or conquest. The enemy can be anywhere. This is still a war. At the same time, I am floating.

Stempel hurries back to me. "Zamosh! Have you got the flag?"

I'm looking for the poplar grove. Of course I have the flag. As a youth
I have made pilgrimage many times to Mount Zion outside the city walls
and there stood on tiptoe to glimpse the crown of the poplars that marks
the vicinity of the Western Wall. I have climbed to the roof of Notre Dame
Hospice and sought with my eyes this same grove. I know exactly where
it is.

Moshe Milo, Zamosh's radioman:

I have not expected the Temple Mount to be so quiet. You hear the
crack of a rifle in the distance, the engine of a vehicle far away—but up
here we move through a world apart. Our boots on the stone make almost
no sound. I think to myself: Now I understand why this site is holy.

Then I see the poplars.

"Zamosh!"

He has spotted the grove, too. These are the treetops I have glimpsed
from Mount Scopus, years ago, knowing what they mean, that the Wall is

Paratroopers of Battalion 71 advance toward the Temple Mount.
Major Uzi Eilam is at center front.

there, nearby but blocked from view, the Wall that I will never reach, never see, never touch, as all Jews, save at rare intervals, have likewise been debarred for two thousand years.

We're near!

Suddenly: gunfire.

Yoram Zamosh, "A" Company commander:

Rifle fire cracks over our heads. About a dozen Jordanians—soldiers and civilians, or perhaps soldiers who have changed into civilian clothes—have taken up a firing position behind a barricade of military trucks, jeeps, and Land Rovers. Our group takes cover behind a low wall and scurries forward toward the gunfire.

A few of our men are ahead, shouting to the enemy to surrender. The foe answers with gunfire. Stempel is with us. We drop flat on our bellies at the crest of a descending flight of steps. The Jordanian position lies below us, thirty or forty meters across a stone plaza. The vehicles have been parked under arches against a row of buildings, apparently to keep them safe from mortar fire.

One of our men, Shimon Arusi, fires two rifle grenades, one after the other. Arusi is a corporal and a formidable fighter. He skillfully skips the grenades under the vehicles, so that they detonate against the wall, directly amid the concentration of Arab Legion soldiers. The carnage is instant and horrific. At once all fire ceases, replaced by shrieks of agony and cries for help. The blast has been contained in the space between the wall and the vehicles, creating a concentrated zone of slaughter.

We leave the enemy to be cared for by our troops following behind us. Our mission is to find the Wall and hoist the flag.

Moshe Milo, Zamosh's radioman:

Now the craziest thing happens. To get to the Wall, we know, we must pass through Sha'ar Mughrabim, the Moroccan Gate. None of us knows where this is or how hard it will be to break through. In fact, we are carrying explosives to blow the gate open once we locate it.

Suddenly, out of nowhere emerges an ancient Arab man wearing a white robe, with a huge key that must weigh half a kilo hanging around his neck.

Yair Levanon commands "A" Company's 1st Platoon. He dashes

straight to this elderly gent, who is clearly confused, frightened, and bewildered. Yair asks him, in English, "Where is the Wailing Wall?"

The old man is too scared to answer. Levanon speaks to him calmly, promising we will not hurt him. "That key around your neck? What is it for?"

Apparently the man is in charge of the Mughrabim Gate. He's the gatekeeper. Haltingly he leads us there. It's a green wooden gate—a small door within a larger door. It's locked.

Zamosh's second-in-command is Lieutenant Rafi Malka. He's speaking to the gatekeeper now in Arabic. One of our sergeants, Ze'ev Parnes, stands beside him. Parnes tells me later that the old man answered in Arabic, very calmly and without fear, referring to 1948 when the Jordanians

The first paratroopers reach the Western Wall. Left to right, Moshe Stempel, Yoram Zamosh, Yair Levanon, Aryeh Ben Yaakov.

drove the Israelis out of Old Jerusalem: "I have been waiting for you for nineteen years. I knew you would come."

He hands Parnes the key and we open the gate.

We cross through and there is the Wall.

Yoram Zamosh, "A" Company commander:

We are on a flight of stone stairs, looking down. The area is nothing like it is today. Instead of a broad stone plaza, we see only a narrow alley, two meters wide, with Arab tenements directly across from it. The space is empty. No soldiers, no civilians. It's a lane, that's all. Patches of weeds sprout from cracks between the stones.

But it's the Wall. I recognize it in an instant.

So does Moshe Stempel. "Zamosh, the flag!"

He orders me to pick one man and send him down to the Wall, to take possession of it. Then he points to a spot high above—a fence or gate made of iron grillwork. We will mount the flag there, Stempel says, then come back down to the Wall.

I pick a sergeant, Dov Gruner, to go down the stone steps to the Wall, and leave a couple of men to cover him. We can hear sniper fire. The fight for the Old City is by no means over. The rest of us, led by Stempel, mount back through the Moroccan Gate.

We're going back the same way we came, trying to find the section of iron grillwork that we glimpsed from below.

Sergeant Moshe Milo:

Somehow a photographer has joined us, Eli Landau, who will one day be mayor of Herzliya. We are hurrying back along the same route by which we approached the steps above the Wall. The iron grillwork we're seeking is not so easy to find.

Someone points to a row of apartments and says the grill must be behind there. But there is no way to approach. We hurry along the plaza, which is very quiet. There's a gate! If we can get through it, the iron grillwork must be somewhere on the other side.

The gate is called the Chain Gate, though no one knows this at the moment. We cross to it, under a row of arches.

Now things get even crazier.

Yoram Zamosh, "A" Company commander:

As we enter the gate, a young man appears—dark haired, tall, and thin. With him are two women, a blonde and a brunette. "It's okay," he says in English. "I'm one of the good guys."

He is an American Jew from Brooklyn, New York, who has converted to Islam and moved to Jordanian Jerusalem to work for an English-language newspaper. His name is Abdallah Schleifer, formerly Mark, though, of course, we have no idea of this at the time. He will go on to become a renowned journalist and Middle East scholar.

The young man opens a door for us. It's his apartment. "Go through," he says. "You are right above the Western Wall."

We pass through and out onto a terrace. The iron grillwork rises straight ahead. We hurry to it. Its siting is perfect, lofty and prominent, visible from all directions, directly above the Wall.

Stempel extracts the flag from under my web gear. "You must write on it, Zamosh."

Stempel's hands are trembling.

I have been awash with emotion all morning. Now suddenly I find I am calm.

"What should I write?"

From my breast pocket I retrieve a pen, a beaten-up ballpoint that I've been using all week for writing situation reports and messages. I set the flag atop my knee, using my thigh as a writing surface.

*This flag of Israel was placed here by paratroopers of
the 55th Brigade,*

"What's the date?"

No one knows. The days have run so together.

"Seven June."

I switch to writing on the edge of the stone step. It's more stable than my knee.

7 June 1967, who have captured the Old City

"Wait, Zamosh!" Stempel stops me. "Not 'captured.' Write 'liberated.'"

I make the change. Scratch out one word and write the new one. We

Hoisting the flag above the Western Wall. Left to right, Shimon Arusi, Aryeh Ben Yakov, Ilan Angel, Moshe Stempel, Avremale Shechter, Yair Levanon, Yoram Zamosh. Moshe Milo is partially hidden behind Stempel.

hang the flag and stand back. The verses of the anthem "Hatikva"—The Hope—croak hoarsely from our throats, finishing with this couplet:

To be a free people in our land
The land of Zion and Jerusalem

Avremale Shechter, sergeant, "A" Company:

We have crossed back down to the Wall. It's unbelievably peaceful. Nobody here. No Arabs, no other paratroopers.

Two nights ago, when the battalion first reached Beit HaKerem, our entry point into Jerusalem, Captain Zamosh had called me aside and asked if I had brought my tefillin. These are Jewish artifacts of prayer, little leather boxes with verses from the Torah inside on parchment. You bind one, the *shel rosh,* to your forehead, and wrap the other, the *shel yad,* around your arm.

I told Zamosh I had brought them.

"Keep them with you."

Avremale Shechter at the Western Wall.

Yoram Zamosh, "A" Company commander:

I have known Avremale and his brothers since we were boys. His father was the kindest, most simple and modest man. He worked all his life for the Tnuva Dairy in Tel Aviv, riding his bicycle to work, raising his boys, asking nothing but to be here as a Jew in this land, but feeling always that our people's return remained incomplete, with the Wall and the Old City in the hands of those who hated us.

Now I see Avremale, with his Uzi with its folding stock under one arm and the tefillin in place on his head and other arm. I know he is thinking of his father.

The others want to pray, too, but none of them knows how. Avremale has to teach them.

My orders from Uzi Eilam are to take the Wall but also to seal one quarter of the Old City. I must rally my company. We still have work to do.

Zeev Barkai, Battalion 71 operations officer:

If everyone who claims to have been first at the Wall really was first, there must've been a mob of a thousand guys. Our group was not first, I know that. Zamosh and Moshe Stempel got there before us.

I was with Uzi Eilam, our battalion commander, and Dan Ziv and Benny Ron and a few others from our headquarters group. We ran into Motta Gur on the steps in front of the Al-Aqsa Mosque. Uzi asked permission to find the Wall. None of us was sure where it was. "Go," said Motta. He had already made his own history that day.

Somehow Uzi found the Wall. We followed down the stone steps. No one was there. We trooped down together. I remember somebody saying that Rabbi Goren had just arrived; he was somewhere up on the Temple Mount, seeking the Wall. Uzi sent one of his soldiers to find him and bring him down to us.

Benny Ron, attached to Battalion 71:

If you were to ask a thousand Israelis, "Who blew the first blast on the ram's horn—the shofar—at the Wailing Wall?" every one of them would answer, "Rabbi Goren." Because of the famous David Rubinger photo in *Life* magazine.

I don't want to take anything away from Rabbi Goren. I love Rabbi Goren. Rabbi Goren stayed at the Wall for hours. He was there when Rubinger took the iconic photograph of the three paratroopers gazing in wonder at the Wall. He was there when Dayan arrived with Rabin and Uzi Narkiss.

But that first blast on the ram's horn was not blown by Rabbi Goren. That was our battalion commander, Uzi Eilam.

Uzi is a trumpet player. He's been playing since he was a kid. When Rabbi Goren first came down to the Wall, he was so overcome with emotion that he couldn't catch his breath. He put the shofar to his lips but no sound came out.

Uzi is a sweet, modest guy. He wasn't trying to make any statement. He just said, in his quiet way, "Rabbi Goren, I'm a trumpet player. May I try?"

I snapped the photo. For years after, when people asked Uzi about that moment, he would never dispute Rabbi Goren's account. He didn't want to take anything away from this legendary personage. Even after Rabbi Goren had passed on, Uzi still would not put himself forward.

He's not that kind of guy.

Photo by Benny Ron.

Major Uzi Eilam sounds the ram's horn at the Western Wall. Rabbi Shlomo Goren stands beside him, with Leizer Lavi adjacent. To Eilam's left is "A" Company commander Yoram Zamosh; to his right, deputy battalion commander Dan Ziv.

BOOK SEVEN

THE DEEP BATTLE

49.

A CAMPAIGN OF ROADS

I have spent this morning, June 6, in cabinet meetings arguing over Jerusalem. I have stood on Mount Scopus and looked out over the Old City, still in Arab hands. Not until afternoon do I have time to turn to events unfolding fast in Sinai.

Moshe Dayan is minister of defense.

Tal and Gorodish have broken through in the north along the El Arish axis; south of Tal, Yoffe's division has reached Bir Laffan; Arik Sharon's division has smashed through the Egyptian stronghold at Um Katef along the central axis. The internal organs of the foe have become exposed. We have entered the belly of the beast.

In the theory of "wars of movement"—as developed and put into practice by the Germans in Poland, France and Belgium and the Netherlands, in Russia, and in North Africa—once an attacking force has achieved breakthrough, it must next bring to battle and destroy the enemy's second line of defense, his divisions held in reserve behind the frontline formations.

Nasser's key second-line elements—the 3rd Infantry Division, the elite 4th Armored Division, and the 6th Mechanized Division (excluding the near-division-size Shazli Force, which has for the moment crossed into Israel and eluded our advance)—wait now in the heart of Sinai. As many as five hundred Egyptian tanks are deployed in the vicinity of Bir Laffan, Jebel Libni, El Thamad, Bir Thamada, and Bir Gafgafa. I know the area well. So do Gavish, Sharon, Tal, Yoffe, Gorodish, and all our commanders.

Our aim is to destroy the Egyptian Army. Where it moves, we will pursue. Where it stands, we will attack.

Warfare in Sinai is a campaign of roads. An armored column seeking to reach the Canal from the east can proceed by one of only three arteries:

Major General Yeshayahu "Shayke" Gavish (in dust goggles),
chief of Southern Command.

the coast highway from El Arish to Qantara, the central road via Bir Gafgafa to Ismailiya, or the southern route through the Mitla, Giddi, or Sudr
Passes to the Great Bitter Lake and the waterway north of Suez.

If Nasser's forces attempt to flee, they must take one or all of these
routes. There are no other avenues of escape.

If our forces can block the enemy's passage along these routes, we can
trap them, bring them to battle, and destroy them.

As our forces press their advantage, however, two elements of supreme
significance come into play and must be taken, by me and by the government, into account.

First is Arab pride and the rulers' imperative to save face.

The Egyptian president and his counterparts in Jordan and other allied states will not be able to admit defeat, or even setback.

Nasser will lie. Hussein will perjure himself. Arab broadcasts will
proclaim phantom victories. This has been happening in fact since early
yesterday morning.

These "news reports," fabricated by Nasser's bureau of propaganda
and abetted by statements from King Hussein, have fortunately served the
cause of Israel so far. They have kept the Soviet Union from pressing for a

cease-fire to preserve the forces of its client states, and they have confused and misled the enemy's own forces and allies.

"Three-quarters of the Zionist air force has been destroyed! Egyptian armored columns are approaching Tel Aviv!"

Can Nasser himself believe these fictions? The habit of pride and the obligation to save face permeate and infuse the Egyptian chain of command from top to bottom, exerting upon junior officers a nearly irresistible compulsion, when reporting to superiors, to fabricate successes and to underreport (or fail to report at all) difficulties or reversals. Who knows what intelligence accounts are being placed before Nasser and his generals? In war, the wish to believe the best can be overwhelming.

If Israeli successes continue, however, and if Nasser comes to recognize their actuality, he will be tempted, even compelled by his office and the mythos of his own invincibility, to seek ways to deflect the shame attendant upon such reverses. He may declare before his people and the world that the United States and Britain have provided Israel with covert support. He may even believe this himself. Surely the Jews cannot be humiliating Egypt's armed forces all by themselves.

One discovers humor in this at his peril. For such fictions may acquire the weight of fact when they are reported by legitimate (or even questionable) news channels and are believed by tens of millions around the globe.

This is exactly what happens, as early as the second day. A letter is dispatched by Nasser to Soviet premier Alexei Kosygin, claiming that warplanes of the American Sixth Fleet are attacking Egypt. The Egyptian president calls for immediate aid. Reports of U.S. intervention are broadcast by government channels across the Middle East. Mobs begin attacking American embassies. Saudi Arabia cuts off all oil to the United States. Nasser recalls his embassy from Washington. Within hours Syria, Iran, Algeria, Sudan, Mauritania, and Yemen have severed ties. Nasser may be getting thrashed on the battlefield, but he is rapidly regaining traction in the arena of propaganda, the province of international politics.

Now the second intangible common to all Arab-Israeli clashes enters the picture. This is the element of the externally imposed cease-fire.

Sponsor states of the belligerents, wishing to shield their clients and to preserve their own spheres of influence (not to mention prevent the outbreak of a third world war) will begin to apply pressure upon these clients to stop the fighting.

How will the Powers do this? They will communicate via international bodies such as the UN, or more immediately through diplomatic channels, via embassies, individuals of influence, and in person-to-person wires and communiqués. In Israel we will hear directly from the Russians. Cables from the Kremlin will menace us with "grave consequences" and "dire outcomes." Kosygin and Brezhnev will warn of impending military action. Israel must take such threats seriously. A growl at us from Moscow is like a bear intimidating a cub. With one paw the Russians can flatten us.

The Americans, on the other hand, will counsel prudence. Johnson, Rusk, McNamara, and their surrogates will urge us to "take the long view," to "let victory lay the groundwork for peace." U.S. diplomacy will advocate "breathing space," a "cooling-off period." Israel must lead by reason, the Americans will argue. She must take the high road. Let her be the first to speak for amity and to act in accord with the world's wish for peace.

The Powers will want Israel to stop fighting before she has achieved complete victory.

Such are the difficulties with which the government and I must contend. The troops in the field know nothing of this. Their aim remains unaltered: Keep advancing at all costs, take as much as you can.

"Bite and eat what is on your plate."

50.

AN UNSEEN RAINBOW

We are out of cigarettes. A search of a wrecked Egyptian truck produces nothing but two of our soldiers shouting to us, "Hey, no looting!" We spy some abandoned tents, park, and go in. Ah, smokes! Cleopatras, a quality Egyptian brand.

Yael Dayan advances with Sharon's division into central Sinai.

We have stumbled into a camp for Egyptian officers. Treasures abound. French cologne, fifths of Johnnie Walker Black, pressed uniforms with riding boots, silk underwear folded in drawers. In a bedside cupboard: Revlon eyeliner kits, makeup, nylon stockings with labels from East Germany.

"See the enlisted men's patch across the way?" says one of our fellows.

"The poor bastards are lucky to have shoes."

"That's enough," says Dov. He pulls us out.

Night. The column crawls in low gear, mounting to a plateau along the roughest road I have ever driven upon. We are advancing toward Nakhl in central Sinai. Reports say that Shazli's force of nine thousand men and two hundred tanks, breaking from El Thamad and Kuntilla, is attempting to flee west. Dov taps Nakhl on the map. "If we get there before the Egyptians, we can cut off their retreat."

But in minutes a jeep of the Recon Company comes slewing back from the head of the column. Minefield ahead! All vehicles halt in place! Combat engineers are called forward to clear a route.

Dov tries a go-around but our jeep bogs down in a wadi. It's getting cold. We return to Arik and the command half-tracks. Sharon is on the net. "A jeep just ran onto a mine," he says. "Two soldiers were killed." Then over the headset he hears something else.

Sharon's face changes.

He tugs the headphone from one ear and turns toward Dov and me.
"The Old City of Jerusalem is in our hands."

Word flies along the length of the column. Dirty, exhausted men pass
the report from tank to half-track, from engineers' bulldozer to ammunition truck. Dov breaks out whiskey and chocolates. Men dismount from
vehicles and cluster in knots of three or four. Verses of "Jerusalem of
Gold" ascend into the frigid air, sung not in triumph or pride, but offered
as a prayer—a prayer that is an answer to so many millions across the
centuries. I wrote later, in *Israel Journal: June, 1967:*

> *We couldn't move, but we had wings. The night was cold and the
> wind brushed us with cutting grains of sand, but there was a
> warmth of surging feelings and an unseen rainbow in the desert sky.*

Daylight brings resupply by air. A helicopter lands with mail and
newspapers. "GAZA STRIP IN OUR HANDS," "RAMALLAH IS
OURS," "WEST BANK CITIES ARE CAPTURED."

We will hear later of my father's arrival at the Wailing Wall with Chief
of Staff Rabin and the head of Central Command, Uzi Narkiss. Dayan
scribbles a few words on a scrap of paper, in accord with tradition, and
slips it into a crack between the stones. "What did you wish for?" a reporter asks.

"Peace," says Moshe Dayan.

That evening in Sinai I hear over the radio—as, I'm sure, do my brothers Assi and Udi in the field with their units, my mother and grandparents,
and every Israeli, as well as Jews all over the world—the full text of my
father's statement from the Western Wall:

> *We have returned to the holiest of our holy places, never to part
> from it again. To our Arab neighbors, Israel extends the hand of
> peace, and to peoples of all faiths we guarantee full freedom of
> worship and of religious rights. We have come, not to conquer
> the holy places of others, nor to diminish by the slightest mea-
> sure their religious rights, but to ensure the unity of the city and
> to live in it with others in harmony.*

Next morning, while wolfing a breakfast of biscuits and canned sardines, Sharon sketches the plan for ambushing the Egyptian column retreating toward Nakhl.

Our armor speeds ahead.

The enemy enters the trap.

Within ninety minutes 150 enemy tanks, along with support vehicles in uncountable numbers, have been rendered into scorched and smoldering wrecks.

This is the Valley of Death for the Egyptian Army.

We drive in silence past the mangled hulks. A sorrow verging on rage oppresses Dov. His sympathy lies with the enemy conscripts, the simple fellahin drafted from the delta who have been abandoned by their commanders.

"How come we hold only one or two Egyptian officer prisoners but hundreds of enlisted men?"

Even Arik, the legendary warrior, looks upon the sight with a countenance drained of animation. "It is horrible," he says. "I hate it."

Nakhl is the biblical wilderness of Paran. To this site Hagar retired with her son Ishmael, cast out by Abraham. It is, I am certain, the ugliest place on earth.

51.

THE LONGEST NIGHT

Ori Orr is the twenty-eight-year-old commander of the Recon Company of the 7th Armored Brigade:

"Five" is military radio nomenclature for a reconnaissance company. It also means the commander of that company. I am "Five." "Twenty" is brigade commander Gorodish. "Forty" is division commander Israel Tal.

It's Thursday, June 8, the fourth day of the war. Just before sunset, Twenty receives a radio transmission from Forty, telling him he has just been informed that the UN is debating a cease-fire resolution. "Twenty, how far are you from the Canal?"

"About thirty kilometers."

"Get there as fast as you can."

At once Gorodish puts together a fast, mobile army in miniature—our company from Recon, a half company of tanks, and a small detachment of artillery. He puts me in command.

"Your people are exhausted, Ori. The road to the Canal will be packed with Egyptian vehicles fleeing. Will you be okay?"

"We'll be fine."

"Wait," says Gorodish. He is very brave. "I'll go with you."

Gorodish radios Forty, who overrules him. "Twenty, you are staying with your brigade. I trust your Five. Let him go."

Menachem Shoval, Recon trooper:

We're on the main road to the Canal. The route is pitch black except for light from burning Egyptian vehicles shot to pieces by our air force and our tanks.

My jeep is sixth in column, behind Ori's jeep, Eli's jeep, Amos's jeep, and two tanks. Trailing us come more tanks. The artillery is last.

Egyptian tanks and trucks are moving on the road with us. We're all traveling in the same direction. The Egyptians are fleeing for safety toward the Canal. We're trying to get there so we can claim all of Sinai before the UN shuts us down.

The Egyptians don't realize that Israelis are among them. They're as stupefied with fatigue as we are. The road itself is blocked at point after point by smoldering hulks and burned-out wrecks. To drive under these conditions requires every ounce of concentration. We're weaving in and out and so are the Egyptians.

We're so tired. We drive like drunks. Twice I have run off the road and only snapped awake when my helmet crashed into the steering wheel as the jeep bellied to a stop in the sand.

In addition, we are mentally blocking out so much trauma: everything that has happened, friends killed, even the massacre of the enemy.

I shout to Eli, asking what time it is. My guess is three or four in the morning.

"Not quite midnight."

Eli Rikovitz, Recon platoon commander:

On this road we are destroying Egyptian armor in a way that is not in the manual. Our jeeps drive on the road; the Patton tanks find their way along the shoulder and off to the side. When we in the jeeps see an Egyptian tank, we spotlight it with our headlamps and make a sign to our tanks to shoot it.

They do, at unbelievably close range.

When an Egyptian tank blows, none of its compatriots stops to help. Each driver has his head down, grinding for the Canal and safety.

Menachem Shoval, Recon trooper:

Suddenly in front of our jeep an Egyptian soldier appears. He's in the middle of the road, flagging us down.

His T-54 is bogged in the sand. He thinks we're Egyptians; he's waving for help. We spotlight the tank with our headlights and call for one of our Pattons to destroy it. Ori's jeep speeds up. Ori calls to the Egyptian soldier, signing to him and his crew to save themselves. In case they don't savvy, he stands and swings in their direction the .30-caliber machine gun that is mounted on the bonnet of his jeep.

The soldier drops his red signal light and bolts into the darkness. The Egyptians cannot believe Israelis are all around them. Our jeep reverses out of harm's way as one of our Pattons pulls up so close to the T-54 that the commander has to duck down into his hatch in case the enemy tank explodes. Point-blank the cannon blows the Egyptian's tracks and front rollers to scrap.

No need to destroy the whole tank. Our wrecking crews will salvage it tomorrow.

Ori Orr, Recon Company commander:

To work this kind of havoc is not fun. It makes the heart heavy. There is great fear, always, even within the fatigue. Any one of these enemy soldiers can open fire from the dark. We have seen how easily life can be taken.

Our young soldiers are trying to do the best they can. They have slept only hours in five days. They are carrying the grief of friends lost and the anguish of enemy slain.

The leader's job is to take onto his shoulders not only the tactical weight of decision, but also the moral burden. Our nineteen- and twenty-year-olds are struggling to think about what they must do and to not think about the consequences.

That responsibility belongs to Eli and to Amos and to me.

Dubi Tevet, nineteen-year-old Recon trooper:

I have not slept for more than an hour in five days. In the jeep, I am in and out of nightmares, flashbacks, and what one might call reality if he could distinguish it from these other states.

Yesterday, or maybe it was two days ago, our brigade command group spotted an enormous cloud of dust to the south. Yes, that was yesterday, Wednesday, June 7. The dust appeared to be moving north.

Eli was summoned to Gorodish's command group, which had drawn up at a spot called Point 68 on the road between Jebel Maara and Bir Gaf-gafa. General Tal, the division commander, was there, too. They were all peering through binoculars at the massive ridge of dust. Gorodish, under orders from Tal, instructed Eli to take two jeeps and advance carefully along the road to the west to find out what was raising those great clouds.

Eli and I set out with a third jeep. I can't remember who was with us. We had a Piper scout plane overhead but our jeeps were all alone, way out in front of everybody. We could see as we advanced that the dust was rising from the primary road south of Bir Gafgafa.

"That's the better part of a division," said Eli.

He speculated that a large Egyptian formation was moving from Bir Thamada to Bir Gafgafa, trying to reach the main east-west route—the one on which our brigade was advancing—so it could flee from there west to the Canal.

Eli Rikovitz, Recon platoon commander:

I radioed back to Gorodish. The road on which the Egyptian column was advancing lay in an open plain with no cover on either side. From the dust it was raising, I estimated the number of its vehicles at above two hundred.

Gorodish instructed us to return at once to his command post at Point 68. He was ordering both of the brigade's tank battalions to prepare for action.

This was the kind of opportunity an armored commander dreams of his entire life.

Patton tanks of Battalion 79 and the Recon Company at Point 68, preparing to move out along the road code-named "Blokada."

Dubi Tevet, Recon trooper:

Gorodish sent us forward again, this time leading the tanks. We advanced along a dirt road called on the code maps "Blokada." Blokada took us straight to the Bir Thamada–Bir Gafgafa road.

We could see the Egyptian tanks and trucks moving from left to right (south to north) before us.

Our jeeps positioned both battalions, 79 and 82, along the crest of a ridge. Below on the road was the enemy column, crawling across our field of fire like ducks in a shooting gallery.

Eli Rikovitz, Recon platoon commander:

The Egyptian column was attempting to escape from the division of Arik Sharon, which was advancing from the southeast, and probably from Yoffe's division pushing out of the east, in addition to our own 60th Armored Brigade, which was paralleling our advance a few kilometers to the south. I was studying the map. The best part of wiping out this Egyptian column here and now was that the wreckage would block this avenue of escape for every other enemy formation in this part of the desert.

Whatever Egyptian forces remained to the south would be at the mercy of Sharon and Yoffe and our warplanes.

Dubi Tevet, Recon trooper:

The brigade's two tank battalions positioned themselves at the top of a ridge about two thousand meters from the enemy column. Two thousand meters is what the manuals call "battle range." The same distance we use in practice on the firing range.

Eli Rikovitz, Recon platoon commander:

Our Pattons and Centurions fired at the vehicles in the front of the column. That blocked all escape forward. At the same time other gunners were sealing the route to the rear. The Egyptians were trapped in the middle. We could see crews abandoning the vehicles and fleeing on foot.

The enemy never maneuvered into a combat formation. They were just trying to get to the main road west, to get away. Perhaps they had orders to flee at all costs, to save whatever they could of themselves and their vehicles.

Dubi Tevet, Recon trooper:

When you have seen your friends dismembered and incinerated before your eyes, it is very satisfying to witness payback. The Egyptians never returned fire. The crews had all run away. Nor did we in Recon have to direct our tank gunners. We sat back and enjoyed the show.

When dark came, we led the tanks back to Point 68, the spot where we had left the main road to advance along the dirt road called Blokada to the plains south of Bir Gafgafa. The tanks went into defensive positions, what they call a "night leaguer."

Eli Rikovitz, Recon platoon commander:

There was no time for celebrating. The tanks were out of fuel and ammunition. The crews remained awake all night working, replenishing lubricants, gasoline, water, ammo for the cannons and the machine guns, and performing the dozens of repair and maintenance tasks that tanks require in the desert—tightening tracks, replacing filters, oiling friction points, cleaning sand and debris out of essential mechanisms like the traversing gears for the turrets.

In Recon we can refuel our jeeps in minutes using jerry cans. But a tank has to take a number, get in line, butt up to a refueling truck, then wait again when something goes wrong with the orders, which it always does. The crews are lucky to wolf down some sardines and biscuits and maybe a mug of tea, heated on a Primus stove or an engine block.

They know they have wiped out most of an enemy division this afternoon. This makes up for losing another night's sleep.

Ori Orr, Recon Company commander:

Now it is two days later, the hours of darkness between Thursday and Friday, the eighth and ninth of June.

The Long Night continues.

My watch says 03:20. We are passing a burning truck with manufacturer's markings from East Germany. This vehicle is, what, the five hundredth so far tonight?

In a way you are lucky to be a commander. Things that might frighten or upset those under you don't produce the same effect on you. Why? Because you cannot let them.

I ask myself sometimes, "Ori, are you afraid?" The answer is, "I have no time to be afraid."

The commander bears responsibility not just for the completion of the mission, but also for the lives of his men. A military unit, particularly a reconnaissance company, is like a street gang. You are closer than brothers. Each life is precious to you. For every man under my responsibility, I see in my mind's eye his mother and father, his girlfriend or wife, his children, even if he has none yet—his children-to-be, and their children as well. All will suffer if he dies. Such a weight makes concerns such as personal fear, loss, even one's own death seem trivial.

War for the commander is not like war for the individual soldier. What is going on in external reality is for me only context. The real war is inside my head.

In my head I must overlook nothing, forget nothing, fail to act on no warning or intuition.

I am lucky. My position denies me the luxury of doubt or hesitation or fear.

Eli Rikovitz, Recon platoon commander:

The scale of destruction along this route is beyond anything I could have imagined. It goes on for kilometer after kilometer.

We started at eight this evening. Another eight hours have elapsed since then. All that time we have been passing wrecked and burnt-out tanks, trucks, ambulances, gun tractors, command cars, three-tonners pulling antitank guns, mobile field kitchens, personnel carriers, and half-tracks. The stench of incinerated flesh has not let up in all that time.

This is what war smells like. Burning rubber and gasoline, gunpowder, cordite, the melting surface of the asphalt road. Egyptian army trucks squat on bare rims in the road and along the sides, their tires burnt to liquid. Of engines nothing remains but the blocks; in cabs, you see only the springs of seats.

Courtesy of Eli Rikovitz.

Between Bir Gafgafa and the Suez Canal.

The road we're on is the main road from Bir Gafgafa to Ismailiya. Bir Gafgafa is a huge Egyptian base, with tanks, infantry, an airfield, everything. That's where most of this traffic is fleeing from. That, and from columns running away from Sharon's and Yoffe's divisions.

Ismailiya is a key crossing of the Suez Canal. The Firdan Bridge is there. The Egyptians are fleeing toward that span.

They are trying to get across the Canal to safety.

Dubi Tevet, Recon trooper:

This night is like a nightmare, where what you see with your eyes seems like some terrible dream, but from which you wake only to realize that it is real and it remains real and you and your friends are still in it. But this night is not the worst. The worst was the first night, at El Arish, counting our dead.

This night is not that bad. This night will end. We will reach the Canal. The war will be over.

52.

THE SEVENTH DAY
OF THE SIX DAY WAR

I am only a major, a helicopter squadron commander, but I can tell you this: No other officer, including Dayan himself, has a bird's-eye view of this war like I do. Why? Because my guys are flying missions in every theater. We are in the West Bank, in Gaza; we are north in the Golan, and west along the Canal.

Cheetah Cohen commands Helicopter Squadron 124.

Morning of the third day: My guys are flying medevacs and emergency resupply missions across three-quarters of the Sinai Peninsula. You can spot the highways from beyond the horizon by the smoke rising from burning Egyptian vehicles.

I feel sorry for the Egyptians. The poor foot soldiers, most of whom are simple fellahin—peasants from the delta—have been abandoned by their officers. They straggle westward in columns of fifty or a hundred, sometimes tens and pairs and even individuals, barefoot and bareheaded. God knows what they are suffering from thirst and heat, grief and shattered pride.

Our helicopters skim over the northern sector of the Bir Thamada–Bir Gafgafa road. Our armor must have shot up three hundred of Nasser's tanks, trucks, and transports. The wrecks are strewn over miles. Bodies litter the slopes. The sand is already drifting over them.

Rafi Sivron is the planner of Operation Moked:

My job was over once Moked had destroyed the Egyptian Air Force. I stayed in the Pit at Tel Aviv for most of the first and second day, performing command and control duties involving ongoing operations. But finally

I went to Motti Hod, my boss, chief of the air force. "I want to fly missions before the war is over."

"Good," he said. "Get out of here."

Cheetah Cohen commands Helicopter Squadron 124:

Rafi Sivron has joined us, coming out from the Pit in Tel Aviv. It's Wednesday, June 7, the third day of the war. I tease Rafi: "So you finally came up from underground!"

Though Rafi is a brilliant planner, he is a flier first. He wants to fly missions.

Rafi has been in helicopters since 1958. He is the bravest copilot and best navigator in the Middle East. He has been awarded the Itur HaMofet and a Chief of Staff Citation for valor, flying covert insertions with me and other teams deep into enemy territory.

Think about the skill it takes to do this. You must cross the border at night, with no lights, in radio silence, flying at such a low altitude to avoid detection by radar that you cannot navigate by landmarks but must find your way using only time, speed, and heading. Now you must find and pick up a special operations team in the middle of the Syrian highlands or in some godforsaken corner of Sinai, knowing that to be spotted by the enemy can cost not only your own life and those of your crew, but the lives of the special operations team as well. And I'm not even talking about the political or national security consequences.

The pilot's job is easy. It's the navigator who carries the weight. Assigned to such a mission, I do not say, "Give me somebody like Rafi." I say, "Give me Rafi or forget it!"

Our squadron is flying north now from Sharm el-Sheikh. We have delivered paratroopers to secure the Straits of Tiran, which had been the trigger point of the whole war when Nasser sent his own paratroopers there in late May. Now, as we fly home along a shoreline of red-gold cliffs and shallows of dazzling aquamarine blue, a transmission comes in from air force headquarters:

Assemble every helicopter you've got; proceed at once to the Golan Heights.

But my guys haven't slept in three days. At Eilat I order the squadron to land. We take over the Red Rock Hotel, fifty or sixty pilots and crew, with no permission and no authorization. Air Force Operations is furious.

I tell them: "Listen—my pilots are so exhausted they can't read their gauges, and neither can I."

"How much sleep do you need?"

"I'll tell you when I wake up."

Uzi Eilam, commander of Paratroop Battalion 71, has just completed the liberation of the Old City of Jerusalem:

Motta Gur calls his battalion commanders together and tells us that the brigade will no longer be operating as a brigade. "You are free to do what you like with your battalions."

I know at once I will take Battalion 71 north to the Golan Heights. Why? Where there is fighting, you must be there.

Cheetah Cohen commands Helicopter Squadron 124:

We fly in to a place called Poriya. Rafi Sivron is with me. He's my copilot.

Poriya is a high point overlooking the Kinneret, the Sea of Galilee, from the west. Over our left shoulders as we fly in, we can see Nazareth, where Jesus grew to manhood. Tiberias, an ancient center of Hebrew learning, passes beneath. Mount Tabor, where Deborah's general Barak defeated the Canaanites, rises to the west. Ahead are the Horns of Hattin, where Saladin routed the Crusaders in 1187. Beyond this lies Capernaum, where a certain person walked on water.

We land in a big field. It's all big fields up there. We have two squadrons—mine, the 124, with seventeen Sikorsky S-58 helicopters, and the 114, commanded by my friend Haim Naveh, flying big French Super Frelons.

Here is Haim's story in four sentences:

Eleven years old, Budapest, 1942, Haim and his parents are herded with hundreds of Jewish families to a bridge in the city center. Father, mother, everyone is packed off to the death camps. Haim escapes. He survives two winters, alone on the streets, before rescue brings him to Mandate Palestine.

Now here he is, twenty-three years later, commanding a helicopter squadron in a fight against other enemies whose aim is to destroy our people.

Across the Sea of Galilee rises the Golan Heights. Looking east from Poriya, we can see the plateau, big and square and high. Volcanic. Tanks need steel tracks there, not rubber like in Sinai.

On the ground, the first person I run into is Danny Matt. His paratroopers are arriving by bus and truck.

"Danny! I thought you were still in Sinai."

"It's over. They pulled us out. We were in Bethlehem and Hebron yesterday, but that's finishing up, too."

I want to hug Danny, but he is a colonel and I am only a major. Instead he hugs me.

"What orders do you have, Cheetah?"

"Me? What orders do *you* have?"

Rafi Sivron:

My orders from Air Force Operations are to set up a forward air command post. I will not be in command of Squadrons 124 and 114, but I will be directing their efforts in coordination with the ground forces.

Together with the commanders of the paratroopers and the infantry, we will figure out what we want to do, what we can do, and what high command will let us do.

Cheetah Cohen:

Rafi and his guys set up their forward CP in the middle of the field. All around them helicopters are landing. The Golan Heights is only sixty-five kilometers long from north to south and between twelve and twenty-five kilometers across. Our birds can ferry Danny's paratroopers anywhere onto the Heights as soon as we get the order.

But will we get the order?

Rafi's improvised command post consists of two tables with radios and other communications gear. We are operating out of our hip pockets, with conflicting reports coming in from all over.

From army headquarters Rafi has learned that ground forces of the Northern Command under General David "Dado" Elazar, joined by others arriving from Sinai and elsewhere, have broken through in the northern sector of the Heights. Elements of the Golani Brigade have captured Tel Fakhr, Tel Azzaziat, and Darbashiya, and other units are advancing as well. The fighting has been furious and bitter, hand to hand in many places, as our troops assault uphill against formidable entrenched positions. Losses have been heavy in men and vehicles. I hear one report of an IDF battalion that started an assault with twenty-six tanks and finished with two.

Rafi Sivron:

Kuneitra is the principal city of the Golan Heights. It's in the north, less than eighty kilometers from Damascus, the Syrian capital. By 10:00 we're hearing reports that Israeli forces, supported by sortie after sortie of Vautours, Mystères, Super Mystères, and Mirages, have cut off the town.

If our ground forces can take Kuneitra, the highway to Damascus will lie wide open.

Cheetah Cohen:

Syrian radio is reporting that Kuneitra has fallen. This report will turn out to be premature. But our radio intelligence guys in Tel Aviv jump on the opportunity and rebroadcast the piece over and over.

Who knows? Maybe it will scare more of the enemy into packing up.

Rafi Sivron:

Syrian forces are withdrawing. Every report confirms this. But we don't know how fast, how many, or from where.

We still have no orders.

At noon Kuneitra falls. Where are our generals? Heading there, apparently. We can't reach them.

We have two squadrons of helicopters and most of a brigade of paratroopers, and we can't get orders from anybody.

Danny Matt:

I'm standing with Cheetah, peering across the Sea of Galilee at the Golan Heights. Both of us are thinking the same thought:

If the Syrians are pulling out of Kuneitra, racing home to defend Damascus, a cease-fire could be imminent. At the UN in New York, Syria's ambassador is no doubt demanding a resolution right now. If such a measure is passed and our government accedes (which it must), cease-fire lines will be established based upon the present positions of the two armies.

Though the Syrians are withdrawing in the north of the Heights, they have not pulled out in the center and the south.

"Danny," Cheetah says, "we can't let this war end with the Syrians still controlling two-thirds of the Heights."

Rafi Sivron:

For three years, between '62 and '65, I was operations deputy in air force headquarters. Two days a week my duties brought me up here to the Galilee. I fell in love with the Golan. No place on earth is more beautiful than the Heights in the spring, when the hills are carpeted with wildflowers. But the fighting up here never stopped.

The Golan Heights is a volcanic plateau, elevation about 3,000 feet, overlooking in its southwest corner the Sea of Galilee, which is 660 feet below sea level. For decades Syrian gunners on the high ground have tormented Israeli farmers in the flatlands below, in violation of the 1948 armistice, firing their Russian artillery down onto the kibbutz fields. This game is not sporting. Our farms are so close the Syrians can throw rocks and hit them. They fire at tractors in the fields and shell the barns and livestock pens and homes and school buildings. The kibbutz children spend half their lives underground.

Since Wednesday, the third day of the war, delegations from these settlements have been besieging Eshkol and Rabin and Dayan, who was born on one of these kibbutzim, Deganiah Alef, and who grew up on moshav Nahalal, only fifty kilometers west.

"Take the Heights!" the farmers plead. "Protect us from the Syrians!"

"Their provocations started this war. We can't let them off scot-free!"

Danny Matt:

Before my paratroop brigade was sent north to the Golan, we were ordered into the West Bank to seize Hebron and Bethlehem. As a young squad leader in the Haganah during the War of Independence, I had fought in this exact place against the Jordanian Arab Legion, defending a cluster of villages called Gush Etzion, the Etzion Bloc.

The campaign lasted from November 1947 till May 1948, when the four primary settlements—Kfar Etzion, Ein Tzurim, Massu'ot Yitzhak, and Revadim—finally surrendered. The Arab Legion massacred every Jew, 127 souls, and looted and burned everything left behind.

This is a score I have very much wished to settle. But when my paratroopers and I get to Bethlehem and Hebron, the enemy has cleared out.

Now here we are in the Golan, presented with another opportunity. We cannot let this one go to waste.

*Pilot Giora Romm has three MiG kills from the first day of
the war:*

The Golan has put me in the hospital. It's my own fault. Day two, I'm
assigned as flight leader with a mission to the Heights. I have no business
leading a formation. I'm twenty-two years old; I have just seen my first
combat twenty-four hours ago. But because I have shot down three MiGs,
I have achieved a certain level of celebrity.

Here is how unconscious I am. I forget that the Syrians know there is
a war going on. I'm thinking it's still day one, that I have to fly below the
radar.

If I had been using half my brain, I would have approached the Golan
Heights at 20,000 feet, well above Syrian triple-A, picked my targets, and
led my planes in high and safe. Instead, I'm hugging the deck, point-blank
above the barrels of the enemy's antiaircraft artillery.

Now I'm in the hospital at Afula, lucky to be alive after taking a hit
directly beneath my seat and barely getting my Mirage safely back onto
the ground at Ramat David. My right leg is full of shrapnel. The nurses
have shot me up with painkillers. I'm wearing one of those ridiculous hospital gowns. I look around my hospital room and say to myself, "Giora,
you can sit out the war reading magazines in this bed or you can show
some initiative and get back into action."

I decide to run away from the hospital. I phone Tel Nof; the air base
sends a truck for me. My flight suit from this morning has burned up. I ride
home in a bathrobe. Back at the base, my squadron commander, Ran Ronen,
won't let me fly because of my shot-up leg. He sends me to the base doctor.
"Giora," says the air force physician, "show me you can move your leg."

So I flex my good leg.

Three hours later I'm back in a Mirage at 20,000 feet over Sinai.

My number one is Motti Yeshurun; number two is Avramik Salmon.
Their planes are leading mine. Suddenly I spot a glint far below. "Visual
contact! Follow me!" This is outrageous for a young pilot to say. I drop my
nose and dive, full afterburner.

You are either a MiG-killer or you are not.

I plunge into an ongoing dogfight, in which my best friend Yigal Sho-
chat in a Super Mystère makes an excellent kill on one MiG-17 and two
others take off to the west. My own partners are far behind. I tell them
over the radio that I'm chasing two MiG-17s. They ask which direction

I'm going. I know if I bring my formation-mates with me, I will never shoot down the two MiGs. At best I'll get one. So I say I'm going east.

I'm going west.

My partners go east and I shoot down the two MiGs, one right away and the other later by the Canal.

No one ever challenges me. No one complains. Why? Because the war is a thousand times bigger than such petty controversies.

And I know I have a fallback position that no one can contest. I can say I made a mistake. I spoke in Japanese, so sue me.

Menahem Shmul is Giora Romm's squadron-mate in Mirage Squadron 119:

Thursday, June 8, I'm with Avramik Salmon over the Canal when the GCI—ground control—tells us we have air targets: four MiG-19s are attacking our infantry and armor. Amazingly, the Egyptians still have planes in the air.

We drop our fuel tanks, dump our bombs. I pick out one MiG-19, miss him first at low level when my primary gunsight fails. I go closer, high speed, put the fixed crosshairs in front of his nose at eighty meters, the MiG looming broad as a barn in my windscreen, pull the trigger, bullets right into his engine, he's gone.

Salmon gets two; I get one.

Next sortie, Jacob Agassi is my leader, a lieutenant colonel, about to be promoted to base commander of Ramat David, flying in our squadron, a great pilot.

Agassi and I are over the same area by the Canal when ground troops call for help over the radio. Egyptian planes are attacking them. It's a great feeling to be the cavalry and be able to rush to the aid of our warriors under fire. I catch an Ilyushin-28, a light bomber, above Bardawill Lagoon, don't even drop the tanks, do a hindquarter attack. He has a 23-millimeter gun aft so I can't come from directly behind. I get him from six hundred meters; he blows right on top of our troops.

The day isn't over. The GCI says, "You have four MiG-21s in your area." We turn back west, half a minute—there they are. I'm younger and quicker than Agassi, so I take one and chase him, down on the deck, pipper on the cockpit, three bullets, the MiG is gone.

So I got three kills in that same day.

Am I thinking of my father? Yes. And of his younger brother Yaakov, my uncle, who at age eighteen in the War of Independence was one of "the Thirty Five" who rushed to the aid of the settlers at Gush Etzion and was tortured and killed by Arab Phalangists in that horrible massacre.

I have had my own war now, the first of five. I have destroyed enemy planes and ground targets, even a ship in Sharm el-Sheikh Bay. I have been shot up by triple-A and brought my Mirage home safely. I have fulfilled my pledge to Ran, my squadron commander, who kept my name on the mission board when he had every right to ground me.

I have maintained unbroken the chain of warriors of my family.

Rafi Sivron:

Cheetah and Haim's helicopters have begun ferrying paratroopers up onto the southern section of the Golan Heights. It has taken all morning to get permission.

I've been waiting beside the ground commander, Elad Peled. High command has hung back, fearing that if we attack and succeed, the Russians will enter the war to protect their Syrian allies.

Finally, early afternoon, Intelligence confirms that the enemy is withdrawing across the length and breadth of the Golan.

I'm on the radio to Rafi Har-Lev at Air Force Operations. "Go," he says. "I'm giving you the green light."

Cheetah Cohen:

The plan is to probe forward with the helicopters. My pilots will take Danny's paratroopers in. Haim's Super Frelons will fly with us, though they're already experiencing mechanical trouble—air filters clogging with volcanic dust.

We will advance onto the Heights, seeking pockets of resistance. When we find them we'll overrun them, then move on to the next.

Danny Matt:

Our forces are in a race now, not just with the Syrians but also with the United Nations. How soon will a cease-fire be declared? How long before the first UN officials appear?

Rafi Sivron:

There is no doctrine for what we are doing. Not even the American airmobile units in Vietnam have a plan for such a situation. We are making it up as we go along.

It goes like this:

Cheetah's helicopters are advancing to road junction Fiq on the ridgeline overlooking the Sea of Galilee along the main road that connects the southern Golan to Kuneitra in the north and to Mount Hermon. His mission is to land a force of Danny's paratroopers, who will secure this intersection and establish an Israeli presence.

I'm on the radio. "Cheetah, where are you?"

"We're at Butamiya."

"What? You're supposed to be back at Fiq."

"We just left there. After a fight, the Syrians pulled out. So we flew after them and took Butamiya."

I can't stand not to be a part of this. When Cheetah returns to Poriya to refuel and pick up more paratroopers, I march straight to his copilot, Moshe Carmeli.

"Moshe, forgive me, I have to fly. I'm taking your seat."

Cheetah Cohen:

The Heights are emptying fast. From the helicopters we can see it with our own eyes. Enemy soldiers are piling onto trucks and racing back to defend Damascus. Our warplanes are already attacking the Syrian capital. At least that's what enemy radio is reporting.

Is it true?

Who knows?

Rafi Sivron:

Our weary pilots, flying on empty and racing against the cease-fire, continue landing troops at critical intersections and strategic points. At Butamiya, sixteen helicopters in formations of two and three land 150 to 180 paratroopers in each sortie. By nightfall we have put on the ground over 500 men.

With this, our forces have sealed off the entire southern Golan.

As the paratroops secure each bridgehead, conventional ground forces come up by vehicle to consolidate the position. Then the heliborne forces leapfrog ahead to take possession of the next strategic point.

Cheetah Cohen:

If Dayan knew what we were doing, he would have a heart attack. If the Russians knew, they would be in here with twenty divisions.

Hey, this is Israeli improvisation!

It is what we do best!

Rafi Sivron:

The helicopters fly all day, till it's too dark to land safely. Night falls on June 10, the sixth day of the Six Day War. From the initial insertion point at Fiq, Israeli paratroopers now control the main arteries of the Golan Heights most of the way to Kuneitra, with ground troops coming up from the south to consolidate these positions.

By evening a cease-fire is technically in place.

No UN teams have arrived yet, however.

Back at Poriya, our pilots collapse in exhaustion in the single tent we've managed to rig for them. I'm the only one still awake and on duty. Suddenly, past midnight, the phone rings.

It's Dado—General David Elazar—chief of the northern front. One of his brigade commanders, named Bar-Kochva, has been wounded on the Heights. Dado wants a helicopter to find this officer and evacuate him.

I point out that the night is pitch black; the Heights are still defended in many places by Syrian troops. No helicopter can land under such conditions (in fact, one has already crashed in darkness this very evening), not to mention that every pilot I've got has been flying for five days straight—they are all dead-out and not even the crack of doom can wake them.

Dado says, "I am giving you an order." He can't really do this; I'm under command of the air force, not the army. But I can see how important this is to him. I promise I will try. Dado says, "Good, get moving, and by the way, I know what kind of soldier Colonel Bar-Kochva is. He will not want to be evacuated."

Dado tells me to bring a pistol.

"I am authorizing you to use force."

On cots in our tent lie twenty pilots. I might as well say they are in graves. Kicks won't rouse them, shouting, nothing works. Finally I get one awake—a brave young flier named Itzhak Segev. He says, "Okay, let's go." The problem is we have no idea where Colonel Bar-Kochva is. We head north, refueling at first light at Kiryat Shmona, the northernmost town in Israel, then set off on our search. Around nine we're flying over a village in the northern part of the Heights when we see below, parked by a soccer field, a grouping of trucks that looks like a command post.

We land.

"We're looking for brigade commander Bar-Kochva."

The colonel is having coffee by the side of the road. The location is in the very north of the Golan Heights, opposite Mount Hermon, near a Druze village called Majdal Shams.

"Sir," I say, "I have an order from Dado to take you out of here."

"I refuse to go."

"Dado was expecting that you'd say that, so he has ordered me to use force. You have been wounded and Dado wants you flown to a hospital."

The colonel sighs and places a hand on my shoulder. "Young man, you are tired. You have not eaten breakfast. Sit down, let my cook fix you something. We'll talk when you have filled your belly."

So we have breakfast and coffee.

Bar-Kochva takes me aside. He indicates his wound, which is in the foot and is slight enough that he has no trouble walking.

"What is your name? Rafi? Listen, Rafi, do you see this fighting here in these hills, on this border? This is the most important thing I have ever done or ever will do. You see I am not bleeding. If I leave my formation, my deputy will take over and he is a blockhead."

This is the seventh day of the Six Day War. Yesterday Dayan and the government formally agreed to a cease-fire. But up here where we are, it is still the Wild West. The northern tip of the Golan Heights remains in Syrian hands.

"Rafi, I will give you a jeep. Follow me. The enemy is running away. We are going to conquer every acre of land that he evacuates. All we have to do is drive and drop off troops. Today is the eleventh of June. I give you my word, by the end of the day, whatever happens, you can take me to the hospital."

We take the jeep. The colonel leads in a command car. Segev and I tie down the helicopter on the soccer field and head off to conquer the northeast corner of the Golan Heights.

From morning till end of day, we drive from crossroads to hilltop to abandoned Syrian post. Here and there the colonel's party encounters resistance. Gunfire is exchanged, minefields must be cleared, but mostly the plateau is quiet, pastoral, beautiful. By late afternoon, when Bar-Kochva completes his loop a few kilometers north of Kuneitra, our forces from the south are driving out to meet him. At the same time from the east comes a UN cease-fire team, accompanied by Syrian officers.

A Syrian colonel hurries to Bar-Kochva, sweating and agitated. "I pray you, stop, stop here! What you've got, you've got. But don't go any farther!"

The UN mission commander declares this moment the official end of the fighting. Here, at this point, both sides must stop.

"Okay, Rafi," Bar-Kochva says to me. "Now you may take me to the hospital."

And that spot became the new cease-fire line and the de facto Israeli-Syrian border, at the official end of the Six Day War, four p.m. on the eleventh of June 1967.

BOOK EIGHT

THE LION'S GATE

53.

THE BIOGRAPHY
OF THE NATION

I never liked Dayan. There were moments when I hated him. I saw him up close many times. I was working sensitive assignments, before the war and after, for Ben-Gurion and others, and my path crossed Dayan's again and again.

Nineteen years after leading the 1948 fighter mission that saved Tel Aviv, Lou Lenart continues to serve Israel as a pilot and in other capacities.

Was anyone smarter than Dayan? Not in Dayan's opinion. He was the brainiest person in any room, and he was not shy about letting you know it. It's one thing to refuse to suffer fools; Dayan didn't suffer anybody. He went where he pleased and took what he wanted. I mean anything. He operated like he was above the law, and no one, including Ben-Gurion, ever called him on it.

Dayan had more charisma than anyone I ever met. He turned it on and off like a light switch. You either loved him or hated him, often both at the same time. I used to ask myself, What is it about this guy that drives people so crazy? Why do his generals kiss up to him one minute, then conspire to steal his credit in the next? Why do the Israeli people put him on a pedestal, then take such pleasure in tearing him down?

One day it hit me.

He is just like they are.

Dayan *is* Israel, more even than Ben-Gurion.

Dayan's strengths are Israel's strengths and his weaknesses are Israel's weaknesses. Sometimes his strengths and weaknesses are the same thing: his brashness, his aggressiveness, his willingness to act as a law unto himself.

Dayan's biography is the biography of Israel: the first child (some say the second) born on the first kibbutz; scion of Labor Party bluebloods; husband of lovely cultured Ruth; father of precocious, ambitious Yael. The Brits throw him in jail in '39, then free him in '41 to fight on their side; he loses his eye fighting the Axis. His brother is killed in battle by the Syrian foe, but Dayan reaches out to this enemy—to the very men who fired the fatal shots—and manages to bring them over to Israel's side. He makes them friends.

As chief of staff, Dayan shapes the army into the image of the "no alternative," "finish the mission," "advance at all costs" state, and of himself.

General Uzi Narkiss, Minister of Defense Moshe Dayan, and Chief of Staff Yitzhak Rabin enter the Old City of Jerusalem, June 7, 1967.

He invents a new kind of Jew and embodies this bold, swashbuckling identity—eye patch and all—for the world to see.

In Sinai and Jerusalem the army that Dayan had invented does exactly what he had taught it to do. It ignores his wishes. It takes decisions on its own. Its officers strike first and read their orders second. Dayan can't stop them.

I started to like him then.

The war is building to its climax. Dayan wants to be Joshua; he wants to be David. But as minister of defense he can no longer operate by the sword alone. He has to be the wise man now. He has to be the statesman. I can see him struggling against his own Old Testament heart.

Dayan once said, "I would rather have to rein in the eager warhorse than to prod the reluctant mule."

Now that horse is history. It's the momentum of events. Dayan controls the steed for as long as he can. He's right to say no to his generals when they first want to take the Old City, and he's right to order "Enter by the Lion's Gate" when he finally does.

Dayan's enemies have accused him of turning the procession to the Western Wall on June 7 into a calculated occasion, a staged opportunity for him to put himself in front of the news photographers and the television cameras. Of course it was. How could it not be?

The Wall is everything. Where else would he go?

Did Dayan deliberately cut Prime Minister Eshkol out of this moment? Hell yes. And he was right to do it. He went to the Wall with the generals, with Rabin and Narkiss.

Why the helmets? Why the buckled chin straps? Why enter by the Lion's Gate?

To make this a warrior's moment, not a politician's. To honor the paratroopers, to tread in their footsteps. To depict for the eyes of the world that Jews have returned to their holiest site *under fire*. Bullets are still flying. We are operating out of military necessity, say the news photos, not from the wish for territorial aggrandizement.

It works.

Give Dayan credit. He knows he's an icon. He knows his jaw and his black eye patch are the face of Israel's armed forces to the world. He is right now to play this role—and to play it to the hilt.

54.

THE OLD MAN

I am sitting with Colonel Shmuel Gorodish, commander of the 7th Armored Brigade, on the east bank of the Suez Canal, June 10, the last day of the war. Gorodish says, "If I get the order, I can go all the way to Mauritania." To the Atlantic. "Nothing between here and there can stop us."

Michael Bar-Zohar is the author of Ben-Gurion: The Armed Prophet, *the authorized biography of David Ben-Gurion. He is a paratrooper attached during the war to Galei Zahal, the IDF radio station.*

That is the feeling of the moment. Earlier in the day I had been farther north, at the Firdan Bridge, where Denis Cameron of *Life* magazine took the photo of Yosi Ben-Hanan in the waters of the Canal that would become one of the iconic images of the war.

Ori Orr was there, the commander of the 7th Armored Brigade's Reconnaissance Company, with his two surviving platoon commanders, Eli Rikovitz and Amos Ayalon. Their unit had suffered terribly. No one knew the numbers then, but we would learn soon that they had lost more men than any outfit of their size in the war. You could see it in their faces, burnt black from soot and gunpowder and from the sun, and in the way they stood alongside one another, as if they trusted no one in the world but themselves.

They were the first unit to reach the Canal and the most decorated. Sixteen men killed, ten Medals of Valor.

Another casualty of the war was Ben-Gurion. Because he had been wrong. He had believed that the armed forces of Israel could not stand up to Egypt, Syria, and Jordan, backed by the Soviet Union, without the help of America or another major power.

Dayan was right.

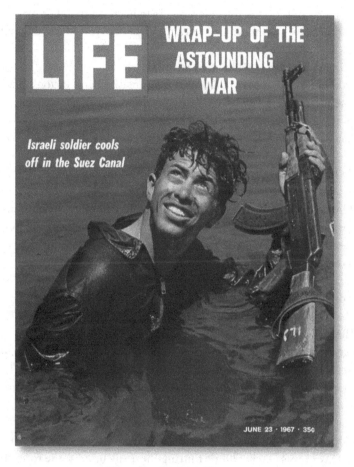

Lieutenant Yosi Ben-Hanan,
photographed by Denis Cameron.

Sharon was right, and Gavish and Tal and Gorodish.

Begin was right. He was a player now.

It was I, four days before the war, who told Dayan that he would be appointed minister of defense the next morning. I chased him all around the country, trying to deliver the news. Each time I got to a place, Dayan had just left. Finally in the evening I caught up with him at his home. "How do you know?" he asked. "I know," I told him.

He said, "You'll come to work for me after the war."

Now on the banks of the Canal a soldier appears. "Is there a Bar-Zohar here? You have a phone call at the communications tent."

I go. Dayan is on the line. He says, "Michael, get to Tel Aviv. You start work tomorrow at eight a.m." I say, "Moshe, do you know where I am? I'm at the Canal!"

"Okay," he says. "Make it eight thirty."

I hitchhiked all night. In Tel Aviv I stopped at Ben-Gurion's place first because I knew he loved to see soldiers coming straight from the front. I was in my uniform, dirty as hell. That was the only time Ben-Gurion ever embraced me. I had worked with him for ten years. Never before had he put his arms around me.

To have known Ben-Gurion in the days of his power was like serving with . . . whom? Moses? That is not far off.

Ben-Gurion founded Israel. He *was* Israel. A stocky little man, remote, often rude, with that crazy shock of white hair. But when prime ministers and heads of state entered his presence, you could see them shrinking. Shrinking! That was the awe in which Ben-Gurion was held.

He loved Dayan. "Michael, come with me," he would say. "We must go to the floor of the Knesset."

"Why?"

"Because Moshe is speaking."

Dayan worshipped Ben-Gurion. One afternoon he and I attended a meeting on the top floor of the Histadrut Building in Jerusalem. The old man was addressing a delegation. "Michael," Dayan said, "you and I will never reach to the ankles of this man. Never."

But now, for Ben-Gurion, the moment has passed.

Before the war he had met with Dayan in a hotel in Beersheba where Dayan was staying while touring the army units at the front. Dayan made Ben-Gurion come to him. This would have been unthinkable a year earlier.

On June 4, the day before the war, Dayan sent his aide Chaim Israeli to inform Ben-Gurion as a courtesy that the war would start the following morning. In public, the old man gave his blessing. But in his diary he wrote, "They are making a big mistake." The next morning, when the news from the Egyptian front was all bad, Ben-Gurion thought, Yes, I will give Moshe a piece of my mind.

Dayan never spoke to Ben-Gurion during the war. This hurt the old man deeply. He realized that he was not needed anymore. That was his real death. I had been urging him for years to write his memoirs. Always he scorned this. "You don't write history, you make it!"

But after the war he told me, "Michael, I am beginning my memoirs."

I didn't understand at first. That was the moment when Ben-Gurion started to change, to reach out to his old enemies, to embrace the role of Father of the Nation.

Dayan is king now. Not in Israel alone, or in the Middle East, but around the globe as well. His eye patch is recognizable in Moscow or Mongolia. He is a celebrity on a par with the most glittering in the world. I tell him, "Moshe, you're bigger than the Beatles."

He does not wish to be prime minister. To perform the tedious duties of state? This is not for a man like Dayan. Sharon, who will in time achieve this office, understands that you cannot govern as a lone wolf. You must build a movement. You must cultivate the Nurses Association and the melon farmers and the crazy rabbis who believe that women are inferior to men.

Dayan grasps the necessity of coalition building. But he cannot do it. He is Joshua. He understands the sword and the land and cares for nothing else.

In a way, Dayan's time is passing, too.

Months after the war, the Arab leaders in the West Bank declared a strike. Dayan called them together, all the notables of Judea and Samaria. He respected them and they respected him. He said, "Listen, I am minister of defense. My concern is security. If you want to strike, I will not stop you unless you provoke violence. So a woman from Tel Aviv who wants to buy elastic bands for her panties will buy them in Tel Aviv instead of Ramallah? I'm pulling the army out of your towns and cities. If you want to strike, strike."

Twenty-four hours later, the strike ended.

But the world is changing. The idea of local autonomy for the Arabs in the occupied territories, this is not good enough. It is not an accommodation that will stand. Jordan won't take the West Bank back, not under conditions that Israel can accept. Hussein doesn't want the Palestinians, either.

We're stuck. Dayan can see this. He can see what is coming. But he has no answer for it.

No one does.

55.

THE GHOST COMPANY

Eli Rikovitz, platoon commander in the Recon Company of the 7th Armored Brigade:

The war has ended. A week has passed. Our brigade has been pulled back from the Canal. Reserve units have come up to take our place.

Our company is quartered now at Bir Gafgafa in central Sinai. Bir Gafgafa is a huge Egyptian base, with an airfield and room for an entire division.

We settle in tents. In daytime we train, to keep busy. But at night there is nothing to do. It begins to hit us, at last, how many of our friends we have lost.

Ori Orr, Recon Company commander:

Because the 7th Armored Brigade is a regular-army unit, the men of our company will not be released and sent home like soldiers in the reserves. We'll get a leave, probably soon. But we in Recon are in regular service and will continue on active duty, some of us for two years or more. Some will make the army their career.

I will. I am in to stay.

Menachem Shoval, Recon trooper:

In the desert you have a fire at night. You gather around. You sing songs, tell stories.

No longer. We can't.

The army is sending entertainers out. Singers and comedians perform for the troops, to keep morale up. Soldiers from other outfits laugh and cheer. Not us. We can stand only our own company, yet when we're together we say nothing.

We don't go over what has happened. We don't speak with one another, trying to make sense of our feelings. We shut up. Everyone stays inside himself.

Dubi Tevet, Recon trooper:

A few Israeli families have gotten permission to come out to Sinai, to seek the places where their dear ones have fallen. They arrive, wordless and grief-stricken, driving their own private cars—Peugeots and Studebaker Larks, Dodge Darts and Citroën Deux Chevaux.

There can be no sight more heartbreaking than that of a mourning mother or, worse, a wife who has become a widow, standing bereft in this wilderness.

Menachem Shoval, Recon trooper:

The euphoria of victory has taken possession of all Israel. Our company is not touched by that. We are totally detached.

At Jebel Libni, the brigade holds a victory parade. Gorodish stands on a platform and makes a speech, some say a great one, which the radio plays over and over. "Be strong and brave, my brothers, heroes of fame!"

This means nothing to us. We don't know what he's talking about.

Eli Rikovitz, Recon platoon commander:

The most celebrated phrase in Gorodish's speech is "We looked death in the eye, and he looked away."

This may be true for the brigade. It is not true for us in Recon. We looked death in the eye, but death did not look away. He took as many of us as he wanted.

Boaz Amitai, Recon platoon commander:

I can take you now to the ditch at the entrance to the Jiradi where I kept my head down when the Egyptian air bursts were coming in, and to the spot at El Arish where I got shot. I can show you the turn of the road where Yossi Elgamis died, the slope where Avigdor Kahalani got burned, the spot where Ehud Elad was killed.

Menachem Shoval, Recon trofoper:

I am carrying Shaul Groag's shaving kit. I took it from the back of his jeep after he was killed. It's crazy to keep it. An army toilet kit. An army towel. There's nothing personal of Shaul at all.

Yet I cannot throw it away. I am carrying it for a month and a half, so that one day I can give it to Shaul's parents and say, what, "This is all that's left"?

Eli Rikovitz:

When a company as tightly bound as ours suffers such losses, the individuals do one of two things. They pull together or they move apart.

Ours is coming apart.

Dubi Tevet:

Someone has made a sign with our unit insignia and this title: The Ghost Company. That is what we are.

It will get worse when we go home.

Eli Rikovitz and Ori Orr at Bir Gafgafa.
The sign reads THE GHOST COMPANY.

Ori Orr:

Eli has come to me and suggested that he and I pay a visit to every family who has suffered a loss.

The first person we go to is Boaz, in the hospital. His wound is healing. "I'll go with you," he says.

Menachem Shoval:

The army has an official system for notifying families of the deaths of their loved ones. But who knows how long this process might take, or how impersonal such a notification might be?

I decide I will go myself, as soon as possible, to the families of those who have been my friends.

Eli Rikovitz:

The hardest is one family who turns us away. The mother looks out through the window and sees me and Ori and Boaz coming up the walk.

"Go back! Get away from here! You have taken my child!" She locks the door and refuses even to speak to us.

We could not visit another family that day.

Ori Orr:

The way the mother chased us, you could see she wasn't blaming us or holding us personally responsible for her son's death. She simply could not accept the reality that her beloved child would never return.

Perhaps she believed that if she never heard the words "Your son has been killed," he would still be alive.

Menachem Shoval:

What can I tell a father who asks me, "How did my son die?" What can I say that will ease his anguish?

I feel so perplexed and so helpless.

And yet the slightest recollection, a joke that the son had told, some silly youthful prank he had played . . . the memory of these means the world. A mother, a father cling to such scraps as these.

"Your son was not afraid."

"He led us forward."

The parents' hearts break, yet they cannot learn enough of acts taken or words spoken by their son.

Moshe Perry:

Chen Rosenberg was my friend. Ten years after he was killed, I am still carrying his photo in my wallet. I am out of the army, married. I have children. Yet Chen's picture is still in my wallet.

Nehama Nissenbaum, mother of Benzi Nissenbaum:

I survived the Holocaust, but my son did not survive the Six Day War. I visit the cemetery once every three weeks. I light a candle, leave a few flowers, and go home and think, If only he were still alive.

But that is what life has given us, what fate has given us.

Bat Sheva Hofert, sister of Shlomo Kenigsbuch:

I lost both my brothers in the Six Day War, and thirty-six years later I lost both my sons. All four are buried in the Kfar Sava military cemetery. In the Jewish tradition, when one visits a grave she sets a small stone as a token of remembrance. But how many stones can one heart carry?

I often think, How happy we would be if they were all still alive. All I know is that it's not in our hands, certainly not in mine. All that remains is the grief and the pain, but still you keep going.

I refuse to give in.

Never.

56.

A WEDDING AT ZAHALA

I did not participate in the postwar euphoria. I had lost dear friends and this overshadowed for me the joy that others seemed to be experiencing so keenly.

Reserve lieutenant Yael Dayan has completed her assignment as a correspondent with Arik Sharon's division and been released from active duty.

The days passed with surprising swiftness. You woke each morning expecting to grasp at last the fullness of the altered reality, and realized with evening that this had eluded you again. Clearly the equation of might had been overthrown. Old borders and armistices were null and void. Israel had become the indisputable power in the region. It could speak in a new language, and must be spoken to in a new way.

Dov and I drove to Jerusalem. He had fought here in the Old City in '48 and knew every turn and alley. But I could not hear his stories. The experience was too overwhelming.

We went to the Western Wall. I was almost surprised to see that it was an actual wall. I had expected, what, a receptacle of tears, an abstraction, a vessel of hope and longing?

My father had told me that in one of the cabinet meetings in which the liberation of the Old City was being debated, two ministers spoke in favor of leaving the holy places in Jordanian hands. Better that these remain a dream, the ministers argued. The same sentiment could be seen in the expressions of the armed soldiers who walked, amazed, among the souks and lanes.

The wall was a wall. Gray blocks of stone, monumental in scale and lovely with age, with sprigs of hyssop sprouting in the fissures. Jaffa Gate, Damascus Gate, David's Tower, the Lion's Gate. I could absorb none of these. It was too soon.

We drove to Bethlehem, to the Church of the Nativity. Yesterday tanks and armored half-tracks had patrolled these streets. Today souvenir hunters haggle for camels carved in wood, exclaiming at the bargain prices, while tourists poke their noses into courtyards of private dwellings as if all belonged to them. I struggled between shame and acceptance. Please, can we get out of here?

Dov drove us back to Mount Scopus. Old Jerusalem lay before us like a dream that had come true but in whose reality one could not yet believe. On the way home Dov asked me to marry him.

I was almost twenty-eight. My brother Assi had set a date to wed his high school sweetheart, Aharona. I knew I had found in Dov the man with whom I wished to spend the rest of my life. With joy we planned a double wedding. The date was July 22—Yud Aleph beTammuz by the Hebrew calendar—the date on which my mother's parents had been married in 1915, and, twenty years afterward to the day, my mother and father as well.

The wedding was held in the garden at Zahala. Ben-Gurion attended, very merry. Danny Kaye came, a longtime family friend. Arik Sharon was Dov's best man. A number of West Bank sheikhs and mayors joined in the celebration as well. They were all friends of my mother and father.

57.

THE WARRIOR JEW

Moshe Dayan:

A few months before the Six Day War, I went to Vietnam. I traveled in the capacity of a journalist. I was writing a series of articles for the Israeli newspaper *Maariv* and for the *New York Times*. But, of course, everywhere I went, I was treated as a soldier.

Americans are the most openhearted people on earth, and none more so than GIs and Marines in the field. I accompanied these young men on many patrols in the jungle, no doubt sowing gray hairs among those officers who were charged with my safety. The field is the only place for me when there is fighting. Maps and dispatches are poor approximations of the reality on the ground, and a joyride in a helicopter 5,000 feet above the jungle tells me nothing.

At first the American soldiers and Marines did not believe that I was the Moshe Dayan they had heard of. They recognized my eye patch from newsreels and television, but they could not give credence to the idea that a "big general" was down there with them, humping through the muck at their sides. Only when I spoke and they heard my Hebrew-accented English did they smile and gather around. What happened then was extraordinary, and it happened over and over. An Airborne lieutenant would speak to me out of earshot of his commanders. "We should be fighting like you Israelis."

"What do you mean?" I would ask.

"I mean get in there and fuck some people up."

Often I was regarded by higher-ranking officers as if I possessed some secret. I was asked how I would fight a war in Southeast Asia. How would the IDF handle this?

I elected not to answer. The Vietnam War was lost the hour it began.

But what struck me was the tremendous respect with which American fighters viewed the Israeli military. I saw again and again wide grins and fist pumps.

Moshe Dayan accompanies American troops in Vietnam
as a journalist a few months before the Six Day War.

I was at army headquarters in Tel Aviv when word came on June 7, 1967, that our paratroopers had reached the Western Wall. I knew I must go at once. I went with Chief of Staff Rabin and head of Central Command Uzi Narkiss. We three must arrive at the wall together, I declared, and it must be in uniform, with helmets.

Why? Not for the Israeli people alone, but for the eyes of the world. For the Marines in the rice paddies. For the Russians and the English and for Diaspora Jews around the globe.

Israel needs America. She needs allies in every land. Ours is not a Jewish story alone. It is a testament for all the world.

When historians set the events of the twentieth century into perspective, such monumental movements as the rise and collapse of totalitarianism, communism, and fascism will be overshadowed, I believe, by the saga of the return of the Jewish people to their ancient homeland. Why? Why do I believe that the destiny of such a tiny country merits such significance?

Because each nation of the earth represents a portion of the collective soul.

The Jewish people stand not for themselves alone, but as an archetype within the greater world psyche. As the British or Romans, say, may be said to represent empire in all its facets, and the races of Africa (and the Arabs to some extent) may be characterized as representing that element of the collective whose lot for centuries has been that of the conquered, the oppressed, and the exploited, so we Jews have come to carry the weight of a people in diaspora, a nation in exile.

Exile means weakness. It means vulnerability. The exile is the whipping boy. He is the last allowed aboard the boat and the first thrown over the side.

At the exile's door are laid the evils of the society in which he dwells as a stranger. On him is projected the wickedness of the hearts of those upon whose succor his survival depends. He becomes inevitably the sinister one, the schemer in secret, the conspirator, the devious, the dark hand. This is true of all exiles in all lands in all centuries.

If there is a universal disease of the modern era, I believe it is the malady of exile. This affliction is experienced on the individual level as well as on the national and the racial—the agony of feeling that one is a part of nothing, that he belongs nowhere and to no one.

Exile is the torment of being held apart (or of holding oneself apart) from one's own deepest essence and his truest, most primal legacy.

What brings a nation or an individual out of exile? Only return—physically, emotionally, and spiritually—to the place of its birth.

In the army of France in the 1890s was an officer of Jewish descent named Alfred Dreyfus. Dreyfus was wrongly convicted of treason and subjected to the most violent and despicable anti-Semitic attacks. Émile Zola wrote his famous editorial "J'Accuse" in Dreyfus's defense in 1898.

Theodor Herzl was a secular Jewish reporter assigned to cover Dreyfus's trial. Herzl was appalled to hear the mob chanting, "Kill the Jew! Kill all the Jews!" That such hatred could exist in a cultured, civilized nation in which the Jewish community had thrived for centuries (and for which tens of thousands of Jewish soldiers had given their lives in France's wars) signified to Herzl the futility of the notion of cultural assimilation.

If this could happen in France, Herzl concluded, it could happen anywhere.

Today, if you walk southeast from the Israeli embassy on the rue Rabelais along the rue du Faubourg Saint-Honoré in the direction of the Place

Vendôme, you will pass the Église Notre-Dame-de-l'Assomption and, continuing on, turn into a quiet, prosperous-looking street called the Rue Cambon. Walk now to the small hotel at no. 36; lift your eyes to the wall above. You will see a white marble plaque with these words in French and Hebrew:

HERE, IN 1895, THEODOR HERZL, FOUNDER OF THE ZIONIST MOVEMENT, WROTE *THE JEWISH STATE,* THE PROPHETIC WORK THAT FORETOLD AND ANNOUNCED THE RESURRECTION OF THE STATE OF ISRAEL.

In the succeeding decades, we Jews came home. There was a mighty justice to this, which the world perceived and of which it approved. A people who had wandered rootless for two thousand years claimed at last its ancient portion. The Jewish people had a home now. We had land. We had guns. By 1948, we had a flag. This repatriation remained incomplete, however, because the eastern half of our ancient capital, Jerusalem, home of our most sacred sites, abided in the hands of our enemies.

The Sinai victory of 1956 put Israel on the map as a military force. But that triumph was rendered inconclusive by the perception that it had been effected under the aegis of the allied powers, England and France. The Jews, it was believed by many even among our own people, could not have achieved this victory alone.

Now in June 1967 this perception has been overturned. On her own, the forces of Israel have repelled powerful enemies bent on her destruction and have prevailed over these foes in spectacular fashion. A new archetype has been born in the eyes of the world: the Warrior Jew.

Now to the names of Joshua and Gideon, Saul and David, Judah Maccabee and Simon Bar-Kochva must be added Rabin and Gavish, Sharon and Tal and Yoffe and hundreds more. The army of Israel has taken its place among the world's elite corps-at-arms. Commanders of the IDF will now be summoned to speak in the halls of the great warrior nations, at Sandhurst and the École de Guerre, at Annapolis and West Point, at war colleges and military academies around the world.

The hearts of Diaspora Jews swell now with pride. Cables and telegrams of congratulations flood our embassies. The wide world seems to share our joy.

This will change, however.

This new conqueror, the Warrior Jew, finds himself responsible now for a million and a quarter Arabs who hate him, who will never be reconciled to his rule, and who would eat him raw in the night.

What will he do?

My every instinct cries for grace, generosity, greatness of heart. Is this folly?

The only time during the war that I lost my temper was when I learned that one of our paratroopers had mounted an Israeli flag atop the Dome of the Rock. I would have flown there on wings and torn that standard down with my teeth.

I have been accused of being too friendly to our Arab neighbors. "He is an Arab," said one minister of me. This man meant that my nature was to lie and cheat, to devise with cunning, and to favor that position only that would advance my own cause.

In this single particular, my accuser is right: I do have the deepest respect and affection for my Arab friends.

When I learned after the cease-fire that our tanks had crossed the Jordan, I ordered all Israeli forces pulled back at once and all bridges destroyed. The message: Israel has no territorial ambitions east of the Jordan River.

When I learned, not long after this, that Arab men and women by the hundreds were fording the seasonably shallow stream bringing farm produce to market in Jordan's East Bank cities, I ordered the spans restored. Temporary bridges were put in place immediately, one at Jericho and another at Damia, below Nablus.

Life for the families of the West Bank involves daily intercourse with relatives and friends on the east side of the river. Farmers and merchants trade, wives go to market, students trek to school.

Let this commerce return. Let us not disrupt it. Let life be as it has been for the people of East Jerusalem and Nablus and Jericho, of Hebron and Ramallah and Bethlehem.

The eleventh commandment asserts the imperative to be strong. But strength, like any weapon, can be misused and misapplied. It can become a liability.

In what manner, then, must we Israelis be strong?

We must be strong enough to yield, when yielding serves the long-term good of all. We must be strong enough to see the other fellow's side, to act with clemency, to extend the hand of friendship.

In the first hours after the cease-fire, I did not dream that Israel would

Moshe Dayan meets with West Bank sheikhs.

hold on to the lands that our forces had captured from Jordan—what we Jews call Judea and Samaria, and the world calls the West Bank. I thought we would give these territories back in a few months. A settlement would be negotiated. King Hussein would promise peace, and we would take it.

But when I traveled to Jericho and Bethlehem during the next few days, I changed my mind. Yesterday I drove in an army command car to the Tomb of the Patriarchs in Hebron. The cave and the fields roundabout are said to have been purchased by Abraham to hold his remains as well as those of Isaac, Jacob, Sarah, Rebecca, and Leah. It had never occurred to me that the state would take possession of this site. I assumed without thinking that it would be returned in due course to Jordan. But when I got there and felt the emotion of the place, I knew that this would never happen.

Judea and Samaria are the lands within which the ancient Israelites dwelt. These hills make up the spine of the biblical kingdom of Israel. Upon these highland slopes, and not on the coastal plain below, our forefathers pitched their tents and grazed their flocks. Our warrior race took root here, on these stony prominences from which their children have been debarred for two millennia.

We shall have these heights back now. We will affirm possession of them, but not to be clutched and held apart from others. Those wrongs that have been done to the Jewish people we must never inflict on others. We must return justice for malice and extend an open hand to a clenched fist. Not only because such acts are right, or because their apparition advances our standing among the nations, but because a gesture of goodwill must eventually be reciprocated by an enemy, if we must wait a thousand years.

Many of my countrymen have accused me of squandering in this hour a once-in-a-lifetime opportunity. War has unbolted the gate, my critics declare. Boundaries may be redrawn. Populations may shift.

Let the Arabs flee, they say. Build a golden highway for them out of Israel. Kalkilya and a hundred other towns will empty overnight, I was told. You have only to stand aside and let it happen.

I could not.

When I was growing up in Nahalal, my family and others shared the land with a Bedouin clan that had grazed its flocks upon these fields for as long as men could remember. Those boys were my playmates. At plowing time they toiled at my side. We took our lunch together among the furrows. I danced at their weddings and they danced at mine.

I collected my brother Zorik's body from a different furrow, in a field not far from those of Nahalal, shot down by Syrian Druzes during the War of Independence. Yet I called to council the very men who had slain him and put to them the case that their lives would be better as part of Israel than beneath the thumb of Syria.

To these tribal warriors, blood for blood is the eternal law. They could not believe that one whose brother had been shot down only days earlier could extend the hand of amity to those who had taken that brave man's life.

Those men became my friends and remain so to this day.

When I would see in the fields an Arab woman bending to light a fire or to care for a child, I saw my own mother. I saw Devorah Dayan and I saw Deborah of the Book of Judges. This land has soaked up the blood of Jew and Arab for almost four thousand years.

Can we not share it now in peace?

Zalman Shoval, Israel's ambassador to the United States, 1990–1993 and 1998–2000:

Dayan saw further than all his contemporaries save Ben-Gurion, who had become by '67 too old. But even he could not see far enough. Who else has?

Arab heads of state work only for their own or their nations' self-interest. The Russians' greed and bellicosity never change. Even the well-intentioned West has been unable to produce a statesman of sufficient vision.

None exists even today.

Mordechai "Morele" Bar-On served as Moshe Dayan's office chief from 1956 to 1957 and later as head of the History Branch of the IDF General Staff. He is the author of numerous works on the history and politics of Israel and the Middle East, including Moshe Dayan: Israel's Controversial Hero *(2012):*

What you must understand about Dayan, in order to make sense of his decisions at this hour, is that he grew up among Arabs. He loved them. He saw the Arabs, particularly the Bedouin, as figures from the Bible.

Dayan had great respect not only for the educated Arab elite but also for the tribesmen and the tenders of flocks. There is a famous story of Dayan's youth. He had a Bedouin friend named Wahsh (Wolf) from a tribe that lived near Nahalal. As boys they plowed together and worked at each other's sides; they shared meals in the fields and became very close. Later, when Dayan was nineteen or so, a dispute arose between this tribe and the Jews of Nahalal. A brawl broke out, in which Dayan's friend Wolf hit him over the head with a club, knocking him unconscious and fracturing his skull.

Still Dayan invited Wolf and the chiefs of his tribe to his own wedding a year later and shook his friend's hand in reconciliation.

This kind of relationship was deep in the bones of Dayan.

His paramount object at first in administering the newly conquered territories was that life go on for the local populace as it had always. Dayan envisioned an "invisible government of occupation." He would displace no mayors or rural councils, alter no local ordinances. No Israeli flag would fly over municipal offices. Military posts, when they were set up, would be tucked out of sight, in the country. "We must permit local Arabs to run their own lives without having to see or talk to any Israeli officials so long as they don't break the law."

Of course, such an arrangement was impossible. No amount of local autonomy, even prosperity, could quench the national aspirations of the Arab people on land they claimed as their own.

In Israel we began hearing a new name: Yasir Arafat, chief of Fatah, the Palestinian guerrilla organization.

Arab bombs began going off in Jewish cities; mines were being planted along roads; Israeli civilians were being shot in the streets.

By August 1967, just two months after the war, the Arab campaign of terror had begun.

Shlomo Gazit, minister in charge of the Territories, 1967–1974, chief of the Military Intelligence Directorate, 1974–1978:

Dayan wrote and delivered a eulogy a decade before the '67 War, which I believed then, and do to this day, to be one of the great speeches of the twentieth century. Certainly it is among the truest.

A young Israeli named Roy Rotberg had moved south from Tel Aviv to take charge of defense and to work the land at Kibbutz Nahal Oz, adjacent to the Gaza Strip. Within meters of the Jewish cultivation sprawled the refugee camps of the Arabs who had been displaced from these lands by war.

One morning on his way to the fields Roy was murdered by a party from these Arab camps.

Here are the words spoken by Moshe Dayan, who was then army chief of staff, over Roy Rotberg's grave, April 19, 1957:

Early yesterday morning Roy was murdered. The quiet of the spring morning dazzled him and he did not see those waiting in ambush for him along the line of the furrow.

Let us not cast blame on Roy's murderers today. It is pointless to remark upon their unquenchable hatred of us. For eight years they have been sitting in the refugee camps in Gaza while before their eyes we have been transforming the lands and the villages, which they and their fathers called their own, into our estate.

It is not among the Arabs in Gaza, but in our own midst that we must seek Roy's blood. How did we shut our eyes and refuse to look squarely at ourselves and acknowledge, in all its cruelty, the calling of our generation? Have we forgotten that this group of young people building a Jewish future at Nahal Oz bears upon its shoulders the heavy gates of Arab Gaza? Behind those gates hundreds of thousands of eyes and hands pray that we will weaken so that they may tear us to pieces. Have we forgotten that?

We are the generation of settlers. We know that without the steel helmet and the cannon's muzzle we will not be able to plant a tree or build a home. Our children will not survive if we do not dig shelters, and without barbed wire and a machine gun we will not be able to pave roads or drill for water. Millions of Jews who were annihilated because they did not have a country cry out to us from the ashes of history, commanding us to settle and build a land for our people.

But beyond the furrow border, a sea of hatred and vengeance swells, waiting for the day when calm will sap our vigilance, the day when we will heed the ambassadors of malevolent hypocrisy who call upon us to lay down our arms.

Roy's blood cries out to us from his torn body. A thousand times we have sworn to ourselves that our blood shall not be shed in vain, but yesterday again we were tempted, we listened, we believed.

Let us make a reckoning with ourselves today. Let us no longer deceive ourselves but instead look facts in the face and see the abiding hatred that fills the lives of the hundreds of thousands of Arabs who live around us, waiting for the moment to shed our blood. Let us not avert our eyes lest our arms slacken.

This is the decree of our generation. This is the choice of our lives—to be prepared and armed, strong and determined, lest the sword be stricken from our fist and our lives be cut down.

The young Roy who left Tel Aviv to build his home at the gates of Gaza and to serve as our bulwark was blinded by the light in his heart. He did not see the flash of the sword. The yearning for peace rendered him deaf to the voice of lurking murder. The gates of Gaza were too heavy for him and they overcame him.

Would the ascension of the Warrior Jew mark a step forward, closer to peace in the Middle East? Or had it propelled us farther along the path to wars without end?

One thing was certain. What was done could not be undone. There was now, and would be in the future, no going back.

58.

"IF I FORGET THEE, O JERUSALEM"

Behind the Al-Aqsa Mosque, the morning our paratroop battalion reached the Western Wall, my eye fell upon a row of water spigots, outdoors behind the holy site, with a concrete sluiceway and drains beneath. For worshippers to wash their hands or feet, I imagined, before entering the sacred precinct.

Yoram Zamosh, commander of "A" Company, Paratroop Battalion 71:

Arab prisoners were being rounded up then—not just soldiers but local officials and dignitaries. They understood now the magnitude of their calamity. I saw more than one brave man sobbing, his face buried in his hands.

Some soldier, we heard, had mounted an Israeli flag atop the Dome of the Rock. In fury Moshe Dayan ordered it taken down. He was right, of course. Let us in this hour of victory show the respect to our enemies' faith that they have not shown to ours.

Paratroopers under orders began releasing the Arab officials. Let them go home. Let normal life return. Let our neighbors worship, let them live, let them work and study and raise their families as before.

The barricades between Jewish and Arab Jerusalem will come down now. The minefields and the barbed wire will be cleared.

We will have one Jerusalem.

I am not the foremost officer in my battalion. Nor was I our commander's favorite. Uzi permitted my formation, "A" Company, to be first through the Lion's Gate primarily because I wanted it so badly. I imagine he thought, Zamosh is religious. Let him be first.

But what does "religious" mean?

The Jewish religion is not a faith that prizes blind obedience or collective adherence to dogma. Our tradition is cerebral. We debate. We argue. The question is always holier than the answer.

The primal Jewish issue is justice. Judaism is a religion of the law, and the seminal concept of the law is that the minority must be protected. In the Jewish faith, you study. You wrestle with issues. You are a scholar. You deliberate, you dispute. A Jew asks over and over, "What is fair? What is just? Who is a good man, and why?"

I spent only one winter in the yeshiva. What I learned, more than Torah, was to love the teachers, Rabbi Zvi Yehuda Kook and "the saintly Nazir," Rabbi David Cohen, who embodied these pursuits with such honor and integrity. I learned not so much from them as through them, by watching their actions, hearing their speech, and observing the way they conducted themselves. I learned the history of the Jewish people, the incredible suffering endured by millions over so many centuries, and of Jerusalem, the centrality of this place in the soul of the people, their *neshama*, and why our return to this site means so much.

The Kotel. The Western Wall, as it is called in English. How did so much hope and passion come to be attached to a wall? Not even the wall of a temple, which the Kotel is not, but even humbler, a retaining wall for the mount upon which the razed temple had once stood. A ruin. How could this mean so much to me? How could it mean so much to our paratroopers who had never studied, who knew nothing of Torah, who did not even know how to pray?

A wall is unlike any other holy site. A wall is a foundation. It is what remains when all that had once risen above it has been swept away.

A wall evokes primal emotion, particularly when it is built into the land, when the far side is not open space but the fundament of the earth itself. When one stands with worshipful purpose before the expanse of a wall, particularly one that dwarfs his person, that rises above him and extends on both sides, an emotion arises from the heart that is unlike the feeling evoked by any other religious experience. How different, compared to, say, worshipping in a cathedral or within a great hall or at the foot of some monumental tower.

One approaches the Western Wall as an individual. No rabbi stands beside you. Set your palms against the stones. Is God present? Will the stone conduct your prayers to Him? Around you stand others of your faith; you feel their presence and the intention of their coming, but you remain yourself alone.

Are you bereft? Is your spirit impoverished? Set your brow against the stone. Feel its surface with your fingertips. Myself, I cannot come within thirty paces of the Wall without tears.

The ancient Greeks considered Delphi the epicenter of the world. This is the Wall to me. All superfluity has been stripped from this site and from ourselves.

Here the enemies of my people have devastated all that they could. What remains? This fundament alone, which they failed to raze only because it was beneath their notice. The armored legions of our enemies have passed on, leaving only this wall. In the twenty centuries since, those who hate us have defiled it and piled trash before it and even relieved themselves against it. They have neglected it, permitted slums to be built up around it. This only makes it more precious to us.

That morning of June 7, I can't remember exactly when this happened—maybe on the way down to the Wall with Moshe Stempel and the others. At some point we were climbing the stairs—Yair Levanon, Dov Gruner, Moshe Milo, and I—when we noticed a scrawl, freshly scratched into the stone, in Hebrew:

IF I FORGET THEE, O JERUSALEM, MAY MY RIGHT HAND
FORGET ITS CUNNING.

This is a verse from Psalm 137, which also contains the line "By the rivers of Babylon, we sat down and wept when we remembered Zion."

It is the lament of an exile. And a vow to return, somehow, to the land from which he has been expelled.

Who could have inscribed this verse? We debated this later. A Jew, for certain. But from where? And when?

Could he have been a soldier—from Canada perhaps, a member of the UN peacekeeping force? The Jordanians permitted foreigners to visit the Old City at certain seasons of the year. Perhaps this Jewish soldier managed to acquire a forged baptismal certificate, as the Jordanians required. He pretended to be a Christian. He got himself included in a party of visitors. Seizing a moment perhaps, unnoticed by the others, he knelt and scratched this prayer into the face of the stone.

Who among us is not in exile? Is not exile the spiritual condition of the human race? Isn't that what we share, when all differences of language, tribe, and history have been stripped away: the sense that we are estranged at our core from—what? From God? From our higher nature? From who we might be or become, from who we truly are?

What, then, does the exile desire beyond all other boons? Home. To come home. To set his feet upon those stones that are his, which belong to him and to which he belongs.

When we of "A" Company entered the Lion's Gate on the morning of June 7, our object, despite the ongoing gunfire and the danger from enemy snipers, was only to reach the Wall. Moshe Stempel had joined us then, my dear friend and our deputy brigade commander. Together we had swept across the Temple Mount and passed through the Moroccan Gate. We were on the steps above the Wall, but had not yet gone down to take possession of it.

Stempel ordered me to send one of my men down while the rest of us followed him back up to find a place above the Wall where we could hang the flag of Israel that I had carried all night and all day and all night and day again.

I picked a young sergeant named Dov Gruner.

This Dov Gruner was not the first to bear that name. The original Dov Gruner, after whom ours was named, had been a fighter for the Irgun Zvai Leumi, the underground paramilitary organization that fought the British during Mandate days, before Israel had achieved its statehood.

English soldiers captured this first Dov Gruner and put him on trial for participating in an assault on the police station at Ramat Gan. He was sentenced to death by hanging. At the final hour he was offered a reprieve, if he would admit his guilt.

Dov Gruner would not.

He refused to defend himself, standing upon the principle that to do so would be to acknowledge the legitimacy of the British court. On the last day of his life Dov Gruner wrote to his commander, Menachem Begin, and to his comrades in the Irgun:

Of course I want to live: who does not? I too could have said: "Let the future take care of the future" . . . I could even have left the country altogether for a safer life in America, but this would not have satisfied me either as a Jew or as a Zionist.

There are many schools of thought as to how a Jew should choose his way of life. One way is that of the assimilationists who have renounced their Jewishness. There is also another way, the way of those who call themselves "Zionists"—the way of negotiation and compromise . . .

The only way that seems, to my mind, to be right is the way of the Irgun Zvai Leumi, the way of courage and daring without renouncing a single inch of our homeland . . .

I am writing this while awaiting the hangman. This is not a

moment at which I can lie, and I swear that if I had to begin my
life anew I would have chosen the exact same path, regardless of
the consequences for myself.

Dov Gruner was hanged at Acre prison on April 16, 1947. As it chanced, his brother's wife had recently given birth to a son, whom they had named Dov.

This boy grew to be our Dov.

Moshe Stempel was asked once by a journalist, "Why did you pick Dov Gruner to be first to the Wall?"

"I did not pick him," Stempel replied. "History did."

Moshe Stempel was killed one year later, in the Jordan Valley, pursuing Palestinian terrorists who had penetrated the border. Stempel was hit in the first exchange of fire, but continued to lead the pursuit, under fire, until he was killed. Years earlier, in 1955, he had been awarded the Itur HaOz for valor on an operation near Khan Younis in which, as happened later when he was killed, he had been wounded but continued to fight until the mission had been completed.

Stempel built our brigade. He put it together, no one else. He had a chest like a bull and wrists as big around as most men's arms.

When we had pinned the flag of Israel to the grillwork above the Wall, our little group stood and sang the national anthem. A photographer, Eli Landau, was recording the historic moment with his camera. Stempel tugged my body between himself and the lens. He hid his face so that no film could be made of his tears.

Stempel held my arm in a grip of iron. Twice he tried to speak and twice his voice failed. He pulled me so close that the brows of our helmets were touching.

"Zamosh!" Stempel said, with such emotion that I can hear the words still, though he spoke them almost fifty years ago. "Zamosh, if my grandfather, if my great-grandfather, if any of my family who have been murdered in pogroms and in the death camps . . . if they could know, somehow, even for one second, that I, their grandson, would be standing here at this hour, in this place, wearing the red boots of an Israeli paratrooper . . . if they could know this, Zamosh, for just one instant, they would suffer death a thousand times and count it as nothing."

Stempel gripped my arm as if he would never let go.

"We shall never, never leave this place," he said. "Never will we give this up. Never."

59.

NECHEMIAH HOUSE

At the end of the war, I flew Arik Sharon out of Sinai in my helicopter. In his 1989 autobiography, *Warrior*, Sharon wrote that I was in tears at the controls because I had just learned of the death of my brother Nechemiah.

Cheetah Cohen, after retiring from the air force in 1974 as a colonel, flew for twenty-five years as a captain with El Al. He was elected to the Knesset in 1999 and served two terms, dedicating himself to drafting a constitution for the state of Israel. He retired for the third time in 2006.

I have no memory of that flight. I know that many have lost brothers and sons and fathers, even entire families, for this idea, this dream of a homeland that belongs to the Jewish people alone.

I think of my grandfather, who grew and sold fruits from his orchards in Turkey, my grandfather Eliezer, after whom I am named, who called his family together in 1918 following the fall of the Ottoman Empire and declared: I will emigrate to start a new life in Jerusalem. Which of you will come with me?

He came to this old-new country, Eretz Yisrael, which was not a country at all but only a farm here, a plot of grazing land there, purchased from absentee Ottoman landlords and registered, one patch at a time, under the British, under Mandate Palestine. Not a country at all, but only a dream, Herzl's dream and Jabotinsky's dream and Joseph Trumpeldor's dream. Yosi Ben-Hanan's family came, to Jerusalem as well, and Moshe Dayan's mother and father came, settling near Galilee on the first kibbutz, and a family named Scheinermann came, hebraizing their name to Sharon, and hundreds and then thousands more came, too.

Today, a child is born in Israel and wishes to grow to be an artist, a musician, to start a family and a business and maybe to get rich. Then, such aspirations seemed decades ahead of us, if they would or could come at all. You dreamed in those days only of the land, the pitiless, beautiful land, of how to make this soil yield enough so that your family could survive one more season in this place, which was our dream, our life, our ancient home. You thought of the land and how to protect it, to shield the young orange trees, to defend the pipelines, to guard the livestock. You learned to keep watch, to fight if you must, to never relax your vigilance, as our European brothers and sisters were so tragically doing at that very hour.

Those families like mine who settled in Jerusalem faced a different kind of struggle. The city was small then and very poor, without industry or trade, confined almost entirely within the one-kilometer-square walls of the Old City. Those Jews who came to Jerusalem came for reasons of the spirit, to be near the holy places. They felt no shame at being poor. To be in this place was everything to them.

My grandfather built his home outside the walls, believing in the city's future. Life was hard. Many could not endure. My brothers and I looked on as families faltered and failed. We watched them as the struggle became more than they could bear.

The father would leave first. "He is traveling to America," the children would say. One day tickets would arrive by post from across the sea. The young ones would vanish next. Finally the wife. The wife was always last. She would slip away in the night. Next day the family's place was empty.

Somehow a nation arose from these few penniless Jews, who dreamed Herzl's dream, Weizmann's dream, Ben-Gurion's dream, and fought to make it come true. I am a fighter pilot and a helicopter squadron commander. My son Amir is a captain in the tank corps; Yuval is a captain and a fighter pilot. Tamar, my daughter, served as operations sergeant in a helicopter squadron.

A nation is born in blood and purchases with blood its right to stand in the ranks with other nations.

Here is how my Six Day War ended.

I flew back to Tel Nof Air Base, that final Saturday, from the Golan Heights. My squadron had been ferrying Danny Matt's paratroopers to various crossroads and strategic points in a mad dash to secure the heights and prevent our enemies from using them again to shell our innocent farmers in the flatlands below.

We had won! The word "victory" was on every man's lips. At Tel Nof the mood was jubilation.

I forget how—maybe somebody called me—but I was summoned to the base commander's office. Colonel Shefer had been wounded and replaced by his deputy, Lieutenant Colonel Jacob Agassi. I knew Agassi well, a good pilot and a good man. He said, "Cheetah, prepare yourself for terrible news."

He told me that Nechemiah had been killed.

"Your brother died on the first day of the war, in the first hours. The decision was taken not to tell you. Your role in the fighting was too important. The air force needed you too much."

I remember nothing after that.

I was in a car, that day maybe, perhaps the day after. Officers were driving me somewhere. I was not capable of driving myself. The automobile pulled up and stopped before my father and mother's house. I remember thinking, I cannot get out of this car. I cannot go into that house.

The most painful part, through those terrible first weeks, was that Nechemiah's body had been buried by his comrades near the spot where he fell, in Gaza, on Kibbutz Be'eri, just south of Nahal Oz. So we could not bring him home to Jerusalem. When I went to the army to apply for restoration of my brother's remains, they told me I could not have them.

You must wait a year, I was told.

That is the law, the religious law.

When I informed my mother of this, I thought she would dissolve in despair. She became first wounded, then grief-stricken, then indignant. Somehow she found her way to Rabbi Goren, the chief religious officer of the army, the man who had sounded the shofar at the Western Wall.

Rabbi Goren sat for an hour with my father and mother. When the appointment ended, my mother was calm again. She had become resigned. If such indeed was the law, as Rabbi Goren had explained, then it must be obeyed.

Nechemiah's body was brought to Jerusalem and buried in the military cemetery on Mount Herzl on May 15, 1968. My father never went to visit the grave. He could not bear it. I survived those days thanks only to my wife, Ela, and to the necessity of continuing to fly missions.

Israel had won a war, but a new war had succeeded it. There would be more wars after that. The need to defend our people was never going to end.

Less than three months after the cease-fire, on September 1, 1967, the leaders of the Arab nations met in Khartoum. At this summit they declared in regard to Israel the notorious "Three No's."

No recognition, no negotiations, no peace.

Waves of terror had already begun. In our helicopters we chased the fedayeen and the terrorist infiltrators, dropping assault forces and interdiction elements.

One day, six months after the war, a phone call came from Avram Arnan, the commander of the Sayeret Matkal, Israel's special forces, in which Nechemiah had served.

"Cheetah, perhaps you are not aware of how deeply your brother was loved by the men of the Unit. We know how modest Nechemiah was. He would never speak of this to you, or to anyone, even if he had known the extent of his friends' devotion."

Arnan told me that he and the men of the Sayeret Matkal had acquired a house in Jerusalem.

"We want to dedicate this house to Nechemiah, to establish it as a special place to honor his memory."

I could not speak. This kind of honor is accorded to generals and to field marshals, not to captains.

Arnan said he wanted to show me the house. "Can you leave your squadron, Cheetah, just for a couple of hours, and come with me in my

Nechemiah Cohen.

jeep? It's a beautiful house, but I want to be sure you approve of it. If not, we will find another."

So we drove, Arnan and I.

When we reached the old British railway station on the Bethlehem Road, I thought to myself, This is the neighborhood of my brother's combat outpost, that day when Ela and I and our children visited him, just before the war.

Arnan's jeep began to climb the hill to Abu Tor.

I said to him, "Did you know that I spoke for the last time with Nechemiah here at Abu Tor, on the terrace of an abandoned Arab house that his men were using as a command post?"

"No, I did not."

Arnan's jeep turned into a final narrow lane. We came out of shadow and into a bright, open space.

"There it is," he said.

It was the house, the same house.

"Avram, did you know? Did you pick this house because it had been Nechemiah's final post?"

"I had no idea."

Tears came to Arnan's eyes. I had never seen him cry before and never saw him cry again.

"Are you sure, Cheetah? Are you sure this house is the one?"

"Of course! I embraced my brother for the last time right there, on that terrace."

The house was dedicated on December 31, 1967. It was given the name Bet Nechemiah—"Nechemiah House."

Two hundred people attended the ceremony. Chief of Staff Yitzhak Rabin took a place up front; Teddy Kollek, the mayor of Jerusalem, stood beside him. The dedication speech was delivered by Ehud Barak, the future prime minister, Nechemiah's dear friend and fellow commander in the Sayeret Matkal, and the only soldier of Israel who would earn as many citations for valor as he.

My family, you must remember, are simple people. For my father and mother, this honor was more than they could comprehend. They knew that their youngest son was a hero. But they had not realized how beloved Nechemiah was as a man and as a friend.

I, too, was overwhelmed. I had come straight from the squadron; I was not prepared for the grief that suddenly overtook me. My family was weeping; they did not know what to make of the illustrious personages attending with such emotion to honor their child. You must remember, too, that everything the special forces did was secret. Even the names of the men were not known outside the Unit.

The feats that Nechemiah had performed were never mentioned in the press or known even within the army; his reputation was not public. He was known only within his own formation.

Ehud Barak in his remarks barely mentioned war, nor did he glorify Nechemiah's deeds or accomplishments. He spoke instead—in plain, simple prose—of how hard my brother had worked to prepare himself and his men for combat, of how diligently he had trained himself and them to achieve excellence, and of how little attention and credit he sought for himself. Barak's tribute could not have been more heartfelt or more eloquent. Yet in truth, I remember little of it. The moment was too heartbreaking.

My brother was gone.

No victory, however sweet, no exploit of arms, no righting of ancient wrongs, not the recovery of the Holy City itself could bring him back, or restore to the nation her other fallen sons, of this war and others.

From this alone could our hearts draw solace: Nechemiah had come home.

Here at last, on these stony slopes where he and I and Uri had played as children, my brother could find rest.

The ceremony ended. Family and friends began, soberly and in silence, to file out. The day was cold and bright. The eye could see for miles in the clear December air.

Outside, on the terrace where my brother and I had parted for the final time, I stopped and looked to the north. From the eminence atop Abu Tor the walls of the Old City seemed close enough to touch. I could see clearly the poplar grove above the Western Wall—and the stones of the Wall itself, lit by the afternoon sun.

I thought, No longer will this site, my nation's holiest, be cut off from the Jewish people. No more will it be desecrated and dishonored. No longer will it reside in the hands of our enemies.

This is our Jerusalem, my brothers' and mine.

We were born here.

The city is our home.

POSTSCRIPT

I was leaning over a news-stand at the time. The owner, reaching for my journal, suddenly went rigid at the sound of the voice. His eyes widened, staring right past me, and he uttered a surprised, "Ah, they've called me up too!"

He stacked his papers and left. Across the street a salesgirl was leaving her store. She stopped a moment in the doorway, her head tilted; then she buttoned her jacket, closed her handbag firmly, and went off. The butcher next door whipped off his apron, pulled down the shutters, and departed. On a nearby lawn stood a group of men huddled round a transistor-radio. With the announcement of a code name, one of them would slip away, then another, then a third, silently, like a bundle of twigs that had fallen apart. Coming towards me was a girl, high heels clacking on the pavement. She, too, was suddenly caught by the voice, and pulled up abruptly. She listened, then turned about, and left. A silence like no other silence enveloped the city.

I have seen cities in moments of destiny. I have seen nations going off to war. I have seen men marching to the blare of ear-shattering loudspeakers. I have seen them crowding the railway stations, embraced by weeping wives and distraught mothers. And I have seen them parading through the streets, receiving the kisses of women standing at the wayside . . .

But never, never have I seen a city rising to its duties in such silence, nor seen a nation go forth into fateful battle so hushed, grim, committed. This is how they went in Nathania and Kiriat Shmoneh, in Jerusalem, Tel Aviv and Beersheba. And these were my people, my people whom I knew not.

Abba Kovner, "After These Things"

IN GRATITUDE

In my experience, the writing of a book is characterized by two qualities. One, the experience is solitary. Two, the research is scholarly. It is book-based.

The Lion's Gate was exactly the opposite.

The process of writing this book was massively collaborative. And despite monumental amounts of reading, the subject matter was absorbed almost entirely through face-to-face conversation and personal contact—interviews (some that went on for days), lunches and dinners, shared expeditions, drives, treks, events, and so forth.

First thanks to David Mamet, who invited me for Shabbat dinner in the summer of 2011 and introduced me to Lou Lenart, Israel's first air force hero, who became the beacon and godfather of this book and to whom it is dedicated.

Lou put me in touch with legendary fighter pilot and retired general Ran Ronen in Israel, who in turn introduced me to IAF lieutenant colonel Danny Grossman, who became my mentor and rabbi, spirit guide and consigliere (more about Danny later).

Big-time thanks, as always, to my peerless editor/agent/partner and friend Shawn Coyne, who has been irreplaceable at every juncture of this project from conception to "Lock the text." Thanks, pard!

Thanks beyond words to Kate Snow, who lived and died with the construction of this ark, cubit by cubit.

Thanks to Randall Wallace for keeping my heart brave at more than one critical juncture.

Profound gratitude to Rabbi Mordechai Finley of Ohr HaTorah Synagogue in Los Angeles, my mentor in all things biblical and Judaic.

To Christy Henspetter, who designed and drew the maps, and to Jasmine Quinsier for her superb computer graphics.

Thanks, too, to Adrian Zackheim and Niki Papadopoulos for their faith in me and belief in this material, and to Kary Perez, who put this book together, shot by shot.

My gratitude to every man and woman, veterans and participants in the Six Day War (and the photographers who recorded it), who sat down with me and patiently answered my questions, who took me around Israel, who translated and tutored and coached and instructed. I'm indebted to all who agreed to appear in this book. The contributions of those who, alas, were not included were in many ways equally indispensable:

Jacob Agassi, Boaz Amitai, Micha Bar-Am, Zeev Barkai, Itzik Barnoach, Morele Bar-On, Danny Baror, Michael Bar-Zohar, Michal Ben-Gal, Joel Bernstein, Shimon "Katcha" Cahaner, Denis Cameron, Eitan Campbell, Eliezer "Cheetah" Cohen and Ela Cohen, Amir Cohen, Ruth Dayan, Uzi Dayan, Yael Dayan, Uzi Eilat, Shlomo Gazit, Roni Gilo, Raanan Gissin, Coleman "Collie" Goldstein, Yoel Gorodish, Yerah Halperin, Motty Havakuk, Shai Hermesh, Sharona Justman, Avigdor Kahalani, Zvi "Kantor" Kanor, Aliza Klainman, Haim Koren, Eli Landau, Arnon Levushin, Gary Littwin, Dana Lustig, Neora Matalon-Barnoach, Danny Matt, Moshe Milo, Nataniel at Givat HaTochMoshet, Ori Orr, Moshe Peled, Yossi Peled, Shirley Reuveni, Benny Ron, Gary Rubenstein, David Rubinger, Jakob "Kobe" Segal, Meir Shalit, Danny Shapira, Avremale Shechter, Menahem Shmul, Menachem Shoval, Zalman Shoval, Smoky Simon, Rafi Sivron, Nancy Spielberg, Dubi Tevet, Bentzi Tal, Matan Vilnai, Aharon Yadlin, Yonni Yaari, Yoram Zamosh, Dan Ziv, and Zvi in the City of David.

Thanks to Michael Kovner, for his gracious permission to quote from his father Abba Kovner's "After These Things" in this book's postscript.

Special thanks to Maya Eshet, who translated Neora Matalon-Barnoach's *A Good Spot on the Side* from Hebrew to English for me.

Yosi Ben-Hanan spent five days with me and Danny Grossman in Paris, not only providing tremendous detail and insight into the 7th Armored Brigade's operations in Sinai but also contributing numerous photos of his own from that campaign, many of which have never been published.

Raanan Gissin, a paratroop battalion commander and former spokesman for Prime Minister Ariel Sharon, spent two days with me in Los Angeles and two more in Israel. His family used to run a stagecoach line. I am indebted to Raanan for his insights, both into the character and history of Ariel Sharon—his youth, his war years, and his legacy—and into the frame of mind and the life of the early pioneers of Palestine.

Rachel Nir (Mrs. Lou Lenart) happened to be watching Tel Aviv Channel 10 one evening when she became engrossed in a documentary titled *We Looked Death in the Eye* . . . about the experiences of the Reconnaissance Company of the 7th Armored Brigade in the Sinai Peninsula during the '67 War. Rachel contacted the film's producer (and a platoon commander of that outfit), Eli Rikovitz, then put me and Eli in touch. Thank you, Rachel!

Eli spent days with me, taking me to Gaza, to the Golan Heights, to training facilities of the contemporary Reconnaissance Company of the 7th Armored Brigade. Eli took me to places I had never heard of and to parts of Israel that I didn't know existed. With endless patience he sat with me, detailing the exploits and tragedies experienced by him and his comrades. Eli introduced me to veterans of that company—the first to reach the Suez Canal—which suffered more casualties and were awarded more decorations for valor than any other unit of comparable size in the IDF.

My gratitude as well to veterans and relatives of this formation whom I did not get to interview but whose words and stories, documented in the film, appear in this book: Gabi Gazit, Tani Geva, Bat Sheva Hofert, Itzhak Kissilov, Zvika Kornblit, Nehama Nissenbaum, Moshe Perry, Moti Shoval, and Moki Yishby. My thanks to Eli's wife, Ruthy, as well.

Giora and Miriam Romm extended the warmest hospitality to me at their home in Savyon, at social events and air force functions, and at their weekend place at Adamit on the Lebanese border. And Giora taught me about the Death Burst, which has proved indispensable in the writing of this book.

Thanks likewise to Uzi and Naomi Eilam, who opened their home to me more than once. Uzi, the commanding officer of Paratroop Battalion 71, and his friend and fellow veteran Benny Ron took me to Jerusalem and walked me, step by step, along the route that they and the paratroopers of Battalion 71 took in their liberation of the Old City.

Yoram Zamosh, commander of Company "A" of that battalion, along with his comrades Moshe Milo (my tutor and advocate in many researches and negotiations) and Avremale Shechter, escorted me along the track through the Lion's Gate, onto the Temple Mount, and to the Western Wall, as they had done as paratroopers on June 7, 1967. Phyllis Gil-Ad assisted as our biblical and historical guide.

The process of researching and writing this book took three years. For a significant portion of that time, Danny Grossman and I were inseparable.

When I arrived in Israel I had in mind the concept and structure of this book. I knew that I wanted to interview the first paratroopers to reach the Western Wall, the first armored corps troopers to get to the Suez Canal, and a number of Mirage pilots who flew in the first wave of Operation Moked. I knew, too, that I wanted to speak to as many individuals as possible who could shed light on the actions and character of Moshe Dayan.

Danny Grossman helped bring that vision into reality. Danny not only set up every interview and accompanied me upon them, he also influenced the book by his suggestions and selections of whom to interview. He took me to Masada; he took me four times to the Western Wall. My first evening in Israel, Danny drove me to a hilltop above his home in Kochav Yair. From that vantage, whose elevation was no taller than a five-story building, we could look east across a modest patch of pastureland to the '67 Jordanian border. Turning west, we could see with ease the Mediterranean coast and the illuminated sky above Tel Aviv.

You didn't have to be an artilleryman to understand what this meant.

When the first draft of this book was finished, Danny's work with me had just begun. He was the one who took the pages back to each participant (except those of the 7th Brigade's Recon Company; Eli Rikovitz took charge of that) and went over the text with him or her to be certain that the details and facts were straight, or as straight as we could get them. He worked with me for hours preparing these pages, before we exposed them to the interviewees, to make certain that my version of events was true not only to the facts as conveyed by the person interviewed but, perhaps more important, to the tone and intent, to the context and nuance.

Through Danny I began to see that Israeli pilots and tankers and paratroopers are not simply Americans who happen to speak Hebrew. They are Israelis, who think, speak, and act differently than we Yanks. Danny, who is an American who made his career in the USAF, then emigrated to Israel and flew for another twenty years in the IAF (winning a medal for valor in a beyond-the-border operation that is classified to this day), exposed me to the subtleties (and not-such-subtleties) to which my GI Joe ears were often tone-deaf.

I told Danny when we first met that his Long Island accent and his sense of humor reminded me of my cousin Bill. Two and a half years later, we finished closer than brothers.

Thanks, Danny (and Lisa and Orli and Nili and Kivi and Ariella and Yonatan), for service above and beyond the call of duty. This book could not have been done without you.

THE FALLEN AND THE DECORATED
OF THE RECONNAISSANCE COMPANY
OF THE 7TH ARMORED BRIGADE

KILLED IN ACTION

Yoram Abolnik

Avi David

Lieutenant Yossi Elgamis

Sergeant Haim Fenikel

Eliyahu Goshen

Lieutenant Shaul Groag

Eliahu Joseph

Lieutenant Shlomo Kenigsbuch

Shmuel "Borvil" Hacham

Ben-Zion Nissenbaum

Michael Polak

Chen Rosenberg

Yaakov Yaakovi

Lieutenant Yaakov Yarkoni

Ben-Zion Zur

Mordechai "Max" Zvili

DECORATIONS FOR VALOR

Itur HaOz (Medal of Courage)

Sergeant Haim Fenikel (posthumously)

Itur HaMofet (Medal of Distinguished Service)

Lieutenant Amos Ayalon

Sergeant Shmuel Beilis

Lieutenant Shaul Groag (posthumously)

Sergeant Major Haim Lavi

Moshe Perry

Lieutenant Eli Rikovitz

Lieutenant Yaakov Yarkoni (posthumously)

Moshe "Moki" Yishby

Uri Zand

Photo by Micha Bar-Am.

BIBLIOGRAPHY

Adan, Avraham. *On the Banks of the Suez*. Jerusalem: Presidio Press, 1980.

Against All Odds: The Six Day War and the Raid on Entebbe. A&E Television Networks/Art and Design, 1996.

Allon, Yigal. *Shield of David: The Story of Israel's Armed Forces*. New York: Random House, 1970.

Aloni, Shlomo. *Arab-Israeli Air Wars, 1947–82*. Oxford: Osprey, 2001.

———. *Israeli Mirage and Nesher Aces*. Oxford: Osprey, 2004.

———. *Mirage III vs. MiG-21: Six Day War 1967*. Oxford: Osprey, 2010.

Avner, Yehuda. *The Prime Ministers: An Intimate Narrative of Israeli Leadership*. New Milford, CT: Toby Press, 2010.

Barer, Shlomo. *The Week End War*. Tel Aviv: Karni Publishers, 1959.

Bar-On, Mordechai. *The Gates of Gaza*. New York: St. Martin's/Griffin, 1999.

———. *Moshe Dayan: Israel's Controversial Hero*. New Haven and London: Yale University Press, 2012.

Bar-Zohar, Michael. *Ben-Gurion: The Armed Prophet*. Englewood Cliffs, NJ: Prentice-Hall, 1966.

———. *Embassies in Crisis: Diplomats and Demagogues Behind the Six-Day War*. Englewood Cliffs, NJ: Prentice-Hall, 1970.

Battle for Survival. Goldhill Video/Scott Entertainment, 1998.

Begin, Menachem. *The Revolt*. Jerusalem: Steimatzky's Agency, 1952.

Bilby, Kenneth W. *New Star in the Near East*. Garden City, NY: Doubleday, 1950.

Borovik, Yehuda. *Israeli Air Force 1948 to the Present.* London: Arms and Armour Press, 1984.

Bowen, Jeremy. *Six Days: How the 1967 War Shaped the Middle East.* New York: Thomas Dunne, 2003.

Byford-Jones, W. *The Lightning War.* Indianapolis: Bobbs-Merrill, 1967.

Churchill, Randolph S., and Winston S. Churchill. *The Six Day War.* Boston: Houghton Mifflin, 1967.

Cohen, Aaron, and Douglas Century. *Brotherhood of Warriors.* New York: HarperCollins/Ecco, 2008.

Cohen, Eliezer "Cheetah." *Israel's Best Defense: The First Full Story of the Israeli Air Force.* New York: Orion, 1993.

Cohen, Rich. *Israel Is Real.* New York: Picador, 2009.

Collins, Larry, and Dominique Lapierre. *O Jerusalem!* New York: Simon and Schuster, 1972.

Cristol, Jay A. *The Liberty Incident: The 1967 Israeli Attack on the U.S. Navy.* Washington, D.C.: Brassey's, 2002.

Dan, Uri. *Ariel Sharon: An Intimate Portrait.* New York: Palgrave Macmillan, 2006.

Dayan, David. *Strike First!* New York: Pitman, 1967.

Dayan, Moshe. *Diary of the Sinai Campaign.* New York: Schocken, 1965.

———. *Story of My Life.* New York: William Morrow, 1976.

———. *Living with the Bible.* New York: William Morrow, 1978.

Dayan, Ruth, and Helga Dudman. *And Perhaps . . . : The Story of Ruth Dayan.* New York: Harcourt Brace Jovanovich, 1973.

———. *. . . Or Did I Dream a Dream?: The Story of Ruth Dayan.* London: Weidenfeld and Nicolson, 1973.

Dayan, Yael. *Israel Journal: June, 1967.* New York: McGraw-Hill, 1967.

———. *My Father, His Daughter.* New York: Farrar, Straus and Giroux, 1985.

Dershowitz, Alan. *The Case for Israel.* Hoboken, NJ: John Wiley and Sons, 2003.

Dog Fights. A&E Television Networks/Digital Ranch, 2006.

Dunstan, Simon. *Centurion Universal Tank, 1943–2003.* Oxford: Osprey, 2003.

———. *The Yom Kippur War: The Arab-Israeli War of 1973.* Oxford: Osprey, 2007.

———. *The Six Day War 1967: Jordan and Syria Campaign.* Oxford: Osprey, 2009.

———. *The Six Day War 1967: Sinai.* Oxford: Osprey, 2009.

Dupuy, Trevor N. *Elusive Victory: The Arab-Israeli War, 1947–1974.* Harper and Row, 1978.

Eilam, Uzi. *Eilam's Arc: How Israel Became a Military Powerhouse.* Brighton, UK: Sussex Academic Press, 2011.

Elon, Amos. *Flight into Egypt.* New York: Pinnacle, 1980.

———. *Jerusalem: Battlegrounds of Memory.* New York: Kodansha International, 1989.

———. *Jerusalem: City of Mirrors.* London: Weidenfeld and Nicolson, 1989.

———. *A Blood-Dimmed Tide: Dispatches from the Middle East.* New York: Columbia University Press, 1997.

Eshel, David. *Chariots of the Desert: The Story of the Israel Armored Corps.* London: Brassey's Defence Publishers, 1989.

———. *Bravery in Battle: Stories from the Front Line.* London: Arms and Armour Press, 1997.

Fallaci, Oriana. *The Rage and the Pride.* New York: Rizzoli, 2001.

Fast, Howard. *The Jews: Story of a People.* New York: Dell, 1968.

Follow Me: The Story of the Six Day War. Israel Film Service, 1968.

Gawrych, George W. *Key to the Sinai: The Battles for Abu Ageila in the 1956 and 1967 Arab-Israeli Wars.* Fort Leavenworth, KS: U.S. Army Command and Staff College, Combat Studies Institute, 1990.

Gazit, Shlomo. *Trapped Fools: Thirty Years of Israeli Policy in the Territories.* London: Frank Cass, 2003.

Gilbert, Martin. *Atlas of the Arab-Israeli Conflict.* London: Orion, 1974.

———. *Israel: A History.* New York: Harper Perennial, 1998.

Giluska, Amos. *The Israeli Military and the Origins of the 1967 War.* London: Routledge, 2007.

Gur, Mordechai. *The Battle for Jerusalem.* New York: Popular Library, 1974.

Halperin, Merav, and Aharon Lapidot. *G-Suit: Pages from the Log Book of the Israel Air Force.* London: Sphere Books, 1990.

Hammel, Eric. *Six Days in June: How Israel Won the 1967 Arab-Israeli War.* New York: Charles Scribner's Sons, 1992.

Hammer, Reuven. *The Jerusalem Anthology: A Literary Guide.* Philadelphia: Jewish Publication Society, 1995.

Heikal, Mohamed H. *Cutting the Lion's Tail: Suez Through Egyptian Eyes.* London: Andre Deutsch, 1986.

Henriques, Robert. *A Hundred Hours to Suez: An Account of Israel's Campaign in the Sinai Peninsula.* New York: Viking, 1957.

Herzl, Theodor. *The Jewish State*. New York: Dover, 1946.

Herzog, Chaim. *The War of Atonement: October, 1973*. Boston: Little, Brown, 1975.

Josephus. *The Jewish War*. Translated by G. A. Williamson. London: Penguin, 1956.

Kahalani, Avigdor. *The Heights of Courage: A Tank Leader's War on the Golan*. Westport, CT: Greenwood Press, 1984.

———. *A Warrior's Way*. Bnei-Brak, Israel: Steimatzky, 1999.

Katz, Samuel M. *Israeli Elite Units Since 1948*. London: Osprey, 1988.

Keinon, Herb. *Lone Soldiers: Israel's Defenders from Around the World*. New York: Devora, 2009.

Kollek, Teddy, and Am Kollek. *For Jerusalem: A Life*. New York: Random House, 1978.

Kollek, Teddy, and Moshe Pearlman. *Jerusalem: A History of Forty Centuries*. New York: Random House, 1968.

Kollek, Teddy, and Shulamith Eisner. *My Jerusalem: Twelve Walks in the World's Holiest City*. New York: Summit Books, 1990.

Kurzman, Dan. *Genesis 1948: The First Arab-Israeli War*. New York: World Publishing, 1970.

Laffin, John. *The Israeli Army in the Middle East Wars, 1948–73*. London: Osprey, 1982.

Landau, Eli. *Jerusalem the Eternal: The Paratroopers' Battle for the City of David*. Tel Aviv: Otpaz, 1968.

———. *Suez: Fire on the Water*. Tel Aviv: Otpaz, 1970.

Lau-Lavie, Naphtali. *Moshe Dayan: A Biography*. Hartford, CT: Hartmore House, 1968.

Lenart, Lou. *Destiny: The Story of My Life*. N.P.: Venice Printing, 2011.

Lew, Alan. *This Is Real and You Are Completely Unprepared*. Boston: Little, Brown, 2003.

Lew, Alan, and Sherril Jaffe. *One God Clapping: The Spiritual Path of a Zen Rabbi*. New York: Kodansha International, 1999.

Lieblich, Amia. *Kibbutz Makom: Report from an Israeli Kibbutz*. New York: Pantheon, 1981.

Loftus, John, and Mark Aarons. *The Secret War Against the Jews: How Western Espionage Betrayed the Jewish People*. New York: St. Martin's, 1994.

Love, Kennett. *Suez: The Twice-Fought War*. New York: McGraw-Hill, 1969.

Luttwak, Edward, and Dan Horowitz. *The Israeli Army*. Harper and Row, 1975.

McNab, Chris. *The Uzi Submachine Gun*. Oxford: Osprey, 2011.

Marshall, S. L. A. *Sinai Victory*. New York: William Morrow, 1958.

———. *Swift Sword: The Historical Record of Israel's Victory, June 1967*. New York: American Heritage, 1967.

Matalon-Barnoach, Neora. *A Good Spot on the Side* (Hebrew). Israel: KIP-Kotarim International, 2009.

Morris, Benny. *1948: A History of the First Arab-Israeli War*. New Haven, CT: Yale University Press, 2008.

Moskin, Robert J. *Among Lions: The Battle for Jerusalem, June 5–7, 1967*. New York: Arbor House, 1982.

Narkiss, Uzi. *The Liberation of Jerusalem: The Battle of 1967*. London: Vallentine Mitchell, 1983.

———. *Soldier of Jerusalem*. London: Vallentine Mitchell, 1998.

Neff, Donald. *Warriors for Jerusalem: The Six Days That Changed the Middle East*. New York: Simon and Schuster/Linden Press, 1984.

Netanyahu, Cela. *Self-Portrait of a Hero: The Letters of Jonathan Netanyahu*. New York: Ballantine, 1980.

Nordeen, Lon. *Fighters over Israel*. London: Guild Publishing, 1990.

Nordeen, Lon, and David Nicolle. *Phoenix over the Nile: A History of Egyptian Air Power, 1932–1994*. Washington, D.C.: Smithsonian Institution Press, 1996.

O'Ballance, Edgar. *The Sinai Campaign, 1956*. London: Faber and Faber, 1959.

———. *The Third Arab-Israeli War*. Hamden, CT: Archon Books, 1972.

———. *No Victor, No Vanquished: The Yom Kippur War*. San Rafael, CA: Presidio Press, 1978.

Oren, Michael B. *Six Days of War: June 1967 and the Making of the Modern Middle East*. Oxford: Oxford University Press, 2002.

Parker, Richard B. *The Six-Day War: A Retrospective*. Gainesville: University Press of Florida, 1996.

Pawel, Ernst. *The Labyrinth of Exile: A Life of Theodor Herzl*. New York: Farrar, Straus and Giroux, 1989.

Quandt, William B. *Peace Process: American Diplomacy and the Arab-Israeli Conflict Since 1967*. Washington, D.C.: Brookings Institution, 1993.

Rabin, Yitzhak. *The Rabin Memoirs*. Boston: Little, Brown, 1979.

Rabinovich, Abraham. *The Battle for Jerusalem: June 5–7, 1967*. Philadelphia: Jewish Publication Society, 1987.

———. *The Yom Kippur War: The Epic Encounter That Transformed the Middle East*. New York: Schocken, 2004.

Romm, Giora. *Tulip Four* (Hebrew). Tel Aviv: Yedioth Ahronoth Books, 2008.

Romm, Miriam. *Ostrich Feathers*. Jerusalem: Gefen Publishing, 2009.

Ronen, Ran. *Eagle in the Sky*. Tel Aviv: Contento de Semrik Publishing, 2012.

Segev, Tom. *1967: Israel, the War, and the Year That Transformed the Middle East*. New York: Henry Holt, 2005.

Shapira, Avraham, ed. *The Seventh Day: Soldiers' Talk About the Six-Day War*. New York: Charles Scribner's Sons, 1970.

Sharon, Ariel, and David Chanoff. *Warrior: The Autobiography of Ariel Sharon*. New York: Simon and Schuster, 1989.

Sharon, Gilad. *Sharon: The Life of a Leader*. New York: HarperCollins, 2011.

Shaw, Robert L. *Fighter Combat: Tactics and Maneuvering*. Annapolis, MD: Naval Institute Press, 1985.

Shlaim, Avi. *The Iron Wall: Israel and the Arab World*. New York: W. W. Norton, 2000.

Six Days in June: The War That Redefined the Middle East (DVD). 2007.

Slater, Robert. *Warrior Statesman: The Life of Moshe Dayan*. New York: St. Martin's, 1991.

Sykes, Christopher. *Orde Wingate: A Biography*. Cleveland: World Publishing, 1959.

Teveth, Shabtai. *The Tanks of Tammuz*. London: Sphere Books, 1968.

———. *Moshe Dayan*. London: Quartet Books, 1972.

Thomas, Gordon. *Gideon's Spies: The Secret History of the Mossad*. New York: Thomas Dunne, 1999.

Vance, Vick, and Pierre Lauer. *Hussein of Jordan: My "War" with Israel*. New York: William Morrow, 1969.

Van Creveld, Martin. *The Sword and the Olive: A Critical History of the Israeli Defense Force*. New York: PublicAffairs, 1998.

———. *Moshe Dayan*. London: Orion, 2004.

Wanderle, William. *Through the Lens of Cultural Awareness: A Primer for U.S. Armed Forces Deploying to Arab and Middle Eastern Countries*. Fort Leavenworth, KS: Combat Studies Institute Press, 1962.

Weizman, Ezer. *On Eagles' Wings*. New York: Berkley Medallion, 1976.

———. *The Battle for Peace*. Toronto: Bantam, 1981.

We Looked Death in the Eye . . . (DVD). Shlomo Avidan/Eli Rikovitz.

Yonay, Ehud. *No Margin for Error: The Making of the Israeli Air Force*. New York: Pantheon, 1993.

Zaloga, Steven J. *The M47 and M48 Patton Tanks*. London: Osprey, 1980.

ILLUSTRATION CREDITS

INDEX

Page numbers in *italics* refer to illustrations.